# Education and Teacher Education in the Modern World

# Education and Teacher Education in the Modern World

*Problems and Challenges*

Edited by

K.G. Karras, P. Calogiannakis,
C.C. Wolhuter and D. Kontogianni

Cambridge
Scholars
Publishing

Education and Teacher Education in the Modern World:
Problems and Challenges

Edited by K.G. Karras, P. Calogiannakis, C.C. Wolhuter
and D. Kontogianni

This book first published 2015

Cambridge Scholars Publishing

Lady Stephenson Library, Newcastle upon Tyne, NE6 2PA, UK

British Library Cataloguing in Publication Data
A catalogue record for this book is available from the British Library

ISBN (10): 1-4438-8004-3
ISBN (13): 978-1-4438-8004-6

# CONTENTS

**Part III: Training, Evaluation and Teaching Practice Issues
in Teacher Education**

# PREFACE

The current volume consists of selected papers presented to the 1st International Symposium in Education and Teacher Education in the modern world, which was organized by and took place at the University of Crete, Department of Primary Education – KEMEIEDE (Centre for the Study and Research of the History of Education and the Teaching Profession) in May 2013 in Rethymno, Crete.

These selected papers by participant researchers are divided into three parts: the first part deals with teacher education in the modern world, the second with professionalism and research in the field of teacher education and the third part presents issues related to the evaluation of training and integration. The editors of this volume believe that the issue of education and teacher education in the modern world is nowadays one of the most important issues in Greece and worldwide. For this reason, distinguished Greek and foreign scholars communicate their experience, their knowledge and their research to form a contemporary and important area of discussion and debate in the field of education and training in the modern educational world. This volume includes new research on teacher education and training and includes original chapters that cover many aspects of what we know about teachers and the teaching profession today from an international perspective.

The editors of this volume would like to thank all the authors from the different countries around the world for their contribution to the contemporary international debate on education and teacher education in the modern world by submitting their original studies and research and Cambridge Scholars Publishing also for undertaking this publication.

This volume brings together significant experiences and practices in the area of teacher education and the teaching profession internationally; it can serve teachers, researchers and all those who are interested in education and teacher education, in the discussion of challenges facing education and teacher education in the pedagogical, educational, sociopolitical, cultural and ideological context of our era.

*K. G. Karras, P. Calogiannakis, C. C. Wolhuter, D. Kontogianni*
*Rethymno, Crete, May, 2014*

# INTRODUCTION[1]

# "NOT FOR A *TECHNE* ... BUT FOR *PAIDEIA*": NOT THE TECHNOCRAT-TEACHER BUT THE PEDAGOGUE-TEACHER IN THE NEW KNOWLEDGE COSMOPOLIS

## ANDREAS M. KAZAMIAS
### EMERITUS PROFESSOR, UNIVERSITIES OF WISCONSIN-MADISON, USA AND ATHENS
### ASSOCIATE MEMBER, ACADEMY OF ATHENS, GREECE

Consequently, Hippocrates, could it be that you believe the instruction/ learning you expect to get from Protagoras, is not of the same kind as the one you got from your language teacher (*grammatistes*), your harp-teacher (*kitharistes*) and your sports instructor (*paidotrives*)? For the kind of learning you received from each of these teachers was not for professional/ vocational purposes, that aimed at some craft/trade (*techne*), i.e. to become a "craftsman", but for educational/cultural purposes, for *paideia*, as befits a citizen and a free man.

(Plato, *Protagoras*, 312b)

In Plato's dialogue *Protagoras,* Socrates, the ancient Greek critical humanist philosopher-pedagogue, draws a distinction between education/ learning/instruction for a particular profession, a craft (*techne*) or a trade, and education/learning/instruction for *paideia*/culture i.e. the cultivation of the mind (development of intellectual character) and the cultivation of the soul (*psyche*), i.e. the development of moral and aesthetic character.

\*\*\*

---

[1] This introduction consists of notes from an oral presentation by Prof. Kazamias.

# Key Concepts of the New Knowledge Cosmopolis

*The political/economic context of teacher education*
- A "techno-scientific knowledge world/society constructed on a new informational epistemological paradigm; a culture of real virtuality; a network society" (Castells, 1996: 66–67).
- A virtual/not virtuous dystopia which emphasizes education and training, not *paideia*; instrumental rationality.
- A cosmos pervaded by materialism and pragmatism – a "denial of intellectual enquiry, aesthetic beauty and public virtue" (Abbs, 1994).
- Emphasis on competences, mostly instrumental. Under-emphasis on ethical dispositions and civic virtues – the "paideia of the soul".
- A philistine empire informed by a philistine ethos (Furedi, 2003).

*The epistemic/educational/cultural context of teacher education: What knowledge and education in the knowledge cosmopolis?*
- Predominantly education and training, not *Paideia.*
- Techno-scientific knowledge/information base, not general liberal education (*Allgemeine Bildung, Culture Générale*).
- Cognitive, vocational and social skills readily assessed and constantly renewable. Competitiveness, entrepreneurship, employability, innovation, creativity, productivity, accreditation.
- Possessive individualism with tangential concomitants, e.g. "critical thinking", "problem solving", "cohesion".
- Emphasis on competences (theoretical, practical, cognitive), mostly instrumental. Under-emphasis on aesthetic and ethical dispositions and civic virtues – the "paideia of the soul".

# Teacher Education in Europe

*The political/economic context*
- Context: Europe of knowledge; European knowledge society/economy – an instrumental rationalist epistemological paradigm.
- Vision – The Lisbon Strategy/Agenda: "To make the European Union the most competitive and dynamic knowledge-based economy in the world capable of sustaining more and better jobs and with greater social cohesion".
- A techno-scientific knowledge/information base; "codified knowledge" for the accumulation of capital in a competitive global economy; knowledge as a trading commodity; sophisticated learning technologies;

emphasis on cognitive, vocational and social skills and mostly instrumental competences (e.g. mathematical and basic competences in science and technology; digital competence; social and civic competences; sense of initiative and entrepreneurship; "learning to learn"; communication in the mother tongue and in foreign languages, and "cultural awareness and expression").

### The neo-European paradigm of pre-service and in-service teacher education/training

In the context of the "instrumental rationalist epistemological paradigm", adumbrated above, schooling is evaluated on the basis of such criteria as "efficiency and productivity", i.e. the criteria of management. Emphasis is placed on "accountability", "standards", "testing", student achievement in mostly cognitively productive areas, e.g. mathematics and techno-scientific knowledge, and in the results of international examinations such as the IEA's TIMSS and the OECD's PISA.

Additionally, there is a trend towards the vocationalization of schooling and an under-emphasis on "general education", particularly of humanistic education, what I would call the "paideia of the soul".

## Teacher Education: The Paradigm of England and Wales

Neo-conservatism in the 1980s and the neo-liberal "marketized educational reforms" were extended to incorporate teacher education. Among other changes:

a. There was a change in the discourse from "teacher education" to "teacher training".

b. Time spent on theoretical studies was reduced in favour of practice in schools – emphasis on "school-based training". Philosophy, sociology and to a great extent psychology have disappeared from the courses for teacher education, being replaced by how to teach a subject and how to control classes.

c. Teacher assessment is based on competences and standards, on performance. Mentors in schools now play a large part in assessing prospective teachers against those standards.

d. "In all the discussions, the question of whether we 'educate' the teachers has been in the forefront, while training rather than education appears to be top priority" (Hilton, 2012: 166).

> We see an emerging generation of teachers who know little of the past and virtually nothing of philosophy, who have an essentially uncritical view of what they do and a managerial language which dims intellectual

perception. Teachers become the technicians of subjects, not the critical guardians of a long culture . . . teachers emerge as an unexpected proletariat in the new technology. They will do the labour but will be told what and how to do it. They become the serving functionaries, not of the life of culture and the intellect, but of either the state or the free market – or a combination of both. (Abbs, 1994: 4–6)

## The English Paradigm: An Example of the Deprofessionalization/deskilling of Teachers

- From a *"pedagogue"* and *"public intellectual"*, whose role has traditionally been to cultivate *"minds and souls"*, i.e., *"to humanize"* the citizen-person, to a *"master technocrat"* whose job becomes one of how to organize and teach effectively, but uncritically, officially-prescribed knowledge (curricula) and methods for high measurable achievement in examinations.
- In the USA, Canada and the United Kingdom, the work of the teachers has been "intensified", "formliazed" and "technicized". It resembles "more the work of a miserable manual laborer, and less that of an autonomous professional" (Hargeaves, 1986).
- "Schools are currently places where commercialism is rapidly intruding. Students, teachers, and leaders rarely critique commercial intrusion (resulting in uncritical consumers and uncritical citizens)." (Boyles, 2005)

## The Finnish Paradigm

### Relative strengths:
- High status/prestige of the teaching profession: "esteemed professionals similar to medical doctors, engineer, or economists". As such, they are given "professional autonomy to practice what they have been educated to do" (Sahlberg, 2010: 76).
- Teaching profession attracts the most able and talented high school graduates (ibid.: 93).
- Teacher education is research-oriented: All teachers "have completed Master's theses accompanied by rigorous academic requirements of theory, methodology and critical reflection equal to any other field of study in Finnish universities" (ibid.: 94).
- Close collaboration between subject faculties and schools of education (ibid. 94).

### Politico-economic and socio-cultural context

Finland has been transformed into an information society and a knowledge-based economy.

- Competitive welfare state with a dynamic knowledge economy. Equitable distribution of income and "state generated social capital" (ibid.: 112).
- Traditional social/cultural values: "law-abiding citizenry, trust in authority including schools, commitment to one's social group, awareness of one's social status and position, and a patriotic spirit" (ibid.: 112). Lutheranism.
- Educational policies/reforms focused on "better knowledge and skills in coherence with creativity and problem solving . . . strong focus on mathematics, science and technology".

Finland has a competitive national economy, low levels of corruption, good quality of life, a strong sustainable-development lifestyle, and gender quality. These qualities make Finland one of the most prosperous nations in the world" (ibid.: 96).

## Teacher Education in the United States

### The Neo-Conservative Market Ideological Context

Schooling is evaluated according to the same criteria as those used by corporations: efficiency and productivity – the criteria of management. Emphasis on accountability, standards, measurement, testing, student achievement in mathematics and techno-scientific knowledge, participation in international studies of achievement such as the IEA's TIMMS and the OECD's PISA.

- "Learning for the sake of learning has been replaced by attention to outcomes; education is measured in inputs and outputs and standardized via test scores" (Boyles, 2005: 34).
- "Primary and secondary schools are no longer meant to develop a democratic citizenry. Too often schools serve as a factory to produce workers or as just another marketing or investment opportunity" (ibid.: 154).

### The "effective schools" concept

The effective school is characterized by high overall student achievement with no significant gaps in that achievement across the major subgroups in the student population. The effective school is built on a foundation of high expectations, strong leadership, unwavering commitment to learning for all, collaboration, differentiated instruction, and frequent monitoring of student progress . . . [There is a focus on demonstrated student results] . . . the effective school is characterized by high overall student achievement with no significant gaps in that achievement across the major subgroups in the student population. (Lezotte & Snyder, 2011: 15, 17–18)

### The discourse: moral and epistemic purposes

*Knowledge:* Content knowledge; general pedagogical knowledge; curriculum knowledge; knowledge of learners; knowledge of educational contexts (schools, communities, cultures); knowledge of educational purposes and values and their philosophical and historical grounds (Shulman, 1987: 8).

*Skills:* Intellectual, assessment, planning, instructional, evaluation, social behaviour management, role modelling skills.

*Dispositions:* Toward self (e.g. reflection on own teaching and its effects on learners, a personal philosophy of education); toward the learner (e.g. respect and value of individual and cultural differences, empathic cooperative relations with and among learners); toward teaching (e.g. engage in critical thinking and problem solving with learners; toward the profession (e.g. act as part of a team, social justice, engage in professional responsibilities within the school, professional organizations and the community (Minnesota Vision for TE).

### "A moral craft" – moral purposes/dispositions
*Humanizing dispositions*:

Commitment to being a learner of diversity and its impact on teaching and learning; Relentless belief in the potential of culturally and linguistically diverse youth; Conviction to coconstruct knowledge with students and their families; Willingness to accept, embrace, and navigate the complexity of teaching and learning in collaboration with others; Persistence in advocating for students and their families. (Murrell et al., 2010: 29–30)

As the University of Southern Maine put it: "Fostering moral dispositions – for equitable and engaging learning – is at the heart of our work as teacher educators" (p. 96).

### Components of powerful teacher education programmes

- A clear vision of good teaching permeates all course-work and clinical experiences.
- Well-defined standards of practice and performance are used to guide and evaluate coursework and clinical work.

- Curriculum is grounded in knowledge and child and adolescent development, learning, social contexts and clinical work.
- Extended clinical experiences are carefully developed to support the ideas and practices presented in course work.
- Explicit strategies to help students (a) confront their own deep-seated beliefs and assumptions about learning, and (b) learn about the experiences of people different from themselves.
- Strong relationships, common knowledge, and shared beliefs link school- and university-based faculty.
- Case study methods, teacher research, performance assessment, and portfolio evaluation apply learning to real problems of practice.

(Darling-Hammond, 2006: 41)

### The University of Wisconsin-Madison Teacher Preparation Program for Majors in English, Mathematics, Science and Social Studies

- Integrated and coordinated course work. Students engage in a coherent, progressive series of courses and experiences that build on their increasing knowledge and skills.
- Course work that links directly to school practice.
- Team learning that fosters dialogue and collaboration. Students are organized into learning communities and learning teams . . . These groups offer students the opportunity for dialogue with faculty, peers and cooperating teachers.
- A commitment to prepare future teachers who can help each child to learn. In course work and field experiences, students explore teaching and learning issues related to ethnic, cultural and language diversity, social class, and students' special needs and abilities.

### The University of Wisconsin-Madison Teacher Education Program – Professional Education Requirements

- Semester 1 – Curriculum and Instruction: Strategies for Inclusive Learning; School and Society; Educational Psychology; Practicum in Secondary Education.
- Semester 2 – Curriculum and Instruction: Language and literacy across the secondary curriculum; Teaching diverse learners; Teaching of subject in secondary schools; Practicum in secondary school subject.
- Semester 3 – Educational Psychology: Human abilities and Learning; Advanced practices in the teaching of the subject; Student teaching.
- Semester 4 – Student teaching; Independent field work.
- Additional State Licensing Requirements: Minority Group Relations and Conflict Resolution.

# Teacher Education and Critical Pedagogy:
# An Interesting Excursus

*Critical pedagogy in teacher education programmes – a call for adoption*

- Grant (2008: 188) states that in a review of articles on social justice, published in refereed journals, several authors argued that teacher education programmes should adopt critical pedagogy in order to help prospective teachers "develop a critical stance to challenge racism and other biases", as one writer put it.
- Bartolome (2007: 264) discusses "the importance of infusing teacher education curricula with critical pedagogical principles in order to prepare educators to aggressively name and interrogate potentially harmful ideologies and practices in the schools and classrooms where they work".

*Paulo Freire and critical pedagogy as a "humanistic and liberating pedagogy"*

- Critical Pedagogy of the oppressed, as a humanistic and liberating pedagogy.
- Critical dialogue and critical reflection leading to praxis (action) by which the oppressed are liberated and become "human".
- Freire's critical pedagogy over-politicizes education by focusing almost solely on using education to transform injustice and oppression. He assumes that by politicizing education you liberate people from oppression and "humanize" them. As such, (a) insufficient attention is paid to the plurality of educational purposes in a democracy; (b) it limits what it means to be human; (c) it narrows the conception of "critical humanist pedagogy": it undervalues the emancipatory power of aesthetic education, the arts and the humanities, what I call the paideia of the soul.

*Critical pedagogy's philosophy of education: over-politicization of education?*

- Individuals are born into a world of domination and oppression, which is (re)produced in schools. Teachers have a moral obligation to be critical pedagogues, to ensure that children become autonomous and can transform the various forms of domination and oppression which exist in society.
- The purpose of education has two aims: critical consciousness and counterhegemonic action. Critical consciousness challenges the framework of thought used in society to give order and meaning to the

social and political world in which we live (Freire, 1974). Counter-hegemonic action aims to prepare students to understand and uncover the construction of power and privilege and to see themselves as agents capable of changing oppressive conditions. (Wheeler-Bell, 2013).

### Socrates as a critical humanist pedagogue (see first page of this introduction)

Socratic pedagogy – the importance of *Elenchus* (questioning/argument/examination/critical play of consciousness)

Critical *Elenchus* (critical examination/questioning): "The unexamined life is not worth living for an individual." "I am a sort of gadfly, given to the democracy by the gods, and the democracy is a large, noble horse who is sluggish in its motions, and requires to be stung into life" (Plato, *Apology*, 30E).

Sustained unrelenting philosophical argument to bear on issues of common concern (as Cicero later put it, "bringing philosophy from the heavens down to earth", an activity which did not please everyone who encountered it (Nussbaum, 1997: 20)).

### Epimythion 1

Both critical theories of education and pedagogy presented here (Freire's and Socrates') purport to be humanist theories, but they prioritize different aspects or elements of humanism. Freire's theory seems to emphasize liberation through dialogue and revolutionary praxis, while Socrates emphasizes liberation through the paideia of both the mind and the soul.

### Epimythion 2

Freire's theory may indeed liberate the "oppressed" and the "alienated", thus creating a more humane society, but to create a wholly human society we must, as Seneca and Martha Nussbaum have argued, cultivate humanity – and to do that we need Socrates' paideia of the soul.

## Toward the Professional Pedagogue-teacher, the Moral Educator with a Scientific/Epistemic Training, *not* the Deskilled Technocrat-teacher

### Clarification of concepts:
a) Teaching as a profession, the teacher as a professional.
b) Teaching as art, craft or science? The teacher as artist, craftsman or scientist?

c) Pedagogy and teaching – the pedagogue *vis-à-vis* teacher; pedagogy as discourse *vis-à-vis* teaching as act.

## Teaching as a profession

- "A profession refers to an occupation that requires specialized education, knowledge, training and ethics . . . Professions are, ideally, made up of people with high ethical standards who have special knowledge and skills." (Taylor & Runté, 1995)
- "The whole question of whether teaching is a profession or can become one, is a red herring. The real issue is the degree to which teachers can resist deskilling and maintain some measure of autonomy within the school bureaucracy". (Taylor & Runte, 1995)
- "A profession has both moral and epistemic purposes . . . professionals are inescapably moral agents whose work depends upon public trust for its success." (Sockett, 2008)

## Teaching: art, craft, or science?—The art of teaching and the science of education I

According to Elliot Eisner, a prominent American philosopher of education, teaching is an art in at least four senses:

a. It [teaching] . . . can be performed with such skill and grace that for the student as well as for the teacher the experience can suitably be characterized as aesthetic . . .

b. Teachers, like painters, composers, actresses and dancers, make judgments based on qualities that unfold during the course of action . . .

c. The teacher's activity is not dominated by prescriptions or routines but is influenced by qualities and contingencies that are unpredicted.

d. Teaching is an art in the sense that the ends it achieves are often created in process.

(Quoted in Alexander, 2001: 273)

## "The moral and epistemic purposes of teacher education" and the teacher as moral epistemon or moral epistemologist professional

Four Models (Sockett, 2008: 48–62):

1. The scholar-professional: "regards knowledge as the purpose of education, so that the teacher is dedicated to imparting wisdom and fostering the life of the mind" (p. 48).

2. The nurturer-professional: "primarily focused on the development of the individual. It describes a teacher whole primary focus is on relationships with children" (p. 48).

3. The clinician professional: "emphasizes the teacher's adaptive expertise, with moral emphases geared to social purposes such as social justice" (p. 49).

4. The moral agent professional: "The model describes the individual teacher with a primarily moral purpose focused on the child's comprehensive development and growth, and its epistemic purposes, for teachers as well as children, are to integrate academic content with intellectual and moral virtues, such as accuracy, consistency, courage, and open-mindedness" (p.49).

### The teacher as pedagogue of the mind and the soul (paidagogos tou nou kai tes psyches)

Key ideas/concepts:

- Teaching as "a moral craft built around a moral relationship between the teacher and the student" (Murrell, 2010: 96).
- "Everything we do . . . as teachers have moral overtones. Through dialogue, modeling, the provision of practice, and the attribution of best motive, the one caring as teacher nurtures the ethical ideal. She cannot nurture the student intellectually without regard for the ethical ideal unless she is willing to risk producing a monster" (Noddings, 1984: 179).

### Pedagogy as discourse vs education/teaching as act or "doing" – Pedagogue vs teacher – Distinction between pedagogy and education/teaching

- "Pedagogy encompasses both the act of teaching and its contingent theories and debates (values, evidence and justifications" (Alexander, 2001: 931).
- "Pedagogy is the discourse with which one needs to engage in order both to teach intelligently and make sense of teaching – for discourse and act are interdependent, and there can be no teaching without pedagogy or pedagogy without teaching" (ibid., 927).
- "A lesson is part of a larger curriculum embodying educational purposes and values, and reflecting assumptions abut what knowledge and understanding are of most worth to the individual and to society" (ibid., 929).

In Italian there is a distinction between *pedagogia* and *educazione,* between "educational doing" and "pedagogical knowing".
"The word *pedagogia* characterizes the reflection about this doing and the knowledge derived from it" (Bohm, 1995: 60).

***Education vs pedagogy II – a modern variation of a classical Greek theme***
Bohm (1995: 59–61) asserts that "contemporary educational thought has added very little to the answers already found in Hellenism". He distinguishes between "education as activity" and "pedagogy as knowledge", between "educational doing" and "pedagogical knowing":

> it is advisable first to draw a careful boundary between education and pedagogy . . . we will denote with the term "education", the educational "doing" that takes place in a concrete (educational) situation, and on the other hand, "pedagogy" will denote critical observation (including projective forethought), reflection, and the knowledge about the "doing".

# Epimython - What Teachers Need to/Should Know and Be Able to Do

According to Lee S. Shulman, content knowledge includes:
- General pedagogical knowledge, including principles and strategies for classroom organization and management.
- Curriculum knowledge, including materials and programmes.
- Pedagogical content knowledge, an amalgam of content and pedagogy that is teachers' special form of professional understanding.
- Knowledge of learners and their characteristics.
- Knowledge of educational contexts, including the characteristics of classrooms, schools, communities and cultures.
- Knowledge of educational ends, purposes and values, and their philosophical and historical grounds.

(Quoted in Darling-Hammond et al., 1999: 35)

# References

Abbs, P. 1994. *The Educational Imperative: A Defence of Socratic and Aesthetic Learning.* London: Falmer.
Alexander, R. J. 2001. *Culture and Pedagogy: International Comparisons in Primary Education.* Blackwell Publishers.

Bartolome, L. I. 2007. "Critical Pedagogy and Teacher Education: Radicalizing Prospective Teachers", in McLaren, P. and Kincheloe, J. L. (eds). *Critical Pedagogy: Where Are We Now?* Oxford: Peter Lang.

Bohm, W. 1995. *Theory, Practice, and the Education of the Person.* Washington DC: Organization of American States.

Boyles, D. (ed.). 2005. *Schools or Markets? Commercialism, Privatization, and School–Business Partnerships.* Mahwah, NJ and London: Lawrence Erlbaum Associates.

Castells, 1996.

Darling-Hammond, L. 2006. *Powerful Teacher Education: Lessons from Exemplary Programs.* San Francisco, CA: Jossey-Bass.

Darling-Hammond, L., Wise, A. E. and Klein, S. P. 1999. *A License to Teach: Raising Standards for Teaching.* Jossey Bass.

Freire, Paulo. 1974. *Pedagogy of the Oppressed.* New York: Herder & Herder.

Furedi, F. 2003. "Afterword: The Downsizing of Intellectual Authority", in *Critical Review of International and Political Philosophy* 6(4), 172–178.

Grant, C. 2008. in *Handbook of Research on Teacher Education* edited by Marilyn Cochran-Smith et al. London: Routledge.

Lezotte, L. W. and Snyder, K. M. 2011. *What Effective Schools Do.* Solution Tree Press.

Murrell, P. C. 2010. *Teaching as a Moral Practice: Defining, Developing, and Assessing Professional Dispositions in Teacher Education.* Cambridge, MA: Harvard Education Press.

Noddings, Nel. 1984. *Caring: A Feminine Approach to Ethics and Moral Education.* Berkeley, CA: University of California Press.

Nussbaum, 1997. *Cultivating Humanity: A Classical Defense of Reform in Liberal Education.* Cambridge, MA and London: Harvard University Press.

Sahlberg, P. 2010. *Finnish Lessons: What can the World Learn from Educational Change in Finland?* New York: Teachers College Press.

Sockett, H. 2008. "The Moral and Epistemic Purposes of Teacher Education", in *Handbook of Research on Teacher Education* edited by Marilyn Cochran-Smith et al. London: Routledge.

Taylor, R. and Runté, R. 1995. *Thinking about Teaching: An Introduction.* Toronto: Harcourt Brace.

Wheeler-Bell, Q., et al. 2013. "Review Symposium of Meira Levinson, No Citizen Left Behind", *Studies in Philosophy and Education* 32(6), 653–666.

# PART I

# EDUCATION AND TEACHER EDUCATION
# IN THE MODERN WORLD

# CHAPTER ONE

# REQUEST FOR AN INTERNATIONAL SURVEY OF THE TEACHING PROFESSION

## CHARLES C. WOLHUTER

PROFESSOR, NORTH-WEST UNIVERSITY, SOUTH AFRICA
PRESIDENT OF SACHES (SOUTH AFRICAN COMPARATIVE
AND HISTORICAL EDUCATIONAL SOCIETY)

**Abstract**

At a time of globalization and the ICT revolution, one of the opportunities for scholars in the field of comparative education is to embark on studies international in scope. Examples of such studies are the IEA surveys and the PISA studies, two international surveys of the academic profession. The Carnegie investigation took place in the 1990s in fourteen countries and the CAP (Changing Academic Survey) survey has just been completed. This survey used a standard questionnaire sent to a sample of the academic profession in 18 countries; it has resulted in a contract for 18 books to be published by Springer and also in over a hundred articles. The author was one of the editors of the recently published *International Handbook on Teacher Education Worldwide* and also of a survey of the social portrayal of the teaching profession in a number of countries. These projects have suggested the need for an international survey of the teaching profession, using a standard questionnaire with a sample of the teaching profession in as many countries as possible. Such a survey should include the following aspects of the lives of teachers:

- biographical particulars
- working conditions
- teaching education
- teaching activities
- views on educational matters
- views on social issues
- community involvement

- relations with school governance
- relations with government, especially with education authorities
- job satisfaction

The purpose of this paper is to test the idea of such a survey, to canvass support and to discuss the content of the questionnaire to be run.

**Key-words**
Teaching profession, Comparative and International Education, Job satisfaction of teachers

# Introduction

At a time of globalization and the ICT revolution, one of the opportunities for scholars in the field of comparative education is to embark on studies international in scope. Examples of such studies are the IEA surveys and the PISA studies, two international surveys of the academic profession. The Carnegie investigation took place in the 1990s in fourteen countries and the CAP (Changing Academic Survey) survey has just been completed. This survey used a standard questionnaire sent to a sample of the academic profession in 23 countries; it has resulted in a contract for 18 books to be published by Springer and also in over a hundred articles. The author was one of the editors of the recently published *International Handbook on Teacher Education Worldwide* and also of a survey of the social portrayal of the teaching profession in a number of countries. These projects have suggested the need for an international survey of the teaching profession, using a standard questionnaire with a sample of the teaching profession in as many countries as possible.

# Research Method

The paper will subsequently survey the three research projects, namely the CAP International Survey of the Academic Profession, the *International Handbook on Teacher Education Worldwide* and the research on the social portrayal of teachers. From the analogy of the fruitful CAP project on the one hand, and the predicament of the teaching profession (revealed by the last two projects), an international survey of the teaching profession will be proposed.

## The CAP International Survey of the Academic Profession

The massification of higher education worldwide, together with the other sweeping changes which hit the higher education environment in the third quarter of the twentieth century, led to the first international survey of the academic profession. This survey, the so-called Carnegie Survey (so called after the Carnegie Foundation which financed the investigation) surveyed the academic profession in 14 countries: Chile, Brazil, Mexico, the United States of America (USA), the United Kingdom, Sweden, the Netherlands, Germany, Israel, Russia, Hong Kong, South Korea, Japan and Australia. The survey took place in the later 1980s and early 1990s and the results were published in Altbach (1996). The acceleration of the changes in the higher education environment brought about a second major international project, the CAP (Changing Academic Profession) survey during 2008, surveying, by means of a uniform questionnaire, the academic profession in the following 18 countries: Argentina, Brazil, Mexico, the USA, Canada, the United Kingdom, Norway, Finland, Germany, Portugal, Italy, South Korea, Hong Kong, China, Japan, Malaysia, Australia and South Africa. This survey has resulted in a contract for 18 books to be published by Springer and also in over a hundred articles. The first of the books was the volume edited by Locke et al. (2011).

## Research Project on the Social Portrayal of Teachers

The author has also been involved in a research project surveying a sample of teachers regarding the social portrayal of teachers in South Africa. The results were published in Wolhuter et al. (2012). This same survey was conducted in Greece, Cyprus, England and Sweden. In the South Africa survey it was found that while teachers are in the profession out of noble motives (to serve as a role model for children, the entered the profession out of love for children) they do experience serious stress in their work environment. This stress revolves around the large number of children per class, time pressure, children with special needs, a shortage of learning material, and the interminable stream of education reform and restructuring. Furthermore they also experience as problematic parents' neglect of their duty of care and education with respect to their children, as well as the poor education background of parents (Wolhuter et al., 2012).

## International Handbook on Teacher Education Worldwide

The author was also involved as editor of the *International Handbook on Teacher Education Worldwide* (Karras & Wolhuter, 2010). This book contains chapters on teacher education in some 90 countries, written by teacher education scholars in those countries. A study of the chapters revealed that teacher education worldwide show a number of distinct trends. These trends occur worldwide, shaped in each case by the national context. These trends pertain to teacher education and its objectives, the roles for which teachers are prepared, the content of teacher education, methods of teacher education, the duration of teacher education, the control of teacher education, teacher educators, access to teacher education, supply/demand balances, internationalization and regionalization, indigenization, in-service and education and training (Wolhuter & Karras, 2011).

## Proposing an International Survey of the Teaching Profession

In an emerging knowledge society, education is more important than ever. A pivotal component in any national education project is the teacher corps. Given the importance of education and of the teaching profession, and the momentous changes currently sweeping through the profession and their training, the author, based on his experience as participant in the CAP project, wishes to plead for an international survey of the teaching profession. Such a survey could also, as in the case of the CAP project, take the form of a uniform questionnaire to be completed by a representative sample of teachers in a number of countries.

Such a questionnaire should cover the following aspects of teachers' professional lives:

- Biographical details: gender, age, years of service in the teaching profession, marital status, family background: number of children, ages of children; socio-economic descent (education levels of parents), years of work outside the teaching profession
- Sources of inspiration/motivation: why the teaching profession was selected as a career
- Training: qualifications, number of years of teacher education, graduate studies, in-service education and training

- Teaching activities: number of hours per week spent on each of teaching, preparing lessons, assessing student work, subject(s) taught, ages and grades of students taught
- Extra-mural activities: number of hours per week, kind of extra-mural activities
- Administrative activities: number of hours per week spent on administrative work, kind of administrative work
- Relations with students
- Relations with parents
- Relations with community and society: the standing of the teaching profession in society, the reason(s) for this standing and how this standing could be enhanced
- Relations with school management
- Relations with government and educational authorities
- Job satisfaction: teachers' views on the extent of and sources of work-related stress.

## Conclusion

For the well-being of the teacher profession and for scholarly inquiry aimed at securing such well-being, an international survey of the teaching profession is essential. This paper ends therefore with the plea that within the remit of this conference, envisaged as the first of a regular annual event, such a survey be planned and carried out.

## References

Altbach, P. G. (ed.). 1996. *The International Academic Profession: Portraits from Fourteen Countries*. Princeton, NJ: Carnegie Foundation for the Advancement of Teaching and Learning.

Karras, K. G. and Wolhuter, C. C. (eds). 2010. *Handbook on Teacher Education World Wide* (Volumes 1 & 2). Athens: Atrapos (republished Athens: Ion Books, 2011).

Locke, W., Cummings, W. K. & Fisher, D. (eds). 2011. *Changing Governance and Management in Higher Education: The Perspectives of the Academy*. Dordrecht: Springer.

Wolhuter, C. C., & Karras, K. 2011. "Global Trends in Teacher Education and the Implications thereof for the Teaching of Comparative International Education at Universities", in N. Popov, C. Wolhuter, B. Leutwyler, M. Mihova & J. Ogunlye (eds), *Comparative Education, Teacher Training, Education Policy, School Leadership and Social Inclusion* (Volume 9), pp. 7–12. Sofia: Bureau for Educational Services.

Wolhuter, C., Meyer, L. & Karras, K. 2012. "Die Suid-Afrikaanse onderwysers se belewing en beskouing van die onderwysprofessie", in E. Gouws, J. Dreyer, A.-M. Dieker & C. Wolhuter (Eds), *Beauty and the Beast: Towards Turning the Tide in Education (EASA 2011 Conference Proceedings)*, pp. 122–129. Cape Town: Digital Print Solution.

# CHAPTER TWO

# DISCOURSES OF QUALITY,
# PRACTICES OF PERFORMATIVITY:
# RESTRUCTURING TEACHER EDUCATION
# AND PROFESSIONAL DEVELOPMENT POLICIES
# IN THE "EUROPE OF KNOWLEDGE"

## GEORGE PASIAS
ASSISTANT PROFESSOR, UNIVERSITY OF ATHENS, GREECE
## AND YIANNIS ROUSSAKIS
RESEARCHER, INSTITUTE FOR EDUCATION POLICY, GREECE

**Abstract**

Since the launch of the Lisbon Strategy, which urged European Union Member States to "attract high-quality teachers", teacher education and professional development have been transversal themes in most initiatives towards the "European Education Space" and the "Europe of Knowledge". The newly-launched "Europe 2020" strategy also underlines the need "to provide adequate initial teacher education … and to make teaching an attractive career-choice".

In this paper, we briefly review, critically analyse and comment on the European Union (EU) policy discourses, initiatives and practices concerning teachers since the launch of the Lisbon Strategy in 2000. We argue that teacher education and professional development policies promoted by the EU stem from international organizations' global discourses of quality, efficiency and effectiveness of education, and create a cult of performativity and quality assurance; they strongly influence the recruitment processes, the curricula, the degree structures, the licensing procedures and the professional careers of educators, signalling a massive restructuring of the teaching profession in Europe.

**Key-words**
"Europe of Knowledge", Teacher Education, European Policies

## Introduction

Since the mid-1990s, teacher education, professional development and practice have been at the foreground of policy debates about the quality and effectiveness of schooling and the role of education for economic development and competitiveness. Expectations from teachers have been aggrandized, and maxims like "no amount of policy reform will make schools more effective unless teachers are a party to the change" (CERI, 1998: 11) or "the quality of an education system cannot exceed the quality of its teachers" (Barber & Mourshed, 2007: 13) are increasingly found in policy documents, research studies and expert reports (OECD, 2005; Caena, 2011; Snoek et al., 2011). "Teacher quality" arguments have been utilized, among others, as utterances of the neo-paternalistic "no excuses" reform movement (Whitman, 2008) or as incantations of social inequalities: "the single most important factor determining whether students succeed in school is not the color of their skin or their ZIP code or even their parents' income – it is the quality of their teacher" ("How to Fix our Schools", 2010).

What is becoming increasingly obvious from this "Scottish shower" of teacher appraisal and inculpation is the attempt of various education stakeholders to construct and study teacher education and practice as a "policy problem", "warranted by empirical evidence and cost-benefit analyses linked to pupils' achievement" (Cochran-Smith & Fries, 2008: 1081). It can also be maintained that this "policy problem" is to a great extent framed by international organizations such as the OECD, the World Bank and the EU, which gradually develop "a shared frame of reference regarding the concept of teacher quality" (ATEE, 2006: 3), overleaping or circumventing different national educational contexts (Grek, 2010).

In this paper, we briefly review, critically analyse and comment on the European Union (EU) policy discourses, initiatives and practices concerning teachers since the launch of the Lisbon Strategy in 2000. We argue that teacher education and professional development policies promoted by the EU stem from international organizations' global discourses of the quality, efficiency and effectiveness of education, and create a cult of performativity and quality assurance; they strongly influence the recruitment processes, the curricula, the degree structures, the licensing procedures and the professional careers of educators, signalling a massive restructuring of the teaching profession in Europe.

## Quality and Performativity: Reshaping Teachers

As we have written elsewhere (Pasias & Roussakis, 2012a; 2012b), we perceive "quality of education" as a "panoptical" discourse connected to market-driven and managerialist reforms, which advocate a minimalist and "evaluative state", envisage an "audit society" and promote "accountability regimes" in education. This discourse is often used to legitimize evidence-based educational reforms, which rely on benchmarking, monitoring and the use of "catalyst data" (Lingard & Sellar, 2013) in order to introduce or facilitate educational change. The "quality" arguments are used to advocate policy and practise control mechanisms: surveillance technology is used extensively in peer reviewing and evaluation in education to achieve concrete learning objectives and to improve educational outcomes (student achievement). Under the influence of the "quality discourse", education is colonized by technocratic-instrumentalist perceptions, and operates through a discerning set of ideological principles and practices. "Quality control" as an "ideological concept", Cowen notes, "along with the equation of educational excellence with 'standards and assessment'", have "melted concern for teacher competence into a powerful new discourse about excellence in education, managerialism, surveillance and a new professionalism" (Cowen, 2002: 10).

Being ideologized, "quality of education" needs what Laclau and Mouffe call a "master-signifier", a "quilting point" in Lacanian terms, which would assume "a universal structuring function" (Laclau & Mouffe, 2001: xi) within the "quality of education discourse", and would give content and meaning to its differential elements. This role, against the backdrop of a changing ontology of the teaching profession, is played by the concept of "performativity". Stephen Ball describes performativity as

> [A] technology, a culture and a mode of regulation, or even a system of 'terror' in Lyotard's words, that employs judgments, comparisons and displays as means of control, attrition and change. The performances of individual subjects or organisations serve as measures of productivity or output, or displays of 'quality', or 'moments' of promotion or inspection. They stand for, encapsulate or represent the worth, quality or value of an individual or organisation within a field of judgment." (Ball, 2004: 143)

In education, Perryman argues, "performativity is manifested by the culture of outcomes, efficiency and accountability" and is "intrinsically linked to the emergence of the evaluative state, accountability in education policy and transparency to the public gaze" (Perryman, 2009: 617, 618). It recasts teacher professionalism along the lines of measured productivity, centre-steered initiatives and "market discipline", away from "professional ethics, collegiality, social responsibility and good practice" (Arthur, 2009: 442).

In essence, performativity vests the "transformative illusion" (Zizek, 1989: 115), which "quilts" teachers in the discourse of quality: it produces a particular profile of the teaching profession, with which teachers should identify themselves and, simultaneously, it discredits or deconstructs competing visions of the "good teacher".[1]

In our analysis, we try to locate occurrences of this "quilting process" between quality and performativity in the EU discourse for teachers.

## EU Discourses, Policies and Practices Concerning Teachers: The Lisbon Strategy and Beyond

The Lisbon Strategy, launched at the dawn of the twenty-first century, aspired to make Europe "the most competitive and dynamic knowledge-based economy in the world, capable of sustainable economic growth with more and better jobs and greater social cohesion" (European Council, 2000). Right from the start, it urged EU Member States to "attract high-quality teachers". Initial teacher education and the professional development of educators, have since been transversal themes in most initiatives towards the "European Education Space" and the European Knowledge Economy-cum-Society.

EU institutional and working group policy documents concerning teachers stress, among others, the need to update teacher education programs, to staff the teaching profession with highly-skilled, adequately qualified individuals, to increase teacher mobility and to establish professional development and lifelong learning structures. The issues they insist on with increasing severity over the last few years are the importance of teacher quality towards raising education outcomes, and the urgent need to restructure the teaching profession in order for the Union to achieve a competitive advantage.

In the inaugural Lisbon Strategy Council Conclusions, European leaders contended that "each European citizen would need a wide range of key competences in order to adapt to the rapidly changing and highly interconnected world" and that "a European framework should define the new basic skills to be provided through lifelong learning" (European

---

[1] See also Moore (2004) for a profound analysis of competing representations of the "good teacher", mainly with reference to the English context.

Council, 2000). They also introduced the Open Method of Coordination (OMC) as a "soft" form of governance, which embodied performative technologies such as "fixing guidelines, specific timetables, quantitative and qualitative indicators and benchmarks, periodic monitoring, evaluation and peer review practices" (para. 37). As a result, a concrete set of standards, indicators and benchmarks gradually became a part of the heart and soul of the European education policy process: "From now on, the production of statistical reports by Member States would double. New categories of educational structures were being invented, and a different European education space was in the making; it would be governed by numbers and quality standards" (Grek, 2008: 213).

Teachers and teacher education became one of the thirteen "concrete objectives" that had to be accomplished by the member-states' systems of education by 2010 (CEC, 2001: 7). Improving the education and training of teachers and trainers (which included defining their required skills, raising the attractiveness of the profession and developing in-service training structures) was considered a *sine qua non* for "raising the quality and standard of learning in order to increase the effectiveness of education and training system in the EU" (CEC, 2001:4). The Commission placed great emphasis on the process of "measuring the achievement of the objective by a limited number of key indicators and the setting up of procedures for the exchange of national and international experiences in key strategic areas" (CEC, 2001:4). To this end it set up an expert Standing Group on Indicators and Benchmarks (SGIB) which would "give advice on the use of indicators as tools for measuring progress towards the common objectives" and an expert Working Group on "Improving the Education of Teachers and Trainers", with a mandate to examine problems, obstacles and policy practices from the member states involving teacher professionalism, to identify "appropriate indicators" and to study quality assurance processes (CEC, 2004).

The Joint Interim Report on the progress of the Lisbon Strategy for Education (CEU, 2004) urged the member states to focus on "reform and investment" in order to enable teachers to meet their changing roles in the knowledge-based society and in transforming the education and training systems". It also noted the need for a European Qualifications Framework (EQF), which would function within the broader context of the Lisbon, Bologna (higher education) and Copenhagen (vocational education and training) processes (CEU, 2004: 12–14). The EQF would use "learning outcomes and competences as descriptors of qualifications", and serve as recourse for "mutually validated quality assurance instruments" (CEU, 2004: 28–29).

In this vein, the quality/performativity nexus became clearly identifiable in the EU discourses and policies concerning teachers and reflected the Union's technocratic-entrepreneurial rationale. The Commission and the Education Council texts stressed that the success of the reforms undertaken at both the European and the member-state level depended on the motivation and the quality of those working in education and training, who should be prepared for their changing roles in the knowledge-based society and for transforming the education and training systems (CEU, 2004).

In 2005 the Commission presented a set of "Common Principles for Teacher Competences and Qualifications" in order to "provide an impetus for developing policies which will enhance the quality and efficiency of education across the Union" (CEU, 2005: 2). The teaching profession in Europe was profiled as a "graduate" and "mobile profession", "placed within the context of lifelong learning" and "based on partnerships". The Commission also proposed a corresponding set of "key competences" that teachers should possess: the ability to work "with others", "with knowledge, technology and information", and "with and in society" (CEU, 2005: 3–4).

In the second half of the Lisbon Strategy decade, teacher quality and the quality of teaching were mentioned in the institutional texts "as key factors in determining whether the European Union can increase its competitiveness in the globalised world" (CEC, 2007b: 3). Raising the quality of the teaching profession became part of the reforms in the areas of the school knowledge and the curriculum, the development of students' new skills and competences as well as school improvement and effectiveness (CEC, 2007b: 3–5). The new rationale of a "techno-preneurial" professionalization of the teachers treated schools as "more autonomous and open learning environments", emphasized "the management of new competences in new learning environments" and demanded that teachers bear "greater responsibility for the content, organisation and monitoring of the learning process, as well as for their own personal career-long professional development" (CEU, 2007b: 8). The Commission and the Council, during that time, subsumed teachers in all their major initiatives, i.e. the key competences for lifelong learning (CEU, 2006), the revised set of comparative indicators and benchmarks (CEC, 2007a) and the European Qualifications Framework (CEU, 2008). They also sponsored a series of "working conferences" and "peer learning activities" (e.g. the "Teachers and Trainers" Cluster) which aimed at "finding solutions to common problems" concerning teachers and teacher education.

Following the lead of the Lisbon Strategy, the "Europe 2020" "strategic framework for European cooperation in education and training", included teachers in the "knowledge triangle" (education–research–innovation) policies and initiatives (CEC, 2008, 2009b). The Commission repeated that "the quality of teachers is the most important within-school factor affecting student performance" and that the enhancement "of innovation, creativity and entrepreneurship, must be reflected in curricula, pedagogies and qualifications" (CEC, 2008: 8, 10). It also urged the EU member states to "revise and strengthen the professional profile of all teaching professions, introducing coherent and adequately resourced systems for recruitment, selection, induction and professional development of teaching staff based on clearly defined competences needed at each stage of a teaching career" (CEC, 2012: 15).

Throughout the Lisbon Strategy period, empirical evidence, mainly in the form of research findings and monitoring reports, became the main input of OMC comparisons and assumptions, which paved the way for EU reactionary reforms in education. In the revised set of indicators and benchmarks, the professional development of teachers and trainers is one of the "16 core indicators for monitoring progress towards the Lisbon objectives" identified by the European Council in May 2007 (CEU, 2007a). The 2009 Progress Report remarks that these indicators enable the Commission and the member states to "underpin key policy messages; analyse progress both at the EU and national levels; identify good performance for peer review and exchange; and compare performance with third countries" (CEC, 2009a: 14). The Report notes that "indicators never tell the full story. But they help to identify differences, similarities and trends and to provide a starting point for further analysis in order to understand better performance and progress" (CEC, 2009a: 15). Despite those words of caution, the "policy by numbers" approach is still the dominant feature of the EU educational strategy: "For the period to 2020, policy cooperation should be supported by benchmarks which fully reflect the identified long term strategic challenges … The future education and training benchmarks should be sufficiently flexible to take account of the targets and indicators in the EU policies beyond 2010" (CEC, 2008: 13).

## Concluding Comments

In this paper, we have argued that the EU promotes a "techno-preneurial" restructuring of the teaching profession through the extended use of numbers, in the form of quality indicators, standards and benchmarks, and the deployment of accountability and performativity audits as policy devices. European policies demarcate a "high surveillance/low trust context" (Mahony & Hextall, 2000: 102), which render teachers "managed professionals" (Codd, 2005: 194), who are constantly challenged to conform their skills and competences to prescribed profiles. Through discourses of quality and practices of performativity, such as those of the EU, teachers resemble J. P. Gee's "shape-shifting portfolio people": they are expected to build up "a variety of skills, experiences, and achievements in terms of which they can define themselves as successful now and worthy of more success later", but also to "stand ready and able" to rearrange their portfolios creatively and redefine themselves "as competent and worthy" if and when circumstances change (Gee, 2004: 96).

But, to quote Biesta (2012: 15), competence "is in itself *never enough*". It needs to be combined with the *phronesis* that will inform "wise educational judgments" (Biesta, 2012: 18). Unfortunately, a measurable "Europe of competences" seems to discard such thoughts.

# References

Arthur, L. 2009. "From Performativity to Professionalism: Lecturers' Responses to Student Feedback", *Teaching in Higher Education* 14(4), 441–454.

ATEE (Association for Teacher Education in Europe). 2006. *The Quality of Teachers: Recommendations on the Development of Indicators to Identify Teacher Quality: Policy Paper* (http://www.atee1.org/uploads/ kennisbank/ quality_of_teachers_atee_def.pdf, accessed 5 February 2013).

Ball, S. J. 2004. "Performativities and Fabrications in the Education Economy: Towards the Performative Society", in Ball, S. J. (ed.) *The RoutledgeFalmer Reader in Sociology of Education*, London: RoutledgeFalmer, pp. 143–155.

Barber, M. and Mourshed, M. 2007. *How the World's Best Performing School Systems Come out on Top*. McKinsey and Co. (http://mckinseyonsociety.com/ downloads/reports/Education/Worlds_School_Systems_Final.pdf, accessed 12 February 2013).

Biesta, G. 2012. "The Future of Teacher Education: Evidence, Competence or Wisdom?" *ROSE* 3(1), 8–21.

Caena, F. 2011. *Literature Review: Teachers' Core Competences: Requirements and Development*. Education and Training 2020 Thematic Working Group on the Professional Development of Teachers. Brussels: European Commission.

CEC (Commission of the European Communities). 2001. *Detailed Work Programme for the Follow-up of the Concrete Future Objectives of Education and Training Systems*. COM(2001)501, Brussels, 07.09.2001.

—. 2004. *Improving the Education of Teachers and Trainers*. Progress Report, Working Group A. Brussels.

—. 2005. *Common European Principles for Teacher Competences and Qualifications*. Brussels (http://ec.europa.eu/education/policies/2010/doc/principles_en.pdf, accessed 5 October 2010).

—. 2007a. *A Coherent Framework of Indicators and Benchmarks for Monitoring Progress towards the Lisbon Objectives in Education and Training.* COM(2007)61final. Brussels.

—. 2007b. *Improving the Quality of Teacher Education.* COM(2007)392final. Brussels (http://ec.europa.eu/education/com392_en.pdf, accessed 16 January 2013).

—. 2008. *An Updated Strategic Framework for European Cooperation in Education and Training.* COM(2008)865final, Brussels.

—. 2009. *Progress towards the Lisbon Objectives in Education and Training: Indicators and Benchmarks 2009.* Commission Staff Working Document.

—. 2009b. *Key Competences for a Changing World.* COM(2009)640final. Brussels.

—. 2012. *Rethinking Education: Investing in Skills for Better Socio-economic Outcomes.* COM(2012)669final. Strasbourg.

CERI (Centre for Educational Research and Innovation). 1998. *Staying Ahead: In-service Training and Teacher Professional Development.* Paris: OECD.

CEU (Council of the EU). 2004. *Joint Interim Report on the Implementation of the Detailed Work Programme on the Follow-up of the Objectives of Education and Training Systems in Europe.* EDUC43, 6905/04, Brussels.

—. 2006. *Recommendation on Key Competences for Lifelong Learning.* OJ L394.

—. 2007a. *A Coherent Framework of Indicators and Benchmarks for Monitoring Progress towards the Lisbon Objectives in Education and Training. Council Conclusions of 25th May 2007.* 2007/C 1083/07.

—. 2007b. *Conclusions of the Council on Improving the Quality of Teacher Education.* OJ C300.

—. 2008. *Recommendation on the Establishment of the European Qualifications Framework for Lifelong Learning.* OJ C111.

Cochran-Smith, M. and Fries, K. 2008. "Research on Teacher Education: Changing Times, Changing Paradigms" in Cochran-Smith, M., Feiman-Nemser, S. and McIntyre, D. J. (eds), *Handbook of Research on Teacher Education: Enduring Questions in Changing Contexts*, 3rd ed., New York, NY: Routledge, pp. 1050–1093.

Codd, J. 2005. "Teachers as 'Managed Professionals' in the Global Education Industry: The New Zealand Experience", *Educational Review*, 57(2), 193–206.

Cowen R. 2002. "Socrates Was Right? Teacher Education Systems and the State", in Thomas, E. (ed.), *Teacher Education: Dilemmas and Prospects: World Yearbook of Education 2002*, London: Kogan Page, pp. 3–12.

European Council. 2000. *Lisbon European Council 23 and 24 March 2000: Presidency Conclusions* (http://ue.eu.int/ueDocs/cms_Data/docs/pressData/en/ec/00100-r1.en0.htm, accessed 15 January 2013).

Gee, J. P. 2004. *Situated Language and Learning: A Critique of Traditional Schooling.* London: Routledge.

Grek, S. 2008. "From Symbols to Numbers: The Shifting Technologies of Education Governance in Europe", *European Educational Research Journal* 7(2), 208–218.

Grek, S. 2010. "International Organisations and the Shared Construction of Policy 'Problems': Problematisation and Change in Education Governance in Europe", *European Educational Research Journal* 9(3), 396–406.

"How to Fix our Schools: A Manifesto by Joel Klein, Michelle Rhee and other Education Leaders." 2010. *Washington Post* (10 October). (http://www.washingtonpost.com/wp_dyn/content/article/2010/10/07/AR2010 100705078.html accessed on 14/2/2013).

OECD 2005. *Teachers Matter: Attracting, Developing and Retaining Effective Teachers*. Paris: OECD.

Laclau, E. and Mouffe, C. 2001. *Hegemony and Socialist Strategy: Towards a Radical Democratic Politics,* 2nd ed. London: Verso.

Lingard, B. and Sellar, S. 2013. "'Catalyst Data': Perverse Systemic Effects of Audit and Accountability in Australian Schooling", *Journal of Education Policy* 28 (in press).

Mahony, P. and Hextall, I. 2000. *Reconstructing Teaching: Standards, Performance and Accountability*. London: RoutledgeFalmer.

Moore, A. 2004. *The Good Teacher: Dominant Discourses in Teaching and Teacher Education*. London: RoutledgeFalmer.

OJ (Official Journal of the European Union). 2009. *Council Conclusions of 12 May 2009 on a Strategic Framework for European Cooperation in Education and Training ("ET 2020")*. 2009/C119/02.

Pasias, G. and Roussakis, Y. 2012a. "'Who Marks the Bench?' A Critical Review of the Neo-European Educational 'Paradigm'", *Journal for Critical Education Policy Studies* 10(1), 127–141.

—. 2012b. "Current 'Policies of Knowledge' in the European Union: Mapping and Critically Assessing 'Quality' in a 'Measurable' Europe of Knowledge", *Revista Española de Educación Comparada*, 20, 303–324.

Snoek, M., Swennen, A. and van der Klink, M. 2011. "The Quality of Teacher Educators in the European Policy Debate: Actions and Measures to Improve the Professionalism of Teacher Educators", *Professional Development in Education* 37(5), 651–664.

Whitman, D. 2008. *Sweating the Small Stuff: Inner-City Schools and the New Paternalism*. Washington, DC: Thomas B. Fordham Institute Press.

Zizek, S. 1989. *The Sublime Object of Ideology*. London: Verso.

# CHAPTER THREE

# TEACHING AND LEARNING POLICIES IN SOUTH AFRICAN SCHOOLS IN THE NEW DEMOCRATIC DISPENSATION: A CRITICAL DISCOURSE ANALYSIS

## TEBOGO MOGASHOA
### LECTURER, COLLEGE OF EDUCATION, UNIVERSITY OF SOUTH AFRICA

**Abstract**

The aim of the research was to establish how teaching and learning policies are implemented by teachers in selected South African schools. A qualitative method was used to gather information. Members of School Management Teams had different views on teaching and learning policies. Learners who are taught in their home language encounter fewer difficulties in learning than those who are taught in a second or third language. There must be a shift from teacher centred to learner centred approaches to teaching, that is, a shift from teaching to learning to enhance thinking and reflection on learners' prior knowledge and experiences. Policy makers have to explore professional development from the side of the participating teachers in order to clearly understand what would be best for changing their classroom practice.

**Keywords**

Curriculum, Involvement, Teacher, Evaluation and Assessment, Critical Discourse Analysis, Perceptions, Forms of Assessment, Criterion Referencing, Assessment Tasks, Progression and Promotion

# Introduction

There have been critics of the South African education policies which condemned the National Department of Education for a curriculum that is said to be irrelevant and uninteresting for the majority of South African learners. Before 1994 the education system in South Africa contradicted world trends by deliberately choosing to serve the education needs of only a section of the South African population. The birth of democracy in 1994 led to the establishment of a new dispensation and that led to a need for the democratization of the education system. The apartheid education system disadvantaged the majority of South Africans, especially the black communities. The situation in the new democracy demanded serious changes in many spheres of life in South Africa, especially in education.

Among other things which were proposed by the Government of National Unity (GNU) was a transformational outcomes-based education. This ushered in Curriculum 2005 with its emphasis on outcomes-based education. According to Kramer (1999: 1), the introduction of outcomes-based education in South African schools and the advent of Curriculum 2005 marked an exciting transformation of the education system. The new curriculum was modelled on William Spady's version of outcomes-based education, defining it as a "comprehensive approach to organising and operating an education system that is focused on and defined by the successful demonstrations of learning outcomes sought from each other" (Spady, 1994: 1). There was a consensus about transforming education in South Africa by different stakeholders in education in order to change the education system and introduce a new curriculum. It was believed that Curriculum 2005 was created to empower all South African learners with knowledge, skills, attitudes and values which would provide productive and valuable agents of social change in creating a better future for all. Outcomes-based education emphasizes that learners should master learning outcomes and be able to work cooperatively.

# Theoretical Frameworks

According to Terre Blanche (2007: 20), refining a research problem involves identifying a theoretical framework upon which to base the research. It is imperative to state the theories that influenced the research problem as well as the research methods that were used. This study was underpinned by a critical discourse analysis theory in which the researcher expressed his comments or judgments based on written or spoken communications, discussions or conversations with educators, learners and the school management team members. It involved an analysis of the merits and demerits of the implementation of education policies in teaching and learning processes in South African schools.

McGregor (2003: 1) sees critical discourse analysis as a tool to help members of the profession understand the messages they are sending to themselves and others and to understand the meanings of the words spoken and written by others (www.kon.org/archives/forum/15-1/mcgreg orcda.html). According to Van Dijk (2001: 4), critical discourse analysis primarily studies social power abuse; dominance and inequality are enacted, reproduced and resisted by text and talk in the social and political context. Lucke (1996: 12) states that critical discourse analysis sets out to generate agency among students, teachers and others by giving them tools to see how texts represent the social and natural world in particular interests and how texts position them and generate the very relations of institutional power at work in classrooms, staffrooms and policy. Furthermore, Locke (2004: 1) argues that language is at the heart of critical discourse analysis. Language is an imperative aspect in teaching and learning as all learning areas/subjects are taught through language.

This study was also underpinned by constructivism. Constructivism is an epistemology (theory of knowledge), a learning or meaning-making theory that offers an explanation of the nature of knowledge and how human beings learn (Abdal-Haqq, 1998: 1). An increasingly dominant constructivist view focuses on the cultural embeddedness of learning, employing the methods and framework of cultural anthropology to examine how learning and cognition are distributed in the environment rather than stored in the head of an individual (Duffy, 2006: 11). Constructivism is a theory of knowledge (epistemology) that argues that humans generate knowledge and meaning from an interaction between their experiences and their ideas (Wikipedia).

The main research question was: How are educators implementing teaching and learning policies in South African schools in the new democratic dispensation?

## Research Design and Methods

Qualitative research assisted the researcher to investigate how teachers implement teaching and learning policies. This method assisted in answering the research questions which are informed by the main research question enabling critical discourse analysis to examine the spoken and written words in detail.

The target group and population of the study comprised experienced teachers who are teaching Grade 4 and 6 learners, and have been in the field of teaching for ten or more years. Only five schools in the Gauteng Department of Education's Gauteng North District were invited to participate in the study. Although the study focused on teachers and learners, other members of the schools' support system like principals and heads of departments were interviewed. This assisted in presenting the views of educators against the background of the ethos and contexts of the individual schools.

## Data Analysis

The researcher used the inductive approach to ensure that the research findings emerge from the frequent, dominant or significant themes inherent in raw data generated. Comparisons were drawn, similarities identified and a discussion of the research was presented. Once the data had been generated, the researcher organized the data and discovered the relationships or patterns through close scrutiny of the data. The data were coded, categorized and condensed. The researcher then interpreted and drew meaning from the displayed data.

## Research Findings and Discussions

***Question: Since the introduction of the new policies on teaching and learning, how has your teaching methodology changed?***

In responding to the question above, some teachers said there are a few changes, while others conceded that they have not changed the way they used to teach. Some teachers added that the new policies did not bring much change as they put more emphasis on spelling, comprehension, group activities and readers when teaching languages. This was vividly depicted by some of the teachers in the following statements:

"There is not that much change actually. Previously more emphasis was on writing and reading, and this is what we are still doing today."

"The difference is only that in the past the teacher was supposed to develop his/her own teaching and learning materials, while today the Department of Education supply us with teaching and learning materials."

"I don't really differ from how I used to teach because in languages I focus on the reading skills and comprehension of texts."

The data presented by the participants indicated that there were few changes from how they used to teach, while others conceded that they have not changed the way they used to teach. The researcher is of the opinion that some teachers were guided by the new teaching methodologies while others continued the way they used to teach.

**Question: What challenges do you encounter in the implementation of the new policies?**

Some teachers who participated in this study complained about the workload while others complained about the resources.

One teacher said: "Workload. It hinders our progress in teaching. I sometimes spend more time dealing with paper work instead of teaching the learners."

Another participant said, "I think the resources and time are our major challenges. Sometimes there are not enough periods to deal with all the learning outcomes and assessment standards."

The researcher found that the manner in which the teachers responded to the questions showed that workload and resources were their major challenges. Teachers mentioned that workload and resources hindered their progress in teaching. The analysis of this state of affairs showed that most teachers who complained about the resources were those in the townships and farm areas. Teachers in the former Model C schools only complained about the workload. This is an indication that the schools are not equally or equitably resourced.

**Question: Tell me more about the workshops you have attended.**

In responding to the question above, teachers had different views. This is supported by the different views below:

"In most workshops the facilitators gave us activities and guided us on how to go through the activities and we were given opportunities to demonstrate how we were going to implement these policies in our classrooms."

"When we attended the workshops on Curriculum 2005 (C2005), the Revised National Curriculum Statement (RNCS) and the National Curriculum Statement (NCS), we were told different things which were confusing. The facilitators were not interpreting the various documents the same way. We were given a lot of papers to fill in. The presentations in the workshops were not appropriate to what we were practically doing in our classes. At least with Curriculum and Assessment Policy Statement (CAPS), it was better".

All teachers interviewed conceded that they received training on various teaching and learning policies. However, teachers had different views of the workshops they attended. This was quite evident to the researcher when some teachers stated that in most workshops the facilitators gave them activities and guided them on how to go through the activities and were also given opportunities to demonstrate how they were going to implement these policies in their classrooms. An indication was also given by other teachers that the presentations in the workshops were not appropriate to what they were practically doing in their classes.

***Question: First, I would like you to comment on your understanding of teaching and learning policies in the new democratic dispensation.***

Members of the school management teams (SMTs) had different views on teaching and learning policies in South African schools in the new democratic dispensation. One said: "There are a number of policies that came into effect. Eh, my understanding is that the education system has changed drastically and many teachers have been confused. This has also affected our learners negatively because they cannot articulate or express themselves on matters of their own needs, or challenges of life. That is why we are having so many learners who are sitting at home, some have passed grade 12, and some have dropped out of schools."

Another SMT member said: "I think they are guidelines. They help us to understand what the Department of Education expects of us and how we should go about as we do our business. Eh, they also help us to do our work professionally". Another SMT member said: "The first thing is, eh, it's a big frustration as the policies change and it makes the management of the school very difficult and the teachers frustrated. If the teachers are frustrated, the child will not benefit. The fact is that we, South Africans, should have our own policies. It is nice to get some policies from Switzerland or England or wherever, but these are first world countries. These policies only benefit white children far more than black children. The black children come from poor circumstances, they don't have access to internet. The gap between the rich and the poor becomes even wider. This is devastating."

Another SMT member said: "We have policies which help us with the day to day running of the school. There are policies like code of conduct for the learners, maintenance, to make sure that the school is managed properly, religious policy to make sure that you don't discriminate, and safety policy to make sure that the learners are safe at school. Prior to 1994 policies were given to us but now we develop our own policies."

Based on the responses of the interviews with members of the SMTs who participated in this study, it was clear that they had different views on teaching and learning policies in South African schools in the new democratic dispensation. This was evident when one indicated that the introduction of the new policies on teaching and learning affected their learners negatively because they cannot articulate or express themselves on matters of their own needs, or challenges of life. Furthermore, the same sentiments were echoed by another member of the SMT when he stated that the new policies brought much frustration and caused the management of the school to be very difficult and frustrated the educators. On the other hand, another member of the SMT stated that the new teaching and learning policies are good guidelines and they helped them to understand and to do their work professionally. The other member of the SMT was not even sure of what teaching and learning policies were. This was evident when she indicated that she does not know policies but will try to respond to the question. The researcher's assumption was that the SMTs' knowledge of policies on teaching and learning were questionable. The above views are an indication that members of SMTs do not manage the implementation of teaching and learning policies appropriately.

*Question: What language do you speak at home?*
In responding to the above question, most learners indicated that their home language is Sepedi. However, some said their home languages are IsiNdebele and Afrikaans. Some mentioned English as their home language. This was an indication that learners speak different languages at home.

*Question: In which language are most of the learning areas/subjects being taught in your school?*
All learners at the four schools mentioned that all learning areas are taught in English. It was in only one school where the learners indicated that some are taught in English while others are taught in Afrikaans.

*Question: How well do you understand this language?*
In responding to the question above, the learners in the four schools where English is the language of learning and teaching complained that they don't understand the language; only very few said they understand the language. The learners who were interviewed in the school that uses Afrikaans and English indicated that they don't have any problems with the languages they are taught in.

# Lesson plan

Most teachers stipulated the learning outcomes and assessment standards that were to be addressed when planning their lessons. However, the learning outcomes and assessment standards were not written in full; only the numbers were written in those columns. When asked if they knew what those numbers represented, all teachers indicated that they referred to the policy documents. The researcher realized that the teachers did not know the learning outcomes and assessment standards that they were addressing in their lesson plans. Although the educators stipulated different resources in their lesson plans, the researcher realized that not all the resources were available and used in the lesson presentations. The researcher in this study reached the conclusion that what appeared on the lesson plans was actually not what the teachers were doing in class. Furthermore, some educators indicated that the duration of their lessons would be 40 minutes, while others indicated time frames of one, two or three weeks. The point to be emphasized is that the researcher observed that the time frames of the lessons did not correspond with the number of learning outcomes and assessment standards to be addressed.

# Lesson Presentation

In the introduction the researcher found that the teachers did not link the known with the unknown appropriately. This was evident from the teacher who instructed learners to open their books on a specific page and started teaching. Some teachers tried to introduce their lessons by asking a few questions but the learners could not respond appropriately. The researcher was then convinced that the learners did not understand the language of learning and teaching as the educator's questions were clear. However, in one school the teacher tested the learners' prior knowledge by asking a few questions and the learners responded appropriately. This further convinced the researcher that learners who are taught in their home language understood the teacher's questions better than those who were taught in a second or third language. The teachers have stipulated the various teaching and learning activities in their lesson plans, but the researcher observed that they were doing different things in the classroom as compared to what they have planned. The researcher in this study reached the conclusion that most teachers did not teach what they had planned for.

# Assessment

Although the learners did not respond appropriately to the questions, all teachers were asking some questions throughout the lesson presentations. This was an indication that teachers understood that assessment should be continuous. The researcher furthermore observed that not all teachers engaged the learners with some assessment activities at the end of the lesson. However, for those who engaged the learners with assessment activities, the researcher was convinced that they were relevant to the lesson though some learners did not respond appropriately.

# Conclusion

It was found that some teachers have changed the way they teach since the introduction of the new teaching and learning policies, while other educators have not changed. The language of learning and teaching has a negative impact on learning and teaching if learners are not conversant with it. SMTs were supportive in some schools while other schools did not have any SMTs. Schools in urban areas were more adequately supplied with teaching and learning support materials than the schools on the farms. Teachers received training on the various teaching and learning policies. However some policies were not deemed appropriate to what teachers were actually doing in their classrooms. This study established that teachers have inadequate knowledge of outcomes-based assessment. Teachers are more comfortable with CAPS and have confidence that it will be easily implemented. Members of SMTs' contradictory views were an indication that they did not understand teaching and learning policies well. The Department of Education provided schools with resources on teaching and learning policies. However, schools did not receive the resources equally or equitably. Though the Department of Education provided schools with assessment policies, members of the SMTs interpreted them differently.

The Department of Education should train members of SMTs on how to monitor, evaluate and support teachers in terms of new teaching methodologies. Education should make learners self-reliant and competent. The researcher recommends that if teachers are not able to teach learners in their home language, they should communicate with learners in that language of learning and teaching at all times so that learners can practise speaking that language. Schools should be provided with sufficient infrastructure to allow easy access to resources for both teachers and learners. The Department of Education is encouraged to give

more financial support to schools in order to provide the basic
infrastructure. Teachers should improvise resources by planning and
executing activities. Policy makers have to explore professional
development from the side of the participating educators in order to clearly
understand what would be best for changing their classroom practice. It is
therefore recommended that for effective implementation of teaching and
learning policies, the Department of Education should provide adequate
knowledgeable curriculum staff to do extensive training both for
classroom teachers and for members of SMTs. Teachers' training or
professional development should be longer, though it might be less than
their initial training. Teachers should collaborate and establish learning
area/subject clusters to resolve mutual curricular challenges. Teachers
should assess learners' achievement of learning outcomes as identified by
the various assessment standards. The researcher recommends that the
Department of Education should provide national templates of lesson
plans for all the schools. The following essential aspects of a lesson plan
should be addressed: lesson details (learning area/subject, grade,
theme/topic, date/s, time allocation/duration); learning outcomes and
assessment standards as well as content analysis (teacher activities, learner
activities, resources, teaching approaches/methodologies, assessment
activities/strategies/methods/tools).

# References

Abdal-Haqq, I. 1998. *Constructivism in Teacher Education: Considerations for
those who would Link Practice to Theory*. Thousand Oaks, CA: Corwin Press.
Duffy, T. M. 2006. *Constructivism: Implications for the Design and Delivery of
Instruction*. Indianapolis: Indiana University.
Kramer, D. 2006. *OBE Teaching Toolkit: OBE Strategies, Tools and Techniques
for Implementing C2005*. Cape Town: ABC Books.
Locke, T. 2004. *Critical Discourse Analysis*. London: Cromwell Press.
Lucke, A. 1996. "Text and Discourse Analysis", *American Educational Research
Journal* 21, 3–17.
McGregor, S. L. T. 2010. *Critical Discourse Analysis: A Primer*. Halifax: Mount
Saint Vincent University.
Spady, W. G. 1994. *Outcomes-based Education: Critical Issues and Answers*.
Virginia: American Association of School Administrators.
Terre Blanche, M. 2008. *Research in Practice: Applied Methods for the Social
Sciences*. Sandston: Juda Academy.
Van Dijk, T. A. 2001. *Critical Discourse Analysis*. London: Sage Publications.
Wikipedia
(http://en.wikipedia.org/wiki/Constructivism_(philosophy_of_education),
accessed 22 September 2011)

# PART II:

# PROFESSIONALISM: MODERN RESEARCH IN EDUCATION AND TEACHER EDUCATION

# CHAPTER FOUR

# EXPLORING THE VIEWS OF PRIMARY SCHOOL TEACHERS ABOUT PROFESSIONALISM AND PROFESSIONAL DEVELOPMENT: A CASE STUDY IN GREECE

## VASILIKI S. FOTOPOULOU
### PHD CANDIDATE, UNIVERSITY OF PATRAS, GREECE
## AND AMALIA A. IFANTI
### PROFESSOR, UNIVERSITY OF PATRAS, GREECE

**Abstract**

This study, which is part of a broader empirical research project, investigates the views of 234 primary school teachers in Achaia, Greece, about professionalism and professional development. Our research data were collected using anonymous questionnaires examining teachers' responses to five parameters of each case. We found that, in relation to professionalism, the majority of teachers tended to value highly the importance of collaboration with their colleagues, parents and students as also their pedagogical concern for the students and their achievement. Regarding professional development, two issues were indicated: the demand for lifelong education and training and for studying specific educational topics. In conclusion, the teachers of our sample highlighted the power as well as the complexities of professionalism and professional development and they closely related them with their personal development and the quality of their work at school.

**Keywords**

Teachers, Primary Education, Professionalism, Professional Development, Achaia, Greece

# Introduction

Nowadays, teachers face a plethora of rapid changes in the educational sector as a result of the broader political, economic and social conditions. In this context, teachers have to cope with the demands of their profession, which in turn entails new roles, skills and responsibilities; it is associated with teachers' active involvement in the implementation of the educational reforms. Consequently, this changing world inevitably affects teachers' work as well as their professionalism and professional development (Day & Smethem, 2009; Hargreaves, 2000).

In particular, the rhetoric of professionalism refers to teachers' ability to respond sufficiently and adequately to the raising roles and responsibilities at school (Day et al., 2007; Evans, 2011; Hargreaves, 2000; Swann et al., 2010). However, several researchers have indicated the difficulty of defining teachers' professionalism due to its inherent complexities (Evans, 2008; Goodson & Hargreaves, 1996; Helsby, 1995). Day (1999:13) attempted to delineate professionalism "as a consensus of the norms, which may apply to being and behaving as a professional within personal, organizational, and broader political conditions". Other researchers have also indicated the existing relation between teachers' professionalism and professional development (e.g. Day, 2001; Evans, 2008; Kirkwood & Christie, 2006).

According to Fullan (1995: 265), professional development is "the sum total of formal and informal learning pursued and experienced by the teacher in a compelling learning environment under conditions of complexity and dynamic change". In other words, professional development implies teachers' reflections and actions, which illustrate the experience and the learning they have already accumulated during their teaching career at school. Similarly, Herdeiro (cited in Heideiro & Costa e Silva, 2013: 181) noted that "professional development can be seen as growing in certain aspects of professionalism and can be legitimately applied to the development of a teacher or a group of teachers in the work context".

The aim of this piece of work is to gain greater insight into primary teachers' perceptions about professionalism and professional development with respect to specific parameters of the two aforementioned notions. Therefore, the data which will be presented are from an empirical study conducted at primary schools in the region of Achaia, in the west part of Greece.

## Material and Method

The survey was carried out during the school year 2011–12 and the sample consisted of primary teachers who were working at state schools in the region of Achaia, Greece. A sufficient number of small and big schools are located in this area (Achaia) for us to get a representative sample of teachers in terms of their teaching experience.

In order to gain insight into teachers' perceptions of certain aspects of professionalism and professional development, anonymous questionnaires were distributed during the working days of the schools. To conduct the survey, we had initially sought the permission of the school principals. At first, a pilot study had also been conducted.

In total, 234 primary teachers completed the questionnaires; the sample size was representative of the population under investigation (response rate: 17% of the sampling frame).

The questionnaire consisted of two parts. The first part contained questions about the background characteristics of the respondents, such as gender, degrees (Master's, PhD, other degrees) and teaching experience. The second part of the questionnaire included five questions. In this study, we are going to present the data that came out from two questions of the questionnaire related to professionalism and professional development.

More specifically, the first question was concerned with teachers' thoughts on five specific parameters of professionalism. Similarly, the second question focused on teachers' professional development and included five sub-questions. Both main questions had been derived from the study of the literature on the topic. The questions were closed-ended and the respondents had to provide answers on a five-point Likert-type scale (scale range: *Not at all, Slightly, Moderately, Fairly, Very Important*).

The questionnaires were processed and analysed with the aid of the SPSS program, version 20.0. The statistical analysis was carried out using the Mann-Whitney (U) and Kruskal-Wallis (H) non-parametric tests.

## Results

### *Characteristics of the sample*
From the total sample of 234 respondents, female teachers (70.1%) outnumbered male teachers (29.9%). Regarding their studies, all the respondents held a Bachelor degree in Primary Education. Additionally, 30.3% of the teachers had attended a two-year training course at the In-

Service Training School, 15% had a second university degree, 6.4% had a Master's degree and a very small percentage (0.9%) held a PhD. Concerning their teaching experience, 10.7% of the teachers had 0–5 years of service. The highest percentage of teachers (46.6%) ranged between 5 and 10 years and 27.7% of the sample was found to have from 15 to 25 years of teaching experience. Finally, 15% of the teachers had more than 25 years of experience.

Table 4.1 provides an overview of the distribution of primary teachers, according to their background characteristics.

**Table 4.1: Distribution of the background characteristics of primary teachers (average percentages)**

| Gender | First degree in primary education | In-service training school cert. | 2nd degree | Master's degree | PhD | Teaching experience (years) | |
|---|---|---|---|---|---|---|---|
| Male 29.9% | 100% | 30.3% | 15% | 6.4% | 0.9% | 0–5 | 10.7% |
| | | | | | | 5–15 | 46.6% |
| Female 70.1% | | | | | | 15–25 | 27.7% |
| | | | | | | 25+ | 15% |

*Data analysis*
*i. Teachers' perceptions of professionalism*
The question regarding professionalism included five sub-questions. The first (1.1) referred to *the teacher, who is acting as a model and is contributing to students' development of moral and social values.*

The majority of teachers (50%) highlighted the importance of this parameter of professionalism, whereas 41.9% of the sample attributed *fair* importance to the same parameter (Fig. 4.1).

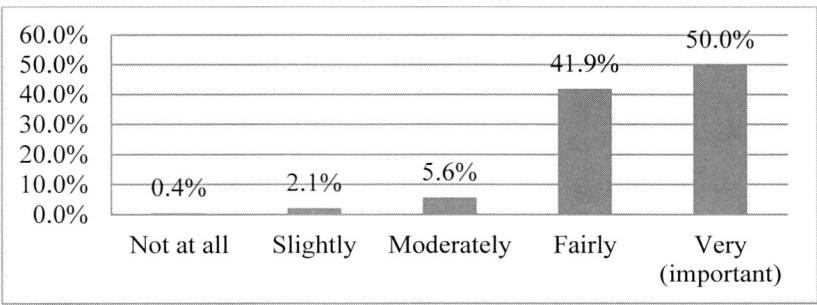

Fig. 4.1. Average percentage of teachers' answers regarding the first parameter of professionalism (The teacher is acting as a model and is contributing to students' development of moral and social values)

The second sub-question (1.2) referred to the contribution of *professional knowledge* to teacher's professionalism. Most of the teachers (45.7%) considered the professional knowledge as *fairly important,* whereas 44% of the sample put a *great importance* to this aspect of professionalism (*very important*). A significant association was also found between teachers' answers and their second university degree, since teachers with a second degree were more likely to attribute greater importance to this aspect of professionalism (U = 2748.5, p = 0.028, r = −0.14) (Fig. 4.2).

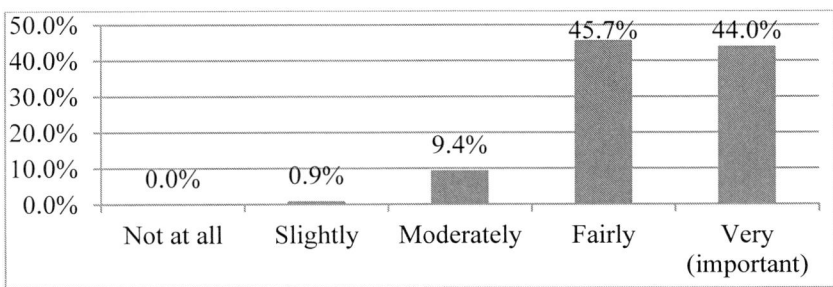

Fig. 4.2. Average percentage of teachers' answers regarding the second parameter of professionalism (The contribution of professional knowledge)

Regarding the third aspect of professionalism (1.3), i.e: *the degree to which the teacher is allowed to apply suitable teaching methods in accordance with students' learning requirements*, a high percentage of primary teachers (47.4%) characterized this aspect as *fairly important,* whereas the 43.6% of the sample underlined it as *very important*. The Mann-Whitney test revealed that the teachers who were holding a second degree attributed greater importance to this parameter (U = 2794.5, r = –0.13) (Fig. 4.3).

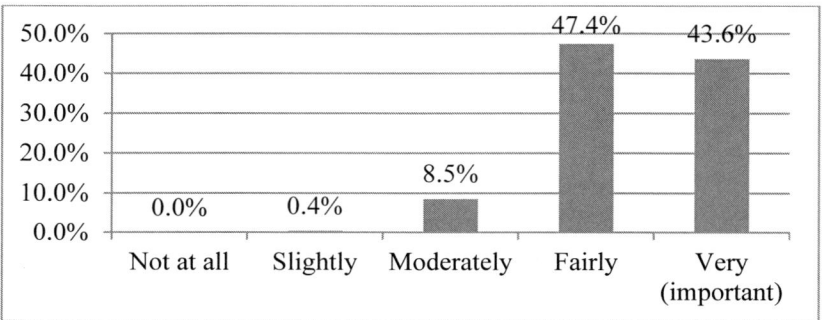

Fig. 4.3. Average percentage of teachers' answers regarding the third parameter of professionalism (The degree to which the teacher is allowed to apply suitable teaching methods in accordance to students' learning requirements)

In relation to the fourth aspect of professionalism (1.4), i.e.: *the collaboration with colleagues, parents, students, etc.*, the majority of the respondents (47.9%) evaluated this parameter at the highest rank order (*very important*). However, the statistical analysis did not reveal any significant difference between this aspect of professionalism and the teachers' background characteristics (Fig. 4.4).

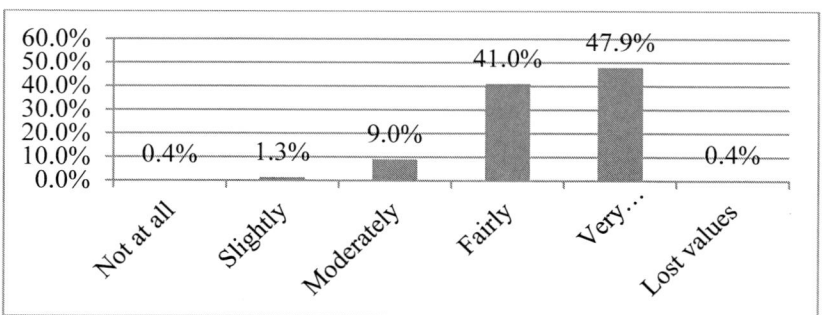

Fig. 4.4. Average percentage of teachers' answers regarding the fourth parameter of professionalism (The collaboration with colleagues, parents, students, etc.)

Finally, the fifth aspect of professionalism (1.5), i.e: *teachers' care, concern, and interest about students and their achievements*, was highlighted as *very important* by the majority of teachers (67.5%), whereas the 27.4% of the sample indicated it as *fairly important*. The comparison of this parameter with the background variables did not reveal any statistically significant difference, according to the Mann-Whitney test (Fig. 4.5).

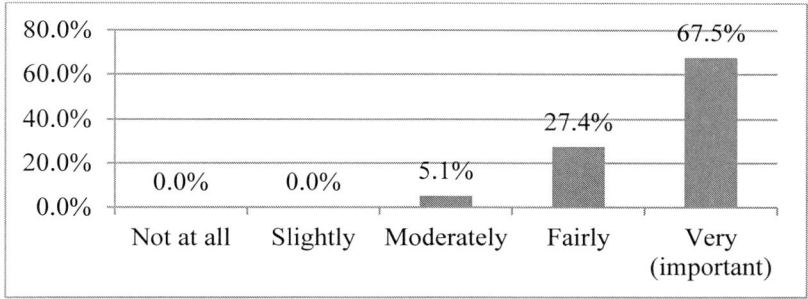

Fig. 4.5. Average percentage of teachers' answers regarding the fifth parameter of professionalism (Teachers' care, concern and interest about students and their achievements)

### ii. Teachers' perceptions of professional development

The question referred to the professional development included five sub-questions, which were concerned with specific aspects of it.

In response to the first parameter (2.1), which was related to *teachers' need for continuing education and training*, the majority of teachers (53.4%) characterized it as *very important*. Other answers were found in descending order as follows: 40.6%: *fairly important*, 4.7%: *moderately important*, 0.9%: *slightly important*. Comparing this factor with the sample's background variables, it was revealed that the teachers who had attended the In-Service Training School were more likely to attribute greater importance to this aspect of professional development, according to the Mann-Whitney test (U = 3562.5, r = −0.25) (Fig. 4.6).

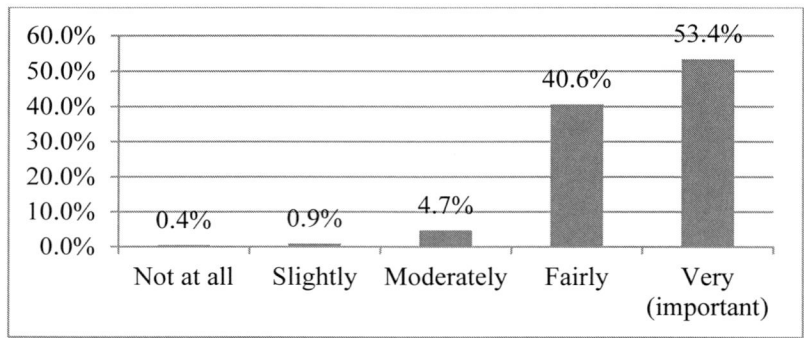

Fig. 4.6. Average percentage of teachers' answers regarding the first parameter of professional development (Teachers' need for continuing education and training)

The second parameter of professional development (2.2), which was related to *teachers' participation in and/or attendance of scientific events (e.g.: conferences, lectures, workshops)*, was characterized as *very important* by the 23.5% of the respondents. The majority of the answers were found in the rank order *"fairly important"*.

The application of the Kruskal-Wallis test brought out that teachers' answers about this aspect of professional development were significantly affected by their teaching experience (H(3) = 10.692, p<0.01). The Mann-Whitney test was then applied. Teachers who were ranged from 15 to 25 years of service at school (Mdn = 4.00, MR = 50.09) attributed greater importance to this parameter, and their answers provided statistically significant differences compared to the answers of teachers with less teaching experience (range: 0–5 years) (Mdn = 4.00, MR = 33.56) (U = 514, r = –0.31) (Fig. 4.7).

The third sub-question (2.3) had focused on *the collaboration with colleagues*, which constitutes an integral feature of teachers' professional development, according to the literature on the topic. Most of the teachers (50.9%) considered this parameter as *fairly important*, whereas 35% of the sample underlined it as *very important* (Fig. 4.8).

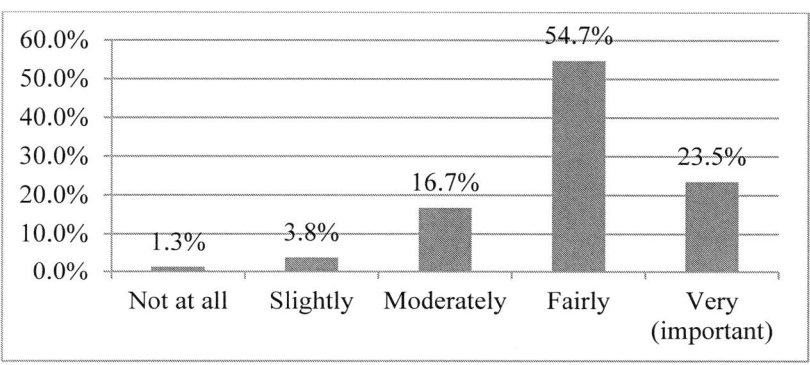

Fig. 4.7. Average percentage of teachers' answers regarding the second parameter of professional development (Teachers' participation in and/or attendance of scientific events (e.g.: conferences, lectures, workshops))

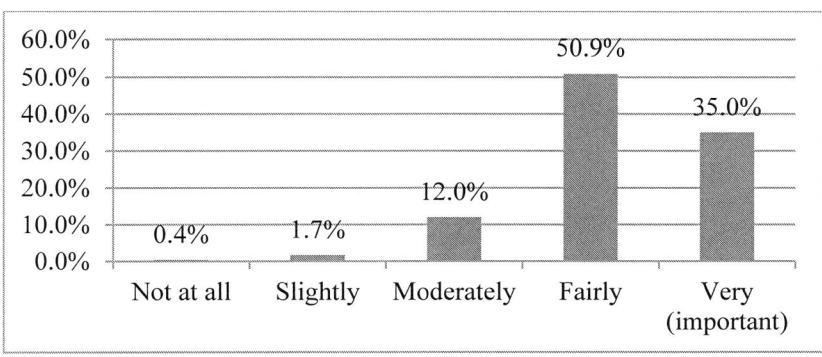

Fig. 4.8. Average percentage of teachers' answers regarding the third parameter of professional development (collaboration with colleagues)

In the fourth sub-question (2.4), i.e.: *the learning through the internet and the application of new technologies*, the majority of the teachers (51.7%) characterized it as *fairly important*. However, the statistical analysis did not reveal any significant correlation with the background variables of the sample (Fig. 4.9).

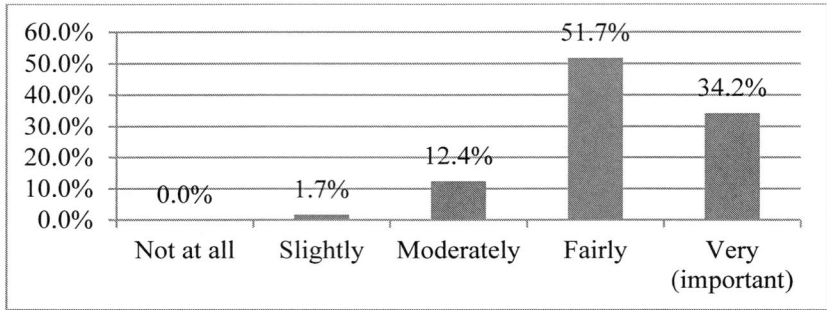

Fig. 4.9. Average percentage of teachers' answers regarding the fourth parameter of professional development (learning through the internet and the application of new technologies)

Finally, the fifth sub-question (2.5) examined teachers' perceptions of their *personal research and study of specific educational issues*. This parameter of professional development was highlighted as *very important* by 49.6% of the sample, whereas 41.9% of the teachers ranked it as *fairly important*. The other findings were ranked as follows: 7.3%: *moderately important*, 1.2%: *slightly important*, 0.0%: *not at all* (Fig. 4.10).

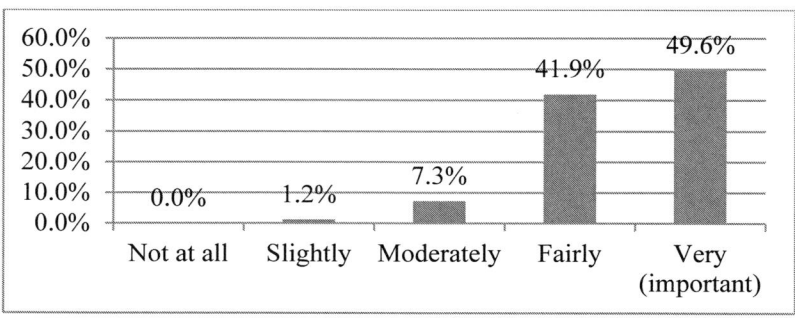

Fig. 4.10. Average percentage of teachers' answers regarding the fourth parameter of professional development (personal research and study of specific educational issues)

## Conclusion

Based on our results and taking into account some main characteristics of professionalism and professional development provided in the literature on the topic, it can be argued that the teachers in our sample acknowledged the significant contribution of basic aspects of professionalism and professional development in their demanding everyday work.

Regarding professionalism, the teachers tended to attribute great importance to the use of the appropriate teaching methods, according to the learning requirements of their pupils. Moreover, teachers' perceptions of professionalism were closely associated with students' development of moral and social values. This outcome was in accordance with teachers' care and concern about their students' achievements.

It is worth mentioning that the care about pupils' achievement, which appears as a main feature of professionalism, was highlighted as a very important parameter by the majority of the teachers in our sample. Such a finding reflects teachers' professional interest and appears to affect their perceptions of professionalism. Moreover, it is in line with other studies that indicate teachers' efforts to contribute effectively to their students' achievements (Antoniou & Kyriakides, 2013; Bredeson & Johansson, 2000; Day, 1999; Garet et al., 2001).

Our data also revealed the power of continuing education and training as a significant parameter of teachers' professional development. This remarkable finding highlights teachers' strong desire for in-service learning, and it is related with the attempt for the upgrading of their professional background and the reinforcement of their professional development. Similar findings are presented in some other studies as well (Ifanti & Fotopoulou, 2010, 2011).

Furthermore, the teaching experience was found to differentiate teachers' perceptions about the influence of their educational experiences upon professional development. It was mainly teachers with teaching experience from 15 to 25 years who emphasized the issue.

Moreover, personal research and studies were recognized as important aspects of professional development. Such a finding has also been considered as particularly important in another study, as it correlates the personal interests of teachers with their professional knowledge and training (Day, 1999). Additionally, this relationship has been perceived to play an important role in shaping the professional identity of teachers (Beauchamp & Thomas, 2009; Beijaard et al., 2004; Goodson & Cole, 1994).

Regarding the use of new technologies in education, our results revealed a negative attitude, which can be attributed to the lack of relevant knowledge on the part of teachers. Hargreaves (2000) and Day (2000) have also pointed out the difficulty teachers have in adopting innovations in their teaching without undertaking the appropriate training.

On the other hand, teachers' collaboration with colleagues, parents and students was rated as a very important issue in our study, and no significant differences were found in relation to demographic characteristics of the sample. The teachers of our sample recognized the various benefits of collaboration, and their views appeared to be in accordance with the results of other similar studies. In fact, it has been indicated that the collaboration with colleagues acts as an "amplifier" for the teachers themselves and their work, as it encourages their active participation in processes leading to professional development (Darling-Hammond & McLaughlin, 1995; Hawley & Valli, 1999; Hunzicker, 2011; Vrasidas & Glass, 2004).

Summing up, the primary school teachers in our sample recognized the significance of various parameters of professionalism and professional development. Data analysis revealed their main concern about students and their achievements at school. Additionally, the need for collaboration in the school environment and the demand for training throughout their career were ultimately underlined. Based on our results and considering the international discussion on professionalism and professional development, it becomes obvious that the views of teachers should be seriously taken into account in any effort to improve teaching and learning at schools.

# References

Antoniou, P. and Kyriakides, L. 2013. "A Dynamic Integrated Approach to Teacher Professional Development: Impact and Sustainability of the Effects on Improving Teacher Behaviour and Student Outcomes", *Teaching and Teacher Education*, 29, 1–12.

Beauchamp, C. and Thomas, L. 2009. "Understanding Teacher Identity: An Overview of Issues in the Literature and Implications for Teacher Education", *Cambridge Journal of Education*, 39(2), 175–189.

Beijaard, D., Meijer, P. C. and Verloop, N. 2004. "Reconsidering Research on Teachers' Professional Identity", *Teaching and Teacher Education*, 20, 107–128.

Bredeson, P. V. and Johansson, O. 2000. "The School Principal's Role in Teacher Professional Development", *Journal of In-Service Education* 26, 385–401.

Darling-Hammond, L. and McLaughlin, M. W. 1995. "Policies that Support Professional Development in an Era of Reform", *Phi Delta Kappa* 76(8), 597–604.

Day, C. 1999. *Developing Teachers: The Challenges of Lifelong Learning.* London/Philadelphia, PA: Routledge/Falmer Press.

Day, C. 2000. "Stories of Change and Professional Development: The Costs of Commitment" in C. Day, A. Fernandez, T. Hauge and J. Moller (eds), *The Life and Work of Teachers: International Perspectives in Changing Times.* London: Falmer Press, pp. 109–129.

Day, C. 2001. "Teacher Professionalism: Choice and Consequence in the New Orthodoxy of Professional Development and Training" in P. Xochellis and Z. Papanaoum (eds), *Continuing Teacher Education and School Development.* Thessaloniki: Department of Education, School of Philosophy, pp. 17–25.

Day, C. and Smethem, L. 2009. "The Effects of Reform: Have Teachers Really Lost their Sense of Professionalism?" *Journal of Educational Change* 10, 141–157.

|Day, C., Flores, M. A., & Viana, I. (2007). Effects on national policies on teachers' sense of professionalism: Findings from an empirical study in Portugal and in England. *European Journal of Teacher Education*, 30(3), 249-265.

Evans, L. (2008). "Professionalism, Professionality and the Development of Education Professionals", *British Journal of Educational Studies* 56(1), 20–38.

Evans, L. 2011. "The 'Shape' of Teacher Professionalism in England: Professional Standards, Performance Management, Professional Development and the Changes Proposed in the 2010 White Paper", *British Educational Research Journal* 37(5), 851–870.

Fullan, M.G. (1995). "The Limits and the Potential of Pprofessional Development" in Guskey, T. R. and Hubernam, M. (eds), *Professional Development in Education: New Paradigms and Practices.* New York: Teachers College Press, pp. 253–267.

Garet, M. S., Porter, A. C., Desimone, L., Birman, B. F. and Yoon, K. S. 2001. "What Makes Professional Development Effective? Results from a National Sample of Teachers", *American Educational Research Journal*, 38(4), 915–945.

Goodson, I. and Hargreaves, A. 1996. *Teachers' Professional Lives.* London: Falmer Press.

Goodson, I. F. and Cole, A. L. 1994. "Exploring the Teacher's Professional Knowledge: Constructing Identity and Community", *Teacher Education Quarterly* 21(1), 85–105.

Hargreaves, A. 2000. "Four Ages of Professionalism and Professional Learning", *Teachers and Teaching: Theory and Practice* 6(2), 151–182.

Hawley, W. D. and Valli, L. 1999. "The Essentials of Effective Professional Development: A New Consensus" in L. Darling Hammond and G. Sykes (eds), *Teaching as the Learning Profession: Handbook of Policy and Practice.* San Francisco: Jossey-Bass, pp. 127–150).

Helsby, G. 1995. "Teachers' Construction of Professionalism in England in the 1990s", *Journal of Education for Teaching,* 21(3), 317–332.

Herdeiro, R. and Costa e Silva, A. M. 2013. "The Quality of Teaching and Professional Development of Teachers: A Portuguese Study", *Teacher Development*, 17(2), 176–194.

Hunzicker, J. 2011. "Effective Professional Development for Teachers: A Checklist", *Professional Development in Education* 37(2), 177–179.

Ifanti, A. A. and Fotopoulou, V. S. 2010. "Undergraduate Students' and Teachers' Perceptions of Professional Development and Identity Formation: A Case Study in Greece", *KEDI Journal of Educational Policy* 7(1), 157–174.

—. 2011. "Teachers' Perceptions of Professionalism and Professional Development: A Case Study in Greece", *World Journal of Education*, 1(1), 40–51.

Kirkwood, M. and Christie, D. 2006. "The Role of Teacher Research in Continuing Professional Development", *British Journal of Educational Studies*, 54(4), 429–448.

Swann, M., McIntyre, D., Pell, T., Hargreaves, L. and Cunningham, M. 2010. "Teachers' Conceptions of Teacher Professionalism in England in 2003 and 2006", *British Educational Research Journal*, 36(4), 549–571.

Vrasidas, C. and Glass, G. V. (eds). 2004. *Current Perspectives in Applied Information Technologies: Online Professional Development for Teachers*. Greenwich, CT: Information Age Publishing.

# CHAPTER FIVE

## PREPARING TO TEACH CHILDREN TO READ AND WRITE IN THE US

### WILLIAM NEW
#### PROFESSOR, BELOIT COLLEGE, BELOIT, WISCONSIN, USA

**Abstract**
In the United States, those committed to whole-language approaches to literacy and those committed to bottom-up, phonics-based approaches have engaged for the past fifty years in what have come to be known as the "reading wars" (Anderson, 2000; Pearson, 2004). This epistemological and ideological conflict has played out in the research community, in policy debates and in classrooms where literacy acquisition is the main business, including college teacher education classes. While the proponents of whole language approaches seemed in the mid-90s to have won the day, no sooner had the sun set than those who stress the importance of phonemic awareness, structural word analysis, fluency and direct and targeted instruction had swept them from the field. At present, some degree of rapprochement has been achieved, but not without accepting conditions that were at one time anathema to the whole-language teachers. The decline of the attraction of whole-language methods of teaching reading and writing can be dated to demands at the end of the last century for accountability, on one hand, and rigorous research support for instructional practices on the other (National Reading Panel, 2000). These two demands were written into the No Child Left Behind Act in 2000, radically changing the way reading and writing were taught, and the way reading and writing were researched. While the qualitative approaches that dominated in the whole-language period were not proscribed in the new law – and these approaches are again deemed valuable in producing knowledge about literacy – for a decade the ruling principle was that if you couldn't count it, then it didn't mean anything.

**Keywords**
Reading, Writing, Children, Teaching, Litteracy, USA.

## Introduction

Nearly constant change in educational policy related to literacy has had a tremendous impact on teacher education. My own career as classroom teacher and university teacher educator/researcher can serve to demonstrate this. I entered the teaching profession without the benefit (or handicap?) of any prior teacher education in 1979. As a new and very amateur teacher, I could draw only on my excellent liberal arts education, my own experience as a student, and the support I received from my principal and fellow educators in creating a teaching practice. Like most young teachers, I brought a great deal of energy, considerable imagination and boundless naïveté to my teaching: I took what might have looked like a "whole-language" approach to reading and writing because that was how I approached reading and writing in my own life, not because I subscribed to a theory of whole-language instruction. During the 1980s I was a graduate student in educational psychology, focusing on language, so I was exposed to the latest cognitive research on psycholinguistic processes and brain-based explanations of reading and writing disabilities (Rayner & Pollatsek, 1989, for example). I did my doctoral research on the mostly unconscious workings of language knowledge in writing. I came to believe, to know scientifically, that learning to read and write was very different from learning to speak, contra the theories of whole-language proponents like Frank Smith (2012), and that one could not reasonably expect most children to infer the complex relationships between speech and print. I came to "understand" that one could not hope to read for meaning if one could not decode, and that all children benefited, if not required, considerable direct instruction related to decoding in order to become fluent expert readers. This was the research base that by the late 1990s convinced policy makers that fundamental changes to how reading is taught were necessary.

One might suppose that when I received my PhD in 1993 and became a teacher educator that – based on my own research and graduate education – I would have emphasized phonemic awareness, automaticity of language functions, and word knowledge more than language experience and dialogue about literature. But my priorities were more influenced by my own literacy practices, and by my personal, non-scientific conviction that student-centred teaching was better in all cases than teacher-centred instruction. I also had gained considerable experience as a classroom teacher with reading-disabled children using a whole-language, rather than phonetic-structural approach, and this experience affected my beliefs about what I should teach my pre-service college students. These academic disputes were highly politicized and publicized. In a political context where "bottom-up" approaches to teaching reading and writing were embraced by conservatives, mostly for reasons having nothing to do with the "science", it was difficult for teacher educators – working in environments where nobody wanted to be seen as a conservative – to leave the whole-language camp in favour of more systematic skills-based approaches to learning to read. The result, in my own case, as a teacher educator specializing in literacy, was that by the early 2000s I found myself very much out of step with what actually was happening in elementary school reading classes. Everything that the public, and the politicians, and public school teachers, were saying about how out of touch with reality university-based teacher education has become seemed, at least on the surface, to be true. Like most of my colleagues, I believed – correctly I would say – that the mechanization of reading instruction, the reduction of literature to a new version of "the rat sat on the mat", was wrong on many levels.

As long as teacher education took place in college classrooms, and teaching children in public school classrooms, it was possible to sustain a bifurcated experience for pre-service teachers, though undoubtedly it did not contribute much to their professional growth. But increasingly, the education of teachers has become more field-based, requiring close cooperation between college professors, cooperating K-12 teachers, and district curricula (Darling-Hammond, 2006). In that context, ideological stridency or radicalism are out of place, and compromise and compliance become more normative. In my literacy class now, for instance, students spend approximately two-thirds of their time in an elementary language arts classroom, and the other one-third in a college classroom. I am with them in both places. Much of students' time in the college classroom is spent learning rather specifically what they need to know in order to teach the children in their classes how to read and write. Whatever intellectual or political agenda I might bring to the teacher education class must be integrated with the practical business of preparing them to teach the curricula mandated by the state and district. That is not to say that the college teacher educator does not have a part in the elementary teaching environments: but that part is to consult with cooperating teachers and pre-service teachers in how to best implement the curriculum, and to provide information and insights about the theories behind the curricula, and about how children best learn to read and write.

From a more traditional understanding about how schools are structured, and the place of a teacher within this structure, the new milieu of literacy instruction might well seem alienating and prescriptive. In the traditional elementary classroom, like the one where I began my own teaching career, the teacher has a great deal of autonomy, bordering frequently on isolation, along with significant control over the content and style of instruction. In present-day elementary schools like the ones where my students learn to teach, teachers even at the youngest levels work in teams, and students move often from room to room for instruction in different subjects and at different levels. Curricula across the third grades across the district, for instance, are completely coordinated, and in step: teachers are expected to be on more or less the same page on the same day. There is a standard set of materials used for instruction, with not much room for deviation, and common assessments are administered according to a prescribed schedule. Systems of classroom management, including the management and differentiation of instruction, are also standardized across the district, to the greatest extent possible, though in practice considerable differences between schools remain. Classroom routines are highly structured and again, to the extent to which central administration can prevail on principals to prevail on teaching staff, standardized across the district. This is the teaching environment for which teacher education would seemingly need to prepare its students, though always knowing that significant changes might be imposed within the school environment at any time, without much notice or time for transition.

The curricular mandates emanating from the state, and from national coalitions, have become increasingly comprehensive and specific, leaving limited room for teachers or college teacher educators to do more than consult about the means of implementation. The smooth operation of school-wide systems justifies or imposes, depending on one's perspective, concomitant standardization of curricular and pedagogical approaches. It goes without saying that all permitted approaches must pass the test of "best practice", that is, their efficacy must be supported by careful research (*No Child Left Behind*, 2002). The notion that creation of the curriculum, or the accompanying pedagogical methods, is the responsibility of the teacher has been effectively taken out of play. For many, this constitutes the "de-skilling" of teachers, but others argue the opposite, that teachers can now express their professional knowledge through their application of scientifically proven methods, their choices of curricular options, and their skill at assessing student progress through the curriculum, i.e. through the development of literacy.

This controversy, though, cannot be resolved in the abstract, or in the highly politicized and polarized contexts of policy debate. The most radical proponents on either side of this debate seem out of touch with the realities of both teacher education and classroom teaching, and do not appear to have spent much time observing how children learn or how teachers teach. For instance, given the extent and complexity of the accumulated knowledge of nearly fifty years of reading research, from all methodological angles, it seems naïve to expect that beginning teachers would be competent to design a reading curriculum for large groups of highly diverse students. On the other hand, the notion that a teacher could be something like a lab technician, simply applying procedures in a prescribed way, belies even a casual acquaintance with the complexity of teaching and learning.

But it might be that the primary danger to education and teaching comes from those who take this latter view: and the plethora of external constraints on teachers reflects this political position more closely than the more common-sense position that teaching a diverse lot of children to read and write is a complex business that requires considerable professional development and many resources. I'd like to highlight just three of the external constraints on (or potential resources for) the exercise of teachers' professional judgment, and by extension, on the content and form of the teacher education meant to produce such teachers:

1. Common core standards for language arts within school systems.
2. Frequent and determinative student assessments; embedding of reading instruction in school-wide behaviour/achievement management systems.
3. Qualifying exams for teacher licensure that address knowledge of language arts and literacy.

The meaning and legitimation of these "innovations" derives in large part from how they function with the overall context of present-day schooling.

The common core standards for English Language Arts (Wisconsin, 2011) were developed by a consortium of experts, including teachers, over the course of more than a decade, and by 2013 they had been adopted by 45 of the 50 United States. These standards represent the best judgment of these experts about what particular skills and knowledge students must have to be college-ready at the end of high school. For instance, at the most general level, the Language Arts Common Core says that students should be able to "read and comprehend complex literary and informational texts independently and proficiently". This seems, on the face of it, fairly uncontroversial. But the standards are highly specified, detailing what students should know at every stage of their literacy education from kindergarten to high school. First graders, for instance, will be expected to "ask and answer questions to help determine or clarify the meaning of words and phrases in a text" (Wisconsin, 2011: 13). Standards such as this focus on comprehension, but the implied approach to instruction seems to favour more intentional, direct methods than the discovery methods more characteristic of the whole-language movement. There are also standards related to foundational skills: the same first grader is expected to "orally produce single-syllable words by blending sounds (phonemes), including consonant blends" (Wisconsin, 2011: 15).

Commercial publishers of educational materials have been involved in the common core movement since the beginning, and the materials now available, and already adopted in most districts, reflect very faithfully the common core standards. That does not mean that literature is not present, but it does mean that a high degree of vocabulary control, for example, is a principle observed in all materials. For teacher educators and their students, student mastery of the common core standards, through the use of the supporting commercial materials, is the pre-constituted goal of teaching, making the goal of teacher education to be the production of teachers who can effectively guide children to mastery of these standards. Naturally, in the spirit of liberal education, a college professor would want to bring some criticism to bear on the common core movement and its presuppositions, but doing so, while at the same time directing all one's energies toward teaching these standards, is problematic.

Language arts instruction in elementary schools is embedded in school-wide approaches to management and instruction, and is structured within and across classrooms through adherence to a framework of balanced literacy. There are many such systems and frameworks, but I will focus on two popular implementations here, mostly because they are common in the schools where I work: Response to Intervention and the CAFÉ method (in conjunction with the Daily Five). Response to Intervention (RTI) began in the special education world as a method to manage (bad) behaviour and accommodate learning and cognitive disabilities. The purpose of RTI when used in the general student population is early identification of problems in learning, and the provision of highly targeted remediation of well-defined problems. RTI presupposes, requires and legitimates a system of continuous assessment of student progress: several times each year the progress of students in meeting the learning goals prescribed by the common core is assessed, and the results are the basis on which RTI is implemented. The presumption of RTI is that all students require some kind of teacher intervention in order to progress (Brown-Chidsey & Steege, 2010). For most students, most of the time, this intervention can be performed in a whole class with little or no differentiation. Everyone, for instance, can listen to the teacher read a children's book, and participate in a question and answer session. But not every student, using this same example, is at the same place with respect to his or her ability to put comprehension strategies to work in understanding the book. A small group of these students – identified through the continuous assessment system – then will meet together with a teacher using a different ("research-based") instructional package: this is a Level 2 intervention. Some students might not be able to make adequate progress even in the small group, with these materials. Those students will require one-to-one instruction, or Level 3 intervention, in which the pace of learning can be carefully controlled.

The Common Core, with its related curriculum materials and assessments – in which context children are identified for specific interventions – structure the literacy teacher's work to a considerable extent, particularly with respect to learning and developmental goals, but they do not by themselves determine what the teacher or the students do to reach these goals. Gail Boushey and Carol Moser (2009) have developed a teaching and assessment framework that many teachers and schools now use to organize literacy instruction. The CAFÉ method of assessment/ research – where CAFÉ stands for comprehension, accuracy, fluency, and expand vocabulary – reflects these goals and provides a means by which students can document and track student progress using criteria congruent with Common Core goals and other reading and writing research. Boushey and Moser show how students can use these four categories as a means to organize instruction and to guide student self-assessment of their own progress, and teacher assessment of student progress. For instance, if a teacher demonstrates the "back up and reread" strategy of comprehension during whole group instruction, she adds it to the comprehension column of the class chart, and then in subsequent lessons and activities students and teachers follow up with practice and assessment of this skill.

The CAFÉ method is used most often in conjunction with Boushey and Moser's (2006) other contribution to literacy instruction: The Daily Five. This is simply a means of organizing time within the literacy block to address different aspects of reading and writing: read to self, read to other, work on writing, spelling/word work, listen to reading. Teachers may use this system in different ways, but the basic principle is that students will move from one of these activities to another at predetermined intervals, often in levelled groups but sometimes independently. In the course of an hour, for example, a second grade teacher might have all four activities for

15 minutes each: teachers will circulate among the groups, providing more direct instruction in some activities – read to others turns out to be guided reading with the teacher – than in others. Word work and spelling, for instance, might be undertaken using computer programs. One primary purpose of the Daily Five is to increase student "stamina" (the ability to stay on task, in small groups or independently) and to develop the ability to manage and assess one's own learning, using the CAFÉ. In some ways, the Daily Five allows teachers to include whole-language or language experience activities within a structure that retains adata-driven, Common Core informed, emphasis of literacy instruction demanded by districts and states.

Pre-service teachers working in schools are exposed, if not indoctrinated, to the use of these methods for literacy teaching, and teacher educators are largely in the position of explaining and justifying the use of the methods, rather than questioning them. The modes and purposes of student learning mandated by the state has a powerfully structuring effect on teacher education and prospective teachers, but that effect is still somewhat indirect. Recently, more direct methods of assessment of teacher candidates have been introduced: an examination of knowledge about reading and writing research and pedagogy, and a comprehensive assessment by external agencies of student teachers' planning, teaching and reflection. Students must meet or exceed the cut-score determined by the State in order to be eligible for teacher licensure, notwithstanding whatever other assessments administered by teacher education programs. The reading test is closely aligned with the research on which the Common Core Language Arts curriculum is based, and the live teacher assessment focuses on the very kinds of planning, teaching styles and reflections (on "data") promoted in the Boushey and Moser methods. While both of these assessments were constructed with the participation of teachers, their administration has been contracted to major private publishers, echoing the ways in which the communally developed common core standards have been rendered commercially viable by the same corporate entities.

Teacher educators in literacy have in this new world limited agency with respect to how or what they teach their prospective teachers about teaching. For a college professor used to the freedom to set his or her own course goals, determine the content, the kinds of pedagogy employed and the methods of assessment, designing and teaching a "methods" class can be very dissonant. The lack of freedom to choose what and how to teach, and the restricted opportunities for critical inquiry and debate, can cause one to believe that teacher education is no longer compatible with liberal education. But if one chooses not to teach the course that the state and the schools seem to require, ethical questions about fulfilling one's responsibilities toward students arise. These, of course, are just the same quandaries that have faced K-12 teachers for many years now.

Space does not permit more than a posing of the problem here, but in my own practice as teacher educator and chair of a teacher education department, two options seem to be before me. First, I can take my colleague's complaints about "deskilling" to heart and advise the Dean that teacher education is not compatible with the mission of the college, notwithstanding my colleagues' desire to save teacher education at all costs short of giving up one's freedom. Or second, I can convince myself that what is being asked of me and my students is appropriate and necessary for the children whose literacy is at stake, and then try to convince my colleagues to stop whining and get with the program. There is some kind of middle way, where I engage my students, the prospective teachers, in dialogue about what the world of teaching is really like, and what it demands, bring up some of the serious issues related to privatization, standardization and the rest of that, but insist that if they want to become licensed teachers they must play the game that is being played. It's not really satisfactory, but that's as far as I've come so far.

# References

Anderson, K. 2000. "The Reading Wars: Understanding the Debate Over How Best to Teach Children to Read", *Los Angeles Times Book Review* (18 June) (http://ssrn.com/abstract=935776).

Boushey, G., & Moser, J. 2006. *The Daily Five*. Portland, ME: Stenhouse.

Boushey, G., & Moser, J. 2009. *The CAFE Book: Engaging All Students in Daily Literary Assessment and Instruction.* Portland, Maine: Stenhouse.

Brown-Chidsey, R. and Steege, M. 2010. *Response to Intervention* (2nd ed.). New York: Guilford Press.

Darling-Hammond, L. 2006. "Constructing 21st-century Teacher Education", *Journal of Teacher Eeducation* 57(3), 300–314.

National Reading Panel 2000. *Teaching Children to Read: An Evidence-based Assessment of the Scientific Research Literature on Reading and its Implications for Reading Instruction,* http://www.dys-add.com/resources/SpecialEd/TeachingChildrenToRead.pdf

*No Child Left Behind (NCLB) Act of 2001.* 2002. Pub. Law No. 107-110, Stat. 1425.

Pearson, P. D. 2004. "The Reading Wars", *Educational Policy*, 18(1), 216–252.

Rayner, K. and Pollatsek, A. 1989. *The Psychology of Reading.* London: Routledge.

Smith, F. 2012. *Understanding Reading: A Psycholinguistic Analysis of Reading and Learning to Read* (6th ed.). London: Routledge.

Wisconsin. 2011. *Common Core State Standards for English Language Arts.* Madison, WI: Wisconsin Department of Public Instruction.

# CHAPTER SIX

# THE NEED FOR TEACHERS
# TO BE PRACTISING RESEARCHERS

## NANA ADU-PIPIM BOADUO
SENIOR LECTURER, FACULTY OF EDUCATION,
DEPARTMENT OF CONTINUING PROFESSIONAL TEACHER
DEVELOPMENT
WALTER SISULU UNIVERSITY, SOUTH AFRICA

**Abstract**
Professional teachers naturally seek answers to questions and solutions to classroom challenges and problems in their work environment to help their students to learn effectively and efficiently. They are decision makers, making thousands of choices on hourly basis regarding the choice of texts, literature, appropriate and relevant technology integration, curriculum, pedagogy, assessment and measurement. They are highly reflective and sensitive to the needs of their students. They encounter failures and successes. However, much of what teachers have to offer remains a secret. Teachers seek multiple means of looking at their world of teaching and learning and that of their students by unlocking the secrets within the classrooms. Their key to success lies in research. This paper addresses the need for all categories of teachers to be practising researchers from empirical and exploratory perspectives.

**Keywords**
Teacher Researchers, Technology Integration, Curriculum, Pedagogy, Assessment, Measurement, Research Paradigms, Action Research, Participatory Research, Classroom Challenges

# Introduction

In the foreword of Boaduo (2011a: 8) a very important message reads:
This book has been specifically prepared for practising classroom teachers
because research has become a major activity among professional
practitioners. In the teaching profession this has become so paramount that
there is need to target classroom professional teachers, especially those in
the first and second cycle institutions and equip them with research
methods to be able to research regularly.

Most institutions for teacher education (faculties of education at
universities as well as teachers' colleges and colleges of education)
provide rudimentary courses in educational research. These courses, in
reality, do not prepare teachers in training to become researchers per se
and apply their research content knowledge and skills acquired while in
training to solve the daily challenges and problems they regularly
encounter in the teaching-learning environment. The aim of such
rudimentary courses is to help the teacher trainee produce a research report
as partial fulfilment of the degree or diploma being sought (Boaduo &
Babitseng, 2006). This is an unforgivable oversight if not an unpardonable
error on the part of the teacher trainers at institutions that train teachers.
This must change immediately and be replaced by long and protracted
training from the first to the final year of study with research modules to
equip teachers with in-depth educational research content knowledge and
skills during their training to be able to research regularly in their working
environment.

In order to be effective and efficient researchers teachers need to become
exceptional teacher-researchers and should engage in regular research to
advance their content knowledge and skills in the classroom and improve
the quality of education for their students (Litchmnan, 2011; Macmillan &
Schumacher, 2006; Kincheloe, 1991). Teachers must engage in the debate
about educational research by understanding meaningful research
themselves; only by engaging in complex critical research will teachers be
able to make a worthwhile contribution in the teaching-learning
environment. Furthermore, teachers should be encouraged to explore their
own voices and begin to renew the enthusiasm for the process of sharing
their own work within a growing teacher-researcher movement.

## Provision of Teachers with Grounding in Educational Research during Initial Training

Teacher education and training initiatives for the twenty-first century should be progressive because teachers will be required to know and understand the characteristics of the twenty-first-century learner. The knowing and understanding should include aspects of pedagogical and content knowledge of subjects that they will teach (Boaduo et al., 2011b, 2011c). These would include the incorporation of languages, cultures and traditions in community contexts as well as technology in the broadest sense (Darling-Hammond, 2006a). Furthermore, the twenty-first-century teacher should understand learners and find a way to nurture their talents (Boaduo, 2011a; Boaduo et al., 2011b, 2011c). To do this, teachers would need research content knowledge and skills to construct and manage their teaching and learning activities, communicate well, use technology efficiently and reflect on their practices, learn and improve continually in order to keep abreast with their profession.

## Research and Powerful Classroom Teaching

Professionally, powerful teaching is very important and increasing in our classrooms because of the stream of dynamic initiatives of human development and evolution in science and technology. Due to these developments and evolution, standards of teaching and learning should be higher in the twenty-first than in the twentieth century. As a result, teachers in training need to acquire additional content knowledge and skills in action and participatory research, both general and specifically related to education, to be able to survive and be successful in the twenty-first-century school environment (Boaduo et al., 2011b, 2011c).

Throughout the world education has become increasingly important to the success of both individuals and nations (Boaduo, 2010a). Growing evidence both published and unpublished demonstrates this. Among all educational resources, teachers' abilities are especially critical to students' learning and consequently the success of a nation to advance in all its development initiatives – industrial, economic, social and political (Darling-Hammond, 2006a). In view of this, teacher education and training need to take on a completely new dimension in the twenty-first century through dynamic curricula that take into account the issue of building bridges across national borders for easy transfer of teachers worldwide (Boaduo, 2010a).

# The Urgent Need for Progressive Teacher Education and Training in the Twenty-first Century

To provide dynamic teacher education and training for the twenty-first century, there is a need to reflect on past teacher education and training by scrutinizing the dilemmas of the past century. During the twentieth century, many countries set out to raise educational attainments in the hope that this would contribute to the growth of national productivity and the extension of economic opportunity to formerly disadvantaged groups in society. The shift of the global economy and the evolving nature of employment required new teacher education and training curricula to be introduced (Kodrzycki, 2002). These led to efforts by nations to reform their education systems to respond to the needs of twenty-first-century development initiatives.

In the past century, teacher education and training policy makers and practitioners, under pressure from opponents of teacher education and training and with incentives for faster, cheaper alternatives, launched weak teacher education and training programmes that underprepared teachers of all categories to render inadequate professional services to their clients (Darling-Hammond & Sykes, 2003). As a result, the attrition of initial teacher education and training continued to increase and the teaching force of most countries increasingly became bimodal (National Commission on Teaching and America's Future, 2003).

The apparent ease of teaching, to the uninitiated, and the range of things teachers actually need to know to be successful with students, is relevant to the dilemmas that teacher education and training programmes contended with in the last century. During this era, many lay people and policy makers held the view that almost anyone could teach reasonably well and that entering teaching required knowing something about a subject and the rest of the simple tricks of the trade could be picked up on the job. These notions, which derived from lack of understanding of what a trained and qualified good teacher actually does behind the scenes and from tacit standards for teaching that were far too low, led to pressure for backdoor routes into teaching. These denied teachers access to much of the content knowledge base as well as skills for teaching, and often to the supervised practice that would have provided them with models of what professionally trained and qualified good teachers did and how they understood their work. These were not adequately provided (Boaduo et al., 2012).

Many such incidents were observed across the globe. For instance, the United States' National Academy of Education Committee's Report (Darling-Hammond & Bransford, 2005: 1–2) wrote that:

> On a daily basis, teachers confront complex decisions that rely on many different kinds of knowledge and judgment and that can involve high stakes outcomes for students' future. To make good decisions, teachers must be aware of the many ways in which student learning can unfold in the context of development, learning differences, language and cultural influences, and individual temperaments, interests and approaches to learning.

In addition to foundational knowledge about the areas of learning and performance listed in the above quotation, teachers need to know how to take the steps necessary to gather additional information that will allow them to make more grounded judgments about what is going on and what strategies may be helpful to them to be able to perform their professional duties and provide guidance to learners (Boaduo et al., 2012; Boaduo, 2011a, 2011b). More importantly, teachers need to keep what is best for their student at the centre of their decision-making. Even though this sounds like a simple point, it is rather a complex matter, which has profound implications for what happens to and for many students in the teaching-learning environment.

For dynamic teacher education and training in the twenty-first century globalized world, teacher education and training institutions must design programmes that will help prospective teachers to know and deeply understand educational research methodologies from a wide array of things about teaching and learning and in their social and cultural contexts. Furthermore, they must be able to put this understanding into practice in complex classroom situations serving increasingly diverse students. If the twenty-first-century teacher is to succeed at this task, teacher education and training institutions must further design programmes that transform the kinds of settings in which both the novices and the experienced teachers teach and become competent teachers. This must consider the environments that most teachers would have to operate after their training. For instance, there should be specific emphasis on training teachers to teach in rural settings especially in the developing world. Unfortunately, no specific attention has been given to this.

This signifies that the enterprise of teacher education and training must venture further and further and engage even more closely with schools in a mutual transformation agenda with all the struggles involved (Boaduo, 2010). Importantly, all teacher education and training institutions must tell education policy makers as well as the public what it actually takes to teach effectively and efficiently. This must be done both in terms of content knowledge and professional methodological skills that are needed and in terms of the school contexts that must be created to allow teachers to develop and use what they know on behalf of their students (Fullan, 2001).

The twenty-first century has in store for teachers surprises of unimaginable proportions especially in terms of the proliferation of technological gadgets. For this reason, many reforms and innovations must be made in teacher education and training to equip initial teacher trainees with the most sophisticated required content knowledge and multiple methodological teaching skills to be able to deal with this proliferation. These reforms and innovations must strengthen both the subject content and pedagogical preparation together with the use of teaching and learning media that join theory and practice. These should effectively and efficiently equip the initial teacher trainee to be able to face all the challenges encountered in the teaching-learning environment in the twenty-first-century classroom (Boaduo, 2011a, 2011b).

One of the many individuals who saw the need for new directions in teacher education and training is the former president of the United States, Bill Clinton. In his *Call for Action for American Education in the 21st Century* in 1996, he indicated succinctly that:

> Every community (and nation, my own words) should have a talented and dedicated teacher in every classroom. We have enormous opportunity for ensuring teacher quality well into the 21st century if we recruit promising people into teaching and give them the highest quality preparation and training.

This is more relevant and important today than it was in 1996.

From the time formal education became the preoccupation of mankind, teacher education and training have been synonymous with the education enterprise and schooling has become a big business. Business people have always been teachers while the main merchandise has always been the student (Boaduo & Babitseng, 2007a). President Clinton was concerned about the talents and dedication of teachers in American schools. He was very optimistic about the mammoth opportunities that existed for teachers if they were given quality education and training. He was also worried about the type of prospective teachers who were recruited for teacher education and training in institutions. Despite the fears that he expressed, he was hopeful and confident that opportunities still existed if teachers were given the highest quality preparation during their initial training that would equip them with the most applicable, relevant, convertible and practical knowledge and skills to be able to do their teaching professionally. That is hopeful for twenty-first-century policy makers.

What needs serious reflection is that teacher education and training of the twentieth century prepared teachers to teach and produce learners who could not use their acquired knowledge and skills to help humanity to live fulfilling lives. This dilemma is expressed by an American school principal in his letter to teachers at the beginning of each academic year (cited by Swart, 1998) which sums up everything that had negative implications for previous generations and even today if nothing is done about reforming teacher education and training in the twenty-first century.

> Dear Teacher, I am a survivor of a concentration camp. My eyes saw what no man should witness. Chambers designed to gas people built by learned engineers, children poisoned by educated physicians, infants killed by trained nurses, women and babies shot and burned by high school and college graduates. So I am suspicious of education. My request is help your students become more human. Your efforts must never produce learned monsters, skilled psychopaths or educated torturers. Reading, writing and arithmetic (biology, physics, chemistry and economics, my own words) are important only if they serve to make children more human.

Teacher education and training of the twenty-first century should not prepare teachers to produce the kind of citizens described in the letter quoted above. The Ministry of Education and Culture in Namibia in a policy document (1993: 37) identified the concern of the above quoted letter thus:

> *Perhaps the most challenge in improving the quality of our education system is to ensure that our teachers are well prepared for the major responsibilities that they carry. More than anything else, it is the teacher who structures the learning environment. It is they who can keep learning exciting and satisfying or alternatively, who make schooling a pain to be endured.*

Since teacher education and training, whether pre-service or in-service, is a deliberate and conscious effort to intervene in the personal and professional development of an individual or groups of individuals, both ethical and practical considerations require some policy statement to guide practice. It is therefore a fundamental assumption that effective teacher education and training programmes rest upon teaching-learning process that is rooted in a consciously developed plan and that effective teacher education and training programmes in turn rest upon well-developed educational policies (Swart, 1997).

## Dynamics of Educational Research Expected in the Twenty-first-century School Environment

Generally, research has undergone a massive metamorphosis over the years, and the changes are not as concise and neatly defined as they once were (Allen & Shockley, 1996). The old formulae do not fit new questions, especially in the technologically advanced twenty-first century. For instance, quantitative experimental research presents a picture of controlled procedures resulting in statistical practice, but classrooms as the playgrounds where teachers regularly interact are dynamic, complex and always evolving. This situation will be even more complex in the twenty-first-century school environment. The rate of flux will place teachers on their toes to live up to the expectations of their students. Therefore, the educational research process should be dynamic and flexible enough to meet classroom contexts and the complexities of the teaching-learning environment. Any research that the teacher engages in should allow for inquiry and be "conducted in the full, messy context of the life of a classroom; providing rich descriptions of people in action" (Atwell, 1993: xiii).

This approach will help teachers to unlock secrets within classrooms that often defy the rigour of traditional experimental conditions. Twenty-first-century teachers, as researchers, should be able to seek multiple means of looking at their world of teaching and learning and that of their students and in-depth content knowledge and practical methodological teaching skills in research can be the instant panacea.

Professionally, teachers should be groomed in a variety of educational research approaches during and after their training. There must be absolute diversity in the educational research activities that teachers would be engaged in. However, all researching teachers need to share common processes of reflecting on their practice, inquiring about it and taking action at the most appropriate time. Generally, teacher-researchers will be required to seek to understand individuals, actions, policies and events that make up their work and working environment in order to make professional decisions. According to Patterson and Shannon (1993: 7) they need to "engage in moments of reflection and inquiry in order to take action that will help their students learn better".

What is excellent about this description is that it recognizes all good teacher-researchers as participants in teacher research. In this process, the key elements are that teacher-researchers ask questions, reflect on their own and students' learning, use multiple data sources which include observation, analysis of artefacts, conferences and seminars and then taking action on the new information that they have come across (Newman, 2002). The new information discovered can open up new vistas for further research and improvement of practice.

## Action and Participatory Research: Methodological Perspectives

To improve their practice, teachers must be forerunners of protracted action and participatory action research.

> Action research is deliberate, solution-oriented investigation that is group or personally owned and conducted. It is characterised by spiralling cycles of problem identification, systematic data collection, reflection, analysis, data-driven, action taken and finally problem redefinition. (http://www.ed.gov/databases/ERIC_Digests/ed355205.html, accessed 20 September 2007)

Boaduo (2011a: 32) describes participatory research as:

> A form of action research carried out in communities, institutions and organizations that are trying to overcome negative and oppressive conditions. The members of the communities, institutions and organizations become actively involved in the research from the planning stages to data collection to the final report compilation.

This does not necessarily indicate that a solution has been found for the problem being researched. It just helps to identify with the procedure to follow to be able to conduct and complete the study being undertaken. This is where the teacher-researcher is at liberty to apply the most appropriate research paradigm that will help to address the research problem.

## The Application of a Variety of Research Paradigms in a Research Study

The significance of methodological paradigms in a research study is the ability to understand and decide on the most appropriate research paradigm that will suit a particular assignment so that the teacher-researcher is able to conduct the study to a successful conclusion. Mouton

(1996) and Boaduo (2011a) are of the view that methodological paradigms – for instance those related to quantitative, qualitative, action and participatory – are not merely collections of research methods with their applicable techniques. Methodological paradigms should always include certain assumptions and values regarding their use under specific circumstances (Boaduo, 2005, 2011a). From the perspective indicated above, the teacher-researcher should be able to make a choice concerning applicable methods, techniques and the underlying philosophy regarding their use in a particular study. In this respect, the philosophy should include the theory of when and why to apply either of the paradigms or approaches and the awareness of the limitations of equally applicable and relevant various methods that could have equally been chosen for the study. In terms of the research being conducted by the teacher-researcher the complete understanding and application of the following are required for introspection.

- Every research paradigm, method or technique is task specific and the task is often defined by the research goal.
- Different research studies use different research paradigms, methods or techniques because they have different objectives.
- In all studies the research paradigm, method or technique must be appropriate and relevant for the task at hand.
- The research paradigm, method or technique should apply to all the aspects of the research study – sampling, questionnaire design, interview schedule, data treatment, analysis, interpretation, findings and recommendations.

## Action Research and the Practising Teacher-researcher

Since the late 1980s, action research has gained the attention of researchers in many fields of study and will gain even greater attention in the twenty-first century (McKernan, 1991; McTaggart, 1992; Masters, 2001; Kemmis & McTaggart, 1988). The teaching profession will find solace in this paradigm. Generally, action research is a process in which groups of people (teachers in this discussion) attain critical understanding and improvement of their situation through participatory plans, practices, observations and reflections. This fundamental feature of action research is part of the well-known spiral propagated by Kemmis and McTaggart (1988). It also becomes a collective reflection by participants on systematic objectifications of their efforts to change the way they work through discourse, organization and power relations to be able to actively contribute to and improve the practice of their profession (McTaggart, 1992).

> Action research is a process for developing practical knowledge for worthwhile purposes leading to health and happiness for people and communities. (Hughes, 2004: 1)

Twenty-first-century teacher-researchers will love to make their communities healthy and happy through the application of practical knowledge.

> Action research is about knowledge and practices that contribute to human well- being and happiness of people in their communities, institutions and organizations. (Reason and Bradbury, quoted by Boaduo and Babitseng (2007b: 186))

Dick (2000) reiterates that action research is for practitioners, especially those of the twenty-first century, who want to improve several aspects of their professional practice or social processes while generating new knowledge. For these reasons, action research can serve different purposes, and provide different ways of understanding knowledge in its relationship to practice and different relationships to people and problems in their context (Bray et al., 2000). This reveals the fundamental differences in our understanding of the nature of inquiry, not simply methodological niceties as proposed by Reason and Bradbury sited by Boaduo and Babitseng (2007) but finding practical solutions to social problems, especially in the teaching-learning environment.

The twenty-first-century teacher-researcher would be required to engage in a careful action research study of identified problems by devising improved ways to assist students to master a specific subject. This can be a beautiful case for introspection. A project of this nature seeks to solve a practical problem for the benefit of students and at the same time add to the stock of knowledge if the findings are published and made available to the world of practitioners (Hughes, 2004).

Action research, therefore, refers to any process with the dual aim of changing a situation and producing knowledge for consumption (Masters, 2001). For this reason, action research has great potential for professional practitioners, especially twenty-first-century teacher-researchers, because it can make teaching practitioners to combine research and improve their professional practice (Chandler & Torbert, 2003). They can also develop collaborative groups to observe their practice, collect and analyse data, reflect on what they have done and plan to improve both their own practice in the industrial, social, political and economic contexts in which they live and work (Hughes, 2004).

## The Participatory Research Perspective

Participatory research is another paradigm that deserves mention to help advance twenty-first-century teachers' research capabilities. Boaduo (2005: 8) indicates that:

> Participatory action research paradigm is self-reflective inquiry in social situations like the ones in which teachers find themselves (in the 21st century classroom). It helps to improve the rationality and justice of the social and educational practices, understanding them and the situations in which they are carried out.

Boaduo further testifies that participatory research plays a liberating role in the learning process by providing the development of critical understanding of social problems, their structural causes and possibilities for overcoming them, especially in the teaching-learning environment. It therefore calls for democratic interaction and intervention between the teacher-researcher and those among whom the research is conducted. Generally, the democratic interaction depends on the practical participation of those involved in conducting the research on the causes of the problem being investigated with the objective of finding a solution.

Twenty-first-century teacher-researchers should know, understand and use the three main interrelated processes of participatory research during their training. These are:

- The collective investigation of problems and issues with the active participation of the constituency in the entire process,
- The collective analysis in which the constituency develops a better understanding of the structural causes of the identified problem (socio-economic, political, educational, cultural or historical), and
- The collective action by the constituency aimed at long-term, as well as short-term solutions of the identified problems.

The integration of these three processes gives participatory research its fundamental strength and power over other research paradigms; they can be identified separately in any participatory research study and each process incorporates aspects of the others. The whole research process begins with people's concrete experiences and situations and moves to include both theoretical analysis and action aimed at change that brings benefits to the constituency.

There are several reasons why twenty-first-century teacher-researchers should be conversant with the principles of participatory research. Basically, it is an educational approach that equips teacher-researchers to help to bring about social change. It is not a recipe for change but a means to help bring about appreciable change. It is a democratic approach to investigation and learning which can be taken by individuals, groups and movements as a tool aimed at social change.

## What must be Considered in the Application of the Participatory Research Paradigm

In any research study where the participatory paradigm is applied, the following research questions must be considered in their entirety, especially during the planning and designing of the research proposal.

- What is the problem to be investigated?
- Who are the subjects?
- Who are the participants?
- How will they participate?
- Who has to learn in the process of investigating the identified problem?
- What has to be learned by the participants?
- Why should the participants learn what they have to learn?
- How will they participate in the whole learning process?

Twenty-first-century teacher-researchers should know the strengths of participatory research. Boaduo (2005), McNiff (1995) and Clark (1972) agree on the following:

- A critical analysis is encouraged throughout the research process and not just at the beginning or termination.
- The approach encourages active involvement on the part of all participants.
- It is positive in initiating and helping to bring about change and improvement.
- By using the classroom (for teachers) or the field as the study environment, the natural behaviour of participants is accommodated.
- As a research framework, it is flexible, relevant, adaptable and applicable.
- Finally, it describes relationships as they develop over time and accommodates changes in thinking which reflect mutations occurring in the context of the study being conducted.

Participatory research helps the researcher to address practical problems with theoretical and applicable practical relevance and transfers the knowledge from the research findings to the participants or the general public for rectification and application.

## The Necessity of Making Actions Substantive for the Solution of Educational Problems

In practical retrospective, teachers of all categories – pre-school, primary, secondary and tertiary – should be socialized into a scholarly lifestyle and be exposed to the values of the educational research tradition especially during training (Boaduo, 2011a; Pease, 1967; Reskin, 1979). During training, the emphasis should be on various aspects of research that are relevant and will help teacher-researchers respond to the needs of their students. Aspects like action and participatory research should be prominent and thoroughly discussed (Boaduo, 2011a; Hunter & Kuh, 1987; Reskin, 1977, 1979).

The training should equip teacher-researchers with both in-depth content knowledge and practical methodological skills as well as the ability to identify problems, design and conduct a progressive study, write up the findings and undergo the refereeing process to get the results published (Hogan, 1981; Hunter & Kuh, 1987; Kuh & McCarthy, 1980; Zuckerman, 1977). The training should emphasize the need to conduct regular research about impending problems that require the attention of the teacher-researcher for their solution (Braxton, 1983; Cameron & Blackburn, 1981; Clark & Corcoran, 1986; Fulton & Trow, 1974; Hunter & Kuh, 1987).

## The Need for Twenty-first-century Teachers to Research

From what have been discussed so far, there is no doubt about the necessity of twenty-first-century teacher-researchers to research regularly. In the teaching-learning environment, they will encounter numerous problems every day. There are problems that may cross the success path of their students, which teacher-researcher would like to eliminate. To do this requires strategies and approaches in research methodologies that will help direct the teacher-researcher towards finding a lasting solution to those problems that may threaten the success of the student. However, teacher-researchers can conduct regular researches if they have been given the in-depth content knowledge and practical methodological skills they need to be able to indulge in regular short or long term research studies.

## How Teachers Should Go about their Research

How should teacher-researchers start and find time to gather data to complete any chosen research? Once schooled in in-depth research studies, the starting point is to:

- Identify the research problem.
- Place it in a simple sentence that can be read and understood without questions.
- State the purpose (statement of the problem).
- Provide main and subsidiary research questions.
- Indicate why the study is being conducted (rationale).
- Conduct a brief literature review to place the study contextually. This indicates that someone has looked at the study from a different perspective. That needs to be identified before one can put the study into proper context.
- Identify the parameters within which the study will be confined (delimitations).
- State the possible problems that may hinder the completion of the study (limitations) and show how these problems will be circumvented.
- Identify the subjects and decide on the size of the sample population for the study.
- Identify a theory or theories that will help to place the study in the research fraternity.
- State the significance and benefits.
- List the data collection techniques and instruments to be used.
- Discuss their validity and reliability with reference to the methodological paradigm that will be used.
- State how the collected data will be treated and analysed.
- Set a time frame (from beginning to the end) for the study.
- (If funds are to be sought from providers) include a budget statement.
- Give a brief description of how the final research report will be compiled (Boaduo, 2005 & 2011a). This is a basic format to help teacher-researchers get started confidently.

The frequency with which teacher-researchers should be engaged in research study should be left to individual judgment. It is known that teacher-researchers will always engage in frequent research if they are confronted by problems regularly. For this reason, there can be no prescription concerning the frequency of research activities and so teacher-researchers are at liberty to make choices about the frequency of research.

## The Need to Make Research into Educational Practice Substantive

Once the study has been conducted to a successful end, a report will be written to make the findings of the study available to members of the teaching professional fraternity. Often, such reports are published in teacher education journals or district or regional educational newsletters for dissemination, to inform professional practice (Boaduo, 2011a; Weiner, 2001; Glickman, 2001; McCall, 2001).

This discussion of twenty-first-century teachers as researchers scenario has touched on the concept of research and indicated the significance of research for the teaching-learning environment. Emphasis has been placed on the need to provide in-depth training with a solid foundation in educational research methodologies by institutions that provide teacher education and training. There has been a is discussion of the most important research tools that teacher-researchers need in order to indulge in regular research with confidence and carry it to a conclusion. The need for teacher-researchers to research has been briefly discussed. However, the frequency of research has been left to the professional teacher-researcher's discretion. It has been indicated that research findings need to be made available to the teaching professional fraternity for dissemination to all practitioners to help improve practice. This is the essence of research in professional practice.

## Conclusion

In this paper, the author has tried to open a very controversial issue for discussion and debate. The thrust of the discussion is that all nations depend on education to achieve their development objectives – social, educational and industrial – and that teachers are significant in this endeavour and should be given fair recognition of their professional education and training. They require registration and certification by globally recognized teachers' councils before practice. If teachers are to ply their profession worldwide, provincial, regional, national and international teachers' councils should merge and formed a global teaching council with offices in each country and a headquarters in a specific country like other international organizations. It is recommended that:

- There should be common-core teacher education and training curricula.
- Research must be considered the master-core subject to equip twenty-first-century teachers with in-depth content knowledge and practical methodological skills in research to be able to attend to day-to-day classroom problems.
- The core curricula should be the preoccupation of the academic and professional faculties of education in universities worldwide. This can begin with the International Society of Teacher Education (ISTE).

It has also been argued that room should be given to protracted practical experience, for at least 24 months, where the teacher is equipped with the necessary relevant, practical, applicable and convertible ammunition to fight the classroom war and win. We cannot do anything better than this for the teaching profession in the twenty-first century.

# References

Allen, J. and Shockley, B. 1996. "Conversations: Composing a Research Dialogue in University and School Research Communities Encountering a Cultural Shift", *Reading Research Quarterly* 31, 220–227.

Atwell, N. 1993. "Foreword" in L. Patterson, C. M. Santa, K.G. Short and K. Smith (eds), *Teachers Are Researchers: Reflection and Action.* Newark, DE: International Reading Association, pp. vii–x.

Boaduo, N. A. P. 2005. "Methodological Choice and Aapplication in a Research Study: A Framework for Practitioners", *African Symposium: Journal of the African Educational Research Network* 5(3), 19–23.

Boaduo, N. A. P. 2010. "Research Methods for Studying Virtual Communities" in B. K. Daniel (ed.), *A Handbook of Research on Methods and Techniques for Studying Virtual Communities: Paradigms and Phenomena.* Ontario, Canada: IGI Publishers.

Boaduo, N. A. P. 2011a. *Practical Educational Research Principles for Practising Teachers.* Saarbrücken, Deutschland (Germany): Lambert Academic Publishing.

Boaduo, N. A. P. 2011b. *Practical Methods for Successful Classroom Teaching.* Saarbrücken, Deutschland (Germany): Lambert Academic Publishing.

Boaduo, N. A. P. 2011c. *Conceptual Educational Theories.* Saarbrücken, Deutschland (Germany): Lambert Academic Publishing.

Boaduo, N.A.P. and Babitseng, S. M. 2006. *How Do We Prepare Educators for a New Role in the 21st Century?* Paper accepted for inclusion in the ACEL Microsoft iNet online conference 4–12 June 2007.

Boaduo, N. A. P. and Babitseng, S. M. 2007a. *New Directions on Teacher Education.* Paper presented at the International Society for Teacher Education (ITE) seminar at the 27th Annual Conference on The Future of Teacher

Education for Professional Development organized by the Institute of Education: University of Stirling, Scotland.
Boaduo, N. A. P. and Babitseng, S. M. 2007b. "The Need for Teachers to be Researchers", *African Symposium: Journal of the African Educational Research Network* 7(1), 183–191.
Boaduo, N. A. P., Boaduo, N. K. K., Boaduo, S. M., Boaduo, N. A. A. and Boaduo, A. A. P. 2011a. *Historical Bases of Education.* Saarbrücken, Deutschland (Germany): Lambert Academic Publishing.
Boaduo, N. A. P., Boaduo, N. K. K., Boaduo, S. M., Boaduo, N. A. A. and Boaduo, A. A. P. 2011b. *Psychological Bases of Education.* Saarbrücken, Deutschland (Germany): Lambert Academic Publishing.
Boaduo, N. A. P., Boaduo, N. K. K., Boaduo, S. M., Boaduo, N. A. A. and Boaduo, A. A. P. 2011c. *Educational Theories for Contemporary Practising Educators – Learning Theories.* Saarbrücken, Deutschland (Germany): Lambert Academic Publishing.
Boaduo, N. A. P., Boaduo, N. K. K., Boaduo, S. M., Boaduo, N. A. A. and Boaduo, A. A. P. 2011d. *Administration, Management and Organization of Schools.* Saarbrücken, Deutschland (Germany): Lambert Academic Publishing.
Boaduo, N. A. P., Danso, M., Mensah, J. and Babitseng, S. M. 2012. *Models of Practical Teaching: Practical Teaching Models for Teacher Education and Training.* Saarbrücken, Deutschland (Germany): Lambert Academic Publishing.
Braxton, J. M. 1983. "Department Colleagues and Individual Faculty Productivity", *Review of Higher Education* 6, 115–128.
Bray, J. N., Lee, J., Smith, L. L. and Yorks, L. 2000. *Collaborative Inquiry in Practice: Action, Reflection and Meaning Making.* Thousand Oaks, CA: Sage.
Cameron, S. W. and Blackburn, R. T. 1981. "Sponsorship and Academic Career Success", *Journal of Higher Education* 52, 369–377.
Chandler, D. and Torbert, B. 2003. "Transforming Inquiry and Action: Interweaving 27 Flavours of Action Research", *Action Research* 1, 133–152.
Clark, P. A. 1972. *Action Research and Organizational Change.* London: Harper & Row Publishers.
Clark, S. M. and Corcoran, M. 1986. "Perspectives on the Professional Socialization of Women Faculty: A Case of Cumulative Disadvantage?" *Journal of Higher Education* 57, 20–43.
Clinton, W. J. 1996. *Call for Action for American Education in the 21st Century.* Washington, DC: White House.
Darling-Hammond, L. 2006a. "Constructing 21st-Century Teacher Education", *Journal of Teacher Education* 57, 1–15.
Darling-Hammond, L. 2006b. *Powerful Teacher Education: Lessons from Exemplary Programs.* San Francisco, CA: Jossey-Bass.
Darling-Hammond, L. and Bransford, J. 2005. *Preparing Teachers for a Changing World: What Teachers Should Learn and Be Able to Do.* San Francisco, CA: Jossey-Bass.
Darling-Hammond, L. and Sykes, G. 2003. "Wanted: A National Teacher Supply Policy for Education: The Right Way to Meet "the Highly Qualified Teacher"

Challenge", *Educational Policy Analysis Archives* 11(33), 1–55 (http://epaa.asu.edu/epaa/v11(33)/).

Dick, B. 2000. *A Beginner's Guide to Action Research.* Lismore: Southern Cross Institute of Action Research (http://www.scu.edu.au/schools/gcm/ar/arp/guide.html).

Fullan, M. G. 2001. *The New Meaning of Educational Change* (3rd ed.). New York: Teachers College Columbia University.

Fulton, O. and Trow, M. 1974. "Research Activity in American Higher Education", *Sociology of Education* 47, 29–73.

Glickman, V. 2001. *Panel Discussion: "From Theory into Practice": Teacher Education/Educator Training: Current Trends and future Directions.* Pan-Canadian Education Research Agenda Symposium Report. Toronto: Canadian Education Statistics Council.

Hogan, T. D. 1981. "Faculty Research Activity and the Quality of Graduate Training", *Journal of Human Resources* 16, 420–5.

Hughes, I. 2004. Action & Research: Action & Research Open Web. Retrieved from http://www2.fhs.usyd.edu.au/arrow/o/m01/rintro.htm

Hunter, D. E. and Kuh, G. D. 1987. "The 'Write Wing': Characteristics of Prolific Contributors to the Higher Education Literature", *Journal of Higher Education* 58, 443–462.

Kemmis, S. and McTaggart, R. 1988. *The Action Research Planner.* Geelong: Deakin University.

Kincheloe, J. L. 1991. *Teachers as Researchers: Qualitative Inquiry as a Path to Empowerment.* London: Falmer.

Kodrzycki, Y. K. 2002. "Education in the 21st Century: Meeting the Challenges of a Changing World: Overview of the Federal Reserve Bank of Boston 47th Annual Conference Themes", *Journal of Teacher Education* 57(CCC).

Kuh, G. D. and McCarthy, M. M. 1980. "Research Orientation of Doctoral Students in Educational Administration", *Educational Administration Quarterly* 16, 101–121.

Lawal, H. S. 2006. "Teacher Education and the Professional Growth of the 21st Century Nigerian Teacher", *African Educational Research Network* 3(2), 1–4.

Litchmnan, M. 2011. *Understanding and Evaluating: Qualitative Educational Research.* London: Sage.

McCall, D. 2001. *Panel Discussion: "From Theory into Practice": Teacher Education/Educator Training: Current Trends and future Directions.* Pan-Canadian Education Research Agenda Symposium Report. Toronto: Canadian Education Statistics Council.

McKernan, J. 1991. *Curriculum Action Research: A Handbook of Methods and Resources for the Reflective Practitioner.* London: Kogan Page.

Macmillan, J. H. and Schumacher, S. 2006. *Research in Education* (6th ed.). London: Macmillan.

McNiff, J. 1995. *Action Research: Principles and Practice.* London: Routledge.

McTaggart, R. 1992. *Action Research: Issues in Theory and Practice.* Paper presented to Methodological Issues in Qualitative Health Research Conference, Deakin University.

Masters, J. 2001. "The History of Action Research", *Action Research e-Reports* 3 (http://www.fhs.usyd.edu.au/arrow/arer/003.htm).

Milondzo, K. S. and Boaduo, N.A.P. 2010. "School-based In-service Education and Training as Intervention Strategy for Teacher Professional Development in the Eastern Free State of South Africa", in T. G. Papanikos and N. Pappas (eds), *Problems and Prospects in Higher Education.* Athens: ATINER, pp. 439–450.

Mouton, J. 1996. *Understanding Social Research.* Pretoria: JL Van Schaick.

Namibia Ministry of Education and Culture. 1993. *Towards Education for All: A Development Brief for Education, Culture and Training.* Windhoek: Jossey-Bass.

National Academy of Education Committee. 1993. *Ministry of Education and Culture.* Windhoek: Jossey-Bass,

National Commission on Teaching and America's Future. 2003. *No Dream Denied: A Pledge to America's Children.* Washington, DC: NCTAF.

Newman, J. 2002. *Participatory Action Research* (http://www.goshen.edu.soan96p.htm).

Pease, J. 1967. "Faculty Influence and Professional Participation by Doctorate Students", *Sociological Inquiry* 37, 63–70.

Popkewitz, T. (ed.). 1987. *Critical Studies in Teacher Education.* Lewes: Falmer Press.

Reskin, B. 1977. "Scientific Productivity and the Reward AStructure of Science", *American Sociological Review* 16, 420–504.

Reskin, B. 1979. "Academic Sponsorship and Scientific Careers", *Sociology of Education* 52, 126–146.

Shaeffer, S. 1990. "Participatory Approaches to Teacher Training" in V. Rust and P. Dalin (eds), *Teachers and Teaching in the Developing World.* New York: Garland.

Swart, P. 1997. *The Transformation of Teacher Education in Namibia.* (Draft Dissertation).

Swart, P. 1998. "Teacher Education: The Key to Continuous School Improvement", in C. D. Yandila, P. Moanakwena, F. R. O'Mara, A. M. Kakanda and J. Mensah (eds), *Improving Education Quality for Effective Learning: The Teacher's Dilemma.* Collection of papers presented at the 3rd Biennial Conference on Teacher Education 26–29 August 1997 at Gaborone, Botswana. Gaborone: Ministry of Education (MOE).

Weiner, H. 2001. *Panel Discussion: "From Theory into Practice": Teacher Education/Educator Training: Current Trends and future Directions.* Pan-Canadian Education Research Agenda Symposium Report. Toronto: Canadian Education Statistics Council.

Zeichner, K. M. and Gore, J. 1990. "Teacher Socialization", in W. R. Houston, M. Haberman, J. P. Sikula, and Association of Teacher Educators (eds), *Handbook of Research in Teacher Education.* New York: Macmillan, (pp. 329–348).

Zeichner, K. M. & Liston, D. P. 1996. *Reflective Teaching: An Introduction.* Mahwah, NJ.: Lawrence Erlbaum.

Zukerman, H. 1977. *Scientific Elite: Nobel Laureates in the United States.* New York: Free Press.

# CHAPTER SEVEN

## COOPERATIVE LEARNING: ONE EFFECTIVE METHOD TO TURN PASSIVE STUDENTS INTO ACTIVE LEARNERS IN THE CLASSROOMS OF BULGARIAN SCHOOLS

### SHAHRZAD KAMYAB

LECTURER, UNIVERSITY OF SAN DIEGO
PROFESSOR, CHAPMAN UNIVERSITY & INTERNATIONAL
EDUCATION CONSULTANT, USA

**Abstract**

Instruction in Bulgarian classrooms continues to focus on preparing good workers and obedient individuals rather than developing twenty-first-century innovators and independent critical thinkers. As Bulgaria plays a more significant role in the democratic world and the global market economy, the schools must be overhauled to undergo major educational reform. To achieve this goal, the Bulgarian teachers – by-products of the old communist era – must be retrained to incorporate creativity and innovative teaching practices into their daily classroom teaching.

The instruction as such is largely lecture based and impersonal, a relic of the communist system. In this system, teaching is a one-way process in which the teacher is a director rather than a facilitator, presenting materials dictated by a textbook and students are largely passive recipients. Group work is not encouraged and students are required to memorize a large quantity of factual knowledge. Overall, this could make schooling look tedious, suffused with anxiety and boredom, destructive of curiosity and imagination; in short anti-educational (Kamyab, 2000).

To alleviate this problem, Kamyab recommends the use of cooperative learning which is an effective teaching strategy to turn passive students into active and enthusiastic learners. Cooperative learning is defined as a collection of teaching strategies that use students to help each other to learn. Cooperative learning has proved to increase students' attention span, raise their motivation level and make them active learners. Overall, it produces significant cognitive, affective and interpersonal benefits (Slavin, 1990).

In addition to cooperative learning, teacher training programmes should include in their pre-service programmes such concepts as metacognitive strategies and multiple intelligences. Multiple intelligences suggest that teachers should create learning environments in which different kinds of students can prosper. One way to do this is to provide students with choices as they learn new content. Those strategies could improve the whole instructional process in Bulgarian classrooms to encourage students' curiosity and imagination to make them active learners and, as a result, make learning more meaningful and enjoyable.

**Keywords**
Cooperative Learning, Bulgarian Classrooms, Effective Teaching Strategies

# Introduction

The instruction in the Bulgarian classrooms continues to focus on preparing good workers and obedient individuals rather than developing twenty-first-century innovators and independent critical thinkers. As Bulgaria plays a more significant role in the democratic world and the global market economy, the schools must be overhauled to undergo major educational reform. To achieve this goal, the Bulgarian teachers, the by-products of the old communist era, must be re-trained to incorporate creativity and innovative teaching practices into their daily classroom teaching. (Mutafchieva et al., 2008)

Instruction in Bulgarian schools is a one-way process in which the teacher directly presents information and skills dictated by a textbook. Students usually remain passive throughout a lesson. Group work is not encouraged, and students are required to memorize a large quantity of factual knowledge. The classrooms are usually arranged in a traditional fashion in which long rows of students' desks face the main instructional area and the teacher's desk. The lesson usually begins with a review of the previous lesson. The teacher then goes over the pupils' homework, listens to memorized material and then accepts or rejects pupils' solutions to problems previously presented. The teacher then introduces new materials and assigns homework, which usually consists of materials to be read or memorized from the book. Interviews with Bulgarian teachers show that although the teachers pose many questions, almost all of the questions asked are at the knowledge and comprehension levels which begin with "what" and "when". High order questions such as "how" and "why" which would promote critical thinking are rarely asked.

In such a system of instruction students are not encouraged to contribute to class discussions by voicing their opinions and supporting their answers; the method of teaching is a didactic one and the acquisition of factual knowledge and memorization are overemphasized. All this could make schooling look tedious, suffused with anxiety and boredom, destructive of curiosity and imagination; in short anti-educational. As the education system in Bulgaria is in a state of transitioning to one that is democratic, humanitarian and humanistic, and as a result teaching in schools is moving from a content centred philosophy to a more child-centered paradigm, Bulgarian teachers should become more equipped with innovative teaching techniques to make the students active in the learning process and to help them develop creativity and to take the initiative in learning.

One effective method that can be incorporated into teacher-training programmes in Bulgaria is cooperative learning, defined as a collection of teaching strategies that use students to help each other learn. One commonly asked question is: Does cooperative learning increase students' attention span in the classroom, raise their motivation level and make all students active in the learning process? The simplest answer to all these questions is that cooperative learning works. Teachers are told that cooperative learning is one of the better researched instructional strategies, and the results of research indicate that it produces cognitive, affective and interpersonal benefits.

Compared to traditional instruction, cooperative learning strategies improve students' achievements both on teacher-made and standardized tests (Slavin, 1990). Slavin attributed these improvements to increased student motivation, greater time on-task, and especially active student involvement.

Slavin (1990) also found that students' self-esteem increased. They felt more in control of their academic success and they began to link their success to their effort, an important factor in motivation. Low achievers tend to attribute their success or failure to luck or other forces outside their control, and cooperative learning helps change this pattern.

Cooperative learning can produce massive improvements in interpersonal relations. When groups were mixed by race, gender and ability, the strategy resulted in improved attitudes toward different ethnic groups and increased interethnic friendships. Bulgarian teachers would benefit from implementing this technique in their multiethnic classrooms. Also, through strategically selected learning activities, teachers can help students to analyse, synthesize, solve problems and even learn to learn. Cooperative learning strategies such as STAD (Student Teams – Achievement Division) and Jigsaw II can be introduced to the teacher training programmes in the form of workshops through role-play.

In STAD, the teacher presents the content or skill in a large group activity in the regular manner such as direct instruction and modelling. Then as opposed to individual study, students are provided with learning materials that they use in groups to master the content. As students are provided with learning materials that they use in groups to master the content, the teacher circulates around the room to monitor group progress and interaction. When students are ready, a test is administered and scored by the teacher, who then uses this information to compute improvement points. These are added up for each team, and teams earning a specific number of improvement points are recognized (e.g., award, free time, certificate of achievement etc.).

The other recommended teaching strategy is Jigsaw II. In addition to learning basic facts, skills and concepts, cooperative learning strategies can also be used to help the students learn organized bodies of knowledge. Jigsaw II, developed by Robert Slavin (1990), assigns students to groups and asks each student to become an expert on one aspect or part of an organized body of knowledge. These experts then are responsible for teaching other team members, all of whom are then held accountable for all the information covered by each member. One of the benefits of using cooperative learning is increased student communication skills. The group discussions provide extended opportunities for students to talk and listen to each other, a powerful tool in developing students' communication skills.

In conclusion, as the Bulgarian school system and especially its teacher training is reforming itself, instruction in the classroom must undergo a major reform. This reform should include a slow move from a didactic approach to a more interactive/conceptual teaching method. In other words, instruction in the classrooms must change from a content-centred approach to a student-centred teaching strategy. For this reform to be effective, the school curriculum must replace emphasis on the acquisition of factual knowledge with an emphasis on process-oriented curriculum that will teach students how to learn, organize, study, judge and solve problems.

Such reform should include in pre-service programmes such concepts as cooperative learning, metacognitive strategies and multiple intelligences. Multiple intelligences suggest that teachers should create learning environments in which different kinds of students can prosper. One way to do this is to provide students with choices as they learn new content. Those strategies could improve the whole instructional process in Bulgarian classrooms to encourage students' curiosity and imagination to make them active learners and, as a result, make learning more meaningful and enjoyable.

# References

Eggen, P., & Kauchak, D. (1988). *Strategies for Teachers: Information Processing Models in the Classroom* (2nd ed.). Englewood Cliffs, NJ: Prentice Hall.

Johnson, D. & Johnson, R. (1991). *Learning together and alone.* (3rd ed.). Englewood Cliffs, NJ: Prentice Hall.

Johnson, D. W., Johnson, R. T. and Stanne, M. B. 2000. *Cooperative Learning Methods: A Meta-Analysis* (http://www.ccsstl.com/sites/default/files/Cooperative%20Learning%20Resear ch%20.pdf, accessed 6 December 2014).

Kagen, S. (1989). *Cooperative Learning: Resources for teachers.* San Juan Capistrano, CA: Resources for Teachers.

Kamyab, Shahrzad. 2000. *Cooperative Learning: One Effective Method to Turn Passive Students into Active Learners in the Russian Classrooms* (http://www.Prof.Msu.Ru/Publ/Omsk1/4_10.html).

Mutafchieva, M., Pojarliev, A. and Kokinov, B. 2008. *Teaching Active Learning and Critical Thinking in Bulgaria's Public Schools: A University in this Formerly Communist Nation Endeavors to Update the Educational System's Soviet-era Pedagogy* (http://www.edutopia.org/global-education-bulgaria, accessed 6 December 2014)

Slavin, R. (1990). *Cooperative Learning: Theory, Research and Practice.* Englewood Cliffs, NJ: Prentice Hall.

# Websites for further reading

http://en.goldenmap.com/Education_in_Bulgaria

http://education.stateuniversity.com/pages/210/Bulgaria-EDUCATIONAL-SYSTEM-OVERVIEW.html

http://www.worldbank.org/en/country/bulgaria

http://www.worldbank.org/en/news/2010/09/13/bulgarian-education-system-more-efficient-further-focus-quality-needed

http://www.unesco.org/new/en/education/resources/unesco-portal-to-recognized-higher-education-institutions/dynamic-single-view/news/bulgaria/

# CHAPTER EIGHT

## EXPERIENCES OF A COMMUNITY OF TESSA FOR TEACHER USERS IN UGANDA AND THE PARADIGM SHIFT TO A LEARNER CENTRED APPROACH TO TEACHING AND LEARNING: THE CASE OF SELECTED PRIMARY SCHOOLS IN UGANDA

### LAZARUS MUGABI
ACADEMIC DIRECTOR, CREAMHILLCOORDINATOR TESSA
PROGRAMME, MAKERERE UNIVERSITY, UGANDA
### AND JULIAN BBUYE
MAKERERE UNIVERSITY, UGANDA

**Abstract**
Uganda's teaching/learning culture at primary level is traditionally a teacher centred approach with a relatively big class of 60 to 100 pupils. In addition to that there are limited resources and poor infrastructure. Lack of textbooks, well facilitated classrooms, chalk and chalkboard are some of the key resources notably unavailable in schools. The teacher centred approach of teaching limits a child's participation and creativity. Having realized the potential of TESSA-OER (Teacher Education in Sub-Saharan Africa – Open Education Resources) materials in primary schools in Uganda to inculcate the child centred approach to teaching/learning among teachers, action research was undertaken in selected schools to identify skills that would enable primary teachers in Uganda to adopt TESSA-OER and use it widely in their teaching and learning.

**Keywords**
Student centred approach, Open Education Resources and Action Research

# Introduction

This paper presents the experiences of a community of TESSA users who are teachers in Uganda. The teachers' experiences were aired during ongoing action research on skills required for the sustainable use of TESSA materials in the context of Uganda. The sharing of findings and case studies is leading the way to the paradigm shift of teacher centred teaching to learner centred teaching.

## *Background*

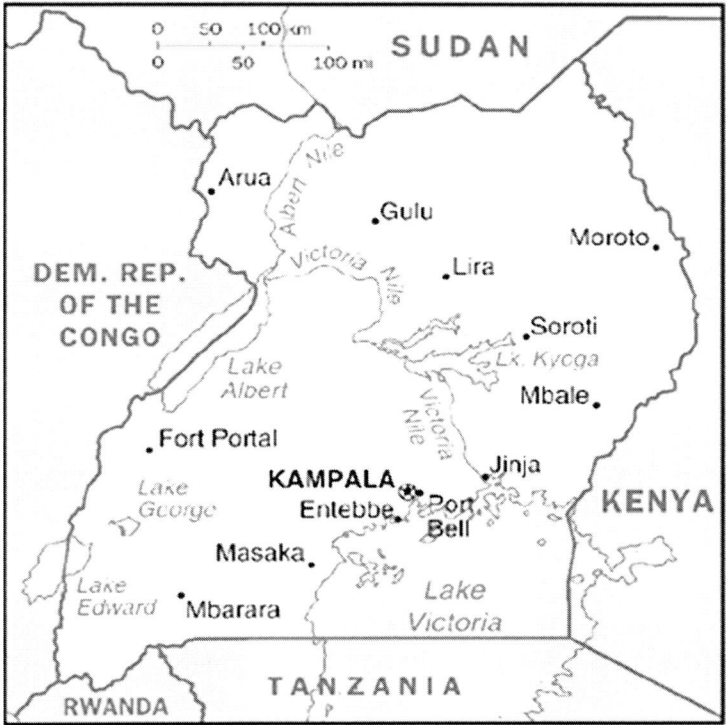

Fig. 8.1. Map of Uganda

Teacher Education in Sub-Saharan Africa (TESSA) is a project based at the Open University, UK, designed to impart basic skills of teaching and learning among teachers based in Africa.

It is important to note that Africa is a continent that faces plenty of infrastructural and socioeconomic constraints in teaching and learning experiences of children in primary schools; Aguti (2002) shows the predicament in Uganda, pointing out the massive numbers in schools, and yet with no commensurable expansion in facilities, teachers or teaching/learning materials. This situation may have compromised the quality of education. The research on which this paper is based arose out of a conviction that it is possible to change teachers' approach, despite their training in a teacher-centred approach, to a learner-centred approach culminating in a change of culture of teaching. In fact Uganda's teaching/learning culture at primary level is the traditional teacher-centred approach with relatively big classes of 60 to 100 pupils. Teaching takes place in a context of limited resources and poor infrastructure (for example, lack of textbooks, classrooms, chalk and chalkboards and a total absence of computers in some schools).

## Problem Statement

Nambogga (2012) points out that schools in Mayuge, one of the districts in Uganda, lack adequate classrooms; many pupils study in mud and wattle structures that are sometimes dilapidated, while some students study under trees. One of the schools with 600 pupils Nambogga points out has only 30 desks. Teaching and learning in such schools therefore require ingenuity to alleviate the impact of difficult conditions. The TESSA approach comes in handy to alleviate such a situation as will be seen later in this paper and that is why the action research on which this paper is based was embarked on, to enable the dissemination of the ability of TESSA materials to assist in teaching and learning in the impoverished schools as well as changing methods of teaching even in the well-to-do schools.

## Objectives of the Action Research

The objectives of this action research were:

1. to find out through the experiences of teachers how a change in the teaching practices of primary teachers in Uganda, from a teacher-centred approach to a learner-centred one, can be achieved through the use of TESSA-OER materials; and
2. to develop specific dissemination practices for the use of TESSA-OER that would bring about a teacher culture of learner-centred approaches among a wider audience of teachers based in the under-resourced schools of Uganda.

# Methodology

This study followed an action research method. The initial stage was a workshop during which teachers from 10 schools were given one TESSA CD-Rom and a hard copy of TESSA materials for Science, Literacy, Numeracy, Social Studies and Study Skills. A follow-up on the utilization of TESSA-OER, challenges and prospects was done by staff of Makerere University. A research team from the university would make appointments with the selected schools and would supervise their lessons, record them, interview the students to assess the impact and take pictures of real learning situations before having an open discussion with the teachers supervised. Follow-up workshops would be organized at the university to assess the impact of the TESSA-OER among the selected schools in relation to the previous trend.

## *Action Research method and the justification for its use in the study*

Action research is a form of research carried out by practitioners into their own practices. It involves observation of processes and gives room for studying a cycle obtaining results and studying a second cycle to improve practice and use TESSA materials effectively. In all these it is paramount to note that practice is always influenced by context.

## *Tools used in the study*

The tools used to aid the action research in this study include a documentary review of previous reports on the use of TESSA materials, gathered from four schools; follow-up visits with observation checklists to the selected primary schools to observe as frequently as possible lessons making use of TESSA materials; case study questionnaires for recording students' learning outcomes and performance in tests of classes that were taught with TESSA-OER materials; questionnaires and intermittent interviews with head teachers.

# Results

Sustainable use of TESSA materials in the teaching and learning in selected primary schools was evident. The teachers' move from a teacher-centred to a learner-centred approach is also evident and teachers now enjoy their teaching experiences, while the pupils look forward to school daily. The experiences shared in the community of TESSA teacher users, rotated around planning for a lesson, thorough preparation, the ability to involve pupils and its impact, the ability to use the local environment, the ability to replicate or adopt a case study to use in your own classroom, the ability to maximize classroom time, and most important of all the ability to get acquainted with the objectives of the lesson by knowing what one needs to achieve at the end of a given lesson and that it should be the starting point. The ability to acquire organization skills, the ability to share and the ability to give the children the foundation to learn and explore are also important.

The following are some of the experiences shared during workshops in the partner schools.

### *The Need to Plan and prepare thoroughly*

Planning was found to be key in preparation of a lesson based on TESSA OER. The teacher preparing to use the TESSA materials should work out the specific steps required to prepare a lesson based on TESSA-OER. One of the teachers, Lukeman of Kiswa primary school, commented:

> Good preparation starts with class environment, in one of the visits to observe lessons at Kabojja Primary school, for example the following scenario surfaced. Teacher Okiror was teaching about road safety in SST and displayed a thorough preparation of the lesson he taught. He prepared pupils to set up their own safety rules in class and the rationale for them. In a democratic manner, the pupils of Primary 3 set up safety rules they would follow in their class. Then afterwards he introduced the road safety rules and took children on the road to test whether they have grasped. While crossing the road to his amazement comments Okiror: "Some had not grasped the idea of looking right then left then right again, some were actually trying to cross even in a dangerous situation. Testing the rules helped them to conceptualize the road safety rules."

### *Acquiring the ability to involve pupils and its impact on learning*

In the teachers' journals were found some of the answers to the guiding questions put before them, especially one that required them to observe and gauge their ability to involve pupils and to give evidence. In their sharing teachers realized that one has to make sure each and every pupil in the class has something to do. Some of the experiences shared in this respect included the following:

> In a lesson observed in a P6 class, Mr. Wamala of Kabojja Primary School had asked pupils to come to class with apples. He was going to teach fractions in Mathematics. With each pupil dissecting his/her own apple, as they observed the teacher doing it, the apple was divided into a half, then a quarter etc, and reassembled again to make a whole. After the lesson each

pupil ate his/her apple and went away happy and yet having grasped the concept of fractions.

### *Ability to survey and use the local environment*

On the issue of surveying the environment, in TESSA review meetings for teachers using the TESSA materials teachers noted that it is important to first of all understand the teaching syllabus and the requirements of the topic you are about to teach and then survey the environment and identify a particular local environment that fits within the syllabus you are using to teach the pupils. Mapping beforehand, and establishing which TESSA materials are relevant to the curriculum, are depicted in the following experience:

> I was teaching graphs in mathematics. I surveyed the environment to find out what elements in the environment would fit my lesson. I decided that the students count all fruit trees on the compound. I grouped the pupils into five groups. Groups were able to tally and record the fruits; for example they counted 10 mango trees, 7 jack trees, three jambula trees, 5 avocado trees. The graphs that came out included bar charts and line graphs; the mathematics class therefore was not in the class, but outside the classroom and pupils looked forward to another adventure.

### *Ability to replicate or adopt a case study to use in your own classroom*

As teachers gave tasks and homework they made use of case studies within the modules.

> Tutor Mary of Makerere University gave an assignment to her students of B.Ed for use in the primary schools they teach in particularly suited for Primary 4.She replicated a case study she saw in TESSA materials and wrote a song on the "Finest Tree" and then asked the students how the song can be used as a basis for teaching English lessons. Teachers came up with interesting suggestions such as, it can be used to introduce pattern writing, it can be used to introduce writing a guided composition, the song can help to teach the skills in language learning, like listening speaking reading and writing, in listening for example the teacher tells the learners the song they are going to learn, he sings the song several times learners join him/her singing.

### *Maximize classroom time*

In the sharing forums, it was found out that classroom time can be maximized with a lot of innovation as in the following example:

> Teacher Sarah was explaining particular concepts of the English language and maximized each and every item she could think of in the classroom, the concepts were " round", "heavy", "light", "soft", "smooth", "rough",

"rectangular," "long" and asked pupils to show all those concepts from the classroom environment. They were able to show the concept of light, using a light bag, to show soft, by touching their skins, to show smooth by touching the blackboard, to show rough by touching their desks, to show rectangular by touching their books and rulers, and to show oval by locating an egg, to show a triangle by displaying a "sumbusa" (something sold in the canteen for them to eat), heavy by trying to lift a desk and a table, light by lifting a polythene bag, and lifting a bucket without water, something long by comparing a short pencil with a long pencil. Whatever they learnt explaining those concepts was in the classroom and they picked the concepts.

### *Ability to make it a rule that a teacher get acquainted with the objectives of the lesson*

Teachers in their sharing realized that each of the teachers, before starting to prepare a lesson, ought to find out what he/she needs to achieve at the end of the lesson.

Drawing from Mary Nabukenya's tasks again, the idea of having objectives of the lesson is well illustrated when she uses a song as she teaches the teachers, in an English class/lecture. The objectives were very clear and are; introduce the writing of poems and songs task, show how replication can be used to reinforce reading skills, mastery of words, order of adjectives, listening, speaking, reading, speaking skills, it was also to enable the teacher to become knowledgeable and skillful in teaching the writing skills, employing songs and poems to teach and one of the objectives also was to show the teachers that the song itself has a motivating effect and writing need not be introduced to the learners as an abstract/hard aspect but as a simple task through making it appealing as in a song. The song makes all pupils activity- engaged. Children learn from known to unknown, a song for example is about the tree, the nest, the egg, the leaf, the branch, the wood which are in their environment.

### *The ability to share*

Sharing helps to open up children's understanding; sharing with fellow teachers is also a skill as the following voice of experience shows:

Teacher Mugeni organized pupils in groups and each group was given materials to perform an experiment and share with the class. Pupil leaders did a wonderful job, introduced participants in their groups and reported, while other groups corrected them. When the video clip was shared with other schools, headteachers urged their teachers to encourage children to use that skill of sharing in class to build their confidence. It also gave teacher Mugeni the ability to identify leaders among the pupils and to teach the pupils leadership skills. The group work also built skills that help learners to search for their own information.

### *Give the children the foundation to learn and explore*

In the teachers' forum, while sharing their experiences, one issue came out vehemently, and that was to encourage children to participate in knowledge construction; once pupils were involved in knowledge construction, they will be able to learn more and not forget what they have learnt. The following is what one of the teachers shared:

> Teacher Lazarus was teaching pollination, took his class in the gardens. Bees and flies were busy pollinating and the pupils saw the two insects live pollinating the plants. The learning was so deep that it involved pupils asking pertinent questions, like how does a bee pollinate a plant with thorns, don't the thorns prick it?

## Discussion

Whereas the results showed mainly the activities of the teachers as they participated in the action research, in the discussion we refer to the reflections of the teachers as required by action research. In order to improve on using TESSA materials teachers ought to turn back and reflect on what went wrong or what was good, what made it better than the earlier one. The teacher ought to be a researcher: What did I learn from what I did? How did the girls perform in relation to boys? What happened when I mixed girls and boys? Generally, there has been identification of skills for the sustainable use of TESSA-OER materials in primary schools in Uganda. This study has provided empirical data, reliable enough to guide those particular primary schools willing to take up use of TESSA materials.

## Conclusion

A change in the teaching practices of primary teachers in Uganda, from a teacher-centred approach to a learner-centred one, can be achieved through the use of TESSA-OER materials by following methods that have been tested to work in classrooms, as observed during this action research. The outstanding issues are that a teacher ought to plan and research thoroughly, should be able to utilize the classroom and school environment in all aspects of teaching involving the students to make use of the resources available and should talk less. Group preparation is an art, and it is therefore important for the teacher to keep on reflecting and improving group management every time he uses it.

Following the conclusion reached in the previous discussion it is recommended therefore that the local environment is a resource that teachers can consistently use to allow the children to enjoy the lessons. Secondly, to get all the pupils involved teachers ought to use methods which are practical and can motivate them, preferably taking place sometimes in a school garden or playground. Thirdly, watching video clips of earlier lessons by the teachers gives teachers a clue on how TESSA materials can be used to make learner-centred lessons. It is also recommended that more funding be poured in the dissemination of TESSA-OER resources to enable the researchers to spread the practice of learner-centred teaching throughout the country. Occasional joint workshops of TESSA users and meetings should also continue to be implemented.

# References and Further Reading

Aguti, J. 2002. *Facing up to the Challenge of Universal Pprimary Education (UPE) in Uganda through Distance Teacher Education Programmes*. Paper presented at Pan Commonwealth Forum on Open Learning, Transforming Education for Development, Durban, 29 August to 2nd September.

Greenwood, D. J. and Levin, M. 2006. *Introduction to Action Research: Social Research for Social Change*. Thousand Oaks, CA: Sage.

Johnson, B. 1993. *Teacher-as-researcher*. (Report No. EDO-SP-92-7). Washington, DC: Office of Educational Research and Improvement. (ERIC Document Reproduction Service No. ED355205)

Kemmis, S. and McTaggart, R. 1982. *The Action Research Planner*. Geelong, Victoria, Australia: Deakin University Press.

Namboga, J. 2012. "Poor Grades Blamed on Lack of Classrooms", *New Vision Newspaper* (Uganda) (25 May), 8.

Nixon, J. 1987. "The Teacher as Researcher: Contradictions and Continuities", *Peabody Journal of Education* 64(2), 20–32.

Somech, B. 2006. *Action Research Methodology for Change and Development*. Maidenhead: Open University Press.

# Chapter Nine

# Teachers' Problem-Solving Activity as a Support for Reconceptualizing their Pedagogical Reasoning in Teaching Multiplication

## Ada Boufi, Angeliki Kolovou
Pedagogics Department of Elementary Education,
University of Athens
## and Koeno Gravemeijer
Eindhoven School of Education, Eindhoven University
of Technology

**Abstract**

This study is part of a professional development programme that aims to support teachers' development of instructional practices that are grounded on students' mathematical reasoning. The design of instructional sequences and their adaptation to students' needs lies at the heart of these practices and requires non-traditional forms of pedagogical reasoning. To this end, we first designed and tested an instructional sequence on early multiplication that aims at fostering derived-facts strategies, which proved to be successful in developing second-graders' multiplicative reasoning. The participants in our programme are teachers who are going to teach multiplication in Grade 2. While designing our collaboration with them, we anticipated that their reflecting on their solutions on a multiplication task designed to evoke derived-facts strategies could serve as a starting point for teachers to develop insight into students' mathematics, to re-examine the mathematics textbooks' approach, and to begin constructing a rationale for the instructional sequence we had designed in the course of a second-grade teaching experiment. The discussion of our data supports our anticipations, as teachers seemed to use their mathematical reasoning as a basis for sound pedagogical arguments.

**Keywords**
Teachers' professional development, teachers' mathematical reasoning, pedagogical reasoning norms, early multiplication, derived-facts strategies

Recent attempts to reform mathematics education necessitate the design of professional development (PD) programmes that aim at helping teachers in developing instructional practices that place students' reasoning at the centre of instructional decision making (Cobb et al., 2003). Building on students' reasoning while at the same time not losing sight of the mathematical ideas that are the goal of instruction is a tension that is endemic in such practices (Ball, 1993; Gravemeijer, 2004). Therefore, PD programmes have to focus on supporting teachers in dealing with this tension. More specifically, these programmes have to provide opportunities for teachers to enhance their understanding of students' reasoning and to use this in designing and enacting their instruction.

Several investigations of the effectiveness of teacher PD programmes point to the difficulties and complexities of supporting teachers in using their students' understandings as a resource in their teaching (Cohen, 2004; Visnovska & Cobb, 2009). Designing instruction on the basis of students' diverse ways of reasoning is not a trivial task for teachers, especially when their current instructional practices are textbook-centred.

In the light of the above considerations, we designed a PD programme for second-grade teachers. This programme is structured in two phases. In the first, teachers are to reconstruct a rationale for an instructional sequence on early multiplication and division that we designed and tested in a second-grade classroom. This sequence was shown to be successful in supporting the students in developing derived-fact strategies. In the second phase of our PD programme, our goal is to support teachers to build on their students' reasoning while fostering the development of derived-fact strategies in multiplicative and divisional situations as taught in their classrooms.

In this paper we report on our experiences from the first phase of our program. These experiences are shaped from our attempts to form conjectures about supporting the learning of the teachers. In order to form these conjectures we did not view teachers' current ideas about teaching and learning mathematics in deficit terms. Instead we considered them as reasonable from their perspectives. Based on the philosophy of the textbooks which the teachers are obliged to use, we assumed that they would view the development of derived-fact strategies as a peripheral goal for an introduction of their students to early multiplication and division. Therefore, our initial conjectured learning trajectory for supporting the teachers' learning had as a starting point the teachers' engagement with a multiplication task designed to evoke derived-fact strategies. This starting point would support them in coming to see as an important goal of an instructional sequence on early multiplication, students' development of derived-fact strategies rather than the learning of the multiplication tables by applying ready-made rules. We also conjectured that this starting point would motivate teachers to delve into questions related to the process of achieving this goal with second-grade students.

The endpoint of the teachers' conjectured learning trajectory was their reconstruction of the rationale of the instructional sequence we had developed in the second-grade teaching experiment classroom. The means of supporting teachers' pedagogical reasoning towards this endpoint included their engagement in activities which would allow them to analyse and discuss students' mathematical reasoning in multiplicative situations. In addition teachers would be involved in an examination of textbooks' activities in order to evaluate the extent to which students' mathematical reasoning is supported. We hoped that both these tools of support would aid teachers to understand the advantages of an instructional sequence aimed to the development of students' derived-fact strategies as opposed to imposing ready-made rules.

As anticipated, we had to adjust our conjectures on the basis of our ongoing analyses of teachers' activity as they interacted with us. The teachers' perspectives on the relevance of students' reasoning to their instruction, as well as on the textbooks' approach, challenged us to redesign the activities we had planned for supporting teacher change.

Our purpose in this paper is to outline the actual learning trajectory of the participants, who were ten second-grade in-service teachers working in Athens. This outline is based on an initial analysis of our data and reflects the norms of pedagogical reasoning that were under formation by this group of teachers (Dean, 2005). Through our data analysis, it will be shown how the teachers' perspectives were dialectically related to our activity as designers of the PD programme. Our data sources consist of video-recordings of the seven PD sessions of the first phase and copies of the teachers' work on the assignments we gave them. It should be noted that apart from the ten second-grade in-service teachers to which our data refer, seven future teachers and four school supervisors also participated in this PD programme. The inclusion of these subgroups will allow us to study issues related to the cooperation of pre-service and in-service teachers, as well as issues related to the power of the institutional setting of teachers' work.

## Theoretical Background and Research Methodology

The interpretation of the teachers' pedagogical activity in our PD programme meetings is guided by an interpretive framework which coordinates cognitive and sociological perspectives (Cobb & Yackel, 1996). Based on an extension of this framework, we view individual teachers' learning and the development of collective norms within the PD group as reflexively related and embedded in the institutional setting of the teachers' work (Cobb et al., 2003).We note that in our results these norms are implicated, as the teachers' learning is documented. These norms are joint accomplishments and they emerge as regularities in teachers' interactions. Cobb et al. (2001) present their method for developing conjectures about the social norms in a classroom. They emphasize the importance of searching for instances where a student appears to violate a conjectured norm. If this violation is constituted as legitimate, it is necessary to revise our conjecture. Otherwise, if it is constituted as illegitimate, the conjecture is supported. Similarly, in conducting an initial analysis of our data, we tried to delineate the extent to which the teachers felt obliged to argue pedagogically in terms of students' mathematical reasoning, i.e. the development of pedagogical reasoning norms in our group of teachers.

As the teachers' change was not independent of our interventions within the PD programme, we adopted the design experiment methodology (Gravemeijer, 1994; Gravemeijer & Van Eerde, 2009), in order to investigate how our interventions supported their learning. Therefore, in outlining the actual learning trajectory of the PD teachers we will refer not only their change but also to the means that supported it. We note that these means of support were designed, tested and revised on the basis of our ongoing analyses of our interactions with the teachers.

## Results

We anticipated that the problem-solving activity the teachers started with would provide them with a basis for analysing students' reasoning in multiplicative situations and for appreciating the rationale of our instructional sequence. In addition, we thought that they could relate their experiences with this activity to their understanding of the textbooks' approach. However, the success of our effort was not straightforward. In the following sections we document the teachers' actual learning trajectory, while divergences from our initial conjectures are revealed.

## Teachers' Problem-solving Activity on the Multiplication Task

We asked the PD participants to solve the problem: "If I buy 18 books that cost 15 euros each, how much do I have to pay?" In addition they were instructed to solve the multiplication problem in as many ways they could, without making use of the multiplication algorithm. In Fig. 9-1, examples of the teachers' activity in this problem are presented.

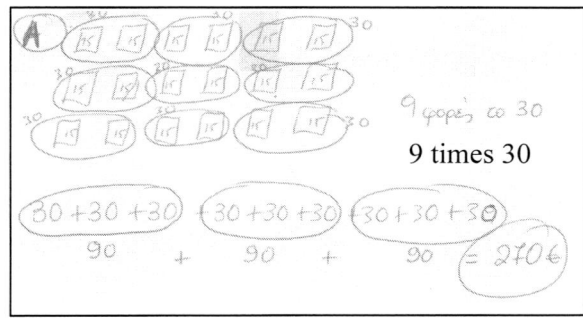

9 times 30

We took 2 times 15

18 is the product of 2×9.

So we need 9 times 30

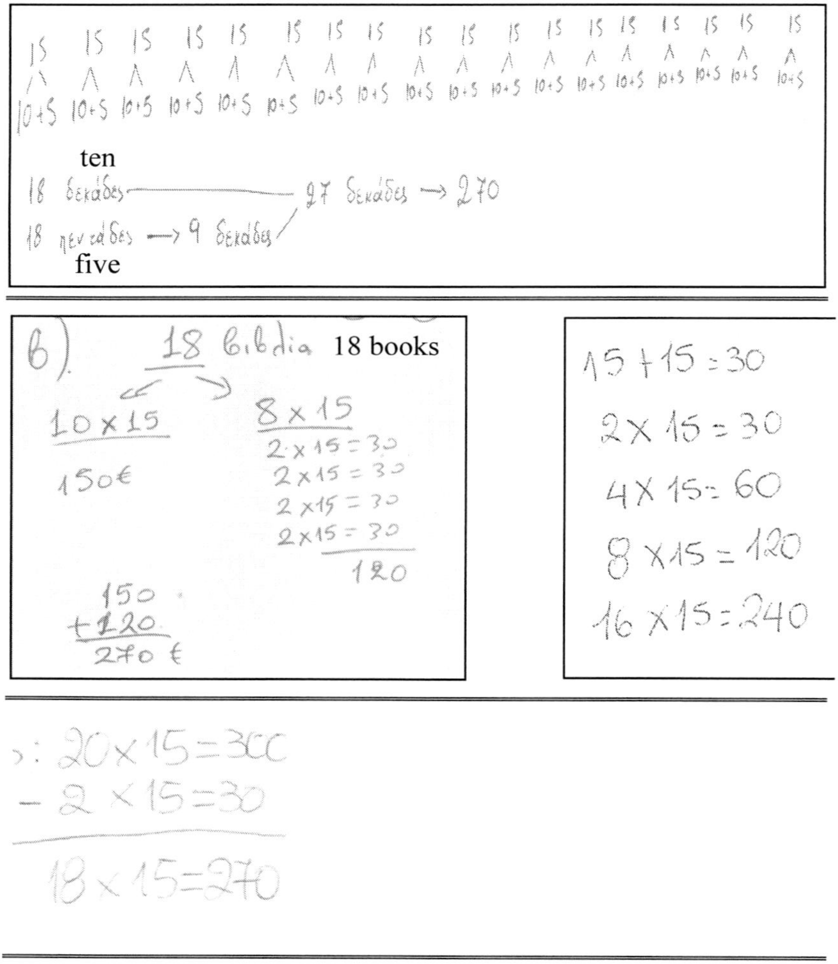

ten

$18$ δεκάδες ─────────── $97$ δεκάδες → $270$

$18$ πεντάδες → $9$ δεκάδες

five

$6)$  $18$ βιβλία   18 books

$10 × 15$

$150€$

$8 × 15$
$2·×15 = 30$
$2×15 = 30$
$2 ×15 = 30$
$2×15 = 30$
─────────
$120$

$150$
$+120$
─────────
$270$ €

$15 + 15 = 30$

$2 × 15 = 30$

$4 × 15 = 60$

$8 × 15 = 120$

$16 × 15 = 240$

$>: 20 × 15 = 300$

$- 2 × 15 = 30$
─────────────
$18 × 15 = 270$

Fig. 9-1. Examples of the teachers' strategies

As can be seen, the calculation of 18×15 is based on the use of already known products and more profoundly on the use of number relations. In this process, we can observe that the teachers' strategies fall into two categories. They reorganize the unknown product: (1) by changing the unit while adjusting the number of its repetitions, or (2) by keeping the unit constant as they built the unknown product by combining known products.

As teachers discussed how their solutions differed from the standard algorithm, they seemed to become aware of the process they actually use in calculating products. Then we asked them to compare their activity with the activity of second-graders coming from our teaching experiment classroom on a similar problem.

## Teachers' Initial Ideas about Students' Reasoning

Teachers were stunned when we presented examples of our second-graders' solutions in calculating 16×15 (see Fig. 9-2). In fact, when students are introduced to multiplication with two-digit numbers in third grade they are only trained in using the standard algorithm. However, one teacher's question: "Were these kids normal?" summarizes not only the teachers' surprise but also their doubts about pursuing such outcomes with second-graders. These doubts might be related to their experiences in using the textbook as a blueprint for teaching multiplication. In this textbook, emphasis is given to the procedural aspects of multiplication and division, rather than to the development of derived-fact strategies. Number relations are built into the textbook's activities, but they are proceduralized to such an extent that they cannot be noticed by the students. As a consequence, the similarities teachers could observe between their own and the students' solutions did not constitute a reason for considering the development of derived-fact strategies as a feasible learning goal for their students. Instead, the teachers felt that our students might have special characteristics or might be gifted. In their view their ways of calculating products as well as our students' ways, were far removed from the conventional procedures emphasized in the textbook.

In order to alleviate their doubts, we organized discussions based on video excerpts from the teaching experiment students' initial and final interviews. Through these excerpts, teachers came to realize that our students' ability was not related to a special capacity. In their initial interviews, our students could not use number relations. For example, Paulina, in her initial interview, was unable to figure out a product (6×5) by using another product (3×5) she had just calculated by counting. On the other hand, the same child in her final interview could build 9×7 by subtracting 1×7 from 10×7. Teachers immediately tied her activity to their own ways of reasoning in the multiplication problem. By discussing the changes in our students' reasoning, teachers had an opportunity to reexamine the development of derived-fact strategies as a plausible goal for their students' learning. In fact, they started asking questions about the process of these students' development and the means of supporting it.

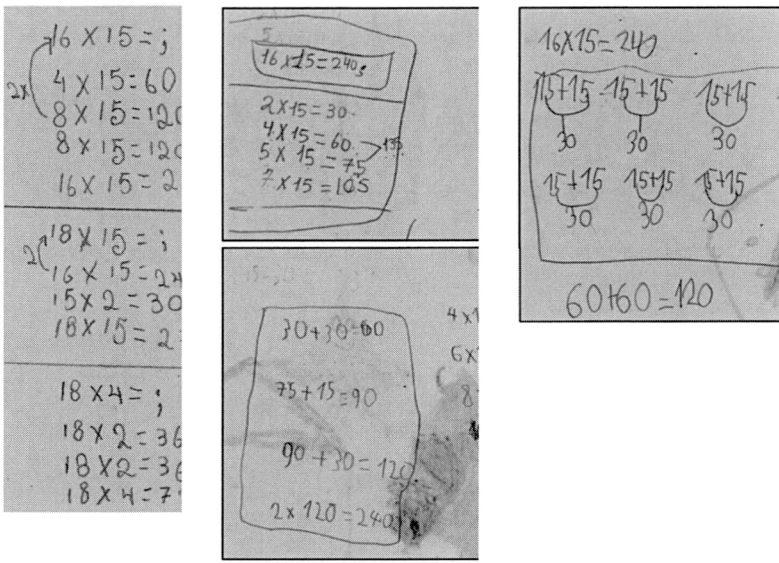

Fig. 9-2. Second graders' strategies in calculating 16×15

## Focusing on Students' Development of Multiplicative Reasoning

As a response to their questions we presented selected video cases of students' work in the context of activities used in the teaching experiment classroom. Teachers seemed to start developing an understanding of the evolving nature of students' activity and to connect it to students' reasoning with appropriate tools of support. For instance, teachers viewed Thanasi in attempting to relate the last two solutions produced by his classmates when structuring a collection of 18 lemons arranged in a 6×3 rectangular crate (see Fig. 9-3). He reasoned that six groups of three lemons are the same as three groups of six lemons because each group of six lemons is made by uniting two groups of three lemons. By analysing the students' activity in similar episodes, teachers had a chance to realize that the students' ability to relate products could be traced back to the design of an appropriate learning environment.

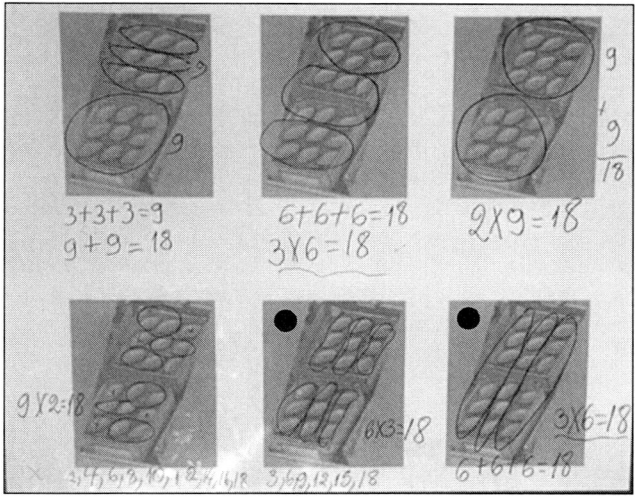

Fig. 9-3. Students' different solutions

Next, we asked teachers to interview some of their students. We expected them to get a handle on their reasoning by detecting possible strengths and weaknesses and to designate starting points for their learning on the basis of this. The tasks for the interviews were designed by us and included bare products and context problems.

It came as a surprise that most of the teachers instructed their students or provided them with a lot of assistance. They did not pay attention to the subtleties of their reasoning. Marina is a characteristic example of the way teachers acted as interviewers. In the written protocol depicting the work of one of her students, it is clear that he is guided to produce three solutions that belong to different levels of reasoning. For example, in calculating 9×7 the student appears to use his fingers in the way prescribed by the textbook. A sketch of his two palms is accompanied by written sentences. Afterwards, he seems to be directed to draw 63 circles in 9 groups of 7 circles each and to connect his drawing to the writing of the addition sentence 7+7+7+7+7+7+7+7+7 and to the process of producing the result. By using pencils of different colors the child writes the steps of calculating in two ways: first by grouping the sevens into pairs and then into trios (sic). After all, it was as if Marina imposed the textbook procedures on her student.

The teachers may have considered themselves accountable for their students' performance, especially those who had taught them some initial lessons on multiplication during the first grade. Their concern to save face by altering or ignoring their students' reasoning may reflect their general perspective on the relationship between teaching and reasoning. For them students' reasoning can only occur as an effect of teaching and cannot serve as an input. Thus, making their students' reasoning visible is avoided because it may be considered as an assessment of their teaching.

We conjectured that teachers' views of their responsibility for their students' ways of working might be challenged by studying the rationale of the textbook activities. We therefore asked them to examine the extent to which certain textbook activities support the development of students' reasoning. In their reports teachers mostly focused on characteristics of the tasks, like the size of the numbers, the phrasing used by the authors and the "transparency" of the pictures used in making the mathematical ideas concrete. In addition, some of the teachers used as a criterion for the effectiveness of a task, the degree of its conformity to the behavioural objectives included in the teachers' guide. Teachers were not inclined to analyse the textbook's activities from the students' point of view. By assuming an observer's perspective instead of an actor's perspective, they were not involved in either trying to anticipate students' difficulties due to the sequencing of the activities, or thinking about the possible contribution of an activity to the development of the students' reasoning.

Our attempt to foster a change in the teachers' perspectives on students' reasoning through an examination of the textbooks was not successful. Their superficial evaluation of the textbooks may be related to them being an integral part of their instruction. For them, looking at the textbooks in terms of supporting students' thinking might be equivalent to criticizing their own instructional practices. It is in this sense that we might say teachers were not experiencing the tension that arises when taking into account both the students' reasoning and the mathematics they are meant to learn. Another reason for our failure to make the teachers aware of this tension might relate to the distinction Daro (2011) makes between teachers who try to teach procedures for finding the right answers to particular problems and those who are concerned about the mathematics that students may learn by being involved in solving a given problem. In our case the teachers did not show any concern for the mathematics that students are learning when they examine an activity. They are mostly focused on answer-getting, as this is reinforced by the textbook's activities. Therefore, we thought of attempting to foster a change in their perspectives on students' reasoning by using the problems we used in the teaching experiment classroom.

## A Change of Orientation: Focusing on Supporting Students' Development of Multiplicative Reasoning

Restarting from the teachers' activity on the multiplication task, we classified the activities of the instructional sequence we developed in the teaching experiment classroom based on the categories in which we had classified their solutions. For each activity, we asked teachers to anticipate students' reasoning. Then we talked about questions they could ask their students in order to support them in creating number relationships. Teachers came to anticipate students' solutions and to propose appropriate questions for enhancing their reasoning (e.g., "How are your solutions related to each other?", "Why does counting by twos takes more time than counting by fours?", "Can you anticipate, how many more groups of five will you make in order to finish your counting?"). They thus seemed to start appreciating and reconstructing the rationale of our activities.

Then, we asked them to compare and contrast students' reasoning in the textbook's activities with students' reasoning in the activities of our instructional sequence. Teachers were now in a position to criticize the textbook activities. For example, they indicated the difference between the use of rectangular arrays in the textbook and in our instructional sequence. As one of the teachers pinpointed: "The child will use the array [in the textbook] in the way it is instructed to and not as he might think. . . . In contrast the boxes with the chocolates [in our sequence] allow children to organize them in different ways and to notice relationships between their own solutions."

Teachers seemed to become aware of the problematic character of their instructional practices as they are obliged to use the textbook. However, they expressed feelings of frustration as they realized the difficulty of seeking activities, like the ones we proposed, for other mathematical units.

## Discussion

In the first phase of our PD programme we tried to support teachers' learning through an iterative process of conjecturing and testing the effect of the means that we used. From our results, it appears that a change in our teachers' perspective on using their students' reasoning has already started. Starting to think about student thinking proved to be a key element in this change in perspective. And it showed that analysing innovative activities with the task to anticipate students' reasoning, while using one's own experience of solving similar problems, helped teachers to let go of their initial observer's point of view. The change, however, is still tentative. More robust evidence for our teachers' learning is sought in the second phase of our programme where teachers are adapting the instructional sequence in their classrooms.

# References

Ball, D. L. 1993. "With an Eye on the Mathematical Horizon: Dilemmas of Teaching Elementary School Mathematics", *Elementary School Journal* 93, 373–397.

Cobb, P., & Yackel, E. (1996). Constructivist, emergent, and sociocultural perspectives in the context of developmental research. *Educational Psychologist, 31*, 175-190.

Cobb, P., Stephan, M., McClain, K. and Gravemeijer, K. 2001. "Participating in Classroom Mathematical Practices", *Journal of the Learning Sciences* 10, 113–164.

Cobb, P., McClain, K., Lamberg, T. d. S. and Dean, C. 2003. "Situating teachers' Instructional Practices in the Institutional Setting of the School and District", *Educational Researcher* 32(6), 13–24.

Cohen, S. 2004. *Teachers' Professional Development and the Elementary Mathematics Classroom: Bringing Understandings to Light*. Mahwah, NJ: Lawrence Erlbaum.

Daro P. 2011. "Against 'Answer-getting'" [Video], http://serpmedia.org/daro-talks/

Dean, C. 2005. *Supporting the Learning and Development of a Professional Mathematics Tteaching Community*. Unpublished Dissertation, Vanderbilt University, Nashville, TN.

Gravemeijer, K. P. E. 1994. *Developing Realistic Mathematics Education.*Utrecht: Freudenthal Institute.

—. 2004. "Local Instruction Theories as Means of Support for Teachers in Reform Mathematics Education", *Mathematical Thinking and Learning* 6(2), 105–128.

Gravemeijer, K. and van Eerde, D. 2009. "Design Research as a Means for Building a Knowledge Base for Teachers and Teaching in Mathematics Education", *Elementary School Journal* 109, 510–524.

Visnovska, J. and Cobb, P. 2009. "Learning about Building Mathematics Instruction from Students' Reasoning: A Professional Development Study", in R. Hunter, B. Bicknell and T. Burgess (eds), *Proceedings of the 32nd annual meeting of the Mathematics Education Research Group of Australasia* Vol. 2. Wellington, NZ: MERGA, 547–554.

# CHAPTER TEN

## LIMITS AND PERSPECTIVES FOR THE PROMOTION OF INCLUSIVE CULTURE AND OF AN INNOVATIVE PSYCHOEDUCATIONAL PARADIGM IN SCHOOL SETTINGS: THEORETICAL CONSIDERATIONS AND EMPIRICAL FINDINGS FROM GREECE AND HUNGARY

ELIAS KOURKOUTAS,
ASSOCIATE PROFESSOR, UNIVERSITY OF CRETE, GREECE
AGNES NEMETHNE TÓTH
ASSOCIATE PROFESSOR, UNIVERSITY OF WESTERN HUNGARY,
HUNGARY
AND ELENA VITALAKI
TEACHING STAFF, UNIVERSITY OF CRETE

**Abstract**

The basic tenets of the "inclusive paradigm" in relation to pupils with Special Educational Needs are presented and analysed in the first section of this paper. Also the findings from recent studies in Greece and Hungary referring to the perceptions of teachers regarding the possibilities of full inclusion of these students in mainstream schools are presented and discussed. Based on these data, the final section of this paper discusses the likelihood of building and implementing an innovative inclusive paradigm in the mainstream school system, based on teachers' needs and the demands and challenges of contemporary social and educational reality.

**Keywords**
Inclusion, Special Educational Needs, Teachers' perceptions, Greece-Hungary

# Introduction

A high number of pupils attending school in Western countries displaying various forms of social, emotional, behavioural and academic (Special Educational Needs) problems cannot become healthy, self-sustaining adults without immediate attention and, in many cases, without specialized support.

Special Educational Needs Students (SENS) and students with school problems in childhood are complex phenomena implying a variety of internal and external processes. Traditional scientific models such as those used in quantitative and qualitative methods are aiming for prediction or categorization of children's disorders, difficulties and disabilities. These intentions, though rigorous and universal, are not always able to give insightful accounts of the structure of the personal experiences and the underlying processes and to thoroughly enlighten the multilevel and dynamic interactions of individual and contextual factors in childhood disorders/disabilities. Accordingly, the traditional medical intervention paradigm still remains dominant (Lloyd, 2008), though recent research shows significant results in improving the psychosocial functioning and the school inclusion of "vulnerable" children, when systemic approaches, child-, family-centred and transdisciplinary/empowering partnership practices are used (Brehm & Doll, 2009; Farrell, 2011; Greenberg, 2003; Kourkoutas & Raul Xavier, 2010).

Research shows that pupils' difficulties, if not treated in an effective way within school context, could worsen and transmute into other more serious forms of broader social emotional and school-academic problems for factors such as the following (Farrell, 2011; Florian & McLaughlin, 2008; Kourkoutas, 2010):

- a dominant intervention philosophy drawn on the bio-medical epistemological paradigm (which disregards the dimensional and developmental aspect of all children's disorders/disabilities by splitting the normal from the abnormal, by using the "syndrome psychiatric narrative" which is exclusively based on external symptoms and deficits, failing to apprehend the child's personal experience and acknowledge, his strengths and assets);
- absence of preventive thinking, reasoning, acting and policy practice;

- extreme emphasis on the clinical individual-based intervention policy overlooking the dimensional and developmental/ transactional aspects of children's problems/dysfunctions;
- insufficient or distorted evaluation and awareness of a child's social, emotional needs; a fragmentary overview of the child's problems from teachers and specialists;
- little effort for an overall review of the child's function in regard to social and other contextual parameters;
- pronounced inability of the parents to manage the problems or difficulties of the child, for a variety of reasons (psychological, economic, social et al.);
- lack of interdisciplinary approach-cooperation among the school, the parents and professionals;
- the absence, in the schools and the community, of psychosocial (non-medical) services that work cooperatively with school staff to support the inclusive policy;
- the absence of real inclusive culture and policy within the educational community;
- stereotyped perceptions of children's problems/SEN exclusively based on personal negative experiences or on the inability to deal with such students;
- low-quality education, absence of psycho-education programmes adapted to the needs of vulnerable or at risk children;
- exclusive use of negative/reprimanding practices to respond to extreme challenges of "dysfunctional" or vulnerable students (students with various forms and degrees of social, emotional, behavioural and learning problems);
- emphasis on competitive educational practice (individual knowledge-centred models and a performance-based educational philosophy) in the school system;
- strong resistance of the community and parents' associations imbued with negative stereotypical thinking/perception about the possibilities, the role and the academic trajectory within the school system of students with various difficulties, disorders and disabilities.

## Special Educational Needs Students (SENS) and Relative Educational Practices

A pupil is considered as having SEN when he/she presents greater difficulties than the rest of his/her classmates to accessing learning according to the curriculum for his/her age. To offset these difficulties, SEN students need significant or not-significant curricular adaptations in several areas of the curriculum. It is also important to mention that the emphasis in contemporary Special and Inclusive Education practice has been placed more on how to support these students to resolve and overcome their multiple difficulties than on thinking about their origin (DfES, 2004). Special Educators and teaching staff in general should focus on developing the necessary strategies and pay the relevant attention to each child who is struggling with difficulties relevant to academic success and learning performance (Farrell, 2011).

Overall, Special Educational Needs (SEN) do not only refer to a certain group of students, such as those displaying learning difficulties, but to a wide range of social, emotional, behavioural and developmental difficulties/disorders. SEN might be permanent or temporary and can be caused by a variety of reasons and factors. In fact, it is believed that they derive from a continuous and dynamic transaction between a wide range of endogenous (individual) and exterior (contextual) factors. In this perspective, it is thought that disabilities have an interactive and social origin. This means that if schools and parents creatively collaborate and provide the necessary assistance and provision, students with special educational needs might be successfully included within the school context and socially promoted (Turnbull et al., 2006). Educational staff should try to find solutions, contribute information about the child and his or her environment, avoid pejorative connotations and focus on the (external or contextual) problem, not the deficit.

Special Educational Needs students can also be classified according to their prognosis and the educational adaptations they need to respond positively to school challenges. Cases of high capacity intellectuals (Gifted) are also considered as students with specific educational support needs, because in this case the curriculum is often easy or even boring for these students. Therefore, it is claimed that a curricular adaptation is a modification or change that takes place in the mainstream curriculum to find a solution for the learning needs of each student. This is, in fact, an individual response for each student, one of the principal bases of inclusive schooling.

In Europe, at the beginning of the twentieth century 2% of children had SEN, whereas today it is around 20% or 25% of the total student population.

Overall, one of the basic premises of inclusive education is that schools should become places where all children, with and without special educational needs, can freely play, learn, perform and interact in constructive ways. Moreover, it is believed that children should be taught in educational environments that permit them to fully develop their social-emotional and academic competencies. Inclusive education focuses on organizational, structural and cultural changes within school contexts and education policy in order to respond effectively to social-school exclusion of pupils with various difficulties (Ainscow et al., 2006). The theoretical background and the policy philosophy of inclusive education has primarily been developed over the last decades as social activism, and also as a scientific endeavour to struggle against social and school stigmatization and exclusion.

## Schooling and Social Pathway of SENS: Assets and Risks

Social contexts and social-educational parameters within school systems are important factors in promoting or hindering pupils' psychosocial and academic development and inclusion. In that sense, it is imperative to abolish the educational inequalities and ensure a cooperative and accepting educational environment. On the other hand, it is also important to develop micro-strategies that help teachers, parents and children better cooperate and overcome or cope with their own personal barriers, limitations and internal or external conflicts and difficulties. Children and youth in conflict and with disruptive behaviour need positive guidance and support from concerned and competent individuals and specialists who are adequately trained in a variety of techniques and models that allow them to have a thorough and complete idea of the children's internal and external difficulties. Integrating systemic thinking in our practice may elicit important systemic modification in the school units and in how we operate as specialists and educators. In addition, the use of evidence based eclectic (psychosocial) techniques at micro-social level melded with the basic principles of the inclusive education framework can be a crucial strategic option to respond to the specific challenges that teachers, families, and children with problems meet in everyday life. It is suggested that educational psychology can contribute to the conceptualization of the nature, appropriateness and effectiveness of inclusive education practices for children with disabilities and special educational needs (SEN) when practitioners are committed to the inclusive project and use analogous counselling/intervention techniques (Farrell & Venables, 2009).

The inclusion approach concerns not only children with special needs (the traditional group) but all children who might, for one reason or another, present psychosocial or educational problems, and who are in need of psychoeducational interventions and of new approaches to their particular needs (Terzi, 2005). Additionally, the goals of the inclusion philosophy encompass on one hand the development of special techniques for dealing with children with complex difficulties, and on the other hand introduces systemic changes to the (competitive and one-sided) educational system, and full acceptance of diversity, which will be made possible in the context of a new philosophy of education and a new (open) school.

To be more specific about the psychology of inclusion and the inclusive education paradigm, the principles arising from it could be summarized as follows (Farrell, 2011; Farrell & Venables, 2009; Greenberg, 2003):

- adaptation of the detailed curriculum and of the goals of education to the heterogeneous needs and particularities of each individual class;
- suitable spatial planning to cover the basic needs (play, socialization, elective activities, safe development of mobility etc.), and also the difficulties of all children;
- individualized and personalized teaching – use of pluralistic multidimensional teaching methodology – alternative psychoeducational programmes;
- use of support structures in close cooperation with the school;
- advancement of the coexistence-collaboration solidarity model;
- reversal of the shortcoming model; emphasis on the special capabilities of children – all children benefit from pluralism;
- inclusion not limited to the "traditional categories" of children with special needs, but extending to all groups of children threatened with exclusion;
- inclusion philosophy against exclusion philosophy; against conventional classification-categorization models (iatrogenic paradigm); emphasis on causes;
- adaptation of the inclusion models/practices based on the needs of the schools and/or the communities.

It follows that the inclusion philosophy does not limit itself to advancing yet another model of special education, but offers a new way of organizing the reality of education and, mostly, changes in the conception and implementation of educational policy (Terzi, 2005). Yet at the same time it also requires and presses for changes in the social representations concerning dysfunctional/problematic behaviour, school-adjustment difficulties and the academic incompetence of a large number of students. In the context of this philosophy it is nevertheless considered that it is possible to educate and train teachers in a way that will help them understand the nature of the difficulties and risks that "vulnerable" children and their families are facing; and mostly help them intervene in a consistent and reliable way, applying supportive (empowering) strategies aiming at reducing the children's dysfunctions and developing a positive atmosphere of acceptance and cooperation in the classroom (Cefai & Cooper, 2009; Terzi, 2005). In many aspects, research shows that although many important modifications have been realized during last decades in the way teachers work and deal with "problematic" students' many problems, such as behavioural dysfunction, are a source of heightened reactions, stress and emotional counteraction on the teacher's part (Cooper & Jacob, 2011).

## Epistemological and Pedagogical Issues in SEN Education and Inclusive Practice

The education of students with SEN has long been the subject of considerable controversy. In fact, there has been massive debate in the last two decades on how SEN are defined and understood. Technocratic and competitive educational systems and policies have often been strongly criticized. Mainstream education culture was often thought to create disabling conditions for children who are "different" and have other learning styles or needs. The radicalization of school and educational culture and the ideological shift towards a wider inclusive perspective that encompasses "different" (diversity) and socially excluded students have been advocated.

Another important issue which is often a source of confusion is the difference between *inclusion* and *integration*. Integration is based on the *normalization* of life of students with special educational needs. Inclusion raises the recognition and appreciation of *diversity* as a *reality* and as a *human right*; it makes their goals always a priority. From the perspective of inclusion heterogeneity is seen as normal, so that the inclusive approach is aimed at all students. Integration is based on pupils with special educational needs that are enabled for certain support, resources and professionals, while the inclusion model is based on a social framework in which the school and the school community are heavily involved; this is thought to lead to the improvement of the quality of education as a whole and for all students. This in itself is inclusive organization, assuming that all members are trained to meet *diversity*. The *integration* proposed curricular changes as measures of overcoming the diversities of students with special needs. Inclusion proposes an *inclusive curriculum*, common to all students, which will implicitly incorporate these adaptations. With *integration,* it is considered that a group of students have been excluded or segregated, in the past, from the ordinary school system. Otherwise, *inclusion* is based on the premise that students with SEN are part of the regular school and they do not have to be included in it, as there is a single curriculum for all. No segregation is justified; all students learn in the same way and with the same educational system and the methodology that this entails. Educational inclusion requires careful consideration of every aspect of schooling and the social context in which children function and live. Innovative approaches to educational inclusion will need to address issues at the macro, micro, personal and interpersonal levels. Connections between school and community cultures have to be made, as well as between educational and community programmes of inclusion. Inclusive education extends beyond special needs arising from disabilities, and includes consideration of other sources of disadvantage and marginalization, such as gender, poverty, language, ethnicity and geographic isolation. The complex interrelationships that exist among these factors and their interactions with disability must be also a focus of attention. Inclusive classrooms promote the participation of all students. To do that, everybody has to take part in the lesson and all the activities they do in that lesson, including opportunities for pupil participation in decision making, positive attitudes and their teacher's knowledge of the learning abilities and difficulties of all the children.

One of the most important things along with the others listed above is that students with special educational needs must respect all the standards of living and requirements like the rest of the children, both inside and outside the classroom, as well as inside the school and outside of it. It is unacceptable for society to treat disabled children or those with some kind of educational need differently from others. This implies a segregative and antidemocratic school system which usually makes those students feel slighted, injured or excluded from the rest of their classmates leading to social disability (Lloyd, 2008).

SENS represent a significant proportion of the school-aged population, and effective models of intervention or of significant changes in the school/educational system and in educators' culture is needed. SENS are widely considered to be the most vulnerable group of learners.

The SEN students might experience: (a) increased risks of experiencing significantly worse academic and psychosocial outcomes through the course of schooling; (b) increased risks of being victimized (physically or verbally) and socially marginalized or academically excluded; (c) risks of developing additional psychosocial and emotional difficulties that might turn to more serious mental health or social professional problems and exclusions in adolescence or early adult life.

## Inclusive Education: Implications for Educational Practice and Critics

Inclusive Education (IE) emphasizes and promotes an epistemological and social-political-cultural shift in the philosophy and scope of educational policy, in the content and directions of the curriculum, in teaching methodology, in teachers' professional role, in moral values, in educational community culture and in teachers' education/training in order to achieve a fully democratic school climate enabling all students with and without disabilities to fully develop their potential (Ainscow et al., 2006, Mittler, 2004). IE has strongly criticized the "standards" paradigm imposed by the prevailing mainstream educational policy. IE stresses that the idea that better educational standards are the key to equal opportunity is mostly based on the needs of industry and has nothing to do with the achievement of individual potential, equity or social cohesion. The central principle of IE is the importance of social justice in and equality of access to education. The difficulties for the rise of a socially equitable education system begin where, under the guise of pragmatism, normalizing "standards" acted to reinforce a highly competitive and hierarchical education system in the UK and all over Europe (Cornwall , 2013). From the other side, Shevlin et al. (2008) in their report, referring to the UK's Ofsted, found that despite certain progress towards inclusion many seemingly intractable difficulties remain as barriers to the realization of the inclusive policy. Furthermore, there is a gap between legislation and implemented practice/inclusive reality all over Europe (Curcic, 2009). It has been argued – against IE – that well intentioned but simplistic ideological arguments may serve as distractions from the real life problems experienced by pupils, families and staff in schools and reinforce instead of challenge the status quo (Cooper & Jacobs, 2011; Kourkoutas, 2010). In other words, the main criticism of this movement is that IE, from a purely sociological stance, seems to prioritize general societal and systemic changes rather than building evidence based practices to promote the psychosocial and academic development of all students. In fact, although there is a broad consensus and understanding that inclusive education is "a process of increasing participation and decreasing exclusion from the culture, community and curricula of mainstream schools" (Booth et al., 2000), this process can take many forms and little is known about the detail of practice at the classroom level (Florian & Black-Hawkins, 2011).

In addition, IE has been criticized for the following (Cooper & Jacobs, 2011; Hornby, 2012; Lindsay, 2007 Terzi, 2010): a very broad definition of inclusion (its definition and use are seriously problematic); prevalence of the ideological discourse over scientific evidence ("too much ideology rather than science"); ideological rigidity ("change the system first in order to change the reality of pupils in need"); extreme rejection of the expert model and idealization of the teacher's role in resolving all students' difficulties; a rationale (for inclusive education) which is seriously flawed; and a lack of empirical evidence to support its effectiveness. Many scholars suggest that the IE model fits students with physical disabilities better than other groups of students (e.g. those with social, emotional and behavioural problems).

Despite many justified or less justified critics, "Inclusive Education", as a new epistemological and philosophical "paradigm" in education and pedagogy, represents a real challenge for a shift in expressed or underlying ideology, rhetoric, agendas and, above all, in the (research or intervention) practice of many related disciplines (such as special education, school psychology, childhood psychopathology and sociology of education). The question is if it is possible for IE to challenge the dominant "medical" paradigm which focuses on categorizing and labelling students with complex difficulties by promoting a new intervention culture/engagement and resisting the ideology of the "marketization" of the educational system (Thomas & Loxley, 2008).

## The Role of the Teacher in Inclusive Education

As schools become more inclusively orientated the role of the teacher changes and different approaches to teaching in an inclusive classroom become more prominent such as the collaborative-consultation model. Mittler (2003) noted that the major obstacle to the progress of inclusive education worldwide was the negative attitudes of teachers, parents, community leaders and politicians. The teacher's role becomes crucial in including SEN or excluded students. Teachers' training in inclusive practice is essential in building inclusive communities/environments (Rouse, 2008). The teacher with an SEN positive relationship is vital in helping these students develop their own potential. In contrast, research has indicated that students who have been identified as having "special" or "additional" educational needs are especially vulnerable to the negative effects of deterministic beliefs about ability held by teachers (Hart et al., 2007). This vulnerability is compounded when teachers also believe that such students need specialist teaching that they have not been trained to provide, a common finding reported in the international research literature on teacher attitudes towards inclusive education (Florian & Black-Hawkins, 2011).

Overall, an essential element of inclusion is a shared responsibility on the part of all educators in the school for the student with SEN. Teachers' beliefs about inclusion might reflect their willingness or unwillingness to engage in inclusive practices and in actions that support the social and academic insertion of SENS within ordinary schools. The traditional way of investigation in teacher training is to explore teachers' attitudes, views and beliefs about specific subjects. The limitation of this approach lies in the eventual gap between teachers' reported beliefs and their real attitudes.

## Previous Studies of Inclusion and Teachers' Attitudes

Many studies have been conducted in order to detect the factors that might contribute to teachers' general attitudes towards inclusion and their eventual engagement in inclusive curricula. It would be impossible to summarize the results of all studies regarding the factors that mediate teachers' attitudes (e.g. age, experience, gender, training, qualification, forms of disabilities, forms of inclusion, academic expectations from SENS etc.). Results are contradictory depending on the methodology, on instruments used and on study samples; some indicative findings are in Avramidis & Norwich, 2002; Avramidis et al., 2000; Boyle et al., 2013; Campbell et al., 2003; Curcic, 2009; Florian & Black-Hawkins, 2011; Ross-Hill, 2009; Rouse, 2008; Sharma et al., 2008; Shevlin et al., 2013; Zoniou-Sideri & Vlachou, 2006).

Demographic variables might influence the attitude of in-service or prospective teachers towards inclusion (Forlin et al., 2007). Teachers with higher educational qualifications (undergraduate or postgraduate) were seen to be more optimistic about students with disabilities in their classrooms than their counterparts with lower qualifications (Sharma et al., 2008). Age did not have an effect on how positive or negative is people's attitude towards inclusion (Loreman et al., 2009). Furthermore, qualifications and gender (female teachers more positive) generally seem to play an important role in developing positive attitudes towards inclusion.

In terms of barriers and concerns related to inclusive project, previous studies have revealed that teachers express concern about inclusive education because of (a) their limited involvement in the process of *integrating* students with disabilities, (b) the progress of all students within the inclusive classroom (Avramidis et al., 2000), and (c) the time and attention required to include students with disabilities (Avramidis et al., 2000).

In summary, the following conclusions, among others, can be drawn from most previous research studies:

a) The successful implementation of inclusive reforms depend largely on the devotion of educators to creating positive environments within school contexts.

b) Teachers with more positive views of inclusion are more confident about accommodating students' diverse needs by adapting suitable classroom material/practices.

c) Teachers with more negative attitudes are found to have low expectations for SENS.

d) A positive school ethos was found to be a significant factor in ensuring inclusive practice.

e) The complex mix of positive teacher beliefs combined with fears and perceived inadequacies is quite common in the evolution of practice towards inclusive learning environments;

f) Social and specialized support is required by most "ordinary classroom" teachers in order for them to successfully work with teachers with SEN.

g) Inclusion is a reality for students in certain societies while in others it remains an aspiration for many.

## Findings Regarding Teachers' Perceptions of Inclusion of SENS in Greece and Hungary

Findings reported in this paper come from three recent studies conducted in Greece and Hungary (Gerassis, 2009; Kourkoutas, 2011; Németh Tóth, 2011). Methodologically, these studies built on previous approaches of international studies and on both qualitative and quantitative study design. We were interested in looking across the interviews and questionnaires we have used to explore some key assumptions we had made about inclusive education and practice (see also Florian & Black-

Hawkins, 2011). These were that inclusive practice requires: (a) rejection of deterministic beliefs about ability and disability (and the associated idea that the presence of some will hold back the progress of others); (b) a shift in focus from the pathology approach to an educational model that is concerned with the promotion of the SEN students' well-being and social-academic development; (c) collaborative work with other professionals and families; and (d) the use of alternative and innovative teaching and psychoeducational methods to strengthen the capabilities of all students (with and without SEN). We used these assumptions to support a deductive approach to the preliminary analysis of these studies' data.

## *Hungary*

The results of the Hungarian study are quite illuminating. In fact, no more than half of teachers at the mainstream schools said that they were informed about terminology of SEN or methodology of integrative education. It is not feasible to make inclusion nationwide.

New educational challenges couldn't really affect teachers with inclusive attitudes at the ten schools studied. It means for the researcher and also for decision makers it's not enough to prescribe something for schools like integration or inclusion without any promotion and/or particular orientation. Many teachers are still negative about students' integration/inclusion probably because of their classical "performance/result orientated" or "competition orientated" teaching practice. We assume they don't or hardly use any innovative methods of competence based teaching like co-operative and/or individual and/or project and social-emotional learning programmes.

One in every five of secondary school teachers do not accept students with SEN either in schools or in classes – compared with elementary school teachers who would undertake and deal with students with SEN, either in school or in their classes. Secondary school teachers' approach should be changed as soon as possible before a large number of students with SEN appear at secondary schools in the next five years.

Mainstream teachers who have experience in integrative/inclusive pedagogy are objecting to their limited teaching methodology, limited teaching tools and limited knowledge in learning organization and also in terms of SEN. It is clear they couldn't learn this kind of information earlier in their professional education at high school or universities. The situation of limited teaching tools is up to school management or its sponsor.

Teachers generally think negatively of postgraduate courses. It may be for many different reasons, such as that the training is too long or too theoretical, or maybe that the lecturer is not adequate to guide teachers and run courses. Experience shows that new postgraduate training courses should be developed for practising teachers by our department but we must attend better to teachers' claims. So courses must be short and practice-orientated and lecturers must be selected for their abilities and their teaching experience. On the basis of the research results we recognized that distance and/or digital learning must be offered to teachers in training.

In summary, in Hungary, many teachers are still hostile to the idea and process of inclusion in their schools/classrooms. Almost half of mainstream school teachers reported not being informed in SEN terminology or in the methodology of inclusive education. According to a sample of 10 schools, new educational challenges can't really affect teachers with inclusive attitudes.

Mainstream teachers reject postgraduate studies and require more specific support measures. One in every five of secondary school teachers does not accept students with SEN either in schools or in classes, unlike elementary school teachers. Mainstream teachers with experience in inclusion adopt a broader conception of the teacher's role, teaching tools/knowledge, teaching methodology etc.

Difficulties in realizing the inclusion of SENS are mainly related to: (a) issues of teaching pupils with SEN (67%) (methodological problems (20%), problems with teaching organization (19%), problems of teaching materials (16%), problems with the curriculum (12%)) and (b) problems of group dynamics in the classroom (15%).

It is impossible to realize a meaningful/comprehensive inclusion policy in schools without adequate information, training, support and genuine awareness/engagement by a large part of involved teachers.

## Greece

A recent empirical study in a large sample of Greek mainstream schools has revealed that the majority of Greek teachers (55–60%) (in a sample of more than 450 mainstream school teachers) recognize the significance of inclusion and are well disposed towards it. However, there are reports of serious precautions/reluctance for both the capability of schools to receive all kind of SEN pupils and the ability of these pupils to access a "mainstream" curriculum. More male than female teachers claim that there is a lack of adequate infrastructure which hinders the successful implementation of an integration policy (Gerassis, 2009). Furthermore, teachers with more years of service are of the view that the implementation of inclusive education will be an additional workload and will exert more pressure and anxiety on them (Gerassis, 2009). Finally, there is a difference in the mean attitude towards inclusion based on the level of qualification (having completed a module or course increases significantly the positive attitude towards inclusion when compared to someone with no special education qualification). In general, female teachers display a more positive attitude towards inclusion.

Another, more recent, empirical study conducted in Central Greece (Larissa, Trikala), Attica, and Crete (Heraklio, Rethimno) asked a sample of 160 Special Education teachers about factors that promote or hinder the successful inclusion of SEN students; the results give an equally strong indication of the quality of inclusive projects in the Greek educational system.

In fact, regarding the factors that hinder the academic inclusion of SEN the following have been revealed: (a) large numbers of children diagnosed as pupils with SEN and limited resources (e.g. lack of time, overcrowded classes, ill-equipped schools etc.); (b) delay of diagnosis and lack of specific intervention guidelines for very difficult cases, by the Diagnostic Centres (KEDDY) officially charged with this function, and in many cases inadequate or incomplete evaluation reports by the DC (KEDDY); (c) large numbers of pupils with serious social-emotional and behavioural problems whom special education and ordinary classroom teachers are not prepared to deal with; (d) a general hostility against the inclusion of pupils with disabilities; (e) a cognitive and performance oriented school system which excludes more vulnerable students; (d) a gap between official policy and rhetoric and practices targeting the full inclusion of many of SENS in the reality of school life.

On the other hand, most Special Education teachers seem not to be aware of the problems related to classic psychiatric classifications. They are likely to consider pupils with SEN as homogenous categories and use general syndrome terms to describe the pupils' difficulties/disorders (e.g. ADHD) in all cases, without questioning the origins of such classifications, the contextual causes of the difficulties and the resulting practices.

Overall, most Special Education teachers do not challenge the prevailing/dominant (deficit-centred) conceptions – models regarding the way pupils are categorized or labekled. Put another way, most SE teachers of this sample are not at all sceptical of the traditional ways of treating students with complex difficulties (e.g. separating pupils with SEN from pupils without SEN, providing segregated treatment outside the classroom). In addition, they don't seem aware of the new approaches in the area of inclusion and childhood disability (e.g. the ecosystemic and holistic character of inclusive practice; the contextual transactional character of many of the social-emotional problems; partnership work). They rather seem to adhere to the conventional mode of special education.

## Summary of Findings Regarding Greece and Hungary

According to the above-mentioned findings about inclusion policy in Hungarian and Greek schools, the following basic points should be mentioned:

- There is a greater recognition of the positive aspects of the inclusion process and the need for schools to expand their respective practices.
- In relation to the full inclusion of SENS, there are differences depending on gender, level of education, years of experience, the kind and degree of difficulty/disability of students, which cannot be adequately summarized and detailed in the present article.
- Most teachers in both countries in order to become better prepared and trained to deal with inclusive practices/ challenges, report the need for a new extended academic curriculum containing/ encompassing SEN inclusion issues, while teachers with more years of service believe to a greater extent that the role of the teacher in the mainstream school is not to educate SENS.
- There is general acceptance of the need for in-service training and support, mainly when dealing with children with disruptive behaviour.
- Although many teachers perceive children's difficulties in a personalized/individualized way, many of them seem easily adhere to the psychiatric model (tending to attribute causes of the psychosocial difficulties to biological factors) in order to understand their students' "dysfunctions".
- Therefore, many of them tend to pathologize their students' difficult or inappropriate behaviour and consequently deny their own responsibility for finding ways to deal with it or to engage in alternative practices.
- Many teachers seek ready-made specific solutions, as well as requiring practical knowledge, which often deprives teachers of the ability to understand the intrapersonal and family/systemic dynamics of the child's pathway/functioning.
- Many Special Education teachers in Greece seem to adhere to the conventional model of Special Education without questioning the

origins of such classifications, the contextual causes of the difficulties and the resulting practices (Kourkoutas et al., 2011).

## Suggestions Based on the Findings of the Greek and Hungarian Studies

Though considerable resistance to working in the classroom with SENS has been revealed, there is now much more acceptance and understanding of what is expected with inclusion and SENS' education in mainstream schools. It should now be a compulsory part of all teacher-training courses, whether as a theoretical subject or more importantly as part of the practical element of the training course (Booth et al., 2003). Interdisciplinary teams of specialists engaged/ working in an inclusive perspective, contesting the medical model (that confuses teachers) should be attached to school units to ensure permanent teachers' support/ guidance. Therefore:

- Both specialist and generalist teaching staff must be willing to compromise, accepting that the curriculum involves various levels of interaction with SEN and students with complex or diverse needs, strengths and weaknesses that might challenge the teacher's role.
- Professionals should adopt a collaborative partnership model to work with teachers in order to include SENS; otherwise teachers feel unsupported and undervalued and are less likely to engage in inclusive issues.
- Despite a push for the inclusion of students with special educational needs into both social and educational perspective, there has been a lack of appropriate planning and training and support for staff, as well as the SENS, in meaningful and comprehensive ways (Boyle et al., 2013). If the key members of the inclusive process (the teachers) are unhappy (because they are not emotionally supported, trained or well guided), they won't be supportive of the fundamental principles of this change process.
- Teachers' positive experience of inclusion should be increased, with successful implementation of meaningful and comprehensive practices.
- Top-bottom or imported models of inclusion fail to achieve important changes within school system and adequately serve the SENS' cause.
- Attachment to school is an important protective factor.

- Social relationships and the theory/model of resilience can prove a very helpful framework in designing and promoting meaningful and comprehensive psychoeducational projects to assist students at risk and create a positive/protective and inclusive whole-school climate (Cefai & Jacobs, 2009; Hart et al., 2007; Kourkoutas & Raul Xavier, 2010).
- Social support for teachers working with SEN is crucial as it has been found to be negatively correlated with teacher burnout in inclusive education; that is, the less social support that the teacher experiences, the higher the level of burnout (Talmor, Reiter & Feigin, 2005).

In fact, the following questions are vital in realizing strategic inclusive policies through the use of comprehensive and innovative teaching methods and whole-school processes in Greek and Hungarian schools: (a) How can we provide a safe and supportive environment in which all students can maximize their learning? (b) How can we remain accessible and responsive to their needs? (c) How can we help our students to develop their ability to cope with challenge and stress?

Innovative models should be grounded in the understanding that the professional development of teachers is fundamental to the success of any innovation. This means developing supportive structures within schools and between schools and their communities, as well as providing teachers with up-to-date knowledge about practice. The curriculum materials should be based on the understanding that young students need to engage actively with ideas and concepts in order to learn. The classroom materials should place the student at the centre of activities, positioning the teacher as a facilitator. Educators should provide the most productive environment for all students, and the health professional specific intervention for selected students who are defined as "at risk" or vulnerable or coming from very complex and dysfunctional family environments and struggling with intense emotional and behavioural or academic problems (Brehm & Doll, 2009). The need for social-emotional support in schools is so great that there is a temptation (seldom resisted) to "do" mental health by bringing in an "expert" for very short intervention (a session or two). The effect of this limited, intervention approach is that the school environment does not shift towards the prevention of social-emotional and school problems and the promotion of wellbeing of most vulnerable students (Wyn et al., 2000). Intervention should be embedded and related to whole-school processes that take a holistic perspective of the problem in consideration (Weare, 2005). Such intervention models usually bring small scale or insignificant benefits to school communities. On the contrary, Mind-Matters represents an ideal example of innovative whole-school programmes aiming at enhancing the development of educational environments where young people feel safe, where they belong and where they develop the skills needed to participate fully with the support of educational and professional staff (Wyn et al., 2000).

## Conclusion

Achieving inclusive education goals within the ordinary school system requires a series of ideological and scientific critical changes and advances in the way child disorder/disability is considered (Zoniou-Sideri & Vlachou, 2006). In fact, a considerable shift in academic training/ education of teachers and other professionals working with SENS is needed to prepare prospective teachers in accordance with inclusive educational standards. In terms of intervention practice, it requires an interdisciplinary perspective, an engagement of all school professionals and staff in a collaborative perspective with families and children with SEN. In addition, integrating expert knowledge/experience in inclusive practice, values and perspective presupposes a paradigmatic change in the way schools and educational psychologists work. School psychologists should be trained and prepared to broaden their way of thinking and consider children's difficulties. They need to develop comprehensive models of intervention that challenge the dominant (medical) taxonomic thinking. In addition, the "commercial" education philosophy, the technocratic pedagogical methodology, the bureaucratic school organization, school isolation from community and families, as well as the teachers' and professionals' traditional roles should be seriously questioned and replaced by alternative and innovative modes of structuring the curriculum and teaching in ordinary schools (e.g. an emphasis on social-emotional learning curriculum). In fact, a curriculum that (equally) prioritizes social-emotional learning fostering relationship and resilient skills and nurturing collectivity and democratic rights values is a priority for schools if they are to be inclusive for all students with difficulties. It is also important to modify from inside the dominant segregative and exclusionary practice with the use of effective practices that adopt an inclusive perspective and are meaningful for ordinary classroom teachers. In addition, it is urgently imperative to provide families and students with complex needs with the necessary support and specialized intervention when necessary in order to strengthen their social and school inclusion and improve their interpersonal and learning skills, their self-concept and self-esteem. Furthermore, it is equally essential to offer teachers suitable support and guidance in order to develop the appropriate educational practices to respond to the wide range of today's children's problems.

In summary, important changes should be realized at (philosophical, cultural and practical) micro- and macro-level in both countries and unhelpful ways of thinking and acting within schools about inclusive education should be abandoned.

# References

Adelman, H. S. and Taylor, L. 2006. "Mental Health in Schools and Public Health", *Public Health Reports* 121, 294–298.

Ainscow, M., Booth, T., Dyson, A., Farrell, P., Frankham, J., Gallannaugh, F., Howes, A. and Smith, R. 2006. *Improving Schools, Developing Inclusion*. London: Routledge.

Armstrong, D. 2005. "Reinventing 'Inclusion': New Labour and the Cultural Politics of Special Education", *Oxford Review of Education* 31(1), 135–151.

Avramidis, E., Bayliss, P. and Burden, R. 2000. "A Survey into Mainstream Teachers' Attitudes towards the Inclusion of Children with Special Needs in the Ordinary School in One Local Education Authority", *Educational Psychology* 20(2), 193–213.

Avramidis, E. and Norwich, B. 2002. "Teachers' Attitudes towards Integration/Inclusion: A Review of Literature", *European Journal of Special Needs Education* 17(2), 129–147.

Booth, T., Nes, K. and Stromstad, M. (eds). 2003. *Developing Inclusive Teacher Education*. London: Routledge/Falmer.

Booth, T., Ainscow, M., Black-Hawkins, K., Vaughan, M. and Shaw, L. 2000. *Index for Inclusion; Developing Learning and Participation in Schools*. Bristol: Centre for Studies in Inclusive Education.

Boyle, C., Topping, K. and Jindal-Snape, D. 2013. "Teachers' Attitudes Towards Inclusion in High Schools", *Teachers and Teaching: Theory and Practice* 19(5), 527–542.

Brehm, K. and Doll, B. 2009. "Building Resilience in Schools: A Focus on Population-based Prevention", in R. W. Christner and R. B. Mennuti (eds), *School-based Mental Health: A Practitioner's Guide to Comparative Practices*. New York: Routledge, pp. 55–86.

Campbell, J., Gilmore, L. and Cuskelly, M. 2003. "Changing Student Teachers' Attitudes towards Disability and Inclusion", *Journal of Intellectual and Developmental Disability* 28(4), 369–79.

Cefai, C. and Cooper, P. (eds). 2009. *Promoting Emotional Education: Engaging Children and Young People with Social, Emotional and Behavioural Difficulties.* London: Jessica Kingsley.

Cigman, R. (ed). 2007. *Included or Excluded: The Challenge of the Mainstream for Some SEN Children*. London: Routledge.

Cole, B. A. 2005. "Mission Impossible? Special Educational Needs, Inclusion and the Re-conceptualization of the Role of the SENCO in England and Wales", *European Journal of Special Needs Education* 20(3), 287–307.

Cooper, P. and Jacobs, B. 2011. *From Inclusion to Engagement: Helping Students Engage with Schooling Through Policy and Practice*. Oxford: Wiley-Blackwell.

Cornwall, J. 2013. "What Makes an Inclusive Teacher? Can Fish Climb Trees? Mapping the European Agency Profile of Inclusive Teachers to the English System", *FORUM* 55, 1.

Curcic, S. 2009. "Inclusion in PK-12: An International Perspective", *International Journal of Inclusive Education* 13(5), 517–538.

DfES. 2004. *Removing Barriers to Achievement: The Government Strategy for SEN*. Nottingham: Department for Education and Skills.

—. 2011. *Support and Aspiration: A New Approach to Special Educational Needs and Disability – A Consultation*. Norwich: Stationery Office.

Farrell, M. 2011. *Debating Special Education*. London: Routledge.

Farrell, P. T., Farrell, P. and Venables, K. 2009. "Can Educational Psychologists be Iinclusive?" in P. Hick, R. Kershner and P. Farrell (eds), *Psychology for Inclusive Education: New Directions in Theory and Practice*. London: Routledge, 117–126.

Florian, L. and Black-Hawkins, K. 2011. "Exploring Inclusive Pedagogy", *British Educational Research Journal* 37(5), 813–828.

Florian, L. and McLaughlin, M. J. 2008. *Disability Classification in Education: Issues and Perspectives*. Thousand Oaks, CA: Corwin Press.

Forlin, C., Loreman, T., Sharma, U. and Earle, C. 2009. "Demographic Differences in Changing Pre-service Teachers' Attitudes, Sentiments and Concerns about Inclusive Education", *International Journal of Inclusive Education* 13(2), 195–209.

Gerassis, D. 2009. *Greek Teachers' Perceptions about Inclusion of Students with Disabilities in Mainstream Schools*. Master's thesis, Department of Political Science, University of Crete.

Glazzard, J. 2011. "Perceptions of the Barriers to Effective Inclusion in One Primary School: Voices of Teachers and Teaching Assistants", *Support for Learning* 26(2), 56–63.

Greenberg, M. T. 2003. "Enhancing School-based Prevention and Youth Development through Coordinated Social, Emotional and Academic Learning", *American Psychologist* 58, 466–474.

Hart, S., Drummond, M. and McIntyre, D. 2007. "Learning without Limits", in L. Florian (ed.), *The Sage Handbook of Special Education*. London: Sage, pp. 499–514.

Heller, F. 2000. "Creating a Holding Environment in an Inner City School", in N. Barwick (ed.), *Clinical Counselling in Schools*. London: Routledge, pp. 81–95.

Hornby, G. 2012. "Inclusive Education for Children with Special Educational Needs: A Critique of Policy and Practice in New Zealand", *Journal of International and Comparative Education* 1, 1.

Kourkoutas, E. 2010. "Education inclusive dans les pays méditerranéens: Réflexions critiques sur les obstacles barrières et les perspectives", in M. Carrozzino & P. Ruffinatto (eds) *Dignity and Effective Citizenship for the Person with Disabilities*. Rome: Nuove Frontiere, pp. 207–233.

Kourkoutas, E. and Xavier Raul, M. 2010. "Counseling Children at Risk in a Resilient Contextual Perspective: A Paradigmatic Shift of School Psychologists' Role in Inclusive Education", *Social & Behavioral Science* 5, 1210–1219.

Leo, E. and Barton, L. 2006. "Inclusion, Diversity and Leadership: Perspectives, Possibilities and Contradictions", *Educational Management Administration & Leadership* 34(2), 167–180.

Lindsay, G. 2007. "Educational Psychology and the Effectiveness of Inclusive Education/Mainstreaming", *British Journal of Educational Psychology* 77, 1–24.

Lloyd, C. 2008. "Removing Barriers to Achievement: A Strategy for Inclusion or Exclusion?" *International Journal of Inclusive Education* 12(2), 221–236.

Loreman, T., Forlin, C. and Sharma, U. 2007. "An International Comparison of Pre-service Teacher Attitudes towards Inclusive Education", *Disability Studies Quarterly*, 27(4).

Mitchell, D. 2007. *What Really Works in Special and Inclusive Education.* New York: Routledge.

Mittler, P. 2003. *Building Bridges between Special and Mainstream Services. Inclusion: Theory and Practice.* Retrieved from http//www.eenet.Org.uk/theor

—. 2004. *Working towards Inclusive Education.* London: David Fulton Publishers.

Németh Tóth, A. 2009. "Teacher Attitudes and Inclusive Education", *Magyar Pedagógia* 109(2), 105–120.

Ross-Hill, R. 2009. "Teacher Attitude towards Inclusion Practices and Special Needs Students", *Journal of Research in Special Educational Needs*, 9(3), 188–198.

Rouse, M. 2008. Developing Inclusive Practice: A Role for Teachers and Teacher Education? *Education in the North* 16, 6–11.

Sharma, U., Forlin, C. and Loreman, T. 2008. "Impact of Training on Pre-service Teachers' Attitudes and Concerns about Inclusive Education and Sentiments about Persons with Disabilities", *Disability & Society* 23(7), 773–785.

Shevlin, M., Winter, E. and Flynn, P. 2013. "Developing Inclusive Practice: Teacher Perceptions of Opportunities and Constraints in the Republic of Ireland", *International Journal of Inclusive Education* 17(10), 1119–1133.

Talmor, R., Reiter, S. and Feigin, N. 2005. "Factors Relating to Regular Education Burnout in Inclusive Education", *European Journal of Special Needs Education* 20(2), 215–229.

Terzi, L. 2005. "Beyond the Dilemma of Difference: The Capability Approach to Disability and Special Educational Needs", *Journal of the Philosophy of Education Society of Great Britain* 39(3), 444–459.

Terzi, L. (ed.). 2010. *Special Educational Needs: A New Look.* London: Continuum.

Thomas, G. and Loxley, A. 2008. *Deconstructing Special Education and Constructing Inclusion.* Buckingham, UK: Open University Press.

Turnbull, A., Turnbull, R., Erwin, E. J. and Soodak, L. C. 2006. *Families, Professionals, and Exceptionality: Positive Outcomes through Partnership and Trust* (5th ed.). Upper Saddle River, NJ: Merrill/Prentice Hall.

Weare, K. 2005. "Taking a Positive, Holistic Approach to the Mental and Emotional Health and Well-being of Children and Young People", in C. Newnes and N. Radcliffe (eds), *Making and Breaking Children's Lives.* Ross-on-Wye: PCCCS Books, pp.115–122.

Wyn, J., Cahill, H., Holdsworth, R., Rowling, L. and Carson, S. 2000. "MindMatters: A Whole-school Approach Promoting Mental Health and Wellbeing", *Australian and New Zealand Journal of Psychiatry* 34, 594–601.

Zoniou-Sideri, A. and Vlachou, A. 2006. "Greek Teachers' Belief Systems about Disability and Inclusive Education", *International Journal of Inclusive Education* 10(4–5), 379–394.

# Chapter Eleven

## The Current State and Challenges Posed by Aggression and Violence in South African Schools: A Multidimensional Approach in Context

### Johan Botha
#### Senior Lecturer, North-West University, South Africa

**Abstract**

A meta-synthesis done in 2009 on aggression in South Africa, as well as a school-based violence report compiled in 2011 by the South African Council for Educators, highlights the pervasiveness of aggression and violence in South African schools. At present, many schools are not able to create the safe and effective teaching-and-learning environments that are a prerequisite for the effective socialization of learners. It is important to note that antisocial or destructive behaviours intersect at various levels (family, school, community and society) and across the divides of age, gender, religion, language and ethnic groups. This article explores the causes and effects of aggression and violence and the challenges these pose for the development and implementation of interactive intervention programmes. It proposes that a multidimensional approach such as communities of practice (CoP) is needed to help to curb aggression and violence in South African school contexts.

**Key-words**

Aggression, Violence, Communities of Practice

# Introduction

The South African Council for Educators (SACE, 2011) overview report on school-based violence in South African society shows that aggression and violence have become rife at various levels in society. This has a negative impact on individuals (Bester and Du Plessis, 2010; Botha, 2006; Bushman and Huesmann, 2010; Collings, 2011; Lau and Stevens, 2010; Muthukrishna, 2011; SACE, 2011). Moreover, the report confirms the serious implications of the high rates of aggression and violence in "both primary and secondary schools, across age, gender, race and school categories" (SACE, 2011: 4). Perpetrators and victims of aggression and violence are common features of society at various social levels such as families (family members), schools (teachers, learners and peers) and communities (community members). Dalling (2008: 12) reports that levels of crimes relating to aggression and violence escalated between 1988 and 2008, with a murder rate of more than 50 people each day.

In many cases aggression and violence result from various social inequalities or inequities brought about by previous and current economic and political policies in South Africa. This cycle of aggressive and violent behaviour reinforces a culture of anti-social or destructive behaviour in society (Botha et al., 2012; Myburgh and Poggenpoel, 2009; SACE, 2011).

The basic assumption of aggressive and violent behaviour as destructive, anti-social or punitive lies in the premise of "intention" to hurt, harm or injure another person physically, verbally or psychologically (Berkowitz, 1993: 11; Fiske, 2010; Louw & Louw, 2007). Berkowitz (1993: 11) maintains that "human aggression is typically an attempt at coercion or an effort to preserve one's power, dominance or social status". Louw and Louw (2007: 199) add that destructive behaviour is applied in order to obtain something, for example status or money (Kassin et al., 2011). This may also be the case when a person wants to obtain and/or maintain power and control (Botha, 2012).

The current high rates of aggression and violence in schools threaten the personal safety and security of teachers and learners (Bushman and Huesmann, 2010; Ngakane et al., 2012; Westraad, 2011). Furthermore, schools find it increasingly difficult to create and maintain safe and effective teaching-and-learning environments (Bushman and Huesmann, 2010, Botha et al., 2012, Westraad, 2011). Since schools are influenced by the mental health and psychosocial problems that ensue, this destructive and anti-social behaviour hinders the school's ability to socialize learners. These situations may even "perpetuate crime and violence in society at large" (Jefthas and Artz, 2007: 46). Bushman and Huesmann (2010: 852) describe aggression as a phenomenon that "directly interferes with [people's] basic [human] needs of safety and security", poses a threat to people's overall well-being and is thus a violation of people's human rights (Botha et al., 2012).

The above scenario underscores the need to use intervention programmes so that schools can fulfil their role of preparing and enabling learners to contribute to society in a significant and meaningful way.

This article is structured as follows: first, the research design and methodology are presented. Secondly, the manifestations of aggression in a South African context are given. Thirdly, attention is given to the various causes and effects of aggression as well as the challenges to multidimensional interactive intervention programmes implemented to curtail aggression. The last part of the paper article argues that a community of practice (CoP) approach should be used in order to address the challenges that aggression and violence present.

## Research Process

*Document analysis*, a qualitative research method, was applied along with an interpretive approach in an effort to gain a holistic understanding of aggression and violence "through the meanings [teachers and learners] assign to [the phenomena under investigation]" (Nieuwenhuis, 2007: 59). Bowen (2009: 27) defines document analysis as a "systematic procedure for reviewing or evaluating documents – both printed and electronic (computer-based and Internet-transmitted) material. This analysis, like any other qualitative analysis, "requires that data be examined and interpreted in order to elicit meaning, gain understanding, and develop empirical knowledge". Bowen (2009: 38) advises that when a researcher makes use of document analysis s/he "needs to determine not only the existence and accessibility but also the authenticity and usefulness of particular documents, taking into account the original purpose of each document, the context in which it was produced and the intended audience". The aim was to determine to what extent aggression and violence is mirrored in schools in order to ascertain the multidimensional interactive approach that should be adopted to eradicate antisocial behaviour.

Bowen (2009: 31) argues that "document analysis requires data selection instead of data collection". In this research, documents served as the source of data during the *data selection* process. The documents selected as data sources were published academic articles, master's dissertations, doctoral theses, a meta-synthesis article on various research on aggression in schools and a school-based report on violence in various South African school contexts. Bondas and Hall (2007:117) suggest that it is important to purposefully include a minimum of 10 to 12 studies in order to generate a meaningful and valid meta-synthesis. However, Bowen (2009: 33) argues that it is not about "how many" sources should be selected but "it should be about the quality of the documents and the evidence they contain" linked with the design and the purpose of the study. Documents offer and hold "evidence, especially when the study is relying heavily or solely on documents" (ibid.). The data selected in this case made it possible to do empirical research on the phenomena of aggression and violence as a conduit of the experiences and voices of teachers and learners in South African schools.

The *data analysis process* involved both *document analysis* and interpretive analysis. Document analysis was used to explore the phenomena as depicted in the documents. Atkinson and Coffey (1997: 47) refer to documents as "social facts". These are "produced, shared and used in social organised ways" (Bowen, 2009: 27). *Interpretive analysis* required that I (as analyst) acknowledge my preconceptions about the data and then suspend these as I explored the data in order to comprehend and interpret it. This entailed a process of "finding, selecting, appraising (making sense of), and synthesising data contained in the documents" and finding the overtones during interpretation of the data (Bowen, 2009: 28; Wellington and Szczerbinski, 2007: 112).

For *ethical* reasons, the documents selected were analysed and referred to within a context of "bearing witness to the past events" (Bowen, 2009: 29). The recording of exact names of authors, researchers, references and details of events within the original context of the data sources was done meticulously throughout the research process to reflect the tracking of changes in and development of the phenomena under investigation over an extended period of time (Bowen, 2009: 31; Yin, 1994).

The *trustworthiness* of the research was enhanced in two ways. The first was that quality documents were selected, and the second was that a detailed description of the research processes and a dense description of the phenomena of aggression and violence in South African schools were provided (Bowen, 2009).

# Results

### Manifestations of aggression and violence in South African schools

South African schools are educational institutions rich in diversity in terms of ethnicity, gender, religion, culture and socioeconomic status.

Political and socio-economic factors have caused a great deal of the aggressive and violent behaviour that has become an entrenched way of responding to the inequalities and injustices caused (SACE, 2011). Accounts of cognitive representations, such as scripts and associations in families and communities, facilitate patterns of aggression and violence (Fiske, 2010). This has a direct influence on families and communities, as well as society at large. People resort to and practise aggression and violent behaviour within the social structures they find themselves in. Vizard (2012: 1–3) adds that aggression is a conduct disorder that is the consequence of poor previous learning experiences (low self-esteem, negative experiences); lack of parenting skills; breakdown of a family; mental health issues such as severe emotional and psychological distress; crime; substance abuse; and media. However, it is important to recognize that school contexts and social structures vary, since the contexts play a prominent and significant role in how and why people develop and resort to aggressive and violent behaviour (Botha et. al., 2012; Richardson and Hammock, 2007).

Aggression and violence appear in various forms and at different levels in South African society. The next section explores possible causes and effects that could explain why people behave aggressively and violently.

### Possible causes and effects of aggression and violence

South African research provides ample evidence of interrelated factors as *possible causes* of the development and reinforcement of aggressive and violent behaviours. For instance, family, friends, school (peers), community and society contexts influence one another, largely as a result of factors such as poverty, drug abuse and availability of weapons (Jefthas and Artz, 2007; Botha, 2006; Botha et al., 2012; Burton, 2007; Myburgh and Poggenpoel, 2009; SACE, 2011). Jefthas and Artz (2007: 50) emphasize that there are "a variety of complex, interrelated reasons" why people act violently. According to the School-based Violence report (SACE, 2011) and the Meta-synthesis on Aggression (Myburgh and Poggenpoel, 2009), there are overlapping internal and external factors that cause people to behave aggressively and violently. Breet et al. (2010: 515) reflect a similar view. They contend that "aggression [and violence] often var[y] with reference to internal factors (emotional and cognitive problems, poor social skills) and external factors (family problems, abuse and neglect)". These varying factors affect how people express aggressive behaviour. Ragins and Winkel (2011: 379) add that "emotional expression is influenced by the social context". Most of the factors that cause aggression and violence are in the realm of the various social contexts such as families, schools, community and society (Botha et al., 2012; Myburgh and Poggenpoel, 2009; SACE, 2011). Factors that could cause aggression and violence are listed in the paragraphs that follow.

- *Family factors*
  Poverty; hierarchical systems; patriarchal systems; excessive drinking; family assaults; family conflict; family violence; rejection by family members; intimate partner violence; and child abuse.
- *School factors*
  Irritation and frustration with teachers; ill-discipline of learners; distrust and disrespect of teachers and peers; learners experiencing academic failure; low level of bonding with the school and the lack of extra-mural opportunities such as sport and cultural activities; learners and teachers displaying intolerance of one another; inconsistent disciplinary systems; unfair treatment such as discrimination; and humiliation.
- *Peer relationship factors*
  Irritation and frustration with peers; gang membership; victimisation; bullying; thwarting; peer pressure; peer exclusion and rejection; poor intercultural communication; and the need for status and power.
- *Community factors*
  Poverty; the availability of weaponry such as guns; availability of drugs; racial prejudices; and the exposure to high levels of violence in the community.
- *Societal factors*
  Social, cultural and political contexts displaying violent and aggressive tendencies such as discrimination, inequalities and a lack of power and control by people in various social contexts.

Aggression and violence result from people experiencing *negative feelings*, developing *negative perceptions* and constructing *negative ideas* such as suicide (Myburgh and Poggenpoel, 2009). Because of poor self-esteem, poor self-control and poor self-awareness, as well as not having emotional control over their feelings, people are not able to verbalize their feelings in appropriate ways. They therefore resort to aggression and violence as defence mechanisms, which affect their development of effective intra- and interpersonal relationships (ibid.).

In South African school contexts, both teachers and learners are exposed to high levels of aggression and violence. As a result they experience sadness, fear, anger, anxiety, stress, post-traumatic stress, shame, loneliness, depression, loss of self-esteem and hardening of their attitudes (Jefthas and Artz, 2007; Myburgh and Poggenpoel, 2009; SACE,

2011). Some teachers and learners experience suicidal thoughts, while others do in fact resort to suicide (Botha, 2006).

It is clear that causes and effects influence and reinforce each other in several ways. People are negatively affected not only in teaching and learning environments but also in family structures, communities and society at large. This has enormous social implications, since aggression and violence are socially learned and constructed in various social systems. The vicious cycle of aggression and violence in families, schools, communities and society spills over from the one level to the other (Botha et al., 2012).

There is an urgent need to address aggression and violence in schools using a contemporary multidimensional intervention approach. However, developing and implementing such an approach would be enormously challenging (McWhirter et al., 2004). Taking an ecological systems perspective would mean acknowledging that the interaction of people and their environmental systems (micro, meso, exo, macro) influence the development of aggressive and violent behaviour (Bronfenbrenner, 1979; Bronfenbrenner, 1989; Donald et al., 2010; McWhirter et al., 2004; Paquette and Ryan, 2001; Visser, 2007). Various theories, including Social Learning theory, Cognitive Neo-association, the Gender Role theory and the ecosystemic approach, emphasize the importance of taking a holistic view of people's continuous interaction with the environment (social and cultural contexts) in which they develop their behaviour.

***Challenges with regard to the development and implementation of multidimensional interactive intervention programmes in order to address aggressive and violent behaviour in South African school contexts***

Steyn et al. (2011: 129) note that "[a solution] by teachers for the negative experiences" with regard to destructive behaviour needs "structural support within [the] education context". Research in South African schools has revealed the urgent need to enable individuals to manage aggression and violence constructively. The skills they will need include the facilitation and development of individuals' self-awareness and positive self-concept, stress management skills, the development of individuals' internal locus of control, assertiveness skills, conflict management skills, interpersonal relationship skills, communication skills and skills to manage environment changes (Botha et al., 2012; Breet et al., 2010; Burton, 2008; Du Plessis, 2008; Myburgh and Poggenpoel, 2009; SACE, 2011). In addition, teachers and school management teams will need substantial support and assistance if aggression and violence in schools are to be curbed. This requires intervention programmes aimed at sensitizing people to aggression and violence in schools, families, communities and society at large. This means that there will have to be formal and functional reporting mechanisms as well as opportunities to establish openness about antisocial or destructive behaviours (SACE, 2011). Botha (2006) argues that knowledge and awareness of the phenomena of aggression and violence are a prerequisite for assisting people to learn about and understand emotional and behavioural problems.

The challenge lies not only in which skills need to be addressed or developed, but also in identifying who needs to take responsibility for developing, implementing and applying such intervention programmes in order to bring about change in people's antisocial behaviour. Role players should include policy makers (Department of Education; schools management teams; curriculum developers), teachers, the South African Council for Educators (SACE), community members and other professionals such as psychologists and counsellors, as well as Mental Health coordinators. Counselling services and community structures will have to be provided to support the collaborative action of role players.

The current situation in South African schools points to ineffective collaboration and incoherent actions between the various role players. The role players seem to resort to inappropriate intervention approaches that do not take a long-term view. Due to financial constraints and a lack of resources, for instance, many schools are not able to offer the services of counsellors or psychologists. Although the South African Department of Education has introduced Life Orientation curricula, which offer teachers opportunities to address behavioural issues, these have either not been implemented or are not understood by teachers as a long-term solution or as a means of collaborative interventions. The role players do not recognize the need to take multiple risk factors at multiple levels into consideration, including family, school, community and society, during the development and implementation of programmes (Ahmed and Suffla, 2007: 89).

### The way forward: A multidimensional interaction approach

Since South African schools are diverse with regard to gender, ethnicity, culture, language and religion, intervention programmes need to be inclusive and relevant to different cultural contexts: all of the community need to be active collaborators (Ahmed and Suffla, 2007). As aggression and violence are socially constructed, programme developers and implementers need to take a multidimensional interaction approach, such as *communities of practice (CoP)*.

A multidimensional approach provides opportunities not only to bring about change in people's antisocial or destructive behaviour, but also to recognize the important role of the community. To be effective, intervention programmes have to be relevant to the needs of people in specific contexts. This approach provides all the stakeholders with opportunities to engage collaboratively in conversation, thus learning cooperatively from one another about aggression and violence. The CoP approach has three distinct dimensions: a collective domain of interests, mutual engagement and a shared repertoire (Ferguson, 2012; Wenger, 1998). The CoP approach offers developers and implementers of intervention programmes an understanding of the significance of engagement and collaboration, working together and learning by way of social participation. This means that the stakeholders (practitioners in a field of study) share a "common concern or interest"; they also engage with one another in a reciprocal manner and take part in mutual conversations that are characterized by shared values projected at "togetherness and empowerment" (Ferguson, 2012; Wenger, 2006). In addition, the stakeholders critically reflect on their own views about the phenomena in their communities (Ferguson, 2012). This provides the "insider interpretations" of the community rather than only the views and interpretations of the programme developer or implementer (Ferguson, 2012: 137). Taking on a CoP approach provides opportunities for taking multiple risk factors (personal and contextual) in a specific context into account, which in turn emphasizes the shared views of relevant intervention programmes.

The CoP approach has the potential to support educational specialists, such as teachers, psychologists and counsellors. It not only focuses on "targeted problems", but also acknowledges that multifaceted behavioural problems require comprehensive, inclusive, multidimensional and integrated response interventions as a long-term approach. It has no interest in "quick-fix" solutions to behavioural issues (Adelman and Taylor, 2009:24).

## Conclusion

Communities of Practice (CoPs) seem to offer a way forward. This multidimensional approach has the potential to strengthen and support the role of teachers, families, counsellors and psychologists, enabling them to engage collaboratively in curtailing aggression and violence. Furthermore, since it makes it possible to conceptualize aggression and violence within a specific context, it creates opportunities for stakeholders to work collaboratively to provide solutions to the challenges that aggression and violence pose to schools.

# References

Adelman, H. S. and Taylor, L. 2009. *Mental Health in Schools: Engaging Learners, Preventing Problems, and Improving Schools*. Thousand Oaks, CA: Corwin.

Ahmed, R. and Suffla, S. 2007. "The Mental Health Model: Preventing 'Illness' or Social Inequalities?" in N. Duncan, B. Bowman., A. Naidoo, J. Pillay and V. Roos (eds), *Community Psychology: Analysis, Context and Action.* Cape Town: UCT Press, pp. 84–101.

Atkinson, P. A. and Coffey, A. 1997. "Analysing Documentary Realities", in D. Silverman (ed.), *Qualitative Research: Theory, Method and Practice*. London: Sage, pp. 56–75.

Berkowitz, L. 1993. *Aggression: Its Causes, Consequences and Control*. New York: McGraw-Hill.

Bester, S. and Du Plessis, A. 2010. "Exploring a Ssecondary School Educator's Experiences of School Violence: A Case Study", *South African Journal of Education* 30, 203–229.

Bondas, T. and Hall, E. O. C. 2007. "Challenges in Approaching Meta-synthesis Research", *Qualitative Health Research* 17, 113–121.

Botha, A. J. 2006. *The Facilitation of Aggression Management in Secondary Schools in Mpumalanga.* (DEd thesis.) Johannesburg: University of Johannesburg.

Botha, J. 2012. "Power and Privilege: White Male Teachers' Experience of Aggression", in C. Roux (ed.), *Safe Spaces: Human Rights Education in Divverse Contexts.* Amsterdam: Sense Publications, pp. 51–168.

Botha J., Myburgh, C. and Poggenpoel, M. 2012. "Peer Aggression by Secondary School Learners in a South African School Setting: Effects of Race, Ethnicity and Gender", *Journal of Psychology in Africa* 22(3), 409–414.

Bowen, G. A. 2009. "Document Analysis as a Qualitative Research Method", *Qualitative Research Journal* 9(2), 27–40.

Breet L., Myburgh, C. and Poggenpoel, M. 2010. "The Relationship between the Perception of Own Locus of Control and Aggression of Adolescent Boys", *South African Journal of Education* 30(4), 511–526.

Bronfenbrenner, U. 1979. *The Ecology of Human Development: Experiments by Nature and Design.* Cambridge, MA: Harvard University Press.

—. 1989. "Ecological Systems Theory", *Annual of Child Development* 6, 187–249.

Burton, P. 2007. *Someone Stole My Smile: An Exploration into the Causes of Youth Violence in South Africa.* Monograph series 3. Cape Town: Centre     for Justice and Crime Prevention, pp. 1–119.

—. 2008. *Merchants, Skollies and Stone: Experiences of School Violence in South Africa.* Monograph series 4. Cape Town: Centre for Justice and Crime Prevention.

Bushman, B. J. and Huesmann, L. R. 2010. "Aggression", in S. T. Fiske, D. T. Gilbert and G. Lindzey (eds), *Handbook of social psychology* (5th ed.). New York: Wiley, pp. 833–863.

Collings, S. J. 2011. "Childhood Exposure to Community and Domestic Violence: Prevalence, Risk Factors and Posttraumatic Outcomes in a South African Student Sample", *Journal of Psychology in Africa* 21(4), 535–540.

Dalling, D. 2008. "Thorns in S.A. Roses", *The Citizen* (23 April), 12.

Donald, D., Lazarus, S. and Lolwana, P. 2010. *Educational Psychology in Social Context: Ecosystemic Applications in Southern Africa* (4th ed.). Cape Town: Oxford University Press.

Du Plessis, A. H. 2008. *Exploring Secondary School Educator Experiences of School Violence.* (Unpublished MA Dissertation). Pretoria: University of Pretoria.

Ferguson, R. 2012. "Let's Find a Way to Learn about our Rights", in C. Roux (ed.), *Safe Spaces: Human Rights Education in Diverse Contexts.* Amsterdam: Sense Publications, pp. 131–150.

Fiske, S. T. 2010. *Social Beings: Core Motives in Social Psychology* (8th ed.). New Jersey: Wiley.

Jefthas, D. and Artz, L. 2007. "Youth Violence: A Gendered Perspective", in P. Burton (ed.), *Someone Stole my Smile: An Exploration into the Causes of Youth Violence in South Africa.* Monograph series 3. Cape Town: Centre for Justice and Crime Prevention, pp. 37–56.

Kassin S., Fein, S. and Markus, H. R. 2011. *Social Psychology.* Belmont: Wadsworth Cengage Learning.

Lau, U. and Stevens, G. 2010. "Exploring the Psychological Exteriority and Interiority of Men's Violence against Woman", *Journal of Psychology in Africa* 20(4), 623–634.

Louw, D. and Louw, A. 2007. *Child and Aadolescent Development.* Bloemfontein: ABC Printers.

McWhirter, J. J., McWhirter, B. T., McWhirter, E. H. and McWhirter, R. J. 2004. *At Risk Youth: A Comprehensive Response for Counsellors, Teachers, Psychologists, and Human Service Professionals* (3rd ed.). Canada: Thomson Brooks/Cole.

Muthukrishna, N. 2011. "Structural Violence Effects on the Educational Life Chances of Children from Low Income Families in KwaZulu-Natal, South Africa", *Journal of Psychology in Africa* 21(1), 63–70.

Myburgh, C. and Poggenpoel, M. 2009. "Meta-synthesis on Learners' Experience of Aggression", *South African Journal of Education* 29(4), 445–460.

Ngakane, M. V., Muthukrishna, N. and Ngcobo, J. E. 2012. "Experiencing Violence in Schools: Voices of Learners in a Lesotho Context", *Anthropologist* 14(1), 39–48.

Nieuwenhuis, J. 2007. "Qualitative Research Designs and Data Gathering Techniques", in K. Maree (ed.), *First Steps in Research.* Pretoria: Van Schaik, pp. 47–68.

Paquette, D. and Ryan, J. 2001. "Bronfenbrenner's Ecological Systems Theory" (http:pt3.nl.edu/paquetteryanwebquest.pdf, accessed 25 Jul 2010).

Ragins, B. R. and Winkel, D. E. 2011. "Gender, Emotion and Power in Work Relationships", *Human Resource Management Review*, 21, 377–393.

Richardson, D. S. and Hammock, G. S. 2007. "Social Context of Human Aggression:    Are we Paying too much Attention to Gender?" *Aggression and Violent Behaviour* 12, 417–426.

South African Council of Educators (SACE). 2011. *School-based Violence Report.* Pretoria: SACE Policy and Research Division.

Steyn, H., Myburgh, C. and Poggenpoel, M. 2011. "Teachers' Experience of Aggression in a Secondary School: A Case Study", *Journal of Psychology in Africa* 21(1), 125–130.

Visser, M. 2007. "The Social Ecological Model as Theoretical Framework in Community Psychology", in N. Duncan, B. Bowman, A. Naidoo, J. Pillay and V. Roos (eds), *Community Psychology: Analysis, Context and Action.* Cape Town: UCT Press, pp. 102–116.

Vizard, D. 2012. *How to Manage Behaviour in Further Education.* Thousand Oaks, CA: SAGE.

Wellington, J. and Szczerbinski, M. 2007. *Research Methods for Social Sciences.* London: Continuum.

Wenger, E. 1998. *Communities of Practice: Learning, Meaning and Identity.* Cambridge: Cambridge University Press.

—. 2006. *"Learning for a Small Planet – A Research Agenda"* Version 2.0 (http:/www.ewenger.com/research).

Westraad, S. 2011. *Changing Schools in Challenging Contexts.* Port Elizabeth: The Repro House.

Yin, R. K. 1994. *Case Study Research: Design and Methods* (2nd ed.). Thousand Oaks, CA: Sage.

# CHAPTER TWELVE

## REALIZING UNIVERSAL PRIMARY EDUCATION IN KENYA

### R. W. ODUORI
#### LECTURER, MOI UNIVERSITY, ELDORET, KENYA

**Abstract**

Kenya reintroduced free primary education in 2003 within the framework of education for all, and with the hope of eliminating illiteracy so as to fully achieve the visions of the millennium development goals within the Kenyan context. The positive effect of this reintroduction was a drastic increase in pupil enrolment in primary schools across the country. This was an indication of the urge for education among the citizens and in the same vein, an indication of the inability of the majority of Kenyans to afford to send their children to school.

The increase in the numbers came with a lot of challenges, ranging from teacher-pupil ratios to provision of basic facilities, putting in question the quality and standards of the education provided. This paper recognizes the efforts made towards realizing universal primary education in Kenya. However, it focuses on the realities and challenges of free primary education in Kenya now, and its implications for the future sustainability of the same. The paper goes further to address how some of the challenges can be addressed to fully realize the aims and benefits of universal primary education in Kenya.

**Keywords**

Free Primary Education, Kenya, Challenges

# Introduction

Since independence in 1963, the Kenyan government has always had the intention and drive to provide free primary education to its citizens. At independence in 1963, the first president of the republic of Kenya, Jomo Kenyatta captured the need for affordable education when he declared that there were three enemies of the people of Kenya that had to be fought hard: illiteracy, poverty and disease. This sentiment has been captured years later under the Kenya government's Poverty Reduction Strategy (PRSP) and the Economic Recovery Strategy (ERS) for Wealth and Employment Creation in which one of the goals is provision of universal primary education by 2015. There have been several attempts and interventions at providing and implementing free primary education since independence. The first attempt was in 1971 and it specifically targeted districts (now referred to as counties) which had poor geographical conditions which made the people in those regions poor. They included Marsabit, Isiolo, Samburu, Turkana, West Pokot, Baringo, Narok, Elgeyo-Marakwet, Olkejuado, Tana River and Lamu.

The second attempt at free primary education was in 1973/74, when the president, during celebrations to mark ten years of independence, abolished tuition fees for standards I-IV countrywide and also ordered a standardized fee structure for standards V-VII. This arrangement never lasted as it was followed by a complete abolition of school fees in all primary schools in the republic. This led to a big rise in enrolment. Those in standards I-IV increased from 1.8 million in 1973 to almost 2.8 million in January of 1974 (Sifuna, 2005). Because of the abrupt nature of this declaration, schools were not well prepared for the sudden change and instantly lost revenues that were used to run the schools. There was hence pressure on physical facilities and on teaching staff because of the rise in numbers. Classes were overcrowded and teaching and learning material strained.

Because of lack of proper planning on the part of the government and the failure to forecast the impact of such declarations, the government's effort failed. The school managements had to find a way to provide for the school's needs like buildings and related infrastructure. Schools introduced what was referred to as a "building levy" basically to raise some revenue. Because of the peculiarities of each school, due to location and population, amongst others, the levies varied across districts. Generally, the levies were higher than the school fees prior to the declaration. As a consequence, parents were frustrated and since they could not afford such high levies, and the quality of education slumped due to high numbers, there were very high dropout rates.

The third intervention affording free primary education came in 1979 when yet again the government, through a presidential declaration, abolished all school levies in all public primary schools in the country. Though it was a presidential directive, it could have been simply an implementation of the 1976 Gachathi Report which had then recommended an extension of the waiver of school fees to the full seven years of primary education by 1980. This recommendation developed from the impact of the 1974 declarations. As a further effort at encouraging more enrolments, the government introduced free school milk in 1980. Although the intention was to encourage children to go to school, it was argued that the purpose was to boost the health and diet of children and institute a milk drinking culture. This effort not only saw enrolment increase by almost 23% and further, it resulted in improvement in school attendance and general health. In 1985, the president ordered the end of all forms of fees in primary schools. This had an impact on the national budget and through sessional paper No.6 on Education and Training for the next Decade and Beyond, it recommended a reduction in recurrent budget for education to sustainable levels. This for the third time saw the beginning of the collapse of free primary education. This was made even worse by the World Bank and IMF-influenced policy on structural adjustment programmes. It required that parents and school committees finance capital and recurrent expenditure at primary and secondary level while the government took care of teachers' salaries, administration and provision of limited school facilities. This brought about the cost sharing policy in the 80s. Although public expenditure reduced, on the negative side there were high dropout rates and poor quality of education. The structural adjustment programmes were a big blow to all the earlier efforts at attaining free primary education.

During the early attempts up to 1980, it is also important to note that the primary education cycle took seven years after which one had to sit an exam, the Certificate of Primary Education (CPE), in order to move on to secondary school level. In 1985, a new system was introduced and this cycle changed to eight years of primary education and the exam at the end referred to as Kenya Certificate of Primary Education (KCPE). In January 2003 the new government which had just come to power reintroduced free primary education. This was a very bold step for a government which politically speaking, other than riding on a reform agenda, came to power with the World Bank and IMF structural adjustment programme still in place. Kenya was also just coming from a regime that had been under economic sanctions for a number of years and as such seemed a big gamble. Bold as it was, there was a sudden surge in enrolments. An estimated 1.5 million children joined primary school. The Ministry of Education's strategic plan for 2006–2011 (page 22) on sustaining the implementation of free primary education states that the enrolment of children increased from 5.9 million in 2002 to 7.4 million in 2004 with the gross rate standing at 108.0% (for boys) and 101.6% (for girls), giving an overall gross enrolment of 104.8%. This was a remarkable improvement over the gross figures of 2002 which were 88.2%. And according to the Ministry of Education's statistical booklet (1999–2004), the children were enrolled in 17,804 public and 1,839 private schools with another 103,628 children enrolled in non-formal schools and centres.

A major achievement of the programme was the provision of instructional materials, especially textbooks. The strategic plan 2006–2011 notes that a World Bank mission evaluation of free primary education showed that the supply of textbooks and other instructional materials improved substantially. The target textbook to pupil ratio of 1:3 in lower primary and 1:2 in upper primary had been achieved in core subject areas. It further noted that there was better pupil performance, improved use of learning material and increased retention of pupils in schools. This particular initiative seemed to generate renewed interest in education: not only were school age children enrolled but even the over-age and adults joined the formal school system. The first cohort under this particular program have gone through the full eight-year primary cycle and even completed the four-year secondary cycle. Assessed on its own merit, it is a near success story. Four cohorts have gone through the eight years of primary education.

All the efforts at attaining universal free primary education and even the need to improve on the gains so far attained have been further enhanced and provided for in the Kenyan constitution of 2008 which clearly states the right to education by all Kenyans. Under the bill of rights in chapter six, part two on rights and fundamental freedoms, it states:

1   Every person has the right to education.
2   The state shall institute a program to implement the right of every child to free and compulsory pre-primary and primary education and in so doing shall pay particular attention to children with special needs.

This constitutional provision therefore makes it mandatory for the government to provide for the education of its citizens and therefore the government's commitment to the attainment of education for all and the attainment of the millennium development goals.

# Challenges

Whereas the constitution provides for the right to education, and the government has moved towards realizing the provision of free primary education, there are several challenges that the sector is facing.

## *Community support*

The term "free" has been understood as such, so there is diminished community support in the implementation of the programme with the government being given the full responsibility of overseeing the success of the programme. This coupled with the constitutional provisions has meant that the government must as a matter of right provide for the educational needs of all the children. This situation is even more real in urban areas, especially in Nairobi, where parents with children in public primary schools do not pay for any activity. In the rural areas, the situation is different. Schools still charge for certain services and the reasoning is that the government delays in disbursing the funds and, because of circumstances unique to the schools, the money released does not fully cater for the needs of the schools. A survey in a few schools revealed that, because of shortage of teaching staff, some schools employ trained teachers but then the school management boards and the parents usually agree on some amount to be paid by the parents so as to sustain the teachers employed by the board. The amount would vary from school to school depending on various variables such as student populations, number of extra teachers required etc.

Parents also pay for other activities like administration of different exams during the term and also enable the children take part in activities like games. It is argued that this is necessitated because the funds budgeted by the government are not sufficient and there are some other activities and needs of the schools that are not factored in by the government thus forcing the schools to fall back to the parents. The fear is that if this is not well controlled by the government it will erode the gains so far attained since some schools will start charging very high levies which will result in children being sent back home.

## *Quality*

Although the Ministry of Education strategic plan 2006–2011 notes that with the implementation of free primary education the quality of education was enhanced, this in essence is a very generalized observation since quality entails several aspects. In this paper, I approach quality from the perspective of the goals of changing the education system from the initial seven years of primary school to an eight-year cycle. One of the objectives of changing primary education from seven to eight years was to provide for a practical and skills based approach to education where, upon completion of eight years of primary schooling, the child would have acquired basic industrial skills to enable him or her engage in income generating activities. The Ministry of Education stated that the 8-4-4 policy was designed to encourage students become more self-reliant and better oriented towards self-employment. This meant therefore that schools needed to have workshops for skills oriented subjects like woodwork and masonry among others. In view of this at the implementation of the eight-year primary system, the number of subjects increased and, practically, the children were overloaded. The success of this approach to education meant heavy investment in infrastructure. Combined with provision of free primary education, it was just untenable. In terms of quality of education, much as the numbers increased, the student-teacher ratio has remained very high in public primary schools and the teaching is oriented towards passing the standard eight exams at the expense of moulding an all-round personality in the children. Because of the need for free universal primary education, the initial objectives of eight years of primary schooling have simply been shelved and forgotten. The only measure of quality is how well the pupils perform at the end of standard eight and therefore transit to secondary school.

### Private Schools

The Kenyan constitution provides for anyone to establish an educational institution. In chapter six, part two on rights and fundamental freedom, it says:

4    Every person has the right to establish and maintain, at that person's own expense, independent educational institutions that comply with the requirements of this constitution and meet standards laid down in legislation.

Although these are efforts meant to caution the government's shortcomings, they pose and create a bigger challenge. One of the biggest challenges is that apart from having a proper policy guideline on the operation of private schools, there is need for an efficient monitoring system. In terms of provision of free primary education, one of the challenges is the proliferation of private schools with some not meeting the standards set by the Ministry. However, these schools still attract pupils because of the parents' urge to see their children pass exams at all costs. Hence, the parents opt to send their children to such schools and not public schools since in most of them the numbers are too high and therefore standards are compromised.

Private schools pose a direct challenge to public schools when it comes to the transition to secondary schools. Parents try to send their children to private schools because of the controlled numbers in most of the schools. Because of this, the schools will strive to register impressive results to attract more students. The result is that the pupils from private schools grab all the positions in the best secondary schools at the expense of those in public primary schools who post results that on average are less than those in private schools. Pupils in public schools are therefore disadvantaged. The ripple effect of this trend is that some public schools, in a bid to compete with private schools and post above-average results, end up imposing a levy, referred to as extra tuition, and because the parents need their children to pass exams, they usually have no option other than to pay the extra levy. With the passage of time, this is likely to kill the government efforts at provision of free primary education. Although the government has banned any extra tuition and hence any extra charges, school management committees in collaboration with the parents normally find ways around such directives.

The most complex challenge is the class structure that is created in society by these schools and depending on which one it is, the fees charged vary with the upper one charging very high fees and defining the boundary between the rich and the poor. This challenge can only be addressed if the government in its effort to provide free education improves the quality of the schools by employing the appropriate number of teachers for the needs of the schools, upgrading the infrastructure in the schools so that there is a near level playing ground for both private and public schools.

*Accountability*

Although there is so little funding for free primary education and there are often delays in disbursements, proper accounting for the funds under various projects has been a major problem. For instance, most of the funding under the Kenya Education Sector Support Programme is hardly visible on the ground and any monies have been spent on projects that have minimal effect on infrastructural development and therefore have no impact on the needs of the schools. The school textbooks project, meant to complement free primary education, came under scrutiny with allegations of fake bookshops and suppliers in which millions of shillings were lost. This led to some donors withdrawing their support. Such a level of corruption and lack of transparency are dangers to the success of the programme.

These problems, coupled with others like overstretched facilities, shortage of teachers and overcrowding in classes, are a real danger to the future of the aims and intentions of free primary education and hence education for all in line with vision 2030.

## *The Future*

Since the reintroduction of free primary education in 2003, unlike the earlier efforts, four cohorts have gone through the system. The future, though it depends on political goodwill, has been protected constitutionally and guaranteed in the Basic Education Act, 2013, Number 14 of 2013, an act of parliament which gives effect to Article 53 of the constitution of Kenya and other enabling provisions among which is to promote and regulate free and compulsory basic education. Part four on free and compulsory education outlines various articles that are geared to protecting and enhancing free primary education. For example:

> The Cabinet Secretary shall implement the right of every child to free and compulsory basic education On the aspect of free tuition, under the devolved government system which Kenya has adopted, although there is some room to levy certain charges, this charges must get the approval of the Cabinet Secretary in consultation with county education board for as long as no child is refused to attend school for failure to pay such charges. . . .
>
> No public school shall charge or cause any parent or, guardian to pay tuition fees for or on behalf of any pupil in the school.

This chapter goes further to state the responsibility of government in ensuring free primary education: article 39 states that it shall be the duty of the Cabinet Secretary to

a) provide free and compulsory basic education to every child;
b) ensure compulsory admission and attendance of children of compulsory school age at school or an institution offering basic education;
j) advise the national government on financing of infrastructure development for basic education.

These legislative documents, which have legal implications, are the instruments that will ensure the continuity of free primary education since on the one hand, demand of the parent to ensure that his or her child is

admitted to a basic education institution and commit the government to
provide for its citizens' educational needs.

Even with all this provision, political goodwill is key in enabling civic
education to sensitize the people to the need to understand their rights,
roles and obligations and those of the government. This is necessary
because many good policies and much legislation have failed either
because people are ignorant of them or the government of the day for
certain reasons does not care or simply incapable of implementing their
own agendas and policies.

## References

Oketch, M. 2010. *Free Primary Education and After in Kenya: Enrolment Impact,
   Quality Effects, and the Transition to Secondary School.* (CREATE Pathways
   to Access Research Monograph No. 37). Brighton: University of Sussex.
Republic of Kenya, Ministry of Education. The Basic Education Act, 2013.
Republic of Kenya, The constitution, 2009.
Republic of Kenya, Ministry of Education. Strategic plan 2006–2011.
Sifuna, D. 2007. "The Challenge of Increasing Access and Improving Quality: An
   Analysis of Universal Primary Education Interventions in Kenya and Tanzania
   since the 1970s", *International Review of Education* 53, 687–699.
Somerset, A. 2009. "Universalizing Primary Education in Kenya: The Elusive
   Goal", *Comparative Education* 45, 233–250.

# Chapter Thirteen

# Language Issues in South African Primary Schools: Supporting the Shift from Apartheid to Post-Apartheid Language-in-Education Policy

## Krish Govender
Post-Doctoral Fellow, University of KwaZulu-Natal, South Africa

## and Reshma Sookrajh
Professor, University of KwaZulu-Natal, South Africa

**Abstract**

One of the challenges facing post-apartheid South African schools with their racially integrated and linguistically diverse learner populations is the language issue. Making the appropriate revisions to outmoded school language policies to address the linguistic needs of the learners is critical. This is especially significant for primary schools with many learners entering formal schooling having been exposed to no other language but their mother tongue. For African learners entering a system in which English as a dominant language of instruction has become entrenched, the challenges are sometimes insurmountable. Making the shift from the old, apartheid Language-in-Education Policy to one which encourages multilingualism and which affirms the previously marginalized African languages has therefore become increasingly urgent. However, changing school language policies and practices, like any other change, can come to nothing if such change is not supported. This paper contemplates the need for support from key stakeholders within the school to sustain language policy and practice change initiated in four South African public primary schools. In interrogating the support received for such change or the lack thereof, the paper explores the extent to which language change in these schools has been enabled or disabled.

**Keywords**
South African Primary Schools, Language-in-Education Policy (apartheid & post-apartheid), Language Policy & Practice Change, Supporting Language Change, Enabling & Disabling Language Change.

# Introduction

The dismantling of apartheid and ushering in of the first democratic government in South Africa in 1994 brought many changes. One of these entailed redressing the language in education policy. The old apartheid language policy in education which entrenched the power of English and Afrikaans was replaced by a new Language-in-Education policy (Department of Education, 1997) that encourages multilingualism, affirms the previously marginalized African languages in education and caters for South Africa's linguistically diverse population.

Hence the challenge facing post-apartheid South African public schools with their racially integrated and linguistically diverse learner populations is the language issue. Making the appropriate revisions to outmoded school language policies to address the linguistic needs of the learners is critical. This is especially significant for primary schools with many learners entering formal schooling having been exposed to no other language but their mother tongue. For African learners entering a system in which English as a dominant language of instruction has become entrenched, the challenges are sometimes insurmountable. In this regard the use of English as Language of Learning and Teaching (LOLT) from as early as Grade 1 for learners whose home language is not English has serious implications. The implications of this practice are that such learners are victims of linguistic deficiency on two fronts. On the one hand, they are expected to move from their home language to English as LOLT at a time when they are not yet functionally literate in their home language. On the other hand, they are required to make a shift to English at a stage where they may not have achieved the necessary competence to cope with English as a LOLT (Macdonald, 2001).

It is now widely acknowledged that learners' linguistic and cultural identities are likely to be enhanced by instructional programmes that attempt to add a second or third language to learners' home language(s).

Conversely, instruction in a second language which is designed to replace the language(s) learners bring to school may undermine the personal growth and linguistic confidence that are critical to academic success (Rosendal, 2008). Hence, the use of indigenous African languages as languages of learning and teaching alongside English in an additive multilingual mode is firmly advocated by language researchers in South Africa and other parts of Africa (Ndayipfukamiye, 1994; Heugh & Siegruhn, 1995; Adendorff, 1996; Arthur, 1994; Martin, 1996; Govender, 1998; Macdonald, 2001; Mukama, 2007; Ankama, 2008; Nkosana, 2011). This theoretical position has become mainstream because language theorists and language research internationally affirm the value of learning through the mother tongue as it is seen to increase the pace of cognitive development and invariably accelerates acquisition of a second or third additional language (Cummins, 1981, 1988; Skutnabb-Kangas, 1988; Hornberger & Vaish, 2008; Wang & Phillion, 2009; Alexander, 2010; Truscott & Malcolm, 2010; Desai, 2012).

Making the shift from the old, apartheid Language-in-Education Policy to one which encourages multilingualism and which affirms the previously marginalized African languages has therefore become increasingly urgent. However, changing school language policies and practices like any other change can come to nothing if such change is not supported. This paper contemplates the need for support from key stakeholders within and outside the school to sustain language policy and practice change initiated in four South African public primary schools. In interrogating the support received for such change or the lack thereof, the paper explores the extent to which language change in these schools has been enabled or disabled.

The paper begins with a selective review of change literature focusing on support as critical to effecting lasting change. This is followed by an overview of the research methodology used in the study and discussion of data analysis and findings. The paper concludes by presenting insights emerging from the findings.

## Supporting School Language Change

While change might occur if individuals accept the need for change, it may only be sustained if there is support for this change. Douglas (1997: 66) argues: "Unless some form of support for the acquired changes is forthcoming, either from the will of the changed individual or the assistance of others or circumstances (e.g. a sufficient gain from the change itself), that change will tend to fade or be displaced."

The need for a network of support to impel the change process and to sustain change is captured in the following observations:

> Great change cannot be durable unless the surrounding network is supportive of that change. (Douglas, 1997)

> Planning for multilingualism, multiliteracy and pluralism through schooling requires the active involvement of agents from the community, as well as the school. Furthermore, these agents must be engaged in developing a school context/culture that supports multilingualism, multiliteracy, and pluralism, beyond that which exists in the societal culture. (Skutnab-Kangas & Garcia, 1995)

In terms of school language change it is the assistance of others within and outside the school that is required to support changes wrought in individuals by the agents of language change and to support the change agents themselves in their quest to sustain the changes they have initiated. Skutnabb-Kangas & Garcia (1995) argue that support for multilingual education should come from individuals within the school and from the surrounding society and that the educational culture of the school should encourage and develop multilingualism. Fullan (2005a) and Shen (2008) consider capacity building to be a key driver in sustaining educational change which involves developing new knowledge, skills, and competencies; new resources; and new shared identity and motivation to work together for greater change. Fullan (2005a, 2005b) also notes that organizational capacity must be built by improving the infrastructure consisting of agencies at local, regional and state levels that can deliver new capacity in the system, such as training, consulting and other support. Fullan's (2005a, 2005b) contention that educational change can only be really sustained and supported through systemic change at the three levels of school, district and nation resonates with Douglas (1997) and Skutnabb-Kangas & Garcia's (1995) network of support for any change to be durable including school language change which shifts the culture of schools from monolingual to multilingual. Katz, Earl & Jaafar (2009), Hord & Tobia (2011) and Fullan (2010) also advocate collaboration among teachers and networking to support changes within a school.

Drawing on applications of chaos theory and complexity theory to the study of school reform, Beabout (2012) distinguishes between the concepts of turbulence and perturbance which are critical to complexity-based theories of educational change. The author defines turbulence as the perception of forces in an organizational environment with the potential to disrupt current modes of operation and perturbance as the social process of actors coming together to adjust organizational practice to fit with the changing environmental context. Beabout (2012) argues that sensible reformers ought to be fostering perturbance while minimizing the harmful consequences of excessive turbulence. Hence, like Fullan (2005a, 2005b) and Hargreaves & Fullan (2012), Beabout (2012) recognizes that creating organizational structures and developing capacity are critical not only to supporting change but also ensuring that change is constructive and beneficial rather than damaging (Douglas, 1997).

## Methodology

The study (Govender 2009) was conducted in four public primary schools in the KwaZulu-Natal province in South Africa. The schools are all ex-HOD (House of Delegates)[1] schools which initially comprised entirely Indian learners but since democratization in South Africa have a more racially integrated learner population with a greater majority of either African or Indian learners.

The study interrogated the attempts by four language change agents to sustain language policy and practice change they had initiated in these schools. Their language change initiatives are captured in an earlier Human Sciences Research Council project (HSRC 2004) investigating the factors promoting and inhibiting the implementation of multilingual education in public schools in South Africa. In each of the four schools one internal change agent worked towards revising the language policy and practices of the school to encourage the use of English and isiZulu[2] as

---

[1] The House of Delegates was part of the Tricameral Parliament which was the name given to the South African parliament and its structure from 1984 to 1994. While still entrenching the political power of the white section of the South African population, it did give limited political voice to the country's Coloured and Indian population groups. The majority Black population group was still excluded. The tricamerel parliament comprised the white House of Assembly, the Coloured House of Representatives and the Indian House of Delegates. Each of these three chambers had power over "own affairs' (as it was termed) of the population group it represented, such as education, social welfare, housing, local government, arts, culture and recreation. The South African population comprises 79.4% Black African, 9.1%White, 8.9% Coloured and 2.6% Indian/Asian. The term "coloured" is still used for the people of mixed race descended from slaves brought in from East and Central Africa, the indigenous Khoisan who lived in the Cape at the time, Bantus, Whites (mostly the Dutch/Afrikaner and British settlers) as well as an admixture of Javanese, Malay, Indian, Malagasy and Asian blood. (Statistics South Africa 2011, SAHO 2008).
[2] English and isiZulu are the dominant home languages of the learners in the four schools. However, prior to 1994, isiZulu, the most widely spoken African

subjects and for instruction, classroom management and school administrative purposes. Two of the change agents were principals, the third a level 1 educator (classroom practitioner) and the fourth the chairperson of a School Governing Body (SGB).[3] Agents R and G were the principals of Piper Primary and Willy Wonka Primary schools respectively; Agent S was a Level 1 educator at Mulberry Primary and L, SGB chairperson and parent of Bo-Peep Primary.[4]

The data was gathered primarily from in-depth interviews with the four change agents. To deepen emerging understandings of the critical role played by support to sustain school language change, opportunistic data gathering (Eisenhardt 1989) was conducted through interviews with significant others (other teachers and a school manager) at each of the schools. The interviews with the change agents comprised initial and follow-up interviews. The follow-up interviews were undertaken after the initial interviews were transcribed and preliminary analysis was done. The purpose was to gain further clarity on issues raised in the initial interviews and to gather additional data to sharpen emerging insights.

## Data Analysis and Findings

It was evident from the experiences of all four change agents that support or lack of it from within and outside the school have enabled or disabled them in their attempts to initiate and sustain school language change. Analysis of the data resulted in the emergence of several themes and sub-themes linked to the issue of support for change. The theme (and its sub-themes) explored in this paper is *In-school Support for School Language Change*.

---

indigenous language in KwaZulu-Natal (Statistics South Africa 2011) was marginalized as a LOLT in public schools in South Africa; Afrikaans and English were the only official languages at the time.

[3] Under the South African Schools Act (No. 84 of 1996), School Governing Bodies (SGBs) are statutory bodies established to provide for a uniform system for the organization and governance of all schools; to redress past injustices in ensuring equitable and democratic transformation in education; and to facilitate community involvement in the education of their children. A SGB is made up of the principal in his/her official capacity and elected members comprising learners (in the 8th Grade or above), educators, a non-educator staff member and parents/guardians of learners in the school. The number of parent members must comprise one more than the combined total of other members of a governing body who have voting rights.

[4] To maintain confidentiality and anonymity pseudonyms have been used for the change agents and research sites.

The data revealed that in-school support for school language change was manifested in the following ways: Staff Support, Learner Support, and Support through Collaboration.

## Staff Support

There was strong support from African teachers at Piper and Willy Wonka primary schools for their Indian colleagues to manage and teach classes comprising a large number of African learners who were minimally proficient in English. African teachers also provided assistance to school management by conducting assemblies in isiZulu to ease communication with African learners, and by facilitating communication with African parents at parents' meetings and when they made school visits through acting as interpreters and translators.

Reportedly, Indian teachers at Piper and Willy Wonka primary schools had been using African teachers as resources to assist them in communicating with African learners who could barely speak English as evidenced in the following responses:

> If the learners are making a noise they call me and I speak to them in isiZulu and they keep quiet ... some days they call me to explain in isiZulu so that the learners can understand.

> Some teachers, like Mrs G, whenever the children don't understand, she says, Barbara come and explain to this learner ... Barbara come I got a problem with this, can I ask you this in English and you can translate in isiZulu so that they can understand.

While it is not the most effective way of dealing with the challenge of teaching in schools with linguistically diverse learners, this approach, nevertheless, confirmed that Indian teachers in the two schools recognized the need to use the learner's mother tongue, particularly in the Foundation Phase, and were being supported to fulfil this need. It was also reported that Indian teachers in these two schools who could speak some isiZulu followed the example of their African colleagues by resorting to isiZulu-English code-switching. They switched to isiZulu to issue simple instructions, provide direction in the completion of tasks and to discipline learners (see Adendorff 1996 for the academic and social functions of classroom code-switching). Concurring with Adendorff's findings, Li (2008) and Ahmad (2009) in the Chinese and Malaysian contexts respectively, contend that code-switching has great potential for helping the bilingual teacher to achieve context-specific teaching and learning goals like clarifying difficult concepts and reinforcing students' bilingual lexicon, as well as providing affective support to learners. Additionally, Li (2008) recommends identifying pedagogically sound and productive code-switching practices, and disseminating good code-switching practices through demonstrations, workshops and teacher-training.

Support from African teachers at Willy Wonka Primary in easing communication with African parents and learners are illustrated in the following responses:

> African parents don't understand English. Now even letters that are being sent to them are written in English and isiZulu. When they come here to pay school fees we have to explain to them in isiZulu. We have to explain to them in isiZulu how to fill a form and even the teacher who has a problem in the class (says) please this is the parent, please explain to him because he doesn't understand English.

> In the assembly when we are making announcements then we have to explain to the learners in isiZulu, to emphasise to them whatever needs to be emphasised.

It is evident that in addition to supporting the school language change process, African teachers also provided a crucial service in making Willy Wonka Primary accessible to a large majority of parents who were perhaps marginalized in the past and in this way created spaces for these parents to participate meaningfully with the school and contribute to the corporate life of the school. Furthermore, the use of isiZulu in forums of mass communication like school assemblies and parents' meetings also affirmed the value of isiZulu and elevated its status so that it enjoyed some parity with English.

African teachers at Piper, Willy Wonka and Bo Peep primary schools had also expressed a strong willingness to hold isiZulu classes in school to assist their Indian colleagues to learn isiZulu. This underscores Fullan's (2005a) contention that one of the drivers critical to effective and lasting change is developing cultures for learning which involve a set of strategies designed for people to learn from each other and become committed to improvement. Apart from African teachers, African support staff at Piper Primary had been providing invaluable support for teachers in the Foundation Phase and Grade R classes in explaining among other things school rules, proper use of ablution facilities and engaging in safe play on the school premises in isiZulu for African learners who had difficulty in understanding English.

This kind of support from teaching and non-teaching staff had created especially at Piper and Willy Wonka primary schools what Skutnabb-Kangas & Garcia (1995) term a multilingual language surround. This is evident in the affirmation of the equal value of both isiZulu and English in these two schools through the use of these languages everywhere, in the offices, corridors, staffroom and playground, in notices to parents, in school signs, posters and articles on bulletin boards and at school assemblies and parents meetings. Affirmation of the L1 (first language) of all the learners through multilingual classroom practices is critical to advancing the cause of multilingual education and especially additive bi- and multilingualism (Hornberger & Vaish, 2008).

In contrast to the support received from Level 1 teachers, management staff in the four schools provided limited support for their teachers to embrace or initiate language policy and practice changes in their schools. Agent S categorically stated that she had not been supported by management in her quest to drive language change at her school. Thus, while Agent S was able to sustain multilingual teaching/learning practices in her own classroom, no support systems were created by management within her school to assist her in her quest to bring about whole school language change.

To address the incapacity of the heads of departments and other management members to provide this support, Agent G felt that input from outside had to be in the form of competent INSET programmes initiated and driven by the education department based on the school improvement plans submitted to the education department as part of IQMS which was mandatory for all public schools. Agent R adopted a different position on assistance for teachers from the school's management staff. He felt that management should be proactive and not wait for assistance from the education department. His position is captured in the following response:

> The other aspect is that while the teacher comes up to the management for assistance the management themselves don't have the capacity to assist. So we have that problem, but that's no excuse really, if you don't have the capacity you put in place programmes that can assist the teachers.

When Agent R spoke of "putting in place programmes" he was evidently referring to management personnel sourcing assistance from within and outside the school so that a structured programme of support could be established as an initiative of the school rather than expecting the education department to initiate such a programme. Agent R's position underscores McLaughlin & Talbert's (2001) contention that strong departmental leadership within schools extends and reinforces opportunities for teacher learning provided by the district and by the school. Additionally, Hord & Tobia (2011) argue that professional learning communities must become the norm in every school and that this can only happen if the leadership of the school supports it and creates working conditions in which professional learning communities can flourish.

Contrary to the position which obtained at the school of Agent S, findings from Wong & Cheung's (2009) study on school reform revealed that the attitudes of senior management to school reform were more positive than those of frontline teachers. However, what was equally significant was the observation that frontline teachers' inadequate understanding of the reform resulted in their inadequate support for the reform. This confirms Agent S's contention that teachers must be capacitated and supported by management to contribute to school language change.

### *Learner Support*

Apart from the staff, learners in all four schools also unconsciously supported the language change process in these schools and were, in a sense, informal language teachers. African learners of their own volition assisted their African peers to learn the target language (English) and to negotiate learning in other subjects across the curriculum by switching to isiZulu in group and pair work. Indian learners also supported their African peers' learning of the target language. In addition, African learners were strategically used by Indian educators in all four schools to support the learning of their African peers by making input in isiZulu in pair and group work and/or to act as translators and interpreters for these educators. There was also evidence that African learners were assisting their Indian peers to learn isiZulu. The following responses from Agents G and S and the IsiZulu language educator at Bo Peep Primary respectively reflect this position:

> I think that generally happens in the classroom where the children code-switch, in fact in certain classes they have their own interpreters. There is a child who comes out and interprets the whole issue, explaining the task, explaining the requirements. Some teachers have developed learners who will do this task in the class.

> And of course I had help from some isiZulu-speaking children ... some of them are more fluent than the others and are able to help their fellow learners and of course I had English L1 learners put in groups to assist them.

When there are many African children in class and then there are some Indian children, I don't know how they are doing this but they learn IsiZulu easier...they are learning from the black children.

Peer learning of the type evidenced in the data is encouraged by Skutnabb-Kangas and Garcia (1995) who support input in the mother tongue in groupwork to assist learners in the emerging bi- or multilingual phase and this is acknowledged by researchers exploring peer support in second language learning (Wheeler, 1994; McLaughlin, 1995; Montague & Meza-Zaragosa, 1999).

Wheeler (1994) and McLaughlin (1995) comment on the usefulness for language learning of L2 learners communicating with L1 peers in group and pair work. Wheeler (1994) found that this kind of peer support increased the L2 learners' confidence and reduced the anxiety that is often found in teacher-dominated classrooms. Montague & Meza-Zaragosa (1999) reflect on the usefulness of teaching in the second language and facilitating peer scaffolding in the native language. Montague & Meza-Zaragosa (1999) examined majority language learners (English speakers) attempting the use of a minority language (Spanish). The researchers concluded that seeing their English-speaking peers struggle with second language use proved to validate Spanish speakers' struggle with English and that the latter most likely saw that their fluency in Spanish was a desired goal for English-speaking peers which could contribute to a validation of their home language. Perhaps what was more affirming for the Spanish-speaking children in the study was that they became "experts" for their English-speaking peers who often sought their assistance in learning Spanish. The position of the Spanish-speaking children is very similar to that of the isiZulu-speaking learners in the present study who also emerged as "experts" assisting the Indian learners to learn isiZulu as suggested by the IsiZulu language educator at Bo Peep Primary.

In a review of research studies in which peer-peer dialogue is linked to second language learning, Swain et al (2002) identify the value of collaborative dialogue, which occurs when learners encounter linguistic problems and attempt to solve them together, and conclude that peer-peer collaborative dialogue mediates second language learning. An extension to peer support is peer correction of written work in English Second Language classrooms which has value even for primary school learners if it is supplemented by teacher feedback and learners are capacitated to provide quality support for their peers (Sultana, 2009).

## Support through Collaboration

The creation of communities of practice (Lave & Wenger, 1991; Wenger, 1998) has important implications for changing school language policies and classroom language practices. In a community of practice members are engaged in the sustained pursuit of a shared enterprise and learning is an evolving, continuously renewed set of relations (Lave & Wenger, 1991). Additionally, Fullan (2010, 2011) advocates collective capacity building through collaborative work among teachers and schools and argues that peers working with peers in a focused deliberate way provide support for change. This implies that collaboration among teachers and between teachers and management staff is critical to supporting and sustaining school language change.

In terms of collaboration between teachers and management on language policy revision, the following comment by Agent G is instructive:

> They (teachers) would rather have it (language policy) developed by the management team and then they would criticize it and thereafter it goes to the SGB. So that's what you call a more expedient route than the proper route, which starts from the teachers first.

The perception created by this comment was that level 1 teachers were apathetic and indifferent and did not embrace opportunities created by the principal and management staff to become involved in policy deliberation or policy revision but instead adopted a negative stance by being unfairly critical of policies developed by management. Agent S contested this view by asserting that from her own experience and that of her level 1 colleagues, management at Mulberry Primary had effectively excluded teachers from policy and development policy revision. Collaborative school reform requires that both teachers as well as managerial staff work collectively to support and sustain any changes initiated in the school. Excluding classroom practitioners from the process might compromise the implementation of such policies for it is really the classroom practitioners who translate policy into practice.

In terms of support that is required to transform classroom practices to meet the agenda of school language change, Agent S suggested pooling of resources within a school and networking schools so that there is a sharing of knowledge and resources among schools to assist educators to learn isiZulu and to improve their competence in teaching the language and teaching through the language. In addition, she suggested a drive by the school to sensitize educators to the value of including isiZulu in the school curriculum. Her suggestions in this respect are captured in the following responses:

> It would be good to have workshops on an ongoing basis ... we could use isiZulu recordings to get the pronunciation right and we could get teachers coming in and doing some lessons ... teachers who are proficient in the language.

> The language teachers can create worksheets in different languages, bilingually for the entire school ... I don't have to do it myself all the time. We can share the responsibility. We could do that with the help of teacher aid books and dictionaries in the two languages.

The suggestion of using multilingual worksheets to support language learning and ultimately advance the school language change process finds resonance in a study by Hornberger & Vaish (2008) who consider illustrative classroom examples of multilingual educational strategies in Singapore, India and South Africa and argue that multilingual classroom practices can be a resource through which children access Standard English while also cultivating their own local languages.

The pooling of resources within and across schools and shared responsibility for driving the language change process in the classroom that Agent S referred to once again raises the importance of collaboration within and across schools to sustain educational reform. Katz, Earl and Jaafar (2009) argue that joint work which they say includes deprivatization and a collective commitment to change may be at the heart of the power of networks and other forms of teacher collaboration. These structures can provide the opportunity for colleagues to address genuinely new and often difficult ideas in a safe environment, away from risk of censure and once the ideas are more fully developed they can be implemented in the network of schools.

## Conclusion

The following insights emerged from the analysis and findings:
- The support provided by African teachers to Indian peers and management staff was critical to sustaining school language change.
- By easing communication with African parents and learners through isiZulu–English code-switching, African teachers not only unconsciously encouraged this type of classroom communication among Indian colleagues but also increased participation of African

parents with the school and affirmed the value of isiZulu so that it enjoyed some parity with English.

- Apart from meeting the school language change agenda, isiZulu support from African support staff was especially critical for Foundation Phase African learners who were functionally illiterate in English when they entered primary school.
- Peer learning among African and Indian learners not only supported language learning and learning through two languages but also affirmed the equal value of both languages and the speakers of these languages.
- Collaboration among teachers and between teachers and management within and across schools can advance school language change especially where there was a paucity of assistance from management staff in individual schools and where pooling of resources can enhance transforming classroom language practices.

The study revealed that meeting the necessary challenge of changing language policies and practices in post-apartheid primary schools depended largely on support. The findings explored in this paper focused on support from within schools, from learners, educators and non-educator staff. This support can be further enhanced from support from other quarters as well, that is support from parents and the education department. As so well enunciated by Douglas (1997), for great change to be durable there must a surrounding network of support for that change.

# References

Adendorff, R. D. 1996. "The Functions of Code Switching among High School Teachers and Students in KwaZulu and Implications for Teacher Education", in K. M. Bailey and D. Nunan (eds), *Voices from the Language Classroom: Qualitative Research in Second Language Education.* Cambridge: Cambridge University Press.

Ahmad, B. H. 2009. "Teachers' Code-Switching in Classroom Instructions for Low English Proficient Learners", *English Language Teaching* 2(2), 49–55.

Alexander, N. 2010. "Mother Tongue Based Bilingual Education: Provincially, Nationally and Internationally", *Leap News* (December), 28.

Ankama, C. 2008. "Namibia: Bilingual or Multilingual Education", *New Era* (28 May) (http://allafrica.com/stories/200805280916.html)

Arthur, J. 1994. "English in Botswana Primary Classrooms: Functions and Constraints", in C. M. Rubagumya (ed.), *Teaching and Researching Language in African Classrooms.* Clevedon, Avon: Multilingual Matters.

Beabout, B. R. 2012. "Turbulence, Perturbance, and Educational Change", *Complicity: An International Journal of Complexity and Education* 9(2), 15–29.

Cummins, J. 1981. *Bilingualism and Minority Children*. Ontario: Ontario Institute for Studies in Education.

—. 1988. "Language Planning in Education in Multilingual Settings", in V. Bickley (ed.), *Language in Education in a Bilingual or Multilingual Setting*. Hong Kong: Institute of Language in Education, Department of Education, pp. 262–264.

Department of Education. 1997. *Language-in-Education Policy*. Pretoria: Government Printer.

Desai, Z. 2012. *A Case for Mother Tongue Education*. (PhD thesis). UWC.

Douglas, T. 1997. *Change Intervention & Consequence: An Exploration of the Process of Intended Change*. London/New York: Free Association Books.

Eisenhardt, K. M. 1989. "Building Theories from Case Study Research", *Academy of Management Review* 14(4), 532–550.

Fullan, M. G. 2005a. "Eight Forces for Leaders of Change", *National Staff Development Council,* 26(4), 54–64.

—. 2005b. "Resiliency and Sustainability", *The School Administrator* (February), 16–18.

—. 2010. *All Systems Go*. Thousand Oaks, CA: Corwin Press. (Ontario Principals Council).

Fullan, M. 2011. *Change Leader: Learning to Do What Matters Most*. San Francisco, CA: Wiley.

Govender, K. M. 1998. *Yebo Nkosingiphile,* you can ask me *Iyini icutin? Zulu-English Classroom Code-Switching Verbal salad or Communicative resource?* (Unpublished Masters dissertation). UDW.

—. 2009. *School Language Change Led by Internal Change Agents*. (PhD thesis). UKZN.

Hargreaves, A. and Fullan, M. 2012. *Professional Capital: Transforming Teaching in Every School*. New York: Teachers College Press.

Heugh, K. and Siegruhn, A. 1995. "Towards Implementing Multilingual Education in South Africa", in K. Heugh, A. Siegruhn and P. Pluddemann (eds), *Multilingual Education for South Africa*. Isando: Heinemann.

Hord, S. M. and Tobia, E. F. 2011. *Reclaiming Our Teaching Profession: The Power of Educators Learning in Community*. New York: Teachers College Press.

Hornberger, N. and Vaish, V. 2008. "Multilingual Language Policy and School Linguistic Practice: Globalization and English-language Teaching in India, Singapore and South Africa", *Compare: A Journal of Comparative and International Education*, 1–15.

Human Sciences Research Council (HSRC). 2004. *Factors Promoting or inhibiting Multilingualism in post-apartheid South African schools*. Assessment Technology & Education Evaluation. The Unit for Language & Literacies Studies.

Katz, S., Earl, L. M. and Jaafar, S. B. 2009. *Building and Connecting Learning Communities*. California: Sage.

Lave, J. and Wenger, E. 1991. *Situated Learning: Legitimate Peripheral Participation*. Cambridge: Cambridge University Press.

Li, D. C. S. 2008. "Understanding Mixed Code and Classroom Code-switching: Myths and Realities", *New Horizons in Education* 56(3), 75–87.

Macdonald, C. 2001. "Eager to Talk and Learn and Think", in I. Moll and G. Gultig (eds), *Learners and Learning*. Cape Town: Maskew Miller Longman.

McLaughlin, B. 1995. "Fostering Second Language Development in Young Children: Principles and Practices", *Center for Research on Education, Diversity & Excellence. NCRCDSLL Educational Practice Reports*. Paper EPR14.

McLaughlin, M. and Talbert, J. 2001. *Professional Communities and the Work of High School Teaching*. Chicago: University of Chicago Press.

Martin, P. W. 1996. "Code-Switching in the Primary Classroom: One Response to the Planned and Unplanned Language Environment in Brunei", *Journal of Multilingual and Multicultural Development* 17, 128–144.

Montague, N. S. and Meza-Zaragosa, E. 1999. "Elicited Response in the Pre-Kindergarten Setting with a Dual Language Program: Good or Bad Idea?" *Bilingual Research Journal* 23(2&3), 289–296.

Mukama, E. 2007. "Rethinking Languages of Instruction in African Schools", *Policy & Practice: A Development Education Review* 4, 53–56.

Ndayipfukamiye, L. 1994. "Code-switching in Burundi Primary Classrooms", in C. M. Rubagumya (ed.), *Teaching and Researching Language in African Classrooms*. Clevedon, Avon: Multilingual Matters.

Nkosana, L. B. M. 2011. "Language Policy and Planning in Botswana", *The African Symposium: An online journal of the African Educational Research Network* 11(1), 129–137.

Rosendal, T. 2008. *Multilingual Cameroon: Policy, Practice, Problems and Solutions*. Gothenburg Africana Informal Series – No.7. University of Gothenburg.

Shen, Y. 2008. "The Effect of Changes and Innovation on Educational Improvement", *International Education Studies* 1(3), 73–77.

Skutnabb-Kangas, T. 1988. "Multilingualism and the Education of Minority Children", in T. Skutnabb- Kangas and J. Cummins (eds), *Minority Education*. Clevedon, Avon: Multilingual Matters.

Skutnabb-Kangas, T. and Garcia, O. 1995. "Multilingualism for All – General Principles?" in T. Skutnabb-Kangas (ed.), *Multilingualism For All*. Netherlands: Swets & Zeitlinger.

South African History Online (SAHO). "Tricameral Parliament" (www.sahistory.org.za>media library>Official or Original Documents).

Statistics South Africa. 2011. (statssa.gov.za/publications).

Sultana, A. 2009. "Peer Correction in ESL Classrooms", *BRAC University Journal* VI(1), 11–19.

Swain, M., Brooks, L. and Tocalli-Beller, A. 2002. "Peer-peer Dialogue as a Means of Second Language Learning", *Annual Review of Applied Linguistics* 22, 171–185.

Truscott, A. and Malcolm, I. 2010. "Closing the Policy–Practice Gap: Making Indigenous Language Policy more than Empty Rhetoric", in J. Hobson, K. Lowe, S. Poetsch and M. Walsh (eds), *Re-awakening Languages: Theory and*

*Practice in the Revitalisation of Australia's Indigenous Languages*. Sydney: Sydney University Press.

Wang, Y. and Phillion, J. 2009. "Minority Language Policy and Practice in China: The Need for Multicultural Education", *International Journal of Multicultural Education,* 11(1) (http://ijme-journal.org/ijme/index.php/ijme/article/view/138/312).

Wenger, E. 1998. "Communities of Practice: Learning as a Social System", *Systems Thinker* (June).

Wheeler, J. 1994. "Overcoming Difficulties in Pair and Group Work", *English Teaching Forum* 32(3), 48–49.

Wong, P. and Cheung, A. C. 2009. "Managing the Process of an Educational Change: A Study of School Heads' Support for Hong Kong's Curriculum Reform", *International Journal of Educational Management* 23(1), 87–106.

# Chapter Fourteen

# Teachers as Assessors:
# A Case Study of Gauteng Province
# (Republic of South Africa)

## Tebogo Mogashoa
### Lecturer, College of Education,
### University of South Africa

**Abstract**

The aim of the research was to establish how assessment was implemented by teachers in selected schools in Gauteng Province. A qualitative method was used to gather information from the different categories of participants. In-depth formal interviewing was used as the main data collection method. The researcher used focus group interviews and individual interviews to collect data. The researcher then interpreted and drew meaning from the displayed data.

Teachers had different views on the process of assessment. There must be a shift from norm-referenced to criterion-referenced type of assessment, that is, shift from assessing learners by comparing one learner from the others.

**Keywords**

Teacher, Evaluation and Assessment, Critical Discourse Analysis, Perceptions, Forms of Assessment, Criterion Referencing, Assessment Tasks, Progression and Promotion

## Introduction

There have been critics of the South African education policies who condemned the National Department of Education for a curriculum that is said to be irrelevant and uninteresting for the majority of South African learners. Before 1994 the education system in South Africa ran deliberately counter to world trends by choosing to serve the education needs of only a section of the South African population. The birth of democracy in 1994 led to the establishment of a new dispensation and that led to a need for the democratization of the education system. The apartheid education system had disadvantaged the majority of South Africans, especially the black communities. The situation in the new democracy demanded serious changes in many spheres of life in South Africa especially in education.

Curriculum 2005 was introduced in 1997 and piloted in selected schools countrywide. Then in 1998, the Department of Education introduced Curriculum 2005 in all schools in South Africa. However, the changes in education had an impact on the attitude, moral and performance of teachers in general as well as assessment in particular. These changes required a paradigm shift on the part of teachers. The introduction of outcomes-based assessment made many demands on both the educators and the education system. Teachers had to change the way they used assess. It is hoped that the study will also inform policy makers about problems experienced by teachers in the implementation of the various methods of assessment. Assessment policy can have a negative impact on teaching and learning if not appropriately implemented.

Drotar (2007: 3) states that in order to be significant, the research needs to exceed the threshold of current scientific work in a specific area. It was appropriate to research how these assessment policies are being implemented and their processes managed in schools and their intended value in teaching and learning. The knowledge this research intended to create will be of significance because teachers play a key role in the process of implementing assessment policies.

## Theoretical Frameworks

According to Terre Blanche (2007: 20), refining a research problem involves identifying a theoretical framework upon which to base the research. It is imperative to state the theories that influenced the research problem as well as the research methods that were used. This study was underpinned by a critical discourse analysis theory in which the researcher expressed his comments or judgments based on written or spoken communications, discussions or conversations with educators. It involved an analysis of the merits and demerits of the implementation of assessment policies. It is for these reasons that critical discourse analysis was used as a framework to engage and converse about the research problem and questions of this study. Critical discourse analysis deals with long term analysis of fundamental causes and consequences of issues. Therefore it requires an account of detailed relationships between text, talk, society and culture.

The main research question was: How are teachers implementing assessment policies in selected schools in Gauteng Province?

## Research Design and Methods

Trochim (2006: 1) states that research design provides the glue that holds the research project together and design is used to structure the research, to show all the major parts of the research projects – the samples or groups, measures, treatments or programmes, and methods of assessment – work together to try to address the central research questions. Tompkins (2008:4) further states that researchers can design a study to characterize a single instance of a phenomenon or draw an inference about a phenomenon in a population via a sample. The research methodology of this study was qualitatively and inductively based. A qualitative method was used to gather information from the different categories of participants on how assessment methods are implemented. Qualitative research assisted the researcher to investigate how educators implement assessment policies. This method assisted in answering the research questions which are informed by the main research question enabling critical discourse analysis to examine the spoken and written words in detail.

The target group and population of the study comprised experienced teachers teaching Intermediate Phase learners. Only five schools were invited to participate in the study. The researcher interviewed five teachers in each school. The above description of the sample is an indication that a purposive sample was used in this research. According to Soanes and Stevenson (2008: 1167), purposive refers to "having or done with a particular purpose". In this study purposeful sampling was used to select for informants with rich information. The sampling involved schools from different socio-economic backgrounds.

## Data Analysis

According to Michelle (2007: 3), qualitative data analysis consists of identifying, coding and categorizing patterns found in the data. Bradley et al. (2007: 5) declare that once the data have been reviewed and there is a general understanding of the scope and contexts of the key experiences under study, coding provides the analyst with a formal system to organize data, uncovering and documenting additional links within and between concepts and experiences described in the data. Plooy (2007: 41) defines data analysis as a process of bringing order and structure to the mass of collected data. Data analysis and interpretation involved the analysis and interpretation of documents related to assessment policies. Data were analysed by selecting, comparing, synthesizing and interpreting information to provide explanation.

## Research Findings and Discussions

*Question: Please give examples of rubrics or marking grids you may have used for assessment.*

Most teachers interviewed mentioned assessment tools such as memos, rubrics and checklists. They all conceded that the Department of Education supplied them with all the tools necessary for assessment.

To establish teachers' requirements for the successful implementation of assessment policies, the following question was asked:

*Question: What are your requirements for the successful implementation of the new assessment policies?*

All teachers who participated in this study indicated that they request the Department of Education not to introduce many assessment policies which always change.

The next question was asked to determine educators' challenges in the implementation of the new assessment policies.

*Question: What training did you receive in respect of the new assessment policies?*

All teachers interviewed conceded that they received training for the National Protocol on Assessment.

In order to identify the various aspects of the training the teachers received, they were asked to elaborate more on the workshops they attended.

*Question: Tell me more about the workshops you have attended*

In responding to the question above, teachers had different views. This is supported by the different views below:

> In most workshops the facilitators gave us activities and guided us on how to go through the activities and we were given opportunities to demonstrate how we were going to implement these policies in our classrooms.

> When we attended the workshops on the National Protocol on Assessment, we were told different things which were confusing. The facilitators were not interpreting the various documents the same way. We were given a lot of papers to fill in. The presentations in the workshops were not appropriate to what we were practically doing in our classes.

All teachers interviewed conceded that they received training on the National Protocol on Assessment. However, educators had different views in terms of the workshops they attended. This was quite evident to the researcher when some teachers stated that in most workshops the facilitators gave them activities and guided them on how to go through the activities and were also given opportunities to demonstrate how they were going to implement these policies in their classrooms. An indication was also made by other teachers that the presentations in the workshops were not appropriate to what they were practically doing in their classes.

**_Question: Did you find the training activities relevant to what you were doing in class? If relevant or irrelevant, explain._**

Most teachers indicated that the workshops were relevant but it was not easy to implement what they were trained for in real classroom environment. This was emphasized by one teacher when he said,

> Yes, but trainings are relevant, but it is totally different from what we do in class. In class there are those who are very slow, and some very intelligent. The training activities are relevant but more challenging to implement in class. When you present in the workshops there are only teachers but when you present in class is a different story. You are faced with a real situation.

The above response was followed by another question to determine teachers' opinions about the knowledge trainers or co-ordinators had of these assessment policies.

**_Question: What is your opinion about the competency level of the trainers and coordinators of the training?_**

The findings of this study indicated that most teachers viewed the facilitators of the workshops for C2005, RNCS, and NCS as not being competent enough. Judging from the responses, there was general agreement that the facilitators of the workshops for CAPS were much better. This implied that the educators are more comfortable with CAPS than the previous policies on teaching, learning and assessment. However, it should be indicated that the teachers have not yet implemented CAPS but were referring to training but not implementation. The researcher's assumption was that the facilitators of the workshops on CAPS were more prepared and could satisfy the educators' expectations.

*Question: Tell me more about assessment procedures you are employing.*

In responding to the question above, the teachers mentioned contradicting statements. A few of the verbatim responses are indicated below:

> As assessment is ongoing, for example, comprehension, you assess two things, reading and comprehending. You ask questions and they respond.

> We get all the guidelines from our facilitators. We know exactly what needs to be done. Under assessment plans, the parents can also see what is happening at school.

> I assess my learners at least every second week by means of tests and letters to write.

> We assess against learning outcomes.

> I can't elaborate much on that.

The researcher noticed that the teachers had contradictory views about outcomes-based assessment. This was evident when some teachers indicated that they assess reading and comprehension, others indicated that they assess by using tests and letters, while some indicated that they assess learning outcomes. Furthermore, the lack of knowledge of outcomes-based assessment was evident when some teachers could not even explain what they understood by the concept outcomes-based assessment. Based on the responses of the teachers who participated in this study, it was clear that the concept of outcomes-based assessment was not well understood by the teachers. The researcher is therefore of the opinion that the facilitators could have given the teachers contradictory statements about outcomes-based assessment.

The next question sought to establish teachers' knowledge of the principles of outcomes-based assessment.

*Question: What are some of the principles of outcomes-based assessment?*

All teachers interviewed indicated that they don't know any principles of outcomes-based assessment.

*Question: What are some of the assessment methods you commonly use when assessing your learners?*

The findings of lack of knowledge of the various assessment methods were shown when some educators could not indicate a clear understanding of the different assessment methods. Lack of knowledge of the various assessment methods was also evident from the teachers' responses. Some teachers indicated that assessment methods are the building blocks of tasks while others mentioned that assessment methods are questions and answers. However, some of the teachers had knowledge of the various forms of assessment as they mentioned aspects such as assignments, investigations, essays, projects and responses to texts. The data presented by teachers in this study showed that some educators knew about the various assessment methods while others had no idea of the new methods used in assessing learners' achievements of learning outcomes.

*Question: What do you understand by different forms of assessment?*

Not all teachers could indicate a clear understanding of the different forms of assessment. This was confirmed by one teacher who said,

> According to policy, it says these different types of assessment are the building blocks of the tasks. Other learners may know how to read but not know how to comprehend.

*Question: Please name a few departmental guidelines you use when planning assessment.*

The researcher noticed that the Department of Education had supplied the teachers with assessment guidelines. However, when responding to the researcher's questions, the teachers mentioned some documents such as mark sheets and grids which are in fact assessment tools. The fact that teachers indicated that they have assessment guidelines but they had challenges in implementing them is an indication that they could not interpret them appropriately.

*Question: Please comment on the school's reporting policy.*

All teachers who were interviewed mentioned that each school has its own policy which is informed by the one supplied by the Department of Education.

The above responses were followed by another question to determine the criteria teachers used for progression of learners from one grade to the other.

*Question: Which criteria are used for progressing learners from one grade to another?*

The teachers indicated that the Department of Education has given them guidelines which they follow when progressing learners from one grade to the other. On analysing the assessment guidelines, the researcher noticed that learners in grades 4 to 8 progress with their age cohort. This contradicted by another guideline that indicated that any decision about progression should be based on the evidence of a learner's performance against recorded assessment tasks. Data further indicated that no learner should stay in the same phase for longer than four years. The researcher is of the view that some learners therefore progress from one grade to the other without having achieved learning outcomes.

*Question: What evidence is there for recording learners' progress?*

The teachers indicated that they keep some recording sheets at school for a long time. In order to ascertain how teachers report learners' achievement of learning outcomes, the following questions were asked:

*Question: How is reporting of learners' achievement done?*

The teachers mentioned that reporting is done quarterly.

# Conclusions

It was found that some teachers have changed the way they used to assess after the introduction of the new assessment policies, while other teachers did not change. Schools in urban areas were adequately supplied with assessment materials than the schools in the townships, informal settlements and on the farms. Teachers received training on the various assessment policies. However some policies were not deemed appropriate to what teachers were actually doing in their classrooms. This study established that teachers have inadequate knowledge of outcomes-based assessment. The Department of Education provided schools with resources on assessment policies. However, schools did not receive the resources equally or equitably. Though the Department of Education provided schools with assessment policies, teachers interpreted them differently. There were problems with regard to time allocation for training workshops and the long distances travelled to the training workshop centres. The researcher also observed that, as a result of the long distances travelled, the teachers arrived late for the workshops and some were already tired by the time they reached the training centres.

The researcher recommends that for the teachers to be effective and efficient in their daily assessment processes there should be in-service training – those education and training activities engaged in by teachers following their initial professional certification and intended mainly or exclusively to improve their professional knowledge, skills and attitudes in order to teach and assess effectively. The Department of Education should train teachers on how to implement assessment methodologies. Education should make learners self-reliant and competent. Schools should be provided with sufficient infrastructure that allows easy access to resources for both teachers and learners. The Department of Education is encouraged to give more financial support to schools in order to provide the basic infrastructure. Teachers should improvise resources by planning and executing activities. Policy makers have to explore professional development from the side of the participating educators in order to clearly understand what would be best for changing their assessment practice. It is therefore recommended that for effective implementation of assessment policies, the Department of Education should provide adequate knowledgeable curriculum staff to do extensive training for both the educators. Teachers' training or professional development should be longer, though it might be less than their initial training. Teachers should collaborate and establish learning area/subject clusters to resolve mutual curricular challenges. Teachers should assess learners' achievement of learning outcomes as unpacked by the various assessment standards.

# References

Bradley, E. H. et al. 2007. "Qualitative Data Analysis for Health Services Research", *Health Services Research* 156, 618–626.
Duffy, T. M. 2006. *Constructivism: Implications for the Design and Delivery of Instruction.* Indianapolis: Indiana University.
Kramer, D. 2006. *OBE Teaching Toolkit: OBE Strategies, Tools and Techniques for Implementing C2005.* Cape Town: ABC Books.
Michelle, B. 2007. "Data Analysis Strategies for Qualitative Research – Research Corner", *AORN Journal* 7, 103–115.
Plooy, G. M. 2007. *Communications Research Techniques, Methods and Implications.* Claremont: Juta.
Soanes, C. and Stevenson, A. 2008. *Concise Oxford English Dictionary.* Oxford: Oxford University Press.
Spady, W. G. 1994. *Outcomes-based Education, Critical Issues and Answers.* Virginia: American Association of School Administrators.
Terre Blanche, M. 2008. *Research in Practice: Applied Methods for the Social Sciences.* Sandston: Juda Academy.

Tompkins, W. G. 2008. *Research Designs: Choosing and Fine-tuning a Design for your Study.* London: Sage Publications.
Trochim, M. K. 2006. *Research Methods Knowledge Base.* Mason: Atomic Dog Publications.

# CHAPTER FIFTEEN

## PERSPECTIVES ON TEACHER EDUCATION FLOWING FROM A COMPARISON OF RELIGIOUS EDUCATION IN MEXICO AND THAILAND

### FERDINAND J. POTGIETER
#### PROFESSOR, NORTH-WEST UNIVERSITY, SOUTH AFRICA

**Abstract**

This investigation into religious education (RE) in Mexico and Thailand seeks to understand in what ways two countries with such different histories, populations and cultures had tackled the problems associated with the provision of RE in their schools. Six implications regarding teacher education are drawn from the comparison: (a) awareness and knowledge of socio-economic conditions as well as the prevailing situation in schools and in society in general; (b) understanding that the state, church, school and parental home are four distinct and independent (also interdependent) societal relationships; (c) realization that the values of any societal relationship should in principle not be imposed on the school; (d) understanding that RE should be granted a place in all schools; (e) treating cultural and religious diversity as national assets and nation-building blocks; (f) understanding how educators could be tolerant of religious differences without sacrificing the core pedagogical principles of schooling.

**Keywords**

Teacher Education, Religion Education, Religious Diversity, Societal Relationships

# On a Methodological Note

For purposes of developing the conceptual-theoretical framework (historical background, teacher education and tolerance issues), I made use of the historical-analytical method, employing an implied and embedded interpretive-constructivist approach to the data (Onwuegbuzie, Johnson and Collins, 2009: 114–139). My analysis of the key words of the investigation led me to draft a theoretical framework in terms of which I could interpretively approach the education systems (and, more specifically, teacher education) in Mexico and Thailand, and with which I could formulate an opinion about the degree to which they seem to be compatible with the implications that I have drawn towards the end of the paper (Ritchie & Lewis, 2003). Since I approached the two education systems descriptively and weighed my findings against the conceptual-theoretical framework discussed below, my research method in analysing RE in Mexico and Thailand can be referred to as descriptive-normative (Creswell & Garrett, 2008).

## *Historical Background*

Contemporary Mexico is rooted in Roman Catholicism which arrived in the territory with the Spanish conquistadors in the sixteenth century. Many struggles ensued between state (supported mainly by anti-clerical Liberals; secularists) and the Church (driven mainly by politically active clergy and pro-clerical Conservatives) (APEC, 2012).

Liberals and Conservatives alternated in power during the period from the War of Independence (1810–21) to the Mexican-American War (1846–48). A liberal constitution (1857) guaranteed basic freedoms. It deprived ecclesiastical orders of the right to own land, and secularized education. In response, conservative forces launched a coup that evolved into a civil war and finally to a clergy-supported occupation by French forces under Maximilian I (1864–67). The final decades of the nineteenth century were marked by the autocratic rule of Porfirio Díaz who allowed the Church and clergy to expand their temporal powers despite the restrictions imposed by the 1857 Constitution (Berkeley Centre, 2012).

In 1917, a new Constitution reaffirmed the liberal principles of the 1857 document, but went further in restricting the authority and influence of the Church (Berkley Centre, 2012). After the uprising of 1929, the state (represented by the Institutional Revolutionary Party) and the Church reached a tacit agreement by which the former reduced its control over Church activities and the latter refrained from criticizing the government. This situation remained in place until the 1980s, although the National

Action Party and its socially conservative positions received tacit support from the Church from the 1930s on (Berkeley Centre, 2012).

In 2011, Mexico's Senate approved constitutional reform that paved the way for religious education in the country's public schools. The reform (following Pope Benedict XVI's visit to the country) is widely seen as a victory for the Catholic Church in Mexico (Rueda, 2012). Article 24 of the Constitution used to grant everyone in the country the right to pick and exercise the religion of their choice. It now also grants people the right to "uphold their ethical convictions, freedom of conscience and religion".

Senators also changed Article 40 of the Constitution so that it described Mexico as a "secular nation", proof, according to certain politicians, that their parties respected the separation of Church and state in Mexico (Rueda, 2012).

Beginning with the colonial period, education had always been the duty of the Catholic Church. After 1810, a public education system was begun out of concern that the Church was imposing its values and beliefs on education and schools. Religious influences of any sort were banned in the public primary schools (grades one through six). The federal government controlled the curriculum and provided the textbooks for primary schools (APEC, 2012). However, the Salinas administration's 1991 proposal to remove all constitutional restrictions on the Roman Catholic Church, approved by the legislature the following year, allowed for a more realistic Church–state relationship (Merrill & Miró, 2012).

In Thailand, Buddhism first appeared during the 3rd century BC. It soon gained wide acceptance because its emphasis on tolerance and individual initiative complemented the Thai sense of inner freedom. King Ramkhamhaeng (AD 1275–1317) established Theravada Buddhism as Thailand's dominant religion. In 1360, Ramathibodi (r.1351–69) declared Theravada Buddhism as the official religion and compiled a legal code based on Hindu legal texts and Thai custom that remained in effect until the late nineteenth century ("Religion", 2012). Although Buddhism became the primary and state religion, Thais have always subscribed to the ideal of religious freedom. From 1972 to 1992 the new government, led by Prime Minister Thanin Kraivichien (an anticommunist), introduced military rule that was more repressive in many ways than the earlier military regimes. Censorship continued and the regime tightly controlled labour unions and purged suspected communists from the civil service and educational institutions (Library of Congress, 2012).

Muslims comprise Thailand's largest religious minority. Islam is said to have been introduced to the Malay Peninsula by Arab traders and adventurers during the thirteenth century. Thailand's Muslims enjoy state support and are free to teach and practise their religion according to their own tenets. Christianity was introduced to Thailand by European missionaries in the sixteenth and seventeenth centuries (US Department of State, 2005). From the mid-sixteenth century Thailand opened up to French Catholic influence until the mid-seventeenth century when it was curtailed and the country returned to a strengthening of its own cultural ideology ("Religion", 2012).

## Teacher education in Mexico and Thailand

In Mexio, elementary education was under the Lancasterian model for most of the nineteenth century (Leal & Romo, 2010: 424). From 1823 to 1887 a few independent teachers, individually trained mainly by personal tutors or in monasteries, were professionally hired by municipal authorities, until the federal government signed a contract with the Lancasterian Company to operate the schools for the training of monitors – teachers for basic teaching skills (counting, reading, writing and individual discipline). The education of these teachers was oriented to the training of advanced students as monitors for the initial pupils in elementary education, by the available teachers professionally appointed by the municipalities (Leal & Romo, 2010: 424). Formally, this system became the Directory for Primary Instruction in the government.

Later on, the National Preparatory School (created in 1867 in Mexico City) became responsible for the training of teachers at the time of its establishment. This model of higher education aimed to put together all available knowledge and sciences as well as their positivist methods of learning. It rapidly expanded all over the country, and was in charge of teacher training but only with a special course of Comparative Pedagogic Methodology in the curriculum of higher middle schools. In 1869, the Normal School for Teachers (*Escuela Normal de Profesores*) was founded. This Normal School was for male student teachers only (*Escuela Normal para Varones*) and a unified curriculum for teachers and pupils in Mexico City and the two Federal Territories were finally established in 1887, putting an end to the contract with the Lancasterian Company. When the government created the office of Secretary of Justice and Public Instruction in 1887, it also authorized the establishment of the School for Female Teachers (*Escuela Normal para Señoritas*). This school was finally founded in 1890.

Outside Mexico City, quite a few schools for teachers were established in San Luis Potosí and Guadalajara (1849), Puebla and Nuevo León (1881), Michoacán, Querétaro and Veracruz (1886). Jalapa, the most influential, had already graduated 275 teachers by the end of the eighties, whilst the one in Mexico City had graduated only 78 teachers. All these normal schools also opened basic schools for children as a space for teachers' practice (Leal & Romo, 2010: 422–423). In 1889, The Mexican State, through the municipalities, extended the number of courses in primary education from four to six years (Leal & Romo, 2010: 423). In 1908, the Law for the School for Primary Teachers was launched to support, in a unified way, the training of teachers for elementary and advanced primary education (Leal & Romo, 2010: 424).

Since the 1940s, an array of different types of teachers and ways of training them can be seen. First, there were those who were trained to provide basic education (reading and counting) by the Lancasterian agencies. As "cultural missioners" they were incorporated mainly as social agents to promote literacy and to help with the creation of schools and community organizations (Leal & Romo, 2010: 432). Secondly, there were the independent teachers who were credited by municipalities, and who were finally incorporated through the Normal Schools (as were those who graduated at Urban Normal Schools, established at the end of the previous century). This model, or type, also made provision for the Rural Schools for Teachers. They worked in what were called "Unitarian Schools" which had offered (and still have to offer) only one or two grades of the six courses that were prescribed for primary school education (Leal & Romo, 2010: 432). Urban teachers worked in more comfortable conditions and salaries in schools that provided the whole set of six courses designed for primary school education. Thirdly, there were those who were trained by the Higher Normal School (also founded in 1924) which was located within the Higher Studies School, and which formed part of the Faculty of Philosophy and Literature in the National University of Mexico. They were considered as highly trained teachers for the Normal Schools in charge of training (primary) teachers. Fourthly, there were those who studied to become teachers after 1984. They could do so, at the time, following a pre-service programme in a normal school, or following an in-service programme in the National Pedagogic University. Both these trajectories would raise them to college level. Fifthly, teachers who have graduated either from a normal school, or from the National Pedagogic University, can enrol for further or postgraduate degrees at any of the private or state universities in the country. Since the normal schools were created, the teaching profession has become a state profession and every one of the graduates from a public normal school is assured of a teaching post and thus of becoming a government employee (Leal & Romo, 2010: 433).

Teacher education in Thailand prior to the requirement of the Licence to Practice, or Teacher Certificate, issued in 2006 can be divided into five phases. Each phase reflected the political as well as social context at the time. These phases are: Western power over Asia and Southeast Asia in 1892–1931; teacher training and teacher education under the democratic constitution 1932–40; teacher education after World War II 1941–73; teacher education after the student uprising in 1974–1980; and the introduction of the teacher and teaching licence from 1999 to the present (Thongthew, 2010: 983).

The Department of Education was established in 1887 during the reign of King Rama V to take charge not only of the development of the curriculum and instructional designs for all schools, but also with regard to the development of education for Buddhist monks in monasteries, for health care personnel in hospitals and for museum personnel. The curriculum and methods of study utilized in Thai schools before the 1950s were influenced by the British system and the Japanese system but later on developed after the United States of America's models (Thongthew, 2010: 977–978). King Rama VI of Thailand had launched the Compulsory Education Act in 1921 to ensure that all Thai citizens from 7 to 14 years old would have access to six years of formal primary school. This Act imposed greater demands on primary school teachers, both in quantity and quality (Thongthew, 2010: 978). During 1936–46, Thailand had undergone rapid expansion of primary education throughout the country to improve literacy levels as well as to familiarize and prepare Thai citizens for the new political system of democracy. The main focus was on the expansion of primary schools to serve students both in Bangkok and in provincial areas. Teacher training schools were then initiated on a much wider scale to provide enough teachers for the newly constructed primary schools (ibid.). After World War II education in Thailand was under the influence of the United States of America. The American liberal concept of education was thus imported into the Thai educational system. Thai teachers and teacher educators were selected and sent to be educated in various renowned teacher training institutions in USA. Upon their graduation, they had brought back "advanced knowledge" and "new concepts" in education, and had initiated the new phase of Thai education (Thongthew, 2010: 979). In 1954 the Department of Teacher Training was established as a formal unit of the Ministry of Education, to ensure that the existing teacher training schools for teachers at all school levels were of compatible standards and aligned to the needs of the nation. As mentioned earlier, prior to 1954 there were various kinds of teaching certificates offered by a number of teacher training institutes: certificates to teach in agricultural schools, in technical schools, in primary schools etc. These teacher training schools were established mainly to serve the public's need for specific kind of certificates. These teacher training schools were also entitled to set their own standards for their graduates (Thongthew, 2010: 985–986).

After the October 1973 student uprising, a major educational reform movement emerged. Students as well as radical educators cried for greater social justice and a more open and relevant curriculum. They wanted to get rid of the previous rigid and restrictive curriculum designed by educators during the time of the military regime. During 1974–80 students had to take up to 140 credits for their bachelor degree in education, covering subject contents in special groups of study as prescribed in the national curriculum as well as general education. Courses offered at most teacher education colleges and universities focused on the understanding of complex issues in society and in the educational system (Thongthew, 2010: 986).

There seem to be at least two major issues as far as teacher education in Thailand is concerned. The Board of Teacher Education Approval and Review (appointed by the Teacher Council of Thailand), established in 2003, has to assure teaching professional standards for all teachers in Thailand. All teachers, especially those who are involved in teacher education, are obliged to try and convince the Board of Teacher Education Approval and Review of their alignment to the professional standards set by the Board. The first major issue emerges as the teacher educators and those responsible for the process of teacher education are trying to align their teacher education programmes with all the requirements of the professional standard. Although teacher education programmes that had been developed and submitted seem to follow the prescribed standards, language format, as well as certain terminology required for the phrasing of these descriptions, it nevertheless seems doubtful whether the submitted and approved teacher education programmes do indeed lead to quality teacher training. The programme quality seems to focus mainly on the quality of the curriculum writer's expertise in document-drafting, especially as it either succeeds in demonstrating (or fails to demonstrate) the alignment of a particular curriculum to the professional standards that had been set, and not in the actual training of the kind of quality teachers that are expected (Thongthew, 2010: 991).

The second issue concerns the lack of theoretical, pedagogical knowledge and most importantly, the critical thinking skills in existing teacher education programs (Thongthew, 2010: 991). The certificates and the approval process have been criticized as the cause for the radical shift to mere teacher training skills as prescribed by the ten categories of Professional Teaching Standards. According to Thongthew (2010: 991–992) the "professional standards" have dominated the Thai teacher education curriculum. The tendency to intellectual inquiry – the very element that allows teachers to engage in the deliberate search to extend knowledge of pedagogic principles and to solve complex issues in education – have been reduced to mere training skills, *per se*. She also argued that to be effective as a teacher, one must not only comply with the teaching professional standards but also engage in research that relates study to the understanding of the social context as well as teacher ideology. To reach the balance between such intellectual inquiry and the required teaching competencies is essential for routine tasks of teaching. Teacher education programmes in Thailand must be reconstructed so as to offer room for more reflective practices (Thongthew, 2010: 992).

*Tolerance issues*

In Mexico, the 1980s and early 1990s witnessed a notable shift in religious affiliation and in Church–state relations in Mexico. Although Mexico remains predominantly Roman Catholic, evangelical churches have dramatically expanded their membership. Dozens of evangelical denominations have engaged in strong recruitment efforts since 1970. Protestants of "evangelical" affiliation – the terminology used by Mexican census officials – surged from 1.8% in 1970 to 3.3% in 1980 and to 4.9% in 1990. The Mormons also reported that membership surged from 248,000 in 1980 to 688,000 by 1993 (Merrill and Miró, 2012).

Motivated in part by the evangelical challenge, the leadership of the Roman Catholic Church has sought greater visibility, speaking out on sensitive public issues and ignoring constitutional bans on clerical involvement in politics. These actions ultimately led in 1992 to dramatic constitutional changes and a resumption of diplomatic relations with the Vatican (Merrill and Miró, 2012). These negotiations resulted in amendments to the Constitution that granted greater freedom to churches (Berkley Centre, 2012). The 1992 Constitution provided that education should avoid privileges of religion, and that one religion or its members might not be given preference in education over another. Religious instruction was prohibited in public schools; however, religious associations were free to maintain private schools, which received no public funds.

The 2001 Constitution explicitly banned discrimination based on religious affiliation. Under the seven decades of PRI rule in Mexico, priests and other religious officials were not allowed to vote until after

1992. However, broadly speaking, the Constitution provided for freedom of religion, and other laws and policies contribute to the generally free practice of religion. The Government generally respected religious freedom in practice; however, there were some restrictions at the local level. There was no change in the status of respect for religious freedom by the Government in the period 2009–10 (UNHCR, 2010).

Incidents of societal abuses or discrimination based on religious affiliation, belief or practice usually occurred in small rural communities in the south. Government officials, non-governmental organizations and evangelical and Roman Catholic representatives agreed that these conflicts were often attributable to political, ethnic or land disputes related to the traditional practices and customs of indigenous communities (UNHCR, 2010).

The emphasis on homogeneously implementing national schooling and curriculum standards without consideration of local context has created a situation where the tension between national standards and local needs could affect the quality of students' education. The educational possibilities for children of indigenous ancestry are particularly at risk. National versus local is a significant topic in Mexico, as is the issue of diverse ethnic groups and the extent to which students will be well served by national curriculum standards (Cisneros-Cohernour, Moreno & Merchant, 1999).

In broad terms, we may distinguish three main periods of multicultural education in twentieth- and twenty-first-century Mexico: the post-revolutionary period of "classic" *indigenismo* (until the eighties), the period of ethnic mobilization and indigenous multiculturalism (during the eighties and nineties) and the current period of official inter-culturalism (since the turn of the century) (Dietz, 2012: 3).

Historically, the relationship between the Mexican state and the private education sector has comprised conflicts and disagreements, as well as tolerance and concurrence. Its complex history is permeated by the ideological alternatives of the Mexican state during the twentieth century, the cyclical dilemma between centralism and federalism, governmental definitions of a national educational project and by the diversity of political, normative and practical actions (Rodriguez & Ordorika, 2011: 9).

In Thailand, the relationship between missionaries and the people was sometimes good and sometimes bad. It depended, first of all, upon the missionaries themselves, in particular on how much attention they paid to the customs of those to whom they preached the gospel. We have inadequate evidence with regard to this matter, because much of the information on it was written by Christians, especially by missionaries themselves. Generally they praised themselves and blamed others. Secondly, the persecution of Roman Catholicism was due to political causes, for example, war between the Siamese and the Spaniards in the course of the first quarter of the seventeenth century. Diplomatic relations were not reopened with European nations until the nineteenth century. During the crisis that ensued, especially while the French soldiers were leaving, the French missionaries and their converts were imprisoned. Finally, persecution recurred in 1769 and 1782, when King Tak Sin went through a spell of insanity. A Thai church history says that one day the King stayed in the temple and told the people that he was a god who could ascend to the heaven. As the missionaries and the Christian converts did not believe in this, he did not permit their existence. A number of Christians were killed; some of them were burnt alive. However, persecutions only made them stronger in their faith. In comparison, persecution of Protestantism was only of brief duration. Persecution usually occurred due to two main factors: first, the people wanted to retain their customs and way of life; secondly, they wanted to preserve their religion. It was understood that anyone who did not care about the nation's social customs was a rebel against Thai society, and had to be punished accordingly (Saad, 1975: 22–27).

Daniel McGilvary (1828–1911), an American Presbyterian missionary who played an important role in the expansion of Protestantism in Northern Siam, realized that the gospel could not be proclaimed unrestrictedly unless religious tolerance were promulgated (Saad, 1975: 22–27). The High Commissioner helped him prepare a petition to the King for a pronouncement on religious tolerance. Fortunately, a favourable reply came from King Chulalongkorn, granting all of his requests. A part of this edict of religious tolerance, promulgated on 8 October 1878, says that religious and civil duties do not come in conflict. Whoever wishes to embrace any religion after seeing that it is true and proper to be embraced, is allowed to do so without any restriction, and the responsibility for a right or wrong choice rests on the individual making the choice. All persons are permitted to follow the dictates of their own conscience in all matters of religious belief and practice. Christians, as well as missionaries of other religions, have been permitted to proclaim their respective faiths throughout the country ever since (Saad, 1975: 22–27). From this conceptual-theoretical framework (historical background, teacher education and tolerance issues), a number of implications for teacher education with regard to religious tolerance in Mexico and Thailand emerge.

*The implications for teacher education of the relative situations in*
*Mexico and Thailand with regard to religious tolerance*

1. During their initial training, prospective teachers should be made aware of the prevailing socio-economic conditions in their country, and particularly in the schools where they will eventually be deployed to teach as professionals. In Mexico, they have to be cognisant of the ongoing conflict between state and church, and about the current uneasy truce between state and church. Future teachers have to be trained not only to understand their place in this conflict, but also to concentrate on their work as professional educators in their schools.

2. Future teachers have to be equipped with the necessary knowledge about the prevailing situation in schools and in society in general, particularly with the ability to refrain from becoming involved or embroiled in any conflict between state and church, despite the fact that the conflict might occasionally also affect the school at which they ply their profession, and on their own work as educators.

3. Their training should contain a solid understanding of societal relationships, so that they would understand that state, Church, school and parental home are four distinct and independent (though also interdependent) societal relationships. They have to realize that the values of neither state nor Church nor parental home (nor any other societal relationship) should in principle be imposed on the school. While this is difficult as far as the state is concerned (because many schools are state schools or state-funded schools), they have to insist on the school maintaining its own pedagogical-analytical values in discharging its pedagogical-analytical duties.

4. Future teachers have to be trained to understand that RE should be granted a place in all schools since it is part and parcel of human life and of being a human being. However, they should also be helped to understand that religion in education should never be used as a divisive factor. To assist them to make up their minds about the place and role of RE in schools, they have to be informed about the various models of incorporating (or banning) of religion in public schools.

5. Prospective teachers should be trained to regard cultural and religious diversity in a nation as an asset, and to employ the diversity for purposes of nation building. They have to be trained to be tolerant of religious and other differences, to understand that in doing so they embrace multiculturalism and multireligionism.

6. The history of Thailand is particularly informative. It would be worth the while of both teacher educators as prospective teachers to study the pedagogical history of Thailand to understand the underlying motive for the renowned religious tolerance of the Thai people. (A study of the situation in Mexico could serve as the counterfoil – why not to become embroiled in state–Church conflict and struggle, and hence to practise intolerance and discrimination against people of different religious conviction.) All these studies might inspire future students to understand how an educator could be tolerant of religious differences without in the process sacrificing the core pedagogical principles of schooling.

## Conclusion

Although Mexico and Thailand are geographically far apart, and as far as could be established had no relations, they seem to have struggled with much the same set of problems regarding the provision of RE in their schools. The comparison brought six implications regarding interreligious tolerance and the training of prospective RE teachers to the surface.

## References

APEC Human Resources Development Working Group. 2012. *Education in Mexico* (http://hrd.apec.org/index.php/Education_in_Mexico)

Berkley Centre for Religion, Peace and World Affairs: Resources on faith, ethics and public life. 2012. Georgetown University (http://berkleycenter.georgetown.edu/resources/mexico).

Cisneros-Cohernour, E.J., Moreno, R. and Merchant, B.M.P. 1999. *Evaluating Curriculum Reform in Mexico: Challenges Addressing a Diverse Population.* Paper presented at the Annual Meeting of the American Educational Research Association, Montreal, Quebec, Canada (http://www.eric.ed.gov/ERICWebPortal/search/detailmini.jsp?_nfpb=true&_&ERICExtSearch_SearchValue_0=ED436474&ERICExtSearch_SearchType_0=no&accno=ED436474).

Creswell, J. W. and Garrett, A. L. 2008. "The 'Movement' of Mixed Methods Research and the Role of Educators", *South African Journal of Education* 28: 321–333.

Dietz, G. 2012. "Intercultural Education in Mexico: In Search of a Contextual Paradigm", IAIE International Conference, Veracruz, Mexico (http://www.iaieveracruz.org/ponencias/1/DIETZ.pdf).

Leal, M. A. N. and Romo, S. G. 2010. "Teacher Education in México: History, Trends and Issues", in K. G. Karras and C. C. Wolhuter (eds), *International Handbook on Teachers Education Worldwide.* Athens: Atrapos, pp. 422–434.

Library of Congress. 2012. *One World Nations Online*, "History of Thailand". (http://www.nationsonline.org/oneworld/)

Merrill, T. L. and Miró, R. (eds). 2012. *Mexico*. Religion: Church-State Relations (http://countrystudies.us/mexico/61.htm).

Onwuegbuzie, A. J., Johnson R. B. and Collins K. M. T. 2009. "Call for Mixed Analysis: A Philosophical Framework for Combining Qualitative and Quantitative Approaches", *International Journal of Multiple Research Approaches* 3: 114–139.

"Religion." 2012. (http://www.hellosiam.com/html/thailand/thailand-religion.htm?vm=r)

Ritchie, J. and Lewis, J. 2003. *Qualitative Research Practice.* London: Sage.

Rodriguez-Gomez, R. and Ordorika-Sacristan, I. 2011. "The Chameleon's Agenda: Entrepreneuralization of Private Higher Education in Mexico", in B. Pusser, S. Marginson, K. Kempner & I. Ordorika (eds), *Universities and the Public Sphere. Knowledge creation and state building in the era of globalization.* New York, NY: Routledge-Taylor and Francis (http://www.ses.unam.mx/publicaciones/articulos/RodriguezAndOrdorika2011.pdf).

Rueda, M. 2012. "Mexico: New Constitutional Reform could Allow for Religious Education in Public Schools", Univision News (29 March) (http://univisionnews.tumblr.com/post/20127084750/constitution-reform-mexico-religion-publicschools).

Saad, C. 1975. *The Christian Approach to Buddhists in Thailand.* Bangkok: Suriyaban Publishers (http://thaicrc.com/gsdl/collect/MIS/index/assoc/D1785.dir/1785.pdf).

Thongthew, S. 2010. "Teacher Training and Teacher Education in Thailand", in K.G. Karras and C. C. Wolhuter (eds), *International Handbook on Teachers Education Worldwide.* Athens: Atrapos, pp. 977–993.

UNHCR. 2010. *Report on International Religious Freedom – Mexico.* (http://www.unhcr.org/refworld/publisher,USDOS,,MEX,4cf2d07f12,0.html, accessed December 2012).

US Department of State. 2005. *Thailand.* (International Religious Freedom Reports), (http://www1.umn.edu/humanrts/research/thailand/religious-freedom-report.html).

# CHAPTER SIXTEEN

## PERSPECTIVES ON TEACHER EDUCATION: A COMPARISON OF RELIGIOUS EDUCATION IN ESTONIA AND SOUTH AFRICA

### JOHANNES L. VAN DER WALT
#### PROFESSOR, NORTH-WEST UNIVERSITY, SOUTH AFRICA

**Abstract**

The question that prompted this investigation into religious education (RE) in Estonia and South Africa was whether two countries from such different parts of the world, with such different populations and cultures though with somewhat parallel histories had tackled the same or similar problems regarding the provision of RE in their schools, and if so, in what ways their solutions with regard to RE and teacher education resemble or differ from each other. The purpose of the paper is to present and discuss some of the parallels, resemblances and differences between RE in the two countries as well as the implications for teacher education that flow from the comparison. Nine such implications are discussed: a number of social theory aspects, a few societal theory aspects (regarding connections between societal relationships such as school and state), the need for prospective teachers to attend to diversity studies and to social capital studies, the importance of studying the personal rights and needs of their learners, the importance of social justice studies, the significance of having future RE teachers understanding the true purpose of RE in schools, the need to cover legislation and didactical aspects during teacher training, the importance of dealing with curriculum issues and of understanding the difference between presenting RE in public or state schools, and private or independent schools.

**Keywords**

Religion, Religion Education, Education, Teacher Education, South Africa, Estonia

# Introduction

This investigation into religious education (RE) in Estonia and South Africa originated in the question whether two countries from such different parts of the world, with such vastly different populations and cultures though with somewhat parallel histories, had tackled the same or similar problems regarding the provision of RE in their schools, and if so, in what ways their solutions resemble or differ from each other. The question assumed that people are the same the world over, and that their problems regarding the provision of RE in schools might be roughly the same, of course depending on the prevailing local and historical circumstances. A secondary question was whether certain principles regarding teacher education could be deduced from the parallels and differences observable between these two countries.

The actual study of the historical, religious, cultural and social conditions in Estonia and South Africa was preceded by a study of what it entails to be a good teacher, and how teacher educators could contribute to the effectiveness of future teachers (cf. Dyer, 2002; Korthagen & Vasalos, 2005: 68). This was then followed by a study of various possible approaches of religious education (RE) and of the imperative to inculcate an attitude of religious tolerance in future teachers and their students (Schreiner, 2005). These insights were used as interpretive instruments for analysing the respective histories of Estonia and South Africa with the purpose of deriving a number of principles that should ideally be adhered to in teacher education, particularly for prospective teachers that might in future become involved in RE. (Interpretivism foregrounds the meaning that individuals assign to their experiences (Loubser, 2005: 65).)

# Some Parallels

## *Both countries in transition*

Christianity was accepted in **Estonia** in the thirteenth century (European Studies on Religion and State Interaction, 2012). Since the Reformation of the sixteenth century, the Lutheran church has played a leading role; the network of public schools that emerged by the end of the seventeenth century was closely associated with that church (Schihaleyev, 2012: 2). No fundamental changes took place in the education system under Russian rule from the beginning of the eighteenth century (European Studies on Religion and State Interaction, 2012). After independence from Russia in 1918, however, RE was excluded from primary schools, but retained as a voluntary subject in secondary schools.

After protests and a referendum in 1923, RE was reintroduced in all schools as an interconfessional and optional subject. Although it was possible to opt out, almost all the pupils took the subject until it was banned in 1940 by the authorities of the Soviet occupation. From then onwards, atheistic ideology was statutorily enforced in Estonia, resulting in religion being shifted to the private sphere (Schihaleyev, 2012: 2).

In August 1991, Estonia became independent from the USSR; its new constitution guaranteed freedom of religion (European Studies on Religion and State Interaction, 2012). RE once more became officially possible in schools (Valk, 2012: 1) as an optional/voluntary non-confessional subject (Schihaleyev, 2012: 6–7; Schreiner, 2005: 5). By the late 1990s, RE was taught in approximately 100 out of the 730 public schools, mostly in primary classes and at the upper secondary school level (Valk, 2012: 1; Schreiner, 2005: 5).

Although the indigenous peoples of **Southern Africa** were religious in their traditional ways, they only began to westernize and convert to Christianity from the fifteenth century onwards. Colonization, coupled with Christian missionary work, led to the large-scale Christianization of the people of Southern Africa. British domination from the beginning of the nineteenth century brought no change in this. After 1652, schools in South Africa were intended to prepare (especially White) children to become fully fledged members of the (Reformed) Christian churches. Both Catholic and Reformed Missionary education (for Black and Coloured children) had the purpose of converting people to the Christian religion and to prepare children to become literate members of the church.

On 31 May 1910, South Africa became independent from Great Britain. Because state and religion were traditionally intertwined, there was no strict separation between state and church. The four provinces of the new Union were each allowed to offer RE as before, and missionary education was continued by the churches as before. This situation prevailed until 1967, when the National Party recast RE to suit the ideals of Christian-national education for Whites. (Non-Christians could apply for exemption from attending RE classes in state schools.) Schools for Blacks, Coloureds and Indians were allowed to offer their own forms of RE, but were tacitly expected to offer Christian RE. Although the theory and practice of Christian-national education were attacked by its opponents, mainly because of its Afrikaner and apartheid links, things did not come to a head before the early 1990s. RE in public schools was inter-denominational – neither inter-confessional nor optional. Indoctrination (in the form of Christian-national RE) was a constant possibility (Giliomee, 2012: 75).

The *Bantu Education Act (no. 47)* of September 1953 made education for Blacks an integral part of "separate development" and left the missionaries, who had until then controlled almost all schools for Africans, in a dilemma: either to hand over their schools to the newly created Department of Bantu Education or to keep them under missionary control without government subsidies (Blumfield, 2008). Many of these schools opted to remain independent church schools. In 1963, Christian-national education (CNE) was extended to the so-called Coloureds by the *Coloured Persons Education Act* (1963) (Blumfield, 2008). In the same year, the *Education Act* of 1963 removed Coloured education from the Provincial and Government departments, vesting it in a Division of Education in the Department of Coloured Affairs. Schools were tacitly expected to offer (Christian) RE. In 1965, CNE was extended to Indians by the *Indian Education Act* of 1965. Two years later, the *National Education Policy Act* (39 of 1967) was passed. For the first time, the central government laid down a comprehensive education policy to be followed for Whites in all four provinces. The Act stipulated that Christian RE should be offered in all schools for Whites, and that non-Christians might apply for exemption. Regulation R1192 of 20 June 1975 laid down that religious instruction based on the Bible was to be a compulsory subject for student teachers, though exemption could be granted (Blumfield, 2008).

After the demise of apartheid, South Africa became a country with a democratic government in 1994. The situation described above remained in place until 1996, when the *South African Schools Act* (Act 84 of 1996) was promulgated. This Act brought an end to CNE, and to the compulsory Christian RE in state schools. Like Estonia, South Africa has since been a country in transition.

The new RE Policy promulgated in 2003 relegated confessional religion education to religious institutions and parental homes. Religion/ Religious Education may now be offered in only two forms in schools: religious observances and formal, academic Religious Studies as a school subject. RE is taught in practically all public schools in accordance with the 2003 Policy. However, some schools still teach confessional (Christian) RE, in contravention of the 2003 Policy. The post-2003 situation has shifted confessional or sectarian religion to the private sphere of the parental home and the church, mosque and synagogue.

# Reform Issues

In **Estonia**, the legal sources describing the relationship between Church and state are national law (the Constitution of the Republic of Estonia and acts which regulate the freedom of religion), international law and the decisions of the courts about fundamental freedom and rights. Article 40 of the Constitution guarantees *freedom of religion* (European Studies on Religion and State Interaction, 2012).

*The Education Act* (RT 1, 12, 192; 1992) states the following as the *general goals of education*: to create favourable conditions for the development of personality, family and the nation; to promote the development of ethnic minorities, economic, political and cultural life in Estonia and the preservation of nature in the global economic and cultural context; to teach the values of citizenship and to set up the prerequisites for creating a tradition of lifelong learning nationwide ("Jewish Community in Estonia", 2012).

The restoration of independence in the early 1990s presented a new opportunity for RE. The interrupted tradition of RE stood between several forces: its historical roots; textbooks for confessional RE translated from Finnish and also doubts about the need for RE in the minds of many people (Schihaleyev, 2012: 6–7). Developing RE in the post-Socialist period after 50 years of atheistic propaganda remains a challenging task (Valk, 2012: 1). Estonia remains a Christian shaped country, but only 23% of the population are members of Christian Churches. Other religious communities are much smaller (European Studies on Religion and State Interaction, 2012). This diversity draws our attention to the issue of religious tolerance in Estonia.

**South Africa's** new Constitution (Act 108 of 1996) entrenches *freedom of religion, belief and opinion* (Art 15). *The South African Schools Act*, No. 84 of 1996, provides as follows regarding religious observances: "Subject to the Constitution and any applicable provincial law, religious observances may be conducted at a public school under rules issued by the governing body if such observances are conducted on an equitable basis and attendance at them by learners and members of staff is free and voluntary." (Art 7.)

The advent of democracy presented the new government with new challenges with respect to RE. The main questions were: (a) how to eradicate the Christian-national education past that had been in force from 1967 to 1994; (b) how to bridge the deep religious, cultural, political, ethnical and racial divide that existed among South Africans at the time; (c) how to promote the values of the 1996 Constitution, among other basic human rights, including tolerance of religious and other differences; and (d) how to formulate a policy on religion in/and education that would be acceptable to most South Africans.

After much deliberation, the Minister of Education proclaimed the present *Policy of Religion in Education* in 2003. This Policy is in line with the Constitution, the Schools Act and the *Manifesto on Democracy, Values and Education* of the Department of Education in 2001. Stipulations were made for accommodating religious observances in public schools. A new curriculum was designed for the new school subject known as Religion Studies, which is the academic (comparative) study of religions. Proselytizing is not allowed and no special emphasis is placed on any specific religion. The legacy of the apartheid regime has made people distrustful of the abuse of religion for political purposes. This could be the reason why South Africans have quietly acquiesced when confessional religion was banned from the public sphere in terms of its new Constitution (Act 108 of 1996), its latest policy on religion in schools (2003) and its Schools Act (Act 84 of 1996).

Just as in Estonia, people wish to find their place in the pluralistic world by themselves. South Africa has never experienced a hiatus in the teaching of RE, but is nevertheless facing serious challenges. There are still two unresolved issues: (a) should confessional RE indeed have been banned from public schools? and (b) what should be the nature of RE in a modern secularized and pluralistic society? Although 70% of South Africans are nominally Christians, only a small percentage regularly attends church. The remaining percentage is made up of Muslims, Hindus, Jews and indigenous religions. This diversity also draws our attention to the issue of religious tolerance in South Africa.

Both education systems seem to struggle with the same set of issues regarding religious tolerance in education:

- intolerance among people and groups, the problem of state domination, and the issue of being societies in transition;
- the issue of diversity, and how to promote religious tolerance and nation building;
- the recognition of human rights;
- the problem of the relationship between state and Church, state (civil life) and religion;
- the issue of how to employ RE as an important educational instrument; and
- attention to various didactical aspects, including the development of a curriculum for RE

# Teacher Education Issues that Emerge from the Comparison of the Two Systems

*Teacher Education in South Africa and Estonia*

Space does not allow for a detailed discussion of the history of teacher education in the two countries. Suffice it to say that in **South Africa** before 2000, initial teacher education for secondary schools took place at Higher Education Institutions (HEIs) such as universities and technikons, and for primary schools at colleges of education. In 2001, the colleges of education were all incorporated into HEIs; all initial teacher education now takes place in HEIs and in some accredited private institutions. Several considerations, including the cost of higher education at universities, have recently forced the Department of Education to consider the reopening of three former teacher education colleges in far-flung areas in Mpumalanga, Kwazulu-Natal and the Eastern Cape (South Africa Info, 2013). Currently, teacher education for **Estonian** and Russian speaking students is offered at universities as well as at a small number of accredited private institutions. Universities have different curricula for the two mother tongue groups. In both countries, parts of the curriculum are the same for secondary and primary student teachers, but other parts differ depending on specialization. While in South Africa pre-schoolers (Reception Year Group or Grade 0) and kindergarten teachers are also trained at universities, in Estonia this training takes place at the Tallinn Teacher Training Seminar (or Pedagogical College) (Kukemelk et al., 2010: 1190–1192).

# At least Nine Aspects of Teacher Education to Attend to

There are at least nine aspects to be attended to in the training (education) of prospective RE teachers.

## Social theory aspects

Prospective RE teachers should be well versed in social theory, particularly theory pertaining to societies in transition. Estonia and South Africa have only recently emerged from a turbulent past, and are still struggling with unresolved issues. As the European Commission (2000: 32) concluded, social diversity in such countries may both create problems and enrich social life. Should social, religious, ethnic and cultural diversity therefore be promoted or rather discouraged? Should confessional/non-confessional, or rather inter-confessional RE be included in the curriculum? What are the advantages and the drawbacks of inclusion/exclusion? Should confessional/non-confessional/inter-confessional RE play a part in the civic education of the students? What role can and should teachers play in the teaching of RE to diverse groups of school students? What is democracy, and how can RE serve the ideals of democracy? How does a teacher find solutions to the problems that he or she encounters in classrooms?

*Societal theory*

Prospective RE teachers should also be trained in societal theory. The histories of Estonia and South Africa prove that teachers should understand how to maintain fundamentally healthy relationships between school, state and Church, the state and religion. Estonians witnessed the situation of state domination during the communist era (1940–91), and South Africa during the era of state-enforced apartheid (1948–94). A healthy distance between school, state and Church must be maintained. State, school and Church must cooperate and maintain a relationship that does not deteriorate into church domination on the one hand, or total secularism (totally nothing to do with church or religion) on the other. RE should be offered in an environment of hearty cooperation and cordial relations between these three societal relationships, and not in a situation dominated by any one of them. Further, as the European Commission (2000: 11) pointed out, the relationship between school and society is a vital ingredient in policy-making.

*Diversity studies and social capital studies*

Prospective RE teachers should be immersed in diversity studies. They should not only understand the notions of diversity, pluralism, exclusivism, inclusivism, pluralism, dialogic pluralism, religious relativism (Vermeer & Van der Ven, 2004), inclusivity, tolerance and non-discrimination, but should learn to understand the roles of such approaches when teaching RE. They should also be trained to guard against missionary work, evangelization and proselytization in schools. They should furthermore appreciate the role that RE can play in the creation of social capital in their country and in their social surroundings, thereby contributing to nation-building.

*Social justice studies*

Future RE teachers should be exposed to social justice studies. They should understand as the principles of social justice: "Each person is to have an equal right to the most extensive basic liberty compatible with a similar liberty for others," and "Social and economic inequalities are to be arranged so that they are both (a) reasonably expected to be to everyone's advantage, and (b) attached to positions and offices open to all" (Rawls, 2007: 571). These principles apply to the basic structure of society. They govern the assignment of rights and duties, and regulate the distribution of social and economic advantages. Justice is fairness (Rawls, 2007: 572, 573). Injustice, Rawls concludes, is simply inequalities that are not to the benefit of all. The teaching of RE should, therefore, contribute to fairness.

### *Understand personal rights and needs of learners*

Prospective RE teachers should understand that their learners have a certain number of constitutionally entrenched and guaranteed human rights, such as freedom of religion, opinion, conviction, expression and conscience. These rights have to be respected, among others by allowing learners to opt out of RE when they feel that what is being taught is in contravention with their personal religious convictions. Teachers must also be taught to tread the fine line between education as leading, guiding and equipping on the one hand and indoctrination on the other.

### *Understand the true purpose of RE*

Future RE teachers should gain insight into the purpose of RE, which is not to indoctrinate or to increase the membership of some church or religion. Its true purpose is to guide the learners to higher levels of personal development and to greater levels of spiritual maturity. If this ideal can only be achieved through confessional RE, the teacher should encourage a learner to opt out of inter- or non-confessional RE in a public school, and to enrol at an independent or private school where such RE is provided. The non-confessional or inter-confessional RE, i.e. teaching and learning *about* the major religions (education about religion [cf. Vermeer & Van der Ven, 2004: 53]) provided in a public school should not indoctrinate or violate learners' basic human rights; it should be constructive, lead to greater spiritual maturity in a world characterized by diversity and pluralism.

### *Legislation and didactical aspects*

Prospective RE teachers should be well informed about the legislation of their country with respect to RE offerings in schools. They should also be well trained in the subject-didactical aspects of teaching RE as a subject.

### *Curriculum issues*

Prospective RE teachers should be expected to master the prescribed curriculum for RE. RE teachers tend to neglect the subject because of the minimal time that is normally allocated to it. They should also resist efforts by the teachers of the "more important" subjects in school to appropriate the time set aside for RE for the students to master the other subjects. RE has a purpose of its own within the curriculum which should not be lost sight of.

### State or public, and private or independent school

Future RE teachers should understand the key difference between RE in a public, state funded or state subsidized school, and a private or independent school, that is completely privately funded (and partially state subsidized). While all the principles regarding the teaching of RE should be adhered to also in a private or independent school, the content of RE may be confessional. This form of RE should, however, also not violate any of the rights of the learners.

## Conclusion

The histories of Estonia and South Africa show such a number of remarkable resemblances that a comparison of the two countries in terms of culture, religion, religious studies/religious instruction, society and diversity was quite viable. They even share dark periods of state and foreign domination, and some of their key dates broadly coincide. Although they are geographically far apart, and had no relations, they seem to have struggled with much the same set of problems regarding the provision of RE in their schools. The comparison brought the following nine clear-cut principles regarding interreligious tolerance and the training of prospective RE teachers to the surface: a number of social theory aspects, a few societal theory aspects (regarding connections between societal relationships such as school and state), the need for prospective teachers to attend to diversity studies and to social capital studies, the importance of studying the personal rights and needs of their learners, the importance of social justice studies, the significance of having future RE teachers understanding the true purpose of RE in schools, the need to cover legislation and didactical aspects during teacher training, the importance of dealing with curriculum issues, and of understanding the difference between presenting RE in public or state schools, and private or independent schools.

# References

Blumfield, B. 2008. *A Timeline of South African Events in Education in the Twentieth Century.* (Unpublished research report). Pretoria.

Dyer, J. 2002. "Characteristics and Behaviours of Effective Social Education Teachers", *Ethos P-6* 10(3), 8–10.

European Commission. Directorate-General for Education and Culture. 2000. *European Report on the Quality of School Education. Sixteen quality indicators. Report based on the work of the Working Committee on Quality Indicators.* Luxembourg: Office for Official Publications of the European Communities. ISBN 92-894-0536-8.

European Studies on Religion and State Interaction. 2012. "Estonia", http://www.euresisnet.eu/Pages/ReligionAndState/ESTONIA.aspx (accessed 16 October 2012).

Giliomee, H. 2012. *Die laaste Afrikanerleiers (The last Afrikaner Leaders.)* Cape Town: Tafelberg Publishers.

Korthagen, F. and Vasalos. 2005. "Levels in Reflection: Core Reflection as a Means to Enhance Professional Growth", *Teachers and Teaching* 11(1), 47–71.

Kukemelk, H., Transberg, K., Ginter, J. and Raam, A. 2010. "Teacher Education in Estonia", in K. G. Karras and C. C. Wolhuter (eds), *International Handbook on Teachers' Education Worldwide. Issues and Challenges* (Volumes I and II). Athens: Atrapos Editions.

"The Jewish Community in Estonia", Estonia official website. 2012. http://estonia.eu/about-estonia/society/the-jewish-community-in-estonia.html (accessed 16 October 2012).

Loubser, C. P. 2005. *Environmental Education: Some South African Perspectives.* Pretoria: Van Schaik Publishers.

Rawls, J. 2007. "A Theory of Justice", in H. La Follette, *Ethics in Practice.* Oxford: Blackwell, pp. 565–577.

Republic of South Africa. 2003. *National Policy on Religion and Education.* Pretoria: Ministry of Education. 4 August. (Extension of National Education Policy Act, No 27 of 1996).

Schihaleyev, O. 2012. "Religion and Religious Education in Estonia in Historical Perspective." Paper read at ISREV Conference, Turku, Finland, July 2012. (Olga Schihaleyev is Researcher Religious Education, Faculty of Theology, University of Tartu, Tartu, Estonia.)

Schreiner, P. 2005. "Religious Education in Europe", Oslo: Comenius Institute, Oslo University, http://resources.eun.org/etwinning/europa2.pdf (accessed 12 December 2014).

South Africa Info. 2013. "SA to Reopen Teacher Education Colleges", http://www.southafrica.info/about/education/teachers-250412.htm#.UWvOKrX3Gfk (accessed 15 April 2013).

Valk, P. 2012. "Some Good Examples about RE Teacher Training in Estonia", www.mmiweb.org.uk/cogree/conferences/vienna/cogree/.../valk.doc (accessed 11 October 2012). (The late Pille Valk was Lecturer in Practical Theology, Tartu University, Tartu, Estonia.)

Vermeer, P. and Van der Ven, J. A. 2004. "Looking at the Relationship between Religions: An Empirical Study among Secondary School Students", *Journal of Empirical Theology* 17(1), 36–59.

# Chapter Seventeen

# Perspectives on Teacher Education in South Africa: A Comparison of Life Skills Education in a Secondary School Musical and Traditional Classroom Context

## Amanda S. Potgieter
### Lecturer, North-West University, South Africa

## Abstract

This paper reports on how participation in a secondary school musical production, within a life skills education programme for the subject Life Orientation, may contribute pedagogically towards equipping learners for meaningful living in a transforming society. It focuses on creating a dialogic-educative space for life skills attainment and practice while staging a secondary school musical. The traditional classroom displays a propensity towards monologism whereas the musical acts as a centripetal force towards dialogue. Four implications regarding teacher education in South Africa are drawn from this comparative study between secondary school musicals, as holograms of reality, and the traditional secondary school classroom as simulated depictions of reality: (a) school musicals are pedagogical practice grounds for life skills attainment, including social justice; (b) they provide a stage for discovering and exercising talents; (c) they offer opportunities for social interaction within a safe dialogic space; (d) participation instils co-responsibility, mutual and reciprocal trust and meaning-making.

## Keywords

School Musical, Dialogue, Monologue, Life Skills Education, Teacher Training

## Dialogic-educative Space

Dialogue is a tool for cultural and pedagogical intervention in human development and learning (Du Preez, 2006: 43; Rule, 2004: 1). Dialogue mediates the cognitive and socio-conventional (i.e. cultural) spaces between all relevant role-players and stakeholders in a musical production, as well as between what the learner (as participant in the musical production) knows and understands and what he or she has yet to learn, know and understand.

One of the principal functions of a secondary school musical production is to provide appropriate and adequate dialogic and educative space to allow for the creation of interactive opportunities and encounters for all relevant role-players and stakeholders (Du Preez, 2006: 44). The fact that these activities seem to develop skills more effectively in extra-curricular activities than in traditional teaching-learning spaces (like classrooms) is also emphasized in the body of scholarship and learners reflected that they had learnt emotional, cognitive, physical, interpersonal and social skills better through participation in organized out-of-school contexts (Wood, Larson & Brown, 2009: 297; Fredricks, 2011: 2; Fredricks & Eccles, 2005: 508). Participation in organized school activities also helps learners to develop life skills such as problem-solving, time management, goal setting, decision-making and leadership skills.

## Secondary School Musicals as Dialogic-educative Space

The secondary school musical provides an opportunity for learners to enter into a safe dialogical space for life skills attainment. Educators usually provide the opportunity for learners to take part but it remains the learners' choice whether they want to participate or not. By participating in the staging of the musical learners acquire reasoning skills through interaction with their peers, as well as their educators and other role players involved in the production (Potgieter, 2012: 121). The interaction between these role players is often confrontational but always encourages dialogue. My study documents a single secondary school experience in a developing country context and highlights the role of extra-mural secondary school musical productions within a Life Orientation education context. It enhances our understanding of the ontological and epistemological limits of Life Orientation education. Musical productions support learners towards a culture in which the South African constitutional and democratic values of human dignity, equality and freedom can be realized as an integral part of the subject Life Orientation.

A secondary school musical essentially remains a pedagogical event, because it represents a purposive socio-conventional intervention in individual and communal human development which is saturated with the values and history of the particular society and community in which it is located and contextualised. As a tool for cultural and pedagogical intervention, dialogue is not only pervasive in its range of use, but also powerful in its pedagogical possibilities. Be it through on-stage dialogue between characters, between members of the cast and the production team, between the production team and the audience, moments of interaction between the cast and the audience, dance, music or eclectic combinations of the above, dialogue mediates the cognitive and socio-conventional spaces between all role-players and stakeholders, as well as between what the learner as participant knows and understands and what he or she has yet to learn, know and understand.

It follows that one of the principal functions of a secondary school musical production is to provide appropriate and adequate dialogic-educative space and to create interactive opportunities for all relevant role-players and stakeholders so that it becomes possible to engineer such mediation.

Weiße and Knauth (1997), Alexander (2005) and Du Preez (2006) reflect on the use of dialogue in educational contexts. Du Preez (2006: 33) critiqued the conceptions of educational dialogue by arguing that dialogue should not be regarded as a commodity to be used to gain a predefined end or become a tool for achieving a preconceived goal. It should be the aim of education to break the traditional mould of the monologue where the educator speaks and where the learner sits quietly absorbing his/her wisdom (Alexander, 2005: 3–4). The nature of the secondary school musical as specific genre is essentially geared towards breaking monologism[1] and promoting dialogue by cultivating a coming together of culturally and religious diverse communities in order to understand and accept each other's life-worlds. It is a vehicle to use dialogue to shape children's thinking and thus the societies they live in (Alexander, 2005:1).

It should never be the aim of the secondary school musical to promote dialogue as a quasi-spiritual practice in order to solve the predicaments of society. This concurs with the view of Weiße and Knauth (1997: 39–42) that diverse experiences are prerequisites for dialogue. The musical production creates space for the exploration of life where interlocutors

---

[1] Monologism in this context refers to humans developing in a void through the perpetuation of cultural essentialism, cultural relativism and traditional communitarianism, where the voices of alternative possibilities are usually deliberately silenced (Du Preez, 2006: 35).

from diverse backgrounds such as educators, learners, parents and other role players who are part of the production meet to compare and reflect on their differences. Although the musical production is currently an extra-mural activity in South African schools, it remains pedagogical in nature and can be adapted for the intramural curriculum as it is a purposive socio-conventional intervention in personal development, drenched with the societal values and history of the community it serves (Alexander, 2005: 2). As such, it provides a safe space for dialogue about social conventions, norms and values where mutual understanding is empathetic rather than critical in nature (Du Preez, 2006: 44).

## The Secondary School Classroom and Lecture Room as Monologic Space

The curriculum provided by the South African Department of Education (2010: 3, 4) for life skills education within a Life Orientation programme envisages a practice ground where individual and communal skills may be acquired and honed by secondary school learners. The traditional classroom has its origins in the factories of the Industrial Revolution where bells regulated time and spaces were shaped by walls and gates (Barret & Smigiel, 2007: 39). In contrast to the scheduled,[2] yet pliable, nature of the musical production where any space may be used for rehearsal and practice, the classroom situation seems to be a space for monologue rather than dialogue. The educator has to create a dialogic space for life skills attainment in a classroom that does not reflect a real life situation. To generate suitable opportunities in which learners are able to practise in a real life environment at least the majority of those life skills, as stipulated by the curriculum, creates a real challenge for educators, especially as principles such as democratic and human rights, social justice, and reconciliation and equity should not only be taught but also instilled (South Africa. Department of Education, 2010: 8).

If educators do not approach Life Orientation and particularly life skills education as an opportunity to realize the potential of the learners as functional individuals and community members they will not be able to contribute to the community where they work and live. The school as extension of the family, given its accountability *in loco parentis*, is obliged to accept its co-responsibility for educating these learners within the

---

[2] It is scheduled, because of, for example, practice schedules and rehearsal slots. These are usually negotiated collaboratively between learners and teaching staff – hence the use of the term "pliable".

framework of the curriculum to acquire those life skills as stipulated by the curriculum for Life Orientation (South Africa. Department of Education, 2010: 3). The aim of life skills education is to teach learners to acquire and apply knowledge, skills, norms and values, and to be able to participate meaningfully in their own communities irrespective of their individual diversity (Griessel et al., 1990: 50; South Africa. Department of Education, 2010: 3). Educators should be aware of the limitations of the classroom environment as monologic space as it does not easily allow for other role players or for transformational conflict to enter the classroom in order to provide input for the creation of a natural dialogue for exploration about life.

## Implications for Teacher Education

Four implications for teacher education in South Africa are drawn from this comparative study between secondary school musicals, as holograms of reality, and the traditional secondary school classroom as simulated depictions of reality.

1. School musicals are pedagogical practice grounds for life skills attainment, including social justice. During their initial training, prospective teachers should be made aware of the importance of life skills attainment and the effective practice ground the secondary school musical provides. Participation in the musical not only teaches the participants new skills but has a corrective effect on existing problems experienced, both on a personal and an interpersonal level. Although life skills could be taught conventionally, they should preferably be practised in an implied, integrated and spontaneous manner and within a secure and safe space. Life skills attainment is, therefore, closely related to lifelong learning.

2. Future teachers have to be made aware of the opportunity a secondary school musical provides for discovering and exercizing talents of the learner-participants but also of the other stakeholders involved in the musical production. Aspects of drama, song and choreography are present in the production and provide opportunities to students and learners to discover and enhance their talents. In the classroom the detection of talents is limited by opportunity and the development of these talents is hampered by time constraints. Technical aspects offer different areas of talent development to students and learners but cannot be fully developed in a traditional classroom environment. According to the data there

is opportunity for all students and learners to participate in a musical production – irrespective of their talents, skills or abilities. Musical ability alone should never be prerequisite for participation in a secondary school musical production. Students and learners (should) become co-responsible for all aspects of the production with educators or senior students as their mentors. The classroom environment rarely provides talent development on this level.

3. Their training should contain an understanding of the impact school musicals offer on creating opportunities for social interaction within a safe dialogic space. Future South African teachers have to be trained to understand the educative importance of a safe space where dialogue can take place. Life skills linked to social interaction include effective communication, cooperation, working together towards a shared goal, mutual trust and acceptance of differences. These skills are best attained when working together as a social community on a shared project that also includes society at large. The musical production provides opportunity for students and learners within a safe dialogic-educative space to share social similarities but also confront social differences. The teaching space of a traditional classroom or lecturing space isolates students and learners, rather than unite them.

   The secure and safe dialogic space provided by the secondary school musical production affords learner-participants the opportunity to face and align those impediments prevalent in their personal lives. As there are educators at hand as mentors, and peers within the cast who have become friends (almost like family) whom they can trust, the adolescents and young adults often feel more secure in dealing with personal and interpersonal difficulties within this secure and safe environment. It is, therefore, important that future teachers be cognisant of the importance of their involvement in this dialogic-educative space provided.

4. Prospective teachers should be trained to value their role in instilling co-responsibility, mutual and reciprocal trust and meaning-making within the dialogic-educative space provided by the school musical production. The musical production encourages co-responsibility, mutual and reciprocal trust, as well as knowledge of otherness and making meaning of social constructs. Trust and co-responsibility are mostly dependent on the presence of the social constructs of sharing and cooperation – which most producers, educators and scholars argue form an intrinsic part of the

pedagogical and educational make-up of any secondary school musical production.

## Conclusion

Four implications regarding teacher education in the South African context are drawn from this comparative study of secondary school musicals as dialogic-educative space and the traditional secondary school classroom.

I have found that secondary school musicals may, curricularly as well as pedagogically, be understood as practice grounds for life skills attainment which also incorporates issues of social justice. The musical production could consequently be a useful pedagogical innovation through which the outcomes of the subject of Life Orientation could not only be taught and practised but also be studied and assessed by students, educators, learners and other role-players and stake-holders.

The secondary school musical production endeavours to entertain and to educate. It becomes an instrument of discovering and exercising human talents as each student or learner finds his/her place in the production. It is restricted in the variety of talent development options, because of time, spacial and subject-pedagogic limitations.

The secondary school musical also facilitates social interaction. The lecturing space and traditional classroom display a propensity towards for monologism whereas the musical is a centrifugal force towards dialogue and social interaction.

Sharing a mutual goal resulted in the participants having to trust their fellow-participants and to believe entirely in their mutual trustworthiness. Within this subculture of shared dialogue created by the musical production, participants are encouraged to practice their interpersonal skills and learn how to get along with and accept diverse people. Although learners are expected to accept diversity within the classroom environment, it remains mostly a simulated situation which is often driven by fear of punishment rather than by true acceptance. Life skills may be explained, but behaviour usually associated with a particular life skill is seldom altered through mere instruction (Fredricks & Eccles, 2005: 508).

Further research on the dialogic nature of secondary school teaching and learning environments sheds light on the implications for students of education in a South African developing country context. Perhaps the problems experienced in our current education system have their roots (of evil?) in the essentially monologic nature of our conventional classroom practices. The ontology of the proposed secondary school musical production and its implementation in education training courses should be clarified. Including a musical production in the Life Orientation programme could remediate contentious social problems and facilitate social justice within South Africa's diverse communities through the creation of dialogic educative spaces for effective knowledge, skills, norms and values education.

I conclude with a quotation from a participant as a summation of this discussion:

> It made me get out of my box, it really did, it really did, it changed my life, after the musical I was never the same again. I know it sounds very corny but it is really like that, it is really true. (P1: R33–35)

> In fact, I remember much more about the musical productions than of the academic part of secondary school. (P7: R12)

# References

Alexander, R. 2005. "Culture, Dialogue and Learning: Notes on an Emerging Pedagogy". Paper presented at the International Association for Cognitive Education and Psychology (IACEP): 10th International Conference, University of Durham.

Barret, M. S. and Smigiel, H. M. 2007. "Children's Perspectives of Participation in Music Youth Arts Settings: Meaning, Value and Participation", *Research Studies in Education* 28(1): 39–50.

Du Preez, P. 2006. *Dialogue as Facilitation Strategy: Infusing the Classroom with Culture of Human Rights.* (Doctoral Dissertation). Stellenbosch: University of Stellenbosch.

Fredricks, J. 2011. "Extracurricular Activities: An Essential Aspect of Education", *Educators College Record*, http://www.tcrecord.org. ID Number: 16414.

Fredricks, J. A. and Eccles, J. S. 2005. "Developmental Benefits of Extracurricular Iinvolvement: Do Peer Characteristics Mediate the Link between Activities and Youth Outcomes?" *Journal of Youth and Adolescence* 34(2), 507–520.

Griessel, G. A. J., Louw, G. J. J. and Swart, C. A. 1990. *Principles of Educative Teaching.* Pretoria: Acacia.

Potgieter, A. S. 2012. *Exploring the Life Orientation Potential of Secondary School Musical Productions: The Case of The Green Crystal.* (MEd. dissertation). Potchefstroom: North-West University.

Rule, P. 2004. "Dialogic Spaces: Adult Education Projects and Social Engagement", *International Journal of Lifelong Education* 23(4), 319–334, http://www.tandf.co.uk/journals.

South Africa. Department of Education. 2012. *National Curriculum and Assessment Policy Statement (CAPS) Life Orientation 7-9*, http://www.thutong.doe.gov.za/Home/PolicyDocuments/tabid/1952/Default.as px?PolicyTypeid=1 (accessed 8 April 2011).

Weiße, W. & Knauth, T. 1997. "Dialogical Religious Education: Theoretical Framework and Conceptional Conclusions", in T. Andree, C. Bakker & P. Schreiner (eds), *Crossing Boundaries: Contributions to Interreligious and Intercultural Education*. Münster & Berlin: Comenius-Institute Publication, pp. 33–44.

Wolhuter, C. C., Van Der Walt, J. L. and Potgieter, F. J. 2009. "Addressing the Discipline Problem in South African Schools by Increasing the Supply of Social Capital in Society: A Position Paper", *Journal of Educational Studies* 8(2), 40–51.

Wood, D., Larson, R. W. and Brown, J. R. 2009. "How Adolescents Come to See Themselves as More Responsible through Participation in Youth Programs", *Child Development* 80(1), 295–309.

# CHAPTER EIGHTEEN

## TEACHER EDUCATION AND ART: PRESENTATION OF A TEACHING MODULE FOR PRIMARY SCHOOLS

### GEORGIA KARELA
EDUCATOR, MSC MANAGEMENT EDUCATION,
UNIVERSITY OF THE AEGEAN,
MSC ADULT EDUCATION, UNIVERSITY OF ATHENS, GREECE

**Abstract**
It is an undeniable fact that we live in a society of constant changes. Many changes occur in the area of education and teachers have to notice and support them. Teacher education leads to the development of both themselves and the educational institution in which they are employed and aims to broaden knowledge and acquire the skills and competencies that will improve the quality of their teaching work.

Aesthetic experience is an important parameter for the all-round development of the child. Towards this, the use of art for educational purposes is a technique that can be applied in the school so that students can reach knowledge in a different and more interesting way and achieve their development.

Perkins (1994: 4–6) pointed out that the approach of art in general and the observation of artworks specifically helps people to learn how to use their mind in a better and more efficient way, to think more correctly not only in the cognitive domain but in all areas of daily life. Dealing with artwork leads naturally and effortlessly to a different way of thinking. This happens once the artworks cause, encourage and require thoughtful behavior of the observer in order to discover their meanings.

In this paper a teaching effort for Primary School that has to do with the right of the child to the game will be presented which can be combined with interculturalism with activities where art holds a leading position.

**Keywords**
Teacher Education, Arts, Primary School

# Introduction

## *Teacher education: Theoretical considerations*
In a rapidly changing world the educational system must be adjusted continuously through educational changes and reforms in order to meet the new conditions and the needs that arise. In this process, among all the new needs and the educational system, continuity is ensured through teacher education, both basic and continuous (Xochellis, 2005: 147).

Our understanding of the role that the teacher has to play has changed. While previously the teacher's role was limited to the implementation of the curriculum, today the teacher is the one who creates it. What the teacher essentially does is that he/she maps out the content of the curriculum according to the needs of students, which was deemed necessary by the cultural pluralism of modern society (Matsagouras & Chelmis, 2002: 7–8). This different perception of the role of the teacher implies differentiation both in the role of education and in the role of further education.

The continuous education of teachers is essential for the improvement and upgrading of educational systems (Goodlad, 1994), as the provided knowledge is expanded and viewed through new methods. Teachers need to have constant access to new data relating to their fields and the corresponding teaching methods.

Another factor necessitating the continuous education of teachers is related to the nature of their work. The "traditional" teacher whose work was the simple transfer of knowledge into passive students contrasts with the teacher of today who seeks for the creative guidance of active students who participate in the discovery and production of knowledge (Cullingford, 1995; Shulman, 1987; Bluma, 1998; all cited in Vitsilaki-Soroniati, 2002: 38–39). This component involves the teacher in a constant process of learning and redefines knowledge, skills and attitude.

The professional development of teachers involves the acquisition or extension of knowledge about various subjects and skills on teaching work as its objectives (Dimitropoulos, 1998). From the above it appears that professional development involves the acquisition of new knowledge and skills or the enrichment of pre existing ones, the amplification of teaching capacity, the strengthening of the ability of cooperation and generally the deeper awareness of the teaching profession (Fullan & Hargreaves, 1992).

In Greece, the pedagogical training of future teachers has the character of superficial and theoretical information on teaching practice. But after studying the training that takes place is not sufficient. Most of the time the training takes the form of a seminar and it is unresponsive to the needs of the teachers. It is common to find a gap between the theoretical knowledge being offered and the everyday teaching process, at all levels.

## Education and Art

The relationship between art and the educational process is an issue that scientists have dealt with since the time of Dewey. In his work *Art as Experience* (1980) Dewey supported the view that the aesthetic experience is the most effective way to cultivate the imagination, which is considered an integral part of the learning process but also of everyday life in general. Each artwork is a "challenge for thought" and enlists the imagination of the person in order to perceive its meanings. Imagination integrates all the components of the project and allows the observer to have a holistic understanding of it.

Apart from Dewey, Gardner (1983) stressed the value of the aesthetic experience for the development of the individual, underlining the potential of aesthetic experience to contribute to the multifaceted empowerment of intelligence, since it offers many symbols for editing.

The "Project Zero" Program of Harvard University is a study that aimed to understand thinking, learning and creativity through art. The researchers pointed out that even six-year-old children can appreciate some aspects of an artwork, such as the style, expression and carriage. Artistic examples can serve as models and subjects are able to familiarize themselves with the content and the example, through artistic creation (Gardner, 1990: 14).

Apart from the scientists already mentioned, Eisner (2002) highlighted the contribution of art to thought processes. The observation of details and the non-literal interpretation of an artwork require complex cognitive thought patterns. Dealing with artwork includes recognizing symbolism, the explanation of what characters in the works represent and their interpretation. The ultimate aim is to make students think and be sensitive, to acquire the necessary knowledge, skills and attitudes in order to experience the aesthetic qualities of an artwork. Arts provide an opportunity to have qualitative experiences in a highly focused manner and to be engaged in a constructive exploration of the effects of a process which is impregnated with imagination.

Efland mentioned that artworks are human achievements that can provide knowledge and aesthetic experience. The use of art in the learning process favours the development of four cognitive functions, cognitive flexibility, interpretation of knowledge, imagination and aesthetic experience (Efland, 2002: 156–171). Cognitive flexibility, the ability to approach each issue with the right strategy, is especially applied in the case of a work of art since it is susceptible to multiple interpretations. Each artwork is part of a particular era and reflects the broader conditions that surround it. When one tries to interpret the artwork with the help of one's imagination, the creation of new ideas is promoted. All these suggest that the aesthetic experience facilitates the learning process (Efland, 2002:157–171).

Perkins supported the use of art in school since it helps the students to improve their way of thinking as they learn to think more correctly. When the student is studying an artwork, he/she implements various cognitive functions, such as analytical thinking, questioning, testing assumptions, arguments (Perkins, 1994: 5).

Thinking is an issue that also interests a scientist, Fowler, who refers to five ways of thinking that promote engagement with art. Fowler claims that the learner is open to new ideas, learns how to use his/her abilities to achieve the goals he/she sets and develops the ability to see the world from different perspectives. Moreover, creativity is encouraged and through his/her acquaintance with other cultures he/she learns to respect diversity (Fowler, 1996: 9–14).

The Eurydice programme that provides information and analyses systems and policies of European education presents some data on the subject of art in education (Education, Audiovisual & Culture Executive Agency, 2009a). According to the report of the project, in Hungary in 2007–08 among the basic purposes of education, knowledge of the importance of aesthetic experience and the creative expression of ideas and emotions in all forms of art were included. In primary school visual arts have an important position in the development of those skills that are useful for a high level of communication in order to improve creativity and enhance diversity in the classroom. It is important that special attention was paid to in-service training of teachers in art (Education, Audiovisual & Culture Executive Agency, 2009c).

In another report of the programme for the Netherlands for the same year, Art seems to hold a special place in the school programme where students broaden their horizons by observing artworks. They are also encouraged to evaluate works of art around them and investigate the expressive potential of materials. Attention is paid to the training of teachers for art themes in collaboration with the school, art schools and cultural institutions (Education, Audiovisual & Culture Executive Agency, 2009d).

In Italy, particular attention is paid to art and the goals of developing skills in music, art and image to students of different ages are distinguished. Young students explore different artworks in order to distinguish the symbolic and communicative meanings. For teachers in-service level activities related to art are organized (Education, Audiovisual & Culture Executive Agency, 2009b).

In the same programme for the case of Malta we observe that arts are considered as a non-verbal mode of communication and it is stated that "Art is the visual language". The value that art gives in diversity is recognized and it is mentioned that it "fosters sensitivity towards cultural differences".

The aim of the school is to teach students "to use feelings, imagination and memory to develop, express and communicate ideas and solutions".

An important fact is that in the curriculum in basic studies art has a special place and offers a range of courses to prospective teachers (Education, Audiovisual & Culture Executive Agency, 2009a).

At this point, after the reference made above to the education and training of teachers in art matters in some countries, it is worth mentioning that in Greece teachers receive optional in-service training in art. A recent example is the Major Training Programme which was attended by a certain number of teachers. During the programme there was a reference to the position art must have in the New School where the student assisted by the teacher holds the primary role.

## Presentation of a Teaching Module through Art

This paper presents a teaching module for the Elementary School relating to the right of the child to a game that can be combined with the theme of intercultural communication. Topics can be accessed by Perkins' Model Analysis of Artworks. Perkins argues that the observation of art works requires thinking and makes reference to the "smart eye", since in collaboration with the mind it allows interpretation and leads to logical conclusions (Perkins, 1994: 13–16).

The "smart eye" requires the contribution of empirical intelligence with the instinctive return to the individual's past experiences (Perkins, 1994: 13–16) and stochastic thinking that provides both the ability to schedule and the evaluation of thoughts and the knowledge of the function of the cognitive system. Perkins suggests a way of approaching art which is based on four principles and is divided into four stages respectively.

In the first stage we have the initial observation of artwork. At this stage the observer places himself a good distance from the artwork and expresses the first questions. Then he turns his eyes elsewhere for a while and looks back at the artwork discovering, perhaps, new information or otherwise interpreting something he had seen previously (Perkins, 1994: 36–42).

In the second stage thinking becomes open and adventurous. Now deeper observation is attempted in order to rebuild the data from a more creative perspective. The observer looks for surprises and detects messages that the artist may want to transfer.

In the third stage, the thought becomes critical and the person compares, deepens, interprets and explains. Here the observer returns to what caused him interest or confused him and attempts to explain it. He may also make mental changes and attempts to provide answers and draw conclusions about questions that emerged in the previous phases (Perkins, 1994: 64–65).

In the last step we look at the whole process. At this stage the observer sees the work holistically and seeks to give his own interpretation.

The artworks were selected to study issues related to the game and intercultural communication. In the first stage we ask students to observe the artwork and express their first comments. Then they stand back and revert to express the first thoughts and their first questions.

In the second stage we have an open and creative observation, where we ask students to find "hidden" stories behind the artwork and urge them to identify what causes them sense. We also ask them to express how they feel looking at the artwork and to recognize technical elements of the works of art and give them the first elements of the project.

In the third stage, students return to the information that surprised them and answer the question of why they were used by the artist. Then, they come back to what interests everyone and try to answer their initial questions and draw conclusions.

In the fourth stage, each student is asked to work individually at the beginning and then take into consideration the whole experience of observation (Kokkos & Mega, 2007: 17–18; Mega, in Kokkos et al., 2011: 48–57).

Students start observing Gyzis's painting with which we negotiate the theme of the game and then with Modigliani's and Savvides's paintings we examine the issue of intercultural communication.

Above there was an indicative plan of negotiating a thematic unity through art. The process requires the active participation of students after making them co-creators of knowledge. The teacher through education and training does not teach them how to think, but offers them his thought with honesty and respect, since they can already think for themselves.

This module can be taught in the fifth grade in the lesson of Social and Political Education. It can also be cross-thematic in wider interdisciplinary curriculum in the fields of Language, Mathematics, Foreign Language and Gymnastics.

Through observation of artworks, students are developed holistically (Anderson & Milbrandt, 2005). They enrich their knowledge in order to observe the artwork. They learn to analyse and synthesize data, cultivate creative thinking as they use their imagination and develop their research spirit. In terms of attitudes students learn to communicate and share their ideas, work together, cultivate empathy and learn to respect each others' ideas.

The evaluation of the module can be formative and takes place after the negotiation of the specific issues with a questionnaire that will be given to the students in order for them to make observations and add other related works of art. Finally, after the completion of the module, to let students explore how they worked with art and if the objectives were achieved.

Fig. 17.1 A little girl playing (N. Gyzis)

Fig. 17.2 A girl with plaits (Modigliani)

Fig. 17-3. Merry Go Round (S. Savvides)

# References

Anderson, T. and Milbrandt, M. 2005. *Art for Life: Authentic Instruction in Art.* New York: McGraw-Hill Higher Education.
Dewey, J. 1934. *Art as Experience.* New York: Minton, Balch.

Dimitropoulos, E. 1998. *Teachers and their Profession: A Contribution to the Development of a Professional Psychology Greek teacher.* Athens: Grigoris. (In Greek).

Education, Audiovisual & Culture Executive Agency 2009a. *Arts and Cultural Education at School in Europe.* European Commission, http://eacea.ec.europa.eu/education/eurydice/documents/thematic_reports/113en.pdf (accessed 17 April 2013).

—. 2009b. *Arts and Cultural Education at School in Europe. Italy 2007/2008.* European Commission, http://mediatheque.cite-musique.fr/mediacomposite/cim/_Pdf/10_40_Italy_EN.pdf (accessed 17 April 2013).

—. 2009c. *Arts and Cultural Education at School in Europe. Hungary 2007/2008.* European Commission, http://mediatheque.cite-musique.fr/mediacomposite/cim/_Pdf/10_40_Hungary_EN.pdf (accessed 17 April 2013).

—. 2009d. *Arts and Cultural Education at School in Europe Netherlands 2007/08.* European Commission, http://mediatheque.cite-musique.fr/mediacomposite/cim/_Pdf/10_40_Netherlands_EN.pdf (accessed 17 April 2013).

Efland, A. 2002. *Art and Cognition: Integrating the Visual Arts in the Curriculum.* New York: Teachers College, Columbia University.

Eisner, E. 2002. *The Arts and the Creation of Mind.* New Haven & London: Yale University Press.

Fowler, C. 1996. *Strong Arts, Strong Schools.* New York: Oxford University Press.

Fullan, M. and Hargreaves, A. 1992. *Teacher Development and Educational Change.* London: Falmer Press.

Gardner, H. 1983. *Frames of Mind: The Theory of Multiple Intelligences.* New York: Basic Books.

—. 1990. *Art Education and Human Development.* Los Angeles: Getty Education for the Arts.

Goodlad, J. I. 1994. *Educational Renewal: Better Teachers, Better Schools.* San Fransisco: Jossey-Bass.

Kokkos, A. et al. 2011. *Education through the Arts.* Athens: Routledge. (In Greek).

Kokkos, A. and Mega, G. 2007. "Critic Contemplation and Art Education: Research Involving Graduate Students of Adult Education in the Greek Open University", *Adult Education* 12, 16–21. (In Greek).

Lawrence, R. L. 2008. "Powerful Feelings: Exploring the Affective Domain of Informal and Arts-Based Learning", *New Directions for Adult and Continuing Education,* 120, 65–77.

Matsagouras, E. and Chelmis, S. 2002. "Educating the Teacher in the Postmodern Era: From Technocrat to Master Critical Thinker", *Science Education* 2, 7–25. (In Greek).

Perkins, D. 1994. *The Intelligent Eye: Learning to Think by Looking at Art.* Los Angeles: The J. Paul Getty Trust.

Vitsilaki-Soroniati, C. 2002. "Lifelong Teacher Education: A Case Sstudy of the 'Uupgrading of Primary School Teachers'", *Science Education* 2, 37–60. (In Greek).

Xochellis, P. 2005. *The Teacher in the Modern World.* Athens: Typothito. (In Greek).

# Chapter Nineteen

## Public and Private Kindergartens from the Perspective of Teachers in Greece: The Case of Crete

### Theodoros Eleftherakis
Lecturer, University of Crete, Greece
### and Vassilios Oikonomidis
Assistant Professor, University of Crete, Greece

**Abstract**

The study of public and private education in Greece has not attracted the interest of researchers to the extent that it should. The present study has examined Greek teachers' beliefs on: a) the differences between public and private kindergarten, b) the reasons which motivate parents to enrol their children in private kindergartens, c) the social status that both of the types of kindergartens have. The results of the study indicate that Greek teachers consider that the main difference between these types of kindergartens are the better facilities that private kindergartens offer (transport by school bus, food provision at school, better (and better equipped) buildings) compared with public kindergartens. These facilities are why parents prefer the private kindergartens. On the other hand teachers take into consideration the social status differences between public and private kindergartens. The teachers' beliefs did not vary according to their educational or social background.

**Keywords**

Public Kindergarten, Private Kindergarten, Kindergarten Status, Preschool Education, Kindergarten Teachers' Beliefs

# Introduction

Public and private are two parallel types of education in Europe, whereas private educational institutions are those that have their own financial resources and those that receive state aid (Eurydice, 2012). The largest proportion of the student population in preschool and compulsory education in Europe (86.5%) attend public schools and a small percentage (13.5%) attend private schools. The percentage in private education presents several variations from country to country. In Malta, France, Spain and especially in Belgium and the Netherlands, where there are private schools subsidized by the state, the percentage at private schools is close to 65%. Regarding Greece, according to European statistics, in 2009 only 6.1% of children of kindergarten and elementary school attended private schools (Eurydice, 2012). It is worth noting that in our country private education is under the supervision of the Ministry of Education with respect to the educational process and issues of teaching staff, but is not financed by the state. Private schools offer kindergarten, elementary and secondary education (high school and lyceum). In this paper we focus on the comparative approach of public and private kindergartens.

# Private and Public Kindergartens in Greece

In the long history of the institution of early childhood education throughout Europe, in Greece the first institutions that operated in this area of education were private. After the creation of the modern Greek state, the care and education of preschool children were the aim of private institutions owned either by individuals (Greeks and foreigners, e.g. Hildner, Hill) or by charitable associations (e.g. Educational Company), or were funded by local municipalities (e.g. Municipality of Piraeus, Municipality of Ermoupolis); they operated with a variety of names (nipioscholeia, kindergarten schools, nursery schools) (Kitsaras, 2001; Chatzistefanidou, 2008; Kyprianos, 2007). The Greek state demonstrated its interest in early childhood education for the first time with the Law BTMΘ/1895 and with the first Greek kindergarten curriculum in 1896, but the establishment and operation of public kindergartens appeared slowly. Only after the liberation of Macedonia and the population exchange of 1923 did the Greek state begin to establish public kindergartens with the main aim of addressing the problem of Greek children who did not speak the Greek language well (Kitsaras, 2001; Kyprianos, 2007). The integration of kindergartens in public education and their subordination to the Ministry of Education was achieved by implementation of Law 4397

*On Elementary Education* in 1929, and the rate of establishment of public kindergartens has varied from then until today (Kitsaras, 2001; Kyprianos, 2007).

The changes in numbers of private kindergartens over time are mainly due to changes in the social and economic conditions of the country (Kitsaras, 2001). The private kindergartens in Greece provide education to a small number of children aged 4–6 years (Kitsaras, 2001; Ministry of Education, 2009˙ ELL.STAT., 2013). Significant increases in the number of children enrolled in private kindergartens occurred during the school years 2007–08, 2008–09 and 2009–10 (Lakasas, 2012; Ministry of Education, 2009), because from 2006 Law 3518 (FEK 272, A/21-12-2006) established preschool education as obligatory and public kindergartens did not have the needed spaces and building facilities to enrol all children from ages 4–6. From the 2009–2010 school year, however, there began a continuous decline in the number of enrolments in private kindergartens, as a consequence of the economic crisis (Lakasas, 2012; Papamathaiou, 2010; Pouliopoulos, 2012). Private kindergartens are either autonomous institutions, part of broader private school clusters or segments of private nursery schools. Private kindergartens are a diverse group: from those targeted at parents with high income and mainly active in wealthy areas of large urban centers with high tuition fees, to those targeted at middle-income working parents covering needs arising from everyday family and working life with lower tuition fees (Lakasas, 2012; Papamathaiou, 2010).

We found no Greek studies regarding the relationship of private and public kindergartens and particularly how teachers face private education. This paper is a first attempt to research this relationship.

The purpose of this paper is to seek the views of teachers employed in public education on private kindergartens. We want to find out their beliefs about the social status accorded by Greek society to private and public kindergartens (Giddens, 1993). This paper presents data from a small part of a broader survey of our research pertinent to the research about the social status of the kindergarten as an educational institution and of the kindergarten teacher as a professional.

## Research Methodology

We are going to take into consideration data from a survey with 343 participating teachers (123 kindergarten teachers, 110 elementary school teachers and 110 secondary education teachers) serving public schools in Crete during the 2011–12 school year. The research questionnaire used an enclosed Likert scale, which was constructed by the researchers, tested during a pilot study and then administered to the participants, asking them to answer questions by choosing one of the statements of the five-point scale 0 = Strongly disagree, 1 = Disagree, 2 = Not sure, 3 = Agree, 4 = Strongly agree. Answers were correlated with participants' educational and socio-demographic characteristics: the educational grade they serve (kindergarten teachers, elementary school teachers, secondary education teachers), age, type of basic/initial education for teacher's bachelor degree, further education and training beyond initial education, years of service, service in urban, suburban and rural areas, social origin criteria with the urbanity of the area in which they upbringing, and educational level of their parents. Research data were coded and analysed using the statistical package SPSS (Nova-Kaltsouni, 2006). The Cronbach coefficient for the total questionnaire was estimated at 0.82, which is considered very satisfactory.

## Results of the Survey

The analysis of the research data gave the following results. On the position that private kindergartens have greater social status than the public kindergartens, participant teachers in our survey have no unambiguous view, though they tend to disagree with this position (M = 1.86 SD = 1.10). Statistically significant differences were found between kindergarten teachers who had any kind of education beyond their initial education for teacher's bachelor degree (M 1.69 SD = 1.08) and those without further education beyond the initial (M = 2.55 SD = 0.90), and t = 4.18 (93.6) p<0.05, with the first tending to believe that private kindergartens have no greater social status than the public ones, and the latter tending to believe the opposite, that private kindergartens have greater social status in the eyes of the public. Similar results were obtained by comparing primary education teachers (kindergarten and elementary school teachers) who had any kind of education beyond their initial education for teacher's bachelor degree (M 1.67 SD = 1.08) and those without further education beyond the initial (M 2.13, SD = 1.07), and t = 3.06 (198.9) p<0.05, with the former tending to believe that private kindergartens have no greater social status than the public ones and the latter having no clear position. The other educational and socio-demographic characteristics of the teachers in this sample do not significantly affect their views on this issue. The points which differentiate private from public kindergartens according to participants in the survey are presented in Table 1.

**Table 1: Points of differentiation between private and public kindergartens. Mean (M) and standard deviation (SD) of the total participant teachers, and statistically significant differences between groups of teachers participating in the survey.**

| Private kindergartens differ from the public in that they: | M of the total survey | SD of the total survey | Statistically significant differences between the M groups of teachers from the survey |
|---|---|---|---|
| provide portability of children | 2.88 | 0.77 | K>E * |
| very often have the capability to accommodate all parents' needs, in contrast with public kindergartens | 2.82 | 0.84 | K>E *, K>S * |
| provide more social services (selective/helpful time etc.) | 2.69 | 0.85 | K>E *, K>S * |
| can provide a meal | 2.62 | 0.88 | K>S * |
| have better buildings, teaching materials | 2.61 | 0.94 | K>E * |
| the child's attendance at a private kindergarten enhances the social prestige of his family | 1.74 | 1.17 | K>E *, K>S * |
| have better teachers | 1.18 | 0.90 | K<S * |

K = kindergarten teachers, E = elementary school teachers, S = secondary education teachers
*= Statistically significant differences p<0.05.

As we see in Table 1, teachers agree that the points which outweigh the private versus public kindergartens concern mainly social benefits to children and families (enrol all children, undertake children's transport to and from school, offer lunch and flexible service hours). Participants in the survey tend to agree about the superiority of private kindergartens in terms of their building comforts, and disagree with the view that better teachers are employed in private kindergartens. Participants do not have a clear view but tend to disagree with the view that a child's attendance at a private kindergarten enhances the social prestige of his family. Although the views of teachers from the total sample converge, by using unvaried analysis of variance (Oneway ANOVA), we found differences depending on the grade at which they serve (kindergarten teachers, elementary school teachers, secondary school teachers). Thus, we applied multiple comparisons with a Bonferroni statistical test to find out the differences between private and public kindergartens among the three educational grades of participants in our survey. The results of these analyses show statistically significant differences between kindergarten teachers and teachers who work in the other two grades of our educational system, as shown in the fourth column of Table 1. For all points of differentiation between private and public kindergartens, kindergarten teachers agree significantly more on the superiority of private institutions, except for employing the best staff in private kindergartens on which they strongly disagree, statistically more than the other two groups of teachers in the sample. The other educational and socio-demographic characteristics of the participants in the survey do not significantly affect their views on this issue.

The responses show that teachers believe that the points of differentiation reported in Table 1 have different importance and constitute the reasons for parents sending their children to private kindergartens. We also identified the same significant differences between kindergarten teachers, elementary school teachers and secondary school teachers presented in Table 1. Yet it seems that primary education teachers (kindergarten and elementary school teachers) who do not have any kind of education beyond their initial education for the teacher's bachelor degree consider that provision of transport and food for children are the most important reasons for parents choosing private kindergartens, compared with the beliefs of their colleagues who have additional education beyond their initial education. Also, kindergarten teachers without additional studies beyond their initial education for the teacher's bachelor degree consider the building facilities of the private kindergartens as the most important reason for parents choosing private kindergarten (M 2.93 SD = 0.85), which is different from their colleagues with additional education beyond their initial education (M 2.55 SD = 0.91) and t = 2.17 (113.0) for p<0.05. The other educational and socio-demographic characteristics of the participants in this survey do not significantly affect their views.

Kindergarten teachers have no unambiguous opinion on whether parents value private or public kindergartens more (M 2.09 SD = 0.91), while elementary school and secondary school teachers themselves do not value private kindergartens more than public ones (M 1.04 SD = 0.98). Educational and socio-demographic characteristics of the participants in this survey do not significantly affect their views on this issue.

# Conclusions

The results show that public teachers employed in public schools have a common view of the social status enjoyed by private kindergartens, with no differences between participants' grade (kindergarten, elementary school, high school), giving the image of a single body with its main feature being employment in public education. The participants' taking no clear view about the superior social status of private versus public kindergarten (or vice versa) may be due to the fact that they do not want to devalue the public school (in which they are employees). On the other hand it may be interpreted by the fact that the differences between private kindergartens are so large and diverse (e.g. eponymous private kindergarten school in North Athens and private kindergarten in the province) (Lakasas, 2012; Papamathaiou, 2010) that ultimately there is no single view of private kindergartens. As for the reasons parents send their children to private kindergartens, the results show that teachers understand that parents choose private kindergartens because they meet everyday social and functional family needs and not because parents consider private kindergartens better than public kindergartens. Maybe all of the above explain the results of a relevant piece of research in Cyprus, where kindergarten teachers from public and private kindergartens did not differ in the social status and recognition that they felt they have in society (Papanastasiou & Zembylas, 2005).

One very significant finding is that teachers who do not have further training and education beyond their initial teacher's bachelor degree tend to believe that the private kindergarten have higher social status than the public kindergarten, unlike their colleagues who have further education and retraining. This finding shows that the confidence of teachers in the work they themselves offer is mainly associated with "larger" and higher studies, and this is reflected in their view of the social status acquired by the institution in which they serve.

The findings about the points of difference between private and public kindergarten are very interesting. According to the teachers these points are associated with features that meet the social and functional needs of a family, such as transport of children to and from school, providing food to children, flexible hours giving special assistance to working parents, who are not served by the hours of all-day and of the classic public kindergarten. Of course, we must emphasize that both for transport and for feeding their children, parents are indeed paying more money to private kindergartens. It is also significant that a very important reason for the superiority of private versus public kindergartens is the possibility of the first to register/enrol all children sent to it (for obvious commercial-economic reasons), something that cannot be done in public kindergartens (Lakasas, 2012), which due to limited building facilities will first of all enroll children aged from 5 to 6 years, and only if there are enough vacancies left children aged from 4 to 5 years. Teachers feel that the best building facilities tend to be one of the elements of positive differentiation of private kindergartens. This finding, together with those indicating that teachers do not believe that the private institutions employ better kindergarten teachers, or that a child's attendance at private kindergarten upgrades the social status of the family, suggests that teachers believe the differentiation of the private kindergarten is not associated either with the quality of educational work (better teachers) or the pursuit of parental social status (child's attendance at a private kindergarten), but is related to the private kindergarten's ability to satisfy (for an additional fee) the social needs of the family and to enrol the child in the kindergarten. We believe the survey shows this view is close to reality. Sometimes the cognitive abilities of private kindergartens' graduates (Xu & Gulosino, 2006) outweigh those of public kindergartens; in other cases there are no differences, while often the cognitive abilities of public kindergartens' graduates outweigh those of private kindergartens' graduates (Carbonaro, 2006). This indicates that the educational process ranks high in public kindergartens, although they have more diverse (national, social, linguistic, cultural) groups of children, which is a characteristic that brings more difficulties in their education process (Carbonaro, 2006; Xu & Gulosino, 2006; Papanastasiou & Zembylas, 2005). Regarding similar results concerning the reasons for choosing private kindergarten by parents, teachers believe that parents are "forced" to choose private kindergartens both because of the possibility of enrolment and because other social benefits are not provided by the public kindergartens. Teachers also believe that parents' criteria for choosing a private kindergarten do not depend on the pedagogical process provided, but on the kindergarten's capability to serve their family life.

    Among all the teachers participating in our survey, the kindergarten teachers emphasize, more than elementary and high school teachers, how important are social benefits for parents, better building facilities and the sense of social upgrading of the family when the child attends a private kindergarten. It seems that the daily contact of kindergarten teachers with parents and the related difficulties they face, the better knowledge that they have about these issues, the daily dealing with related problems – children who arrive at or depart late from kindergarten because of their parents' working hours, frequent harassing by parents to collect their child before the end of school hours, children coming from home with no breakfast or lunch at the all-day kindergarten etc.), the difficult position they place themselves in when they cannot enrol all children in the kindergarten they work at – lead kindergarten teachers to understand how important these points are both for the social status of the institution and for the parents' selection. In the same way we interpret the differences between the views of kindergarten teachers and those of teachers from other grades, about the importance of buildings (building rooms, room layout, teaching materials) in order to improve the social status of kindergarten and to be chosen by the parents. Preschool teachers daily experience many problems related to the unsatisfactory building facilities of many public kindergartens (Koulaidis, 2006); they know how important this is for pedagogical and educational processes in kindergarten (Dafermou et al., 2006; Oikonomidis & Linardakis, 2011), as opposed to elementary and secondary education, where although space and teaching materials are very important factors in education they do not have such a central role. It is probably due to this specific knowledge and daily experience that kindergarten teachers agree more than other teachers that a child attending a private kindergarten enhances the prestige of his family.

Kindergarten teachers, in comparison with elementary and high school teachers, support more strongly the statement that teachers in private kindergartens are no better than themselves. This finding may be interpreted both as a kindergarten teachers' need to defend their own work and also as a view arising from knowledge of the educational characteristics of their colleagues in private kindergartens: all kindergarten teachers are graduates of the same university-level studies, while kindergarten teachers employed in public kindergartens were previously able to qualify by means of in-service education in University Teachers' Inservice Education Departments (KANEP/GSEE, 2009). Research shows that teachers employed in public kindergartens have higher levels of education than their colleagues in private kindergartens (Xu & Gulosino, 2006; Papanastasiou & Zembylas, 2005).

The finding that kindergarten and elementary teachers without further training and education beyond their initial teacher's bachelor degree believe that the social benefits and better building facilities provided by private kindergartens are elements that improve private kindergartens' social status and influence parents' choice may indicate that more qualified teachers consider that the quality of the educational process, in which their training is important, should affect the social status of educational institutions and parents' choice and not other factors.

Finally, the finding that elementary and high school teachers do not value private kindergartens more than public ones can be interpreted on the one hand as a part of what is discussed above, and on the other hand as a way of defending the public education system in which they serve.

Kindergarten teachers avoid taking an unambiguous view about how parents value private compared to public kindergartens. This finding is interpreted by those outlined above, regarding what private kindergartens offers to children and to their parents, compared to public kindergartens. We believe that the kindergarten teachers' view is quite modest and is shaped by daily communication with parents, an element that gives objectivity.

The most important conclusions of our research are the following:

- The teachers participating in our survey tend to assume that private kindergartens have no greater social status than public ones and they do not value them more highly, thus supporting the public school system in which they are employees.

- Teachers, and especially kindergarten teachers, consider that strong points of differentiation between private and public kindergartens, and reasons for choosing private over public kindergarten by parents, are the social benefits (enrolment, transport, feeding all children) and building facilities rather than the quality of teachers who work in kindergartens. Therefore, private kindergartens are more responsive to the needs of families of preschool children than the public kindergartens.

- The more education beyond their initial education for teacher's bachelor degree teachers have, the less they value private kindergartens. This, possibly, indicates the confidence teachers feel in their proficiency and therefore the work done in the public schools.

The findings and conclusions of our research have constraints and lead to the suggestions listed below:

- The teachers participating in our survey come from a single geographic region of Greece, from one administrative and educational region, the island of Crete, with few private kindergartens located in the urban centres of the island, aimed at families with average budget. The expansion of the research to teachers serving in the rest of the country would give a more representative picture of the public school teachers' views of the issue in question.

- Exploring the issue with another research tool (e.g. interview) will allow fuller study of the issue.

- It is also advisable to seek the views of private kindergarten teachers, so as to have a more integrated approach comparing public and private kindergartens.
- It is very important to seek the views of parents who chose either the public or the private kindergarten for their children, in order to find out how the wider Greek society (apart from the teaching profession) sees the two institutions.

In terms of educational policy, the research findings lead to the following suggestions:

a) The establishment of new kindergartens and operation of new sections employing the necessary number of teachers will increase the number of available spaces provided, and may include all preschool children in public kindergartens. It is obvious that in these difficult economic times prevailing in Greece, the implementation of this proposal seems utopian and unworkable. But it is precisely this economic situation, at a time when families are experiencing unprecedented deprivation, that requires the state to give all children the chance to attend a public kindergarten free of tuition fees, providing educational structures. In this way the state will respond both to the constitutional obligation ("Education is core mission of the State": *Constitution of Greece* (2001), Art.16, 2) and will exempt families from additional financial burdens on the education of their children. Besides, investing in education is the best foundation for the course of a society towards development (Heckman, 2006; Kitsaras, 2001).

b) All-day kindergartens should be provided generally. It is obvious that the type of classic kindergarten operating from 8:00 to 12:30 no longer serves the needs of working parents. These families need their children to attend for extended school hours (from 7:00 to 16:00) with the possibility of rest time and a meal (which children bring from home) (Eurydice, 2009); this provides better education for the children (McClelland et al., 2006; Blok et al., 2005; Carbonaro, 2006; Doliopoulou, 2003).

c) Improving the building facilities of kindergartens is sine qua non of offering quality education in early childhood and is one of the most urgent needs in Greece (Koulaidis, 2006; Oikonomidis, 2010).

The research about social status and differences between the private and the public kindergarten presented in this paper, essentially highlights the need to improve the supply of public preschool education.

# References

Blok, H., Fukkink, R. G., Gebhardt, E. C. and Leseman, P. P. M. 2005. "The Relevance of Delivery Mode and other Program Characteristics for the Effectiveness of Early Childhood Intervention with Disadvantaged Children", *International Journal of Behavioral Development* 29, 35–47.
Carbonaro, W. 2006. "Public-Private Differences in Achievement among Kindergarten Students: Differences in Learning Opportunities and Student Outcomes", *American Journal of Education* 113(1), 31–65.
Chatzistefanidou, S. 2008. *History of Early Childhood Education.* Vol A. Thessaloniki: Kyriakidis Bross. (In Greek).
Dafermou, Ch., Koulouris, P. and Basagianni, E. 2006. *Kindergarten Teacher's Guide: Educational planning, Creating Learning Environments.* Athens: School Book Publishing Organization (OEBD). (In Greek).
Doliopoulou, E. 2003. *The Day Kindergarten in Greece and 12 other countries.* Athens: Ellinika Grammata. (In Greek).
ELL.STAT. 2013. [Greek Statistical Authority.] *Primary Eeducation: Preschool Education (Schools). Students. Contact Start the School Year 2012–2013.* http://www.statistics.gr/portal/page/portal/ESYE/PAGE-themes?p_param=A1401&r_param=SED11&y_param=2012_00&mytabs=0 (accessed March 2013). (In Greek).
Eurydice. 2009. *Early Childhood Education and Care in Europe: Tackling Social and Cultural Inequalities.* Brussels.
—. 2012. *Key data on Education in Europe.* Brussels.
Giddens, A. 1993. *Sociology.* Cambridge: Polity Press, 1993.
Heckman, J. J. 2006. "Skill Formation and the Economics of Investing in Disadvantaged Children", *Science* 5728, 1901–1902.
KANEP/GSEE (Centre for Education Policy Development General Confederation of Greek Workers). 2009. *Study on Education in Greece: Primary and Secondary Education.* Athens: GSEE. (In Greek).
Kitsaras, G. 2001. *Preschool Pedagogy.* Athens. (In Greek).
Koulaidis, B. (ed.) 2006. *Depiction of the Educational System – School Grades.* Athens: Centre for Educational Research. (In Greek).
Kyprianos, P. 2007. *Child, Family, Society: History of Early Childhood Education from its Beginnings to the Present Day.* Athens: Gutenberg. (In Greek).
Lakasas, A. 2012. "Planning Rescue for Private Schools: After Constant Leaks, Students, Discounts and Elongation of Records", *Kathimerini* (5 February), http://news.kathimerini.gr/4dcgi/_w_articles_ell_4_05/02/2012_471410. (In Greek).
Law 3518/2006. *Restructuring of sectors of the Pension Fund Engineering and Public Works Contractors (TSMEDE) and regulate other matters of competence Ypourgriou Employment and social protection.* Article 73, paragraph 1. FEK 272, vol. A. 21-12-2006. (In Greek).
McClelland, M. M., Acock, A. C. and Morrison, F. J. 2006. "The Impact of Kindergarten Learning-related Skills on Academic Trajectories at the End of Elementary School", *Early Childhood Research Quarterly* 21, 471–490.

Ministry of Education, Lifelong Learning and Religious Affairs. 2009. *Primary Education Public & Private throughout Greece: School Population by Sex, Number of Schools – Sections – Graduates – Teachers. School Year 2008–2009,* http://users.sch.gr/mpratis/2010/st5.pdf (accessed March 2013). (In Greek).

Nova-Kaltsouni, C. 2006. *Empirical Research Methodology in Social Sciences: Data Analysis using the SPSS 13.* Athens: Gutenberg. (In Greek).

Oikonomidis, V. 2010. "The Introduction of Compulsory Preschool Education in Greece", in E. J. Pyrgiotakis & V. D. Oikonomidis (eds), *Dialogue On Education.* Rethymnon: University of Crete. School of Education. Department of Elementary Education, pp. 99–113. (In Greek).

Oikonomidis, V. and Linardakis, M. 2012. "The Quality of the Classroom in Kindergarten: Activity Corners and Equipment", in A. Trilianos, G. Koutroumanos & P. Alexopoulos (eds), *Quality in Education: Trends and Prospects. Proceedings of the National Conference with International Participation* Vol A. Athens: National and Kapodistrian University of Athens. Department of Education, pp. 770–781. (In Greek).

Papamattheou, M. 2010. "Crisis Brings Economic Loss to Private Schools: Not even Discounts Make certain to Contain the 'Leakage' of their Sstudents to the Public. *To Vima* (4 September), http://www.tovima.gr/society/article/?aid=352215 (In Greek).

Papanastasiou, E. C. and Zembylas, M. 2005. "Job Satisfaction Variance among Public and Private Kkindergarten Sschool Teachers in Cyprus", *International Journal of Educational Research* 43(3), 147–167.

Pouliopoulos, G. 2012. "Study, my Son, in Public School: What Parents say about their Decision to Switch from Private to Public Schools", *To Vima* (12 February), http://www.tovima.gr/society/article/?aid=443174 (In Greek).

Xu, Z. and Gulosino, Ch. A. 2006. "How Does Teacher Quality Matter? The Effect of Teacher–Parent Partnership on Early Childhood Performance in Public and Private Schools", *Education Economics* 14(3), 345–367.

# CHAPTER TWENTY

# TEACHERS' DEPARTMENTS: A FORGOTTEN ASPECT OF THE DEBATES ABOUT EDUCATION IN GREECE

## LEONIDAS GOMATOS
PROFESSOR, SCHOOL OF PEDAGOGICAL AND TECHNOLOGICAL EDUCATION, PATRAS, GREECE

**Abstract**
Secondary schools can fulfil their pedagogical role only if their teachers have the necessary pedagogical and teaching qualifications. In order to discover whether Greek secondary teachers do possess these qualifications, the curricula of several university faculties are studied here. These faculties belong to the so-called "teachers' faculties" or "teachers' departments". The curricula are studied regarding the extent to which they provide pedagogical and teaching qualifications. The study was carried out in spring 2009 and at the beginning of 2013. Law 3848 was passed in 2010. Conducting the study again in 2013 allows us to investigate if there have in the interving years been some changes in these teachers' faculties as an impact of this law. Results show that the term "teachers' departments" is not justified. Organized teacher training was not found to be a general feature of these departments either before or after the introduction of the aforementioned law. The majority of secondary education teachers do not possess the necessary pedagogical and teaching qualifications obtained through an organized study programme. (Exceptions exist and they are discussed below.)

**Keywords**
Teachers' departments, Pedagogical qualifications, Secondary education, Greece

# Introduction

In the various reforms of the educational system attempted from time to time in Greece, there exists a demand to "relieve" senior high schools of being a prelude to the selection of students for tertiary education. This would allow senior high schools to play an autonomous pedagogic role. A question arises however, which is directly related to the possibility of fulfilment of the pedagogical role of secondary schools in general: to what degree do secondary education teachers have the necessary pedagogical and teaching qualifications? In a number of studies and bodies of research (Eurydice 2006; Gomatos, 2010a; Patouna et al., 2005) a lack of pedagogical and teaching preparation of secondary teachers has been discerned. This constitutes an eternal educational problem in Greece (Kassotakis, 2010, for further analysis). Despite the conviction of pedagogic scholars that something "has to be done" and despite efforts to introduce an obligatory pedagogical and teaching preparation for all secondary teachers (L.2525/97, L.3848/2010), the problem seems to resist solution.

Law 2525/97 contemplated a global regulation concerning teachers' access to secondary education: no one would be accepted to work in secondary education (gradually from 1998 and globally from 2002 onwards) without having completed a year-long programme of pedagogical and teaching preparation in a University or in ASPETE (still named SELETE at the time). The only exception, according to this law, concerned the graduates of the departments of Philosophy-Pedagogy and Education of the National and Kapodistrian University of Athens (NKUA) and the equivalent departments. This law's provisions concerning pedagogical and teaching preparation were never applied on a large scale. In 2010 law 3848 was passed. This reintroduces the pedagogical and teaching preparation as a necessary qualification for participation in national teacher recruitment contests, it determines the ways available to obtain the pedagogical and teaching qualification, as well as the prescriptions of relevant programmes, and it defines among other things the minimum duration of such programmes, which is an academic semester.

What constitutes pedagogical and teaching preparation (PTP), according to European texts and practices? There are certainly differences from country to country concerning the manner and the content of PTP programmes. Some initiatives have been developed nevertheless by European organizations (Euridice, 2006) or through international projects (Ginestié, 2006), in order to determine commonly accepted models of description. It is broadly accepted for example that a PTP programme must have a minimum duration (this is very often an academic year) and it has to comprise three distinct units: subjects that aim at general pedagogic knowledge and competences (regardless of a teacher's specialization), pedagogical subjects related to the teacher's specialization and practical teaching exercises which take place partially or entirely in school establishments. These exercises are not conceived of simply as an application of theory in praxis but they are considered as a generator of questions which support pedagogical training as a whole (Chevallard & Cirade, 2009). The IUFM (University Teacher Training Institutes), developed in France from 1990 for two decades, constitute a characteristic example from international experience on the subject (Gomatos, 2010b for a short description).

To what extent is Greece concerned with the aforementioned specifications concerning PTP? To start with we can say, as far as primary education is concerned, that all the issues mentioned earlier exist in the undergraduate programmes of primary school teachers' faculties. The problem arises with secondary education teachers and specialist school teachers working in primary schools. The difference between primary and secondary teachers regarding pedagogical preparation is huge. As a consequence the outdated perception noted by Kassotakis (2010: 295), that pedagogical studies are associated with primary teachers' training, is strengthened and contributes to the stereotypes which hinder the organized introduction of PTP for secondary school teachers.

Secondary education teachers in Greece are graduates of the so-called "teachers' departments" (departments of mathematics, language, science etc.) or graduates of educators' departments of ASPETE (School of Pedagogical and Technological Education) or, finally, graduates of other departments (sociology, economics, engineering or other higher education departments). The graduates of this last category have to complete the annual PTP program (EPPAIK) provided by ASPETE if they want to have access to secondary education. This programme offers fourteen pedagogical semester subjects, Practical Teaching Exercises (seven teaching practices altogether by each student throughout the year) as well as a dissertation, which means a complete academic year of studies. For the undergraduates of ASPETE, this programme is spread over 8 semesters, with a ratio of 75% for the subjects of each department and 25% for the PTP subjects (Gomatos, 2010b). Despite its weak points, which certainly exist, this system provides the idea of an overall conception of a PTP programme in accordance with the specifications developed earlier. The vast majority of in-service secondary teachers possessing a PTP qualification have done their PTP in ASPETE. However, the percentage of secondary school teachers with a PTP qualification is low. It does not exceed 25% of the secondary school teachers' population. What is actually happening in the so called "teachers' departments"? This is the subject of this inquiry: to what extent do the teachers and candidate teachers who have graduated from a "teachers' department" have the necessary pedagogical and teaching qualifications?

## Method

In this research the curricula of 14 university departments belonging to the spectrum of the so-called teachers' departments are studied. These departments have been chosen so as to represent different teaching specializations (mathematics, physics, languages, history/archaeology, biology, geology) from various Greek universities. The study programmes and the curricula were studied with regard to whether they provide PTP to their students. The research was carried out twice: in Spring 2009, and at the beginning of 2013. Law 3848 was passed between these dates i.e. in 2010. This law determines that PTP is obligatory for all candidate secondary school teachers in the recruitment contests which are to follow, with the exception of the two first contests. The sample of departments is the same so as to allow a judgment upon eventual changes in the study programmes as a result of the new law.

The axes of analysis of the study programmes are as follows:

i) In order to discover whether an overall PTP for the students of those departments exists (which is implied by the term "teachers' departments") all the mandatory pedagogical courses are noted.

ii) In order to verify if the opportunity for a PTP, based on an overall conception of a PTP programme, exists for the students who want it, the orientations and the optional pedagogical courses are noted.

iii) In order to determine if there have been any changes resulting from the establishment of Law 3848, data from the years 2013 and 2009 are compared.

## Results

Table 20-1 presents the number of obligatory pedagogical courses provided by the departments covered in our research:

| Department of | Number of obligatory pedagogical courses | |
|---|---|---|
| | 2009 | 2013 |
| Physics, University of Patras | 0 | 0 |
| Physics, University of Crete | 0 | 0 |
| Chemistry, Aristotle University of Thessaloniki | 0 | 0 |
| Chemistry, University of Ioannina | 0 | 0 |
| Biology, NKUA | 0 | 0 |
| Biology, Aristotle University of Thessaloniki | 0 | 0 |
| Geology and Geoenvironment, NKUA | 0 | 0 |
| History and Archeology, NKUA | 2 | 2 |
| History and Archeology, University of Ioannina | 1 | 1 |
| Philology, University of Patras | 0 | 0 |
| English language and Philology, NKUA | 2 | 2 |
| Mathematics, University of the Aegean | 0 | 0 |
| Mathematics, University of Patras | 0 | 0 |
| Mathematics, University of Crete | 0 | 0 |

**Table 20-1. Obligatory pedagogical courses in 14 undergraduate programs of teachers' departments. Source: Study regulations and study programmes.[1]**

It is clear that the term "teachers' departments" is not justified at least regarding the undergraduate programmes which we have studied. Those programmes are far from providing PTP to their graduates. It must certainly be mentioned that many of these departments have introduced a number of pedagogical courses which are usually free choice out of lists where the majority of the courses offered are not pedagogical. In some of the departments the orientation "education" is proposed, whereas in most of the departments some optional pedagogical courses exist. These possibilities are presented in Table 20-2.

---

[1] These data have been taken from the study guides and regulations and from the study programmes of the departments, appearing on the respective websites (during the period from 1 March to 5 April 2009). For 2013 the websites were utilized again, as referenced in the bibliography.

| Physics, University of Patras | Four free choice courses are offered (three of them are offered in one of the orientations provided in the 4th year of studies). The picture corresponds to the one in 2009. |
|---|---|
| Physics, University of Crete | A large number of free choice courses, chiefly from the field of Physics Education. Additionally, teaching practice in physics (which includes observing 10 lessons and doing two teaching practices in schools) exists, the same as in 2009. |
| Chemistry, Aristotle University of Thessaloniki | One of the 4th years' orientations is named "Theoretical Chemistry & Chemistry Education". It includes 5 free choice pedagogical courses, chiefly in the didactics of the subject. There is no special reference to teaching practice. Compared with 2008–09 we just find changes in the titles of some courses. |
| Chemistry, University of Ioannina | One free choice pedagogical course, as in 2009. |
| Biology, NKUA | One free choice pedagogical course, as in 2009. |
| Biology, Aristotle University of Thessaloniki | Two free choice courses: "Environmental Education and Awareness" and "Biology Education" offered to all three orientations in the 4th year, one of which is called "General Orientation – Education". The same happened in 2009. |
| Geology & Geo-environment, NKUA | One free choice pedagogical course in the 8th semester, as in 2009. |
| History and Archeology, NKUA | Apart from the two obligatory courses, there is encouragement for two free choice courses in the 5th and 6th semesters as well as for an additional one of the student's choice (offered by the department of Philosophy, Pedagogy and Psychology) in order to "strengthen pedagogic training". The picture is similar to the one in 2009. |
| History and Archeology, University of Ioannina | One obligatory course. No reference to PTP. Additionally, there is at least one free choice course in the 7th semester. The picture corresponds to the one in 2009. |

| Philology, University of Patras | An obligatory course is offered (Didactics of Language) in the linguistics specialization. Three free choice courses are also offered. The picture corresponds to the one in 2009. |
| --- | --- |
| English language and Philology, NKUA | Apart from the two obligatory courses, a large number of free choice courses are offered which have to be chosen for the PTP (more than 5). Teaching practice in the 8th semester. Overall conception and design of a PTP programme entitled "Initial education in Didactics of English". The picture is similar to the one in 2009. |
| Mathematics University of the Aegean | Two free choice courses and a large number of optional (6) are offered, chiefly from the field of mathematics education. Teaching practice is not clearly designed. The picture corresponds to the one in 2009. |
| Mathematics University of Patras | Two free choice courses and a large number of optional courses concerning Mathematics education. Students who are interested in those courses can choose up to 5. Teaching practice is not clearly designed. The structure of the program, regarding PTP, remains the same as that of 2009. |
| Mathematics University of Crete | A large series of free choice pedagogical and mathematics education courses as well as Teaching Practice. An overall conception of a PTP. A standard program extended from the $5^{th}$ to $8^{th}$ semester is proposed in order to obtain the PTP qualification. This possibility was already provided for before the establishment of Law 3848/10. |

**Table 20-2. Opportunities to follow an adequate number of pedagogical courses or a PTP program leading to qualification in 14 undergraduate programmes of teachers' departments.**

It is clear from the table that the pedagogical courses offered are in most cases very few. Even if the student follows two or three courses this is just patchwork compared with the standards of a PTP. Only three departments (English language and Philology NKUA, Mathematics of Crete and Physics of Crete) seem to offer the opportunity of a complete PTP, four others are close to it (Chemistry of Thessaloniki, History and Archaeology NKUA, Mathematics of Patras and Mathematics of the

Aegean) whereas the remaining seven departments are far from providing the possibility of following a PTP. Moreover, no trend towards increasing the number of the pedagogical courses offered is apparent: they are generally the same as those existing in the academic year 2008–09 and as those noted in an older thorough study by the Center of Educational Research (Patouna et al., 2005).

## Conclusion

It follows from the data presented that the majority of the graduates from the departments which were studied in our research do not possess a pedagogical and teaching qualification, as they graduated from programmes which did not, for the most part, provide this opportunity in a systematic way. None of the departments analysed provides PTP to all its students and very few of the departments provide the possibility of following a PTP to the students who want to, as is shown in Table 2. In this respect, PTP is conceived of as an organized study programme, as developed in the introduction, leading to qualification. Moreover, the situation depicted in Table 1 is exactly the same for 2009 and 2013, as if Law 3848 had never been introduced. Concerning the possibility of PTP, the situation is again the same apart from some additional references to the term "pedagogical and teaching qualification" in the study guides of some departments – without, however, any reference to Law 3848.

We can strongly hypothesize, on the basis of the aforementioned results, that the teachers' department graduates holding a pedagogical and teaching qualification constitute a narrow minority of the total. (Some caution is however necessary as our inquiry is not exhaustive regarding the departments. Moreover, entire categories of undergraduate programmes of teachers' departments such as Theology and Physical Education are not represented in our sample.) Nonetheless, all teacher departments' graduates, no matter which orientation they had chosen during their studies and no matter which series of courses they had attended, were accepted by the Ministry of Education to work in secondary education. They are still accepted and they will be accepted in the next two national contests. The low level of implementation of Law 3848 leads ineluctably to doubts regarding whether the exception will only apply to the next two contests. It is worth mentioning that in EU records concerning science teachers' preparation in the member states (Euridice, 2006), Greece is one of the few countries not to have provided enough data. The aforementioned results fully explain it: which system of PTP can our country refer to, when this either does not exist or is segmented? Finally even the cases of a satisfactory PTP which surely exist are not enough to testify to an overall conception and a clear educational policy.

It must be said that a series of changes during the past 10 years have made it rather difficult for someone to work in secondary education without having been at least "informed" of the serious pedagogical and teaching demands of his task. Candidate teachers participate in the national contest (ASEP) for teachers. In this contest 50% of the overall mark awarded concerns the performance in the Pedagogical and Teaching part of the contest. Moreover, for several years introductory training for newly employed teachers has been introduced in the Centres of Teacher Training (PEK). However, those new realities do not negate the need for an organized PTP. The teachers' contest (ASEP) has its own role as an evaluation system and not as an educational system. It may even be asked here how a coefficient of 50% is given to the Pedagogical-Teaching part of the contest, when the possibility of following PTP has not been provided to all the graduates that take part in the contest. Regarding PEK, the introductory training is important but it cannot be a substitute for a PTP. Besides, the introductory training exists for primary education teachers as well, who already have a solid preparation regarding the pedagogical aspects of their vocation: introductory training in PEK is an important complement to a solid previous PTP of candidate teachers.

The above statements are not intended to cast doubt on the efficiency and the scientific adequacy of the departments whose programmes have been studied in this research. They may be excellent departments each one in its particular subject, but they do not deserve to be called "teachers' departments". They prepare scientists in their respective scientific fields but, in most cases, not teachers.

To close, one can wonder if the lack of organized PTP may possibly be covered through encouraging operation of such programmes in university faculties. Maybe an overall policy, at national level, has to be developed. The latter could possibly designate the operation of at least one PTP university programme in each administrative region simultaneously, which would contribute to the elimination of socio-geographical access differentiations to these programmes.

# References

Chevallard, Y. and Cirade, G. 2009. "Pour une formation professionnelle d'université: Éléments d'une problématique de rupture", *Recherche et Formation* 60 (Lyon : INRP), 51–62.

Euridice, le réseau d'information sur l'éducation en Europe. 2006. *L'Enseignement des sciences dans les établissements scolaires en Europe: Etat des lieux des politiques et de la recherche.*

Ginestié J. 2006. *Formation des enseignants: Au-delà des apparences, quelles différences? Une étude internationale sur la formation des enseignants en éducation technologique.* Union Europeéne, Europe Aid, programmes Alfa.

Gomatos, L. 2010a. "La Place de la Didactique dans les Programmes de Préparation des Enseignants de Physique et de Technologie en Grèce", *Review of Science, Mathematics and ICT Education* 4(2) (University of Patras-Metaichmio), 85–99.

Gomatos, L. 2010b. "Preparation of Teachers of Ttechnological Subjects in Greece and in France: A Ccomparative Study", *Preparation of teachers of secondary vocational education in Greece. SEP-ASPETE.* Proceedings of the conference for the 50 years of SELETE-ASPETE, Athens 11th and 12th December 2009, 219–227. [in Greek]

Kassotakis, M. 2010. "The Problem of Pedagogical and Teaching Training of Secondary Education Teachers and the Efforts to Resolve it after the Political Changeover", *Preparation of teachers of secondary vocational education in Greece. SEP-ASPETE.* Proceedings of the conference for the 50 years of SELETE-ASPETE, Athens 11th and 12th December 2009, 293–317. [in Greek]

Official Gazette, Law 3848/2010 (No Α΄/71), http://www.et.gr/index.php?option=com_wrapper&view=wrapper&Itemid=10 4&lang=el (accessed 1 October 2011).

Patouna, A., Stellakou, V., Koutouzis, M., Verevi, A. and Thomadaki, E. 2005. "Pedagogical Courses in Study Programs and the ASEP Contest: Indications for Training Needs of Teachers", in G. Bagakis (ed.), *Training and Professional Development of Teachers.* Athens: Metaichmio, pp. 263–275. [in Greek]

*University websites*
Department of Physics, Patras University, Study Regulations, http://www.physics.upatras.gr/main.php?categoryId=4&subCategoryId=4 (accessed 22 February 2013).

Department of Geology and Geoenvironment, NKUA, http://www.geol.uoa.gr/attachments/article/487/geologiko_odig_spoydon_201 2_2013_SITE.pdf (accessed 2 March 2013).

Department of Philology, University of Patras, Study guide, http://www.philology-upatras.gr/files/content/Odigos%20Spoudwn%202012-13_site.pdf

Department of Chemistry, Aristotle University of Thessaloniki, new program of studies, http://www.chem.auth.gr/index.php?rm=5&mn=631 accessed 2 March 2013).

Department of Biology, NKUA, http://www.biol.uoa.gr/fileadmin/biol.uoa.gr/uploads/PDF_Files/Odigos_Violo gias_2012_2013.pdf (accessed 3 March 2013).

Department of Mathematics, University of the Aegean, http://www.math.aegean.gr/in/index.htm (accessed 3 March 2013).

Department of Mathematics, University of Crete, http://www.math.uoc.gr/ep_spoud/ug-programme.html (accessed 3 March 2013).

Department of Mathematics, University of Patras, http://www.math.upatras.gr/media/Ops_gr_12-13.pdf (accessed 3 March 2013).

Department of Chemistry, University of Ioannina, http://www.chem.uoi.gr/sites/default/files/O_S_XHMEIAS.pdf (accessed 3 March 2013).

Department of Biology, Aristotle University of Thessaloniki, http://www.bio.auth.gr/content/programma-proptukhiakon-spoudon (accessed 3 March 2013).

Department of English Language and Philology, NKUA, http://www.enl.uoa.gr/fileadmin/enl.uoa.gr/uploads/pdf/os_12_13a.pdf (accessed 4 March 2013).

Department of History and Archaeology, NKUA, http://www.arch.uoa.gr/fileadmin/arch.uoa.gr/uploads/proptyxiakes_spoudes/o dhgos_spoudwn_2012_2013.pdf (accessed 8 March 2013).

Department of History and Archaeology, University of Ioannina, http://www.hist-arch.uoi.gr/pdfs_docs/odigos_spoudon_new_2012_2013.pdf (accessed 9 March 2013).

Department Physics, University of Crete, http://www.physics.uoc.gr/files/undergrad_guide_2009_sm.pdf (accessed 9 March 2013).

# Chapter Twenty-One

## Political Ambiguities of Lifelong Education: Between Humanism and Technocratism

### Kalerante Evaggelia
#### Assistant Professor, University of Western Macedonia, Greece

**Abstract**

In the present paper the lifelong education model is being examined – as an education rationalization procedure, so that the "educational draft" is redefined – which functions as an alternative intrinsic educational model by which the transition from traditional educational structures to alternative educational solutions is brought about and is conducive to the most rapid adjustment to the changing socio-professional roles. The individuals' corresponding socialization in flexible forms of work and their assimilation by the post-modern form of labour roles, as they are formulated within differentiated "economic areas", are included in the "educational draft".

Emphasis is placed on how interaction and exchange mechanisms with social and political domains are developed by lifelong education, so that, through a total of conjunctions and disjunctions, a different educational field is formulated in which the partial ideal type regulations compose an idiosyncratic individual as the notion of individual completion, progress and prosperity is typically or non-typically redefined within spatio-temporal realities which are formulated on the basis of the prevailing economic paradigm.

**Keywords**

Lifelong education, rationalization, educational draft, economic paradigm.

## Introduction: Lifelong Education as an Educational Reality

The lifelong educational model is incorporated in the new "educational constructions" directly related to the "economic paradigm" imposing compliance policies through special political instruments. Reference could be made to the educational policy imposed by the European Union on member-states (Passias, 2006; Tsaousis, 2007). A general view on the association between lifelong education and economy emphasizing the change in education apparently affects all educational grades and imposes corresponding adjustments in the educational bureaucratic structures of educational micro-society and curricula (Cobb, 2013). The effect of the economic model on the educational system of countries facing economic crisis is very interesting. This is the case of Greece where the cost curtailment policy distracts and disorganizes structures while interventions in the cognitive fields, namely cognitive areas, are intensified (Kalerante, 2011).

A system of traditional educational grades is gradually being formulated and directly associated to individuals' expectations to integrate into the labour market. During a period of economic insecurity and uncertainty individuals are gradually adjusting to new flexible labour relations in which a solid reference to labour time, salary, security and pension is absent. Individuals invest more time on work and simultaneously more time on acquiring "packages of knowledge" so that they use the economic model. There is no possibility of escape as integration in labour is identified both with economic and social needs because labour is a value tied to the acceptance by and integration into the social whole and the corresponding social status.

Within the European Union framework the acceleration of educational and training transformations are accentuated so that a model of education and training corresponding to the general framework of the committees' goals for performance harmonization with education is reinforced. Symbolically speaking, it is the articulation of a highlighted policy on prosperity and social coherence in Europe (Dienel, 2003). According to the national reports of countries ever since 2004 (House of Lords, 2005) there have been detailed data about the promotion of lifelong education. Emphasis is particularly placed on policies reinforcing the promotion of the corresponding transformations, adjustments, programmes and carriers tied to the implementation of a lifelong education policy in the systemic view of the European social model.

Acquisition of "functional knowledge", both formal and piecemeal, is reinforced by the educational policy toward a conservative perception of education in which knowledge and skills are separate. Meanwhile the individual is also separated from pursuing the essence of knowledge which could form the "self", in humanistic terms (Veugelers, 2011).

Lifelong education is formed and acts in the context of a post-modern bio-authority which monitors and guides individuals, as units, in an economic system. Besides, there is a continuous readjustment of its productivity, undermining interests and values of the lower social strata, corrupting and distorting individuals' existence and social life. Thus, individuals are not able to define their lives in the social and political system. As social subjects they experience the fear of rejection when unemployed because they ought to readjust structures and relations in their broader social environments. Life plans conducive to experiencing the pleasure of nature, social company and love are concurrently cancelled. Individuals are apparently enfeebled and depend on the economic paradigm which regulates and defines their lives in various phases. They live in a confined, mass-like world in which diversity is replaced by a homogeneous mass, defined by similar figures moving at a loss in the space-time system. In this respect the self becomes valueless as the creative dimension is dissolved. Emotions are simultaneously limited since everyday reality is intensified within an undefined continuum of imposed work either in the form of labour or education.

Lifelong education for the lower strata is incorporated in the transformation of methods for monitoring individuals as they continuously define their life in the educational system, associating it with labour. In other words functional knowledge is traded for participation or incorporation in labour on the basis of new labour conditions, namely flexible, insecure "economic areas". The definition of lifelong education is unstable and vague since knowledge as well as the individuals' role and right to education are not included in it. Moreover, it is not tied, in humanistic terms, to notions about personality development, self-cultivation and the link between educational policy and other social fields like political morality.

Lifelong education is the means by which the relation between the individual and the economic system is rewritten, shaping a form of education in which individuals are incorporated as potential economic subjects (Rouse, 2010). Thus, through education there is a legalization of schematized authority relations. Meaning is given to obedience and discipline relations in an economic model, cancelling aspects of social life and self-fulfilment. The irrational functioning of the labour market is enhanced by functional arrangements implemented through education by mingling education with "labour morality" within the context of irrationalism and a broader model of progress and social prosperity conceptualization. The association of progress and prosperity with economy and how subjects are "exhausted" by the economic system in their striving for reincorporation in undefined economic conditions is very interesting (De Vogli, 2013).

Individuals' morality on the basis of their role and adaptability in the economic environment is redefined. Moreover, utility, prosperity and progress are defined in economic terms. In this sense, individual self-fulfilment is lost through education and labour. There is also a cancellation of emotions which would be conducive to love, understanding, companionship and groupings of the established defined patterns of labour and education areas. These areas are apparently unified in a continuum in which the amorphous figures of trainees/employees move. They receive specific packages of knowledge but their personal needs are not taken into account. The only thing that matters is what is defined as necessary by the economic system.

References to other systems or to underlying individual needs or predispositions are enfeebled by the dynamics of the economic system. In humanistic terms, emphasis could be placed on the loss of emotions resulting in the cancellation of personality traits within a model in which individuals apparently trade off their feelings and thoughts with the political-economic system to avoid marginalization. Thus, the question is whether one could state one's thoughts and feelings when one is forced to adapt to changing economic conditions. In political terms, we see the gradual cancellation of the policy of rights. In other words, the stability of democracy and the related acknowledgment of citizens' rights (conducive to the creation of security by which they could define their lives) fade.

In the post-modern field of uncertainty and insecurity – also formed on an international level and especially affecting marginalized people (Bauman, 2000, 2011a, 2011b) – lifelong education suspends or cancels the essence of knowledge tied to democratic principles of equality, social solidarity and humanism. Reference is made to the cancellation of any moral or values system through the formation of new correspondences conducive to insecure and uncertain conditions (Bauman, 2007). As regards lower social strata, long-term education in fields of their choice is rejected since families are not able to support long-term studies with no direct relation to the labour market. It should be pointed out that humanitarian studies, the relation to higher culture, namely art and music, and principles like solidarity and the recognition of the other tied to social co-existence and the essence of democracy, are all downgraded. In this respect the rise of extreme right wings could be deemed the outcome of deficient humanistic capital (Kalerante, 2013b; Kalerante, 2013c).

Lifelong education functions as an imposed form of education from which choice and the individuals' potential decisions on the cognitive fields of their desire are absent. According to Sen (1992; 2010) the social and political formation of preferences and choices are attuned to the broader model of justice which is formulated in a democratic environment. To perceive the deconstruction and the new conceptual fields, the broader changes of social values and systems should be incorporated in the time-space compression, to use Harvey's terms (1989). Thus, despite the disproportions in a new globalized system, internationalized policies and globalized conditions of social deconstruction or decay are apparently strengthened (King, 1995).

Lifelong education is about another form of education whose compositional nature is conducive to shifting educational policy from knowledge to functional knowledge. In this sense there is a transfer from a constructive active situation to imposed conditions in which knowledge is transformed into limited "packages" including data necessary for changing and unstable labour areas. The content of the emerging knowledge and its transformation into "shared areas of knowledge" is confined to meet the needs defined by the economic environment (Kalerante, 2013a).

These new "packages" contain value patterns, as void elements, legalizing the gradual unfolding of a globalized policy to reinforce social inequality and limitation of rights in a regulating procedure towards reworking of the capitalist system in which the renewed perception of efficiency and performance in education is defined. According to Knopp & Bale (2012) the educational model is tied to post-modern societies through the reinforcement of the capitalist system emphasizing structural components and model functionality.

## Lifelong Learning as a Form of Legal Violence

As foretold, lifelong education legalizes the individual's disdain and assimilation in labour areas following the gradual cancellation or de-legalization of the policy of rights. Although lifelong education is, theoretically, the individuals' choice, if they lack it they are not able to enter the labour market. They are explicitly based on this type of education so that they are selectable by the labour market. Reference is made to individual conventions in which each one depends on lifelong education to acquire the packages of knowledge.

The lower social strata are primarily entrapped in the new economic conditions and the corresponding political arrangements. As a result, they are turned into a labour force which is continuously re-educated pursuing their incorporation in flexible forms of labour through relevant and legalized functional knowledge. According to Sennett (2007) flexible labour and insecurity is tied to the new capitalist development model. Consequently, choice is cancelled and lifelong education is not tied to selected knowledge. No meaningfulness is given to the individual's selection of cognitive fields as poles of interest. On the contrary, the essence of knowledge and the concept of choice are undermined. The individual is entrapped in a condition in which non-compliance results in one's questioning and rejection by a system promoting uniformity as an end to its maintenance through the citizens' disdain.

This turn of education apparently signals the decay of humanitarian studies as this type of education is not correspondent to the technocratic form of functional knowledge. In a period when reformulated values model and the individuals' attitudes and behaviours, like their choices, are based on efficiency and performance the concept of "moment", as a time signified, incorporates choices containing interpretations of the economic condition and the individual's relation to labour areas interpreted in social and economic terms.

The brief character of labour opportunities as taxonomic criteria in a period of economic crisis makes difficult the free selection of cognitive fields. Besides, the enforced functional knowledge prevails through the invocation of fears of rejection and the individual's disapproval or marginalization which defines its incorporation in the labour market concurrently as a social and economic subject.

The invocation of these fears, mainly by individuals from lower social strata, reinforces the reception of the prescribed forms of flexible zone. Additionally, they are established as "consumers" of functional knowledge rejecting any form of knowledge on an abstract or symbolic level which is contradicted by the labour market. The change of the economic paradigm formulated during the period of economic crisis leads to "educational transfer", the representation of which is lifelong education. The manipulation mainly of the lower strata is conducted through it by means of bodiless violence which monitors people's life and represents an intense lifelong process of panoptic supervision.

In confining terms, a "bricoleur" with prescribed knowledge and skills is formulated through lifelong education, having misappropriated the new values of submission and discipline, and is to be integrated into the "mass", supporting the asymmetric development of economy on a globalized level, through the restriction of the policy of rights. The general view on discipline systems and the formation of obedience and discipline conditions through supervision and along the formation of regularity and non-regularity in terms of behaviour is of special interest (Foucault, 1995).

## Humanistic and Technocratic Knowledge: Contradictory Co-statements in the Class Model

Lifelong education forms a labour market-related educational model which reinforces social inequality as functional knowledge is formulated as content knowledge, mainly for the lower social strata. Additionally, it will be re-integrated in unstable, insecure, fluid professional environments. This is a model related to the convergence of interests during the economic crisis period between the economic core and state educational policy.

Lower social strata individuals are observed to function within a sterile technological and cognitive environment in which emotions, creative thinking and the highlighted choices and preferences about the present and the future are destroyed (Sennett, 2000). According to D. Cohen, a *homo economicus* unable to experience happiness and success off the economic paradigm is formed while his life and experiences are fluid and the pleasure of wishes and dreams is absent. His bonds to the economic environment are tied by means of shaping his identity. On the other hand, personal pleasures, even those ones which, as a *homo empathicus*, could be available in family, friends and companions, are lost (Cohen, 2012).

People are apparently trapped and dependent on lifelong education and labour areas. It is a "post-modern paranoia" which is conducive to people's isolation, in political terms, since they are defined as trainees or workers pointing to confining relations through their gradual disdain. People's political assimilation is accelerated in labour areas by lifelong education which also accomplishes a functional compliance with post-modern labour conditions by preventing ideological or social conflicts which would be incompatible within a globalized rhetoric of counter-riot and submission.

Times of work and times of no work are hard to distinguish. Times of no work include lifelong education which, being integrated in the social field, redefines the individual's position in relation to labour. Both times of work and times of no work have a social political and moral dynamic in which the individual is defined and profiles his/her position in the social whole while trapped in imposed defined time from which he/she cannot be diversified. Thus he/she cannot be creative in an active game of dialogue full of thoughts and emotions which, in humanistic terms, would bring him/her close to his/her fellows and, in sociopolitical terms, would be conducive to the perception of ideological capital in which it would move as a political subject by exercising political control toward the prevention of deconstructing democratic principles.

There is no time between the time of work and the time of no work so that individuals could eventually formulate a different perspective on their position within the economic and political system. Cancelling the policy of rights is conducive to the gradual disdain of the individual's social existence while the reformulation, under stricter terms, of inequality, subordination, dependence and "de-humanization" systems is obvious. The schematic distinction between upper and lower social strata is incorporated in their relation to lifelong education and the labour market. Social classes are reorganized within the prevailing labour relations of flexibility and insecurity (Kerbo, 2011), perhaps on stricter terms. These relations are explicitly or implicitly generated in various social environments. People from upper social strata, even if they are integrated in formal lifelong education, are able to choose "packages of knowledge" which they will additionally enrich with new "free fields of knowledge".

Although a decrease of social inequality in western societies has been achieved during recent years through the reinforcement of democratic institutions, policies of rights and the enhancement of long-term education, a system of acute social inequalities with unpredictable consequences is now to be seen. Nussbaum and Ferguson's viewpoints on the troubling situation in society are interesting. More analytically, liberal systems are not in favour of the citizens' confidence in the institutions and the right to dream is absent. In other words the lower social strata's right to achievement and distinction in societies allowing, even theoretically and in a confining amount, the transfer from one society to another does not exist (Ferguson, 2012; Nussbaum, 2012).

Lifelong learning is about the possibility of the upper social strata managing information networks and adjusting to decision policies, benefiting from the advantages by which they can define themselves under different correlations and strategies by taking initiatives and transforming organizational forms and compositional processes. Thus they are incorporated in the labour market on different terms, have political discourse and position and are capable, through consolidated timeliness tactics, of defining their standpoint by confirming their class dynamics towards the utilization of the historic instance and economic dynamics.

Upper social strata seem to benefit from the economic crisis through an internal redistribution of educational, social and economic capital which, typically or atypically, redistributes information and benefits through a centripetal tendency which is enhanced in contradistinction to the process of de-democratization (Tilly, 2007). In this process not only do people of lower social strata benefit from privileges, but the policy of rights and subsequent opportunity structures are also lost. Even though inequality has not been eliminated in recent years, the aforementioned structures were conducive to the reinforcement of the subjects' political protection and the possibility of defining themselves within a dynamic sociopolitical environment. Furthermore, they were legalized and able to manage cognitive fields through increased free time and solid labour relations resulting in emotional and mental enhancement and democratic cognitive forms of school organization.

Lifelong education is the expression of deeper educational transformation following a model of functional knowledge provision for the lower social strata whose contact with this form of education is increased during periods of unemployment and decreased during the corresponding periods of employment. Given the insecure and fluid labour status of lifelong education as well as people's dependence on incomplete packages of knowledge, the formation of new subjects will be expanded. In the light of confined cognitive fields people will not be able to be autonomous, to vindicate their rights or to function as political individuals (Sennet, 1992). Thus, the possibilities of questioning or inversion of dependence and submission relations will be minimized.

# Conclusion

The capitalist system, by means of lifelong education, perpetuates its relation to individuals by monitoring the knowledge provided which is transformed into functional, defined, prescribed and controlled knowledge. The provision, distribution or enforcement of functional knowledge is established in the new economic, national and international legal requirements.

In other words, lifelong education is eventually deemed the subject of economy and politics. Thus, it functions as a form of educational super-simplification through the combined use of functional knowledge and skills closely related to new technologies. As a result, an educational model in constructed that reinforces moving and flexible forms of labour in which the individuals' new functional code in the labour areas will be incorporated.

The individual is ruptured from social bonds and political pockets which would associate it with the democratic function of societies, political deliberation and, eventually, the movement action. All this is due to the fact that lower social strata are engaged in a process of working without labour rights, unemployment, lifelong education and loss of free time.

# References

Bauman, Z. 2000. *Liquid Modernity*. Cambridge: Polity Press
—. 2007. *Consuming Life*. Cambridge: Polity Press
—. 2011a. *Collateral Damage: Social Inequalities in a Global Age*. Cambridge: Polity Press.
—. 2011b. *Culture in a Liquid Modern World*. Cambridge: Polity Press
Cobb, J. 2013. *Leading the Learning Revolution: The Expert's Guide to Capitalizing on the Exploding Lifelong Education Market*. USA: Cobb.
Cohen, D. 2012. *Homo Economicus*. Paris: Albin Michel.
De Vogli, R. (2013). *Progress or Collapse: The Crises of Market Greed*. London: Routledge.
Dienel, C. 2003.*Visions of Europe: Europavisionen*. USA: Peter Lang.
Ferguson, N. 2012. *The Great Degeneration*. USA: Penguin Press.
Foucault, M. 1995. *Discipline and Punish: The Birth of the Prison*. 2nd edn. New York: Vintage Books.
Harvey, D. 1989. *The Condition of Post-modernity*. Oxford: Blackwell.
House of Lords. European Union Committee. 2005. *Proposed EU Integrated Action Programme for Life-Long Learning: Report: 17th Report of Session 2004–05*. United Kingdom: Stationery Office.
Kalerante, E. 2011. "Instrumental Financial Management of Education: Ideological and Political Extensions of its Dominance in the Immigrants' Education". 4th International Scientific Conference. *The role of social policy today, critical approaches and challenges*. (in press).
—. 2012. *Greek Educational Policy in recessionary Times: Does liberal educational Policy take its toll on the Leisure Activities of the lower social Strata?* Cambridge Scholars Publishing.
—. 2013a. "Shared Areas of Knowledge in the Educational Process or Lifelong Education as an Economic Condition" in *Institutions in Greece after the Political Changeover. Evaluation of a contradictory period*. Athens: Papazisis.
—. 2013b. "The Youngsters' Participation in Extreme Right Political Parties in Greece: The Case of Students-supporters of 'Chrisi Avgi'", *American Journal of Educational Research* 1(6), 199–204.
—. 2013c. "Extreme Right Political Discourse and its Educational Dimensions as they are Projected in the Formal Form of the Greek Extreme Right Political Party of 'Chrisi Avgi'", in International Academic Conference on Social Sciences, *Conference Proceedings,* 88–94.
Kerbo, H. 2011. *Social Stratification and Inequality*. London: McGraw-Hill Humanities.

King, A. 1995. "The Time and Spaces of Modernity" in Featherstone, M., Lash, S. & Robertson, R. (eds) *Global Modernities*. London: Sage.

Knopp, S. and Bale, J. 2012. *Education and Capitalism: Struggles for Learning and Liberation.* Chicago: Haymarket Books.

Nussbaum, M. 2012. *Not for Profit: Why Democracy Needs the Humanities.* Princeton: Princeton University Press.

Passias, G. 2006. *European Union and Education: Institutional Discourse and Educational Policy (1950–1999).* Athens: Gutenberg.

Persson, B. M. and Goddard, M. 2000. *Literacy within Lifelong Learning: Elements of Good Practice in Ffive European Countries: England, Portugal, Slovenia…* Slovenia: Ljubljana.

Rouse, W. 2010. *The Economics of Human Systems Integration: Valuation of Investments in People's Training and Education, Safety and Health.* Canada: Wiley

Sen, A. 1992. *Inequality Re-examined.* USA: Harvard University Press.

—. 2010. *The Idea of Justice.* United Kingdom: Penguin Books.

Sennett, R. 1992. *The Fall of Public Man.* London: W.W. Norton & Company.

—. 2000. *The Corrosion of Character: The Personal Consequences of Work in the New Capitalism.* London: W.W. Norton & Company.

—. 2007. *The Culture of the New Capitalism.* USA: Yale University Press.

Tilly, C. 2007. *Democracy.* Cambridge: Cambridge University Press.

Tsaousis, D. G. 2007. *The Educational Policy of International Organisations: Global and European Dimensions.* Athens: Gutenberg.

Veugelers, W. 2011. *Education and Humanism: Linking Autonomy and Humanity.* Canada: Sense Publishers.

# PART III:

# TRAINING, EVALUATION AND TEACHING PRACTICE ISSUES IN TEACHER EDUCATION

# CHAPTER TWENTY-TWO

## ARISTOTELIAN RHETORIC COUNSELLING METHODS FOR TRAINING TEACHERS IN GREECE AND EUROPE

### S. TRIANTARI
ASSISTANT PROFESSOR, UNIVERSITY OF WESTERN MACEDONIA, GREECE

**Abstract**

Aristotle's *Rhetoric* and *Protrepticus to Themisona* is a communicative tool for the modern teacher who is an active critical political subject; it helps widen the limits of democracy in school and society. This study aims to show the practical and theoretical use of *Rhetoric* and *Protrepticus* based on a consultative method with an international perspective in the training of teachers. The teacher acts in the field of communicative interactions and conflicts with the main aim of promoting social and educational relationships. The teacher as an orator-adviser of education must acquire the communicative ability of persuasion to convey knowledge, to develop characters and transform the "art" and "artless" rhetorical proofs into rules of teaching method. Also, the philosopher teacher-adviser must acquire self-awareness and self-control, helping actively in meaningful social and educational change.

**Keywords**
Rhetoric, rhetorical proofs, communication, teacher, adviser, consultative, training, prudence, empathy

## Introduction

One of the basic problems faced by modern educators across Europe is the students' problematic behaviour and the need to communicate with students, parents and among each other within a modern communicative and collaborative framework. Aristotle's *Rhetoric* and *Protrepticus to Themisona* can be a teaching tool for the Greek and European educator, which, if adapted to the needs and requirements of the modern educational system, can be a consultative training method for teachers. There are two classical Aristotelian works from which the *Rhetoric* provides the educator with suitable verbal structures and styles of argument. *Protrepticus* as a consultative discourse constructs interpersonal relations and mutual communication between teacher and student. Thus Aristotelian rhetoric could form a consultative training method for educators at an international level, by providing balance between the philosophy of Greek and European educators. On the one hand, in this view, the knowledge of Aristotelian rhetoric can help the modern educator fulfil his role. On the other hand the educator and his students can examine, within a quite good communicative environment, any problems which concern them when working towards a solution.

## Rhetoric as the Beginning of Modern Counselling

The original meaning of counselling implies giving or getting advice. Counselling is the evolutionary form of one out of three types of rhetorical discourse, which is consultative discourse. According to Aristotle's *Rhetoric*, in consultative discourse "the listener judges topics of his concern; therefore, what has to be proved is that facts are as they are told by the consultative orator" (Aristotle, Rhetoric, 1345b). This Aristotelian parameter for consultative discourse is more than the modern meaning of counselling which is merely the process of mutual communication of the competent adviser-orator with the listener or listeners on the individual or individuals' issues and considerations (Dellis, 2005: 39, 120). The focal point of modern counselling is the improvement of the individual's interpersonal relations. Therefore, the adviser's basic pursuit is to lead the individual to self-control, self-awareness and self-criticism. Thus counselling evolves to a dynamic self-revelation of the individual's intellectual potential towards their activation (Papanoutsos, 1957: 98–131).

The counselling background is reinforced by two fundamental essays, Aristotle's *Rhetoric* and *Protrepticus*, which are the practical and theoretical framework of counselling. The timely contribution of rhetoric is the constitution of discourse through a rational reasoning process which, along with the orator's ethos and special qualifications, forms the manner of persuasion (Triantari, 2012: 11–12). The *Protrepticus* forms the theoretical construction of the modern adviser's word of advice about human self-examination and self-control further aimed at self-determination in life and work (Triantari, 2011: 503). The *Protrepticus* is definitely this kind of consultative rhetoric discourse and is deemed likely to be Aristotle's work. It provides a distinctive method of argumentation aspiring to persuade people to philosophize, by pinpointing the reconciliation of rhetoric with philosophy for individual and collective well-being (Hutchinson & Johnson, 2006: 62–63).

Within a period of economic, social and political changes which is also characterized by a profound and growing moral and social crisis, to the extent that people do not pursue self-control and self-criticism to improve their interpersonal relations, modern educators should inspire their students with good interpersonal relations and proper communicative behaviour, instead of being merely a transmitter of knowledge. Aristotelian rhetoric could be a consultative method in the process of educators' training in Greece and Europe, by framing both the theoretical and the practical part of personality formulation not as a mere educator but as an educator-adviser.

## Rhetoric as Training in the Adviser-educator's role

Rhetoric is an equivalent art and the beginning of counselling. Therefore, rhetoric is potentially conducive to the educator's training and, in particular, to the educator's consultative role throughout the educational process. Within this framework an attempt is made to delineate some basic traits of Aristotelian rhetoric through the formulation of a training draft related to the modern educator's role as an adviser. It is widely accepted that no significance has been given to the educator's training regarding his consultative role to children. Nonetheless, the consultative role forms the basic parameter for the child's smooth integration into school and afterwards into society (Brouzos, 2009: 72). The educator's credibility is the first and essential principle of fulfilling the consultative role. Persuasion is the art of rhetoric itself which is elevated through the orator's expert and fully poised discourse (Gagarin, 2003: 31–32). Therefore rhetoric, as a competence of the orator (adviser-educator-politician-public speaker), is the location of persuasive traits and should not be overlooked during the educational process (Aristotle, Rhetoric, 1355b). According to the determinant meaning of rhetoric in the educational system the educator should be trained in the basic evolutionary periods of rhetoric taking into account basic representatives like Gorgias, the formulator of rhetoric into the science of persuasion (Zuntz, 2003: 95).

Provided that the relation between rhetoric and counselling is inextricable and indissoluble, the traits of the educator's consultative role towards the formation of students' attitude limits and behaviour should be sought after. The modern educator is provided by Aristotle with three ways of gaining students' confidence: students are addressed with respect and appreciation while the educator can comprehend them, discuss with them and give them advice to their problem. More specifically, the educator's training should be oriented towards three goals: character cultivation and improvement; the process of understanding and expressing emotions; and proved persuasive argumentation towards truth (Aristotle, Rhetoric, 1356a; Kennedy, 2000: 94).

These three  are the starting point towards the educators' training further aiming at the improvement of the educational system within a modern European framework. The first parameter related to the educator's character is his primary obligation to a change "from inside out". Aristotle is perhaps the only philosopher accentuating the orator's honesty as the essential trait of the rhetoric art (Aristotle, *Rhetoric*, 1356a). Honesty presupposes the educator's autonomy, self-awareness and freedom. The educator's free will is the utilization of himself through wise and scheduled actions. These traits are expanded to interpersonal relations and communication with students and parents (Brown & Prywansky-Shulte, 2006: 501–502; Triantari, 2011: 112–113).

The second parameter is concerned with the development and improvement of the educator's ethical and psychological stability and balance. He approaches his students through his warmth and friendliness by expressing, through his own emotions, his students' emotions. The educator is the constructor of an interpersonal relation ending in an honest communication with children. Within this communicative interaction the educator's insights and skills are elevated to the extent that children can be armoured with mental power, their self-confidence and self-control being reinforced while any insecurity or negative thought about the future is overturned (Brouzos, 2009: 167).

The third parameter could be deemed pivotal in reinforcing and facilitating interpersonal relations and throughout the instruction process. The correct constitution of argumentation entails correct reasoning which proves that the educator is language cognizant so that he accurately and clearly transfers his viewpoints to students (Aristotle, *Rhetoric*, 1413b). The lucidity of argumentation is conducive to empathy, to empathetic listening and communicating empathy. Aristotle in *Nicomachean Ethics B΄* (1106b) posed the issue of emotional intelligence according to which the educator adviser understands and empathizes with students' problems and considerations. Emotional intelligence contains one more similar parameter, mutual transfer, acknowledgment and comprehension of the other's experiences. Experiences' transfer as a step to empathy was John Dewey's base for teacher-student communication (Dewey, 1997: 5–6; Triantari, 2008: 275). Dewey particularly accentuates the importance of rhetoric and references communication from a particularly verbal connection of words, in which according to Aristotle, customs are attributed (Aristotle, *Rhetoric*, 1407b) to a manner, a communicative method bringing people close to each other so that there are mutual achievements in a democratic society (Triantari, 2012: 63).

The third parameter is the peak of the educator's competence to be oneself as well as his psychic composition, as this is obvious in his authentic behaviour, the elevation of behaviour to a position equal to self-awareness, a point towards which the educators' training should be oriented. Aristotle, in his rhetorical plan, bequeathed to both the Greek and European educator the means to a complete training, which concerns the implementation of "art" and "artless" evidence in the modern European framework.

## "Art" and "Artless" Rhetoric Evidence as a Modern Communicative Teaching Method

Two kinds of evidence were elevated in Aristotle's *Rhetoric*, "artless" ones which pre-exist (accounts, confessions etc.) and "art" ones which, through rhetoric, can be constructed by people (Aristotle, *Rhetoric*, 1335b; Brauw, 2010: 195–196). Both kinds are important to education. "Art" evidence is the background of modern "visual" rhetoric in lifelong education teachers' training included (Fow, 1982: 56–57; Foss, 2004: 312–313). Reference is made to the modern form of "artless" evidence which is the teacher–student communication channels. "Art" evidence is reinforced by Aristotle through reference to "indications" on the basis of which argumentation is constituted. "Indications" are the information towards the formation of a judgment or suggestion (Aristotle, *Rhetoric*, 1357b). In modern reality "indications" are represented by the points, that is the signifier and the signified of semiotics. These points give meaning to the content of a text both verbally and non-verbally. Through the combination of "artless" evidence and "visual" rhetoric (Ehninger, 1972: 3) with semiotics, the educator is provided the audiovisual methods of teaching (power point, video, music etc.). The teacher–student communication is blunted by these methods as through a picture, an incontrovertible confession, emotions are expressed and both verbal and non-verbal reactions are emanated.

This form of audiovisual communicative method is a teaching method in which the modern educator should be trained. It is therefore realized that rhetoric is necessary as a subject for both teacher and student and throughout the educational act. The educator's communicative and consultative perspective is completed through the correct constitution of discourse with the relevant use of verbal schemata and elegant verbal style (Aristotle, *Rhetoric*, 1407a-b, 1408a-b) in combination with body movement, facial expressions or gestures (Pernot, 2005: 346). In this sense it is clear that educators' training as advisers is a hard process also including self-education (Plato, *Politeia*, 377b, 1-cl-5; Triantari, 2005: 130–131). This is done in the form of self-awareness and control through the educator's own completion and self-fulfilment in order to achieve the students' completion and self-fulfilment. Self-fulfilment is the hallway to a humanistic education by which the educator's role is altered in the classroom. Aristotle's *Protrepticus* is a guide for counselling towards the educator adviser's training conducive to this change of role.

## *Protrepticus* as a Guide for Counselling Educators in the Modern World

*Protrepticus to Themisona* (353/351 BC) is deemed by scholars a work of Aristotle since there are essential traits elevating Aristotelian thinking (Düring, 2003: 162). It is a consultative discourse in which Aristotle pinpoints a basic pedagogical standpoint to Themisona, king of Cyprus, and persuades him to engage in philosophy (Triantari, 2012: 423). *Protrepticus* is a timeliness consultative discourse whose basic reverberation until today is the study of philosophy as a guide and tool of modern man towards the completion of his personality through self-control and self-criticism (Triantari, 2012: 431). Through *Protrepticus* Aristotle constructs the art of rhetoric on the basic philosophical concepts of bliss, justice, self-restraint, leniency, wisdom as well as to what is good and beneficial. These concepts empower the basic qualifications of the educator-adviser who, through his personality and behaviour, potentially gives his own specifications for a good student and future active citizen.

Aristotle's *Protrepticus* could be the basic guide to training of an educator who actually assumes the adviser's role. As a guide to practical life *Protrepticus* offers an educational process, a combination of meditation with the formulation of moral behaviour. Through *Protrepticus* the educator-adviser could be an enthusiastic inspiration for students not only in lessons but throughout any involvement in life. The educator through his personality can merely activate students' psyche. Psychic activity is the outcome of Aristotelian teaching in the sense that life is given to alert and wise men and not to dopey and unwise ones. Psychic activity signals the pleasure of living (Aristotle, *Protrepticus to Themisona* 90, p. 565).

The educator's training should explicitly turn towards the development and inextricable dynamics of the teacher-student relation. A turn towards philosophy will essentially be conducive to this development as Aristotle suggested, since the pleasure of life is the outcome of the involvement with philosophy being primarily the art of living (Aristotle, *Protrepticus to Themisona* 91, p. 567) and any kind of living, particularly students' living throughout the educational process. Unfortunately, both rhetoric and philosophy are absent in both the school curriculum and educators' training. *Protrepticus* introduces a basic parameter according to which the art of rhetoric in combination with philosophy could be a determinant factor for the educator-adviser's role. The modern educator should primarily aim to heal the psyche through intervening to improve students' behaviour by encouraging the expected behaviour and by presenting his personality as a means to help them love school and cooperate with him (Karageorgou, 2010: 45).

Moreover, the *Protrepticus* offers the educator-adviser a systematic rhetoric consultative discourse of a technical nature which could be used as coaching to exercise discourse and thinking for the educator truly wishing to be trained and develop his students' potential for the formation of complete active citizens. In this framework the acts of intellect are apparently the acts of psyche from which human virtues emerge, wisdom in particular (Aristotle, *Protrepticus to Themisona* 67, p. 553; Triantari, 2012: 479–492; Terezis, 1999: 417). The educator should be armoured with wisdom to change his role through training and in the light of various and complex problems faced by him in his collaboration with students and parents.

## Conclusion

The aim of the present paper is to examine the utility of Aristotle's *Rhetoric* and *Protrepticus* through the transformation of these two works of the philosopher into a practical method in the context of the educator's training as an adviser in education. Both *Rhetoric* and *Protrepticus* could be positively conducive to the improvement of teacher–student and parent communication in school as well as to the educator's scientific upgrading as the recipient of an overflow of exclusively technical information and insights through the reception of formulaic behaviours. These cannot purge the educational system, let alone the educational process. Rhetoric and philosophy basically generate true beliefs in people who think creatively while the virtues of discourse and morality are highlighted. All these traits are remote from present-day education as educational policy is not apparently conducive to educating active citizens in an era of economic, moral and social crisis.

# References

Aristotle. 2002. *Rhetoric A'*. Introduction – Translation – Remarks. D. Lipourlis. Thessaloniki: Zitros.
—. 2012. *Rhetoric to Alexander and Themisona Protrepticus. Introduction: Rhetoric and Philosophy in Aristotle*. Introduction – Translation – Remarks: S. A. Triantari. Preface: V. Kalfas. Thessaloniki: Zitros.
Brouzos, A. 2009. *The Educator as an Adviser: A Humanistic View of Education*. Athens: Lychnos.
Brown, D. and Pryzwansky-Shulte, A. C. 2006. *Psychological Dialectic Counselling: Introduction to Theory and Practice*. Scientific editing Chr. G. Chatzichristou. Translation Aik. Labropoulou. Athens: Typothito-Dardanos.
Brauw, M. de. 2007. "The Parts of the Speech", in *A Companion to Greek Rhetoric*. Ed. Ian Worthington. Oxford: Wiley-Blackwell, 187–202.
Delis, I. G. 2005. *Philosophical Counselling. Philosophy as "Healing"*. Athens: Typothito-Dardanos.
Dewey, J. 1997. *Democracy and Education: An Introduction to the Philosophy of Eudcation*. USA: Simon & Schuster.
Düring, I. 1961. *Aristotle's Protrepticus: An Attempt at Rreconstruction*. Gütenberg: Studia Graeca et Latina Gothoburgensia XII.
—. 2003. *Aristotle: Presentation and Interpretation of his Thinking*. 2nd ed. Vol. B'. Translation A. Georgiou-Katsivela. Athens: Educational Institute of National Bank.
Ehninger, D. 1972. *Contemporary Rhetoric: A Reader's Coursebook*. Glenview, IL: Scott, Foresman.
Foss, S. K. 2004. "Framing the Study of Visual Rhetoric: Toward a Transformation of Rhetorical Theory", in *Defining Visual Rhetorics*. Ed. Charles A. Hill and Marguerite Helmers. Mahwah, New Jersey: Lawrence Erlbaum, pp. 303–313.
Fow, Sonja K. 1982. "Rhetoric and the Visual Image: A Resource Unit", *Communication Education* 31, 55–56.
Gagarin, M. 2003. "Persuasion and the Natural: Plato and early Greek Rhetoric", in*Persuasion: Rhetoric*. Selection-Editing: Dimow G. Spatharas & Lenia Tzallila. Athens: Smili, 31–62.
Hutchinson, D. S. and Johnson, M. R. 2006. *Protrepticus and Antidosis*. Portland, Oregon.

Karageorgou, E. 2010. "The Teacher's Consultative Role in Problems Management in School", *Educational News* (online journal: http://thess.pde.sch.gr/jm/periodiko/teyxos01/teyxos_1.pdf) A'(1), 40–49.

Kennedy, G. 2000. *History of Classical Rhetoric*. Translation N. Nikoloudis. Athens: Papadimas.

Papanoutsos, E. P. 1957. *The Pedagogical Love: Philosophy and Education*. Athens: Ikaros.

Pernot, L. 2005. *Rhetoric in Antiquity*. Translation Xanthipi Tzelepi. Athens: Daidalos / I. Zacharopoulos.

Terezis, Ch. 1999. "Metaphysics and politics in Aristotle", in *Aristotle's Political Pphilosophy and its Effects*. Proceedings of the 2nd International Conference. Editing and Publication D. N. Koutras. Athens: "To Lykeion" Aristotelian Studies Society, 403–421.

Triantari, S. 2005. *History of Philosophy. Vol. A'. From Antiquity to Medieval Times*. Thessaloniki: Antonis Stamoulis.

—. 2008. "Experience as a Teaching Tool in John Dewey" in *Scientific Issues: History, Philosophy and Teaching*. Proceedings of 4th Meeting in Athens (28–30 September 2007). Athens: Nisos, 273–284.

—. 2011. "Intercultural Rhetoric and Dialectic Counselling in Education", *Science of Education* 3, 103–117.

Triantari, S. A. 2012a. *The Philosophy of Pragmatism in Education: Update of Dewey's Study "Democracy and Education"*. Translation Il. Nikolaidou. Thessaloniki: Antonis Stamoulis.

Triantari, S. A. 2012b. *Rhetoric of Aristotle in Lifelong Education*. Germany: Lap Lambert Academic Publishing.

Zuntz, G. 2003. "The Style of Early Attica Novel (the Second Tetralogy of Antifontas)" in *Persuasion: Rhetoric*. Selection-Editing: Dimos G. Spatharas-Lenia Tzallila. Athens: Smili, 86–113.

# Chapter Twenty-Three

# Kindergarten Teachers' Perceptions of In-Service Training as a Factor which Enhances Professionalism

## S. Karagianni,
Msc, PhD candidate, University of Ioannina, Greece
## M. Sakellariou
Associate Professor, University of Ioannina, Greece
## and C. Vassi
PhD candidate, University of Ioannina, Greece

**Abstract**

The transition from modernity to postmodernity was accompanied by the restructuring of political, cultural and economic fields. In this context, education is a key factor as it is reflected by the reforms in the educational systems of the member states of the EU. To this end, emphasis is placed on teacher training in order to meet the new standards. The purpose of this study is to explore kindergarten teachers' perceptions of the type and content of in-service education they wish to have in order to develop a broader model of professionalism.

**Keywords**

Teachers' education; kindergarten teacher-professionalism.

## Introduction

The rapid changes which characterize our era are attributed to the transformation of knowledge and the development of technology. According to research, these changes are connected with the emergence of a new era defined as post-modernity (Sakellariou, 2010–2013). It has been noticed that the distinctive traits of this era are doubt about the one and unique truth, the objectivity and rationalism of the scientific method, the expansion of global systems of communication, the erosion of national, cultural and linguistic identities, the change in the composition of population due to immigration, the loss of self-value of knowledge and its commercialization as the main productive power (Asimaki, Koustourakis, Kamarianos, 2011: 104–105). On the other hand, it can be argued that post-modernity is not a new era but all the above are the consequences of the principles and practices of modernity (Giddens, 2001: 17) or rupture which reflects the need for improvements in the frame of modernity. Modernity is defined as the chronological era which dates back to the middle of the seventeenth century and it is based on the principles of Enlightenment: its main characteristics are faith in objectivity and the perception that the problems which plague humanity will be solved through objective and scientific methods (Lyotard 1993: 10; Asimaki, Koustourakis & Kamarianos, 2011: 109). Taking the above into account, there is no widely accepted definition of post-modernity due to the pace, the width and the content of these changes in current societies (Sakellariou, Zebylas & Petrou, 2010: 33; Giddens, 2001: 21).

In this study we adopt the opinion that "postmodernity can be approached as an interpretative-explanatory social theory which is possible to contribute to the analyses and processing of the data related the field of social action, civilization social class, scientific and financial life as well as family relations" (Asimaki, Koustourakis & Kamarianos, 2011: 103). On this spectrum, it is possible to argue that post-modernity has influenced to a great extent the organization of current societies in the political, financial and social field whether it is considered to be a new historical era, a rupture or a consequence in the frame of post-modernity. It is claimed that the post-modern school is the answer to the modern one which was based on strictly centralized structures in order to help the state exert more control. This move from modern to post-modern schools has resulted in changes to the structure and function of schools as a mechanism of socialization, to the targets of socialization, to the typical practices which are formed at school as well as to changes in the structure of knowledge itself, to the values taught by school and to the motives that school offers for the dissemination of knowledge.

In several research projects, post-modernity is considered as a set of ideas, principles and attitudes "which supports new ways of understanding of the conceivable world" and in this way it is possible to be the basis of a new paradigm for the education (Sakellariou, Zebylas, Petrou, 2010: 33). More particularly, it is stated that post-modern schools can function curatively concerning the existing problems and contribute to the "creation of an education absolved from the doctrines where the progress coincides with civilization" (Sakellariou, Zebylas & Petrou, 2010: 36). On the other hand, the fact that this era is regarded as a transition of a reconstruction of school is connected with a conflict between the modern and postmodern trends in the educational field (Hargreaves, 1994: 3). In particular, this conflict is held between the "deeply anachronistic structure" of modern schools, which function in a vague and inflexible frame, the rapid change, the complexity of technology, the cultural diversity and the change in the nature of knowledge. All the above characterize and affect the post-modern perception of school (Hargreaves, 1994: 3). "The realization of the educational reform is a chance for positive change or a mechanism for exerting stricter control and restriction" (Hargreaves, 1994: 4).

As a consequence, the role of teachers as a vehicle for these changes is reconsidered. These changes are carried out through reforms to the initial training of teachers, the introduction of new curricula and the implementation of programmes which aim to form a new culture among teachers, which responds to continually changing, social, cultural and financial needs (Grollios, 1999: 124–128; Sakellariou, 2001: 13; Mavrogiorgos, 1987: 16).

This reconstruction of the teacher's role is connected with the idea of teachers' professionalism, which has influenced educational reform in Britain and in the countries whose educational systems are organized according to the British model. The issue of teachers' professionalism was posed in Greece in the mid-1990s and was accompanied by changes in teachers' induction at state schools, their assessment, the introduction of new curricula and the way of teaching itself (Noutsos, 1993). The discussion about teachers' professionalism is presented more painstakingly in the following section.

## Sociological Approaches to the Issue of Teachers' Professionalism

The matter of teachers' professionalism was initially posed in Britain in the mid 1920s and reached its peak during the 1960s (Ozga, 1998: xi). The main sociological approaches which try to interpret it are the functional, the Marxist and the Weberian. Two main directions have been developed in the frame of the functional approach. The first one focuses on the professions, examining their relation with state. In this frame, professions are considered to be entities which ensure social stability and unity (McDonald, 1999: 2; Nixon et al., 1997: 7). Two models of teachers' professionalism have been developed in the field of education with the state guaranteeing teachers' interests (Hatcher, 1994: 55). These models, known as embodied professionalism, cover the period from 1960 up until today (Furlong, 2001: 118; Furlong et al., 2000: 19–20). Starting with the model of the academic professional, which was based on the general knowledge acquired by teachers during their initial training and the absence of national curricula, we pass to the model of the autonomous professional (1976–1984), the expert professional (1984–1992) the competent professional (1992–1997) and finally the new professional (1997– today). The transition from one model to the other is accompanied by the gradual technicalization of teachers' work, the introduction of national curricula, the implementation of rigid systems of assessment, the introduction of managers, the increasing accountability and the strictly defined role of higher education (Furlong, 2001: 126). For the deeper understanding of this study, it is worth noticing that the initial training of teachers has been limited to fields connected with teaching. To illustrate it, certain fields of the sciences of education such as the sociology of education, the history of education, the philosophy of education etc. are not considered necessary in the curricula of the corresponding faculties (Sacks, 1997: 268–272; Barton et al., 1994: 536–537). In the second direction, defined as the "traits approach", teachers' professionalism is studied in relation to the procedure of professionalization. Professionalization refers to meeting certain criteria and this, which according to its proponents, seems to be the dominant version of the ideal model of the professional. These criteria are autonomy, knowledge and responsibility (Bennet & Hokenstand, 1973: 28).

The Marxist approach examines teachers' professionalism through its relation with the state but from a different aspect. It is argued that teachers' professionalism is an ideology which covers the introduction of market laws in education and the reduction of their autonomy. They contrast the procedure of professionalization to that of the proletarianization, arguing that teachers' professionalization results in their proletarianization, since it leads to the technicalization of their work and the reduction of their autonomy through national curricula, strict systems of assessment and the restriction of their cognitive basis (Dale, 1997: 273–279; Ball, 1990: 68; Ball, 1998: 29–31; Ball, 1994: 89; Hatcher, 1994; Apple, 1993: 51).

The Weberian approach regards the issue of teachers' professionalism as a self-interesting strategic, in order to obtain power through conflicts and negotiations (Blackledge and Hunt, 1995: 423). It argues that teachers can achieve professionalization by expanding their cognitive basis. We should also mention Larson's "professional project", according to which professionalization is defined as " a certain type of organization and action which aims to the interpretation of an array of rare sources – specialized knowledge and skills – to another which is social and financial rewards" (Macdonald, 1995: 10).

This study adopts the Weberian approach because we consider that the broadening of teachers' knowledge, which can be achieved through the total representation of the sciences of education in the content of their training, will provide them with the appropriate cognitive basis so that a broader, professional model will be created.

# The Research

Taking the above into account, it can be argued that knowledge is a significant criterion for the promotion of teachers' professionalism. The aim of this study is to examine whether the perceptions of Greek kindergarten teachers concerning the type and the content of the in-service education they wish to have are in line with a broader model of professionalism.

This research is of a particular interest because knowledge offers teachers "significant tools of analyses and understanding of the deeper relations referring to the function of school" (Diamantis, 2005: 154). This has a double meaning. First, it helps them to understand the social orientation of their work because "their task is not just a pedagogical act for the dissemination of knowledge but a political procedure with social repercussions" (Sianou, 1995: 35). Second (and as a consequence of the first), the knowledge which teachers obtain enables them to evaluate and broaden their "relative autonomy" as far as the choice of methods and the content of teaching are concerned.

Two questions were put for the purpose of this study:
1. What are the kindergarten teachers' perceptions of the type and content of in-service education they wish to have?
2. Is the formation of these perceptions influenced by the level of their studies?

## Methodology
50 questionnaires were sent to the kindergartens in the area of Agrinio for the purpose of this research. After the necessary explanations had been given, 37 questionnaires were answered and sent back.

The choice of the sample was random. Thus, it is considered to be representative of the population examined (Cohen & Manion, 1994). It represents 52% of the total population of 71 teachers.

## Description of the sample teachers

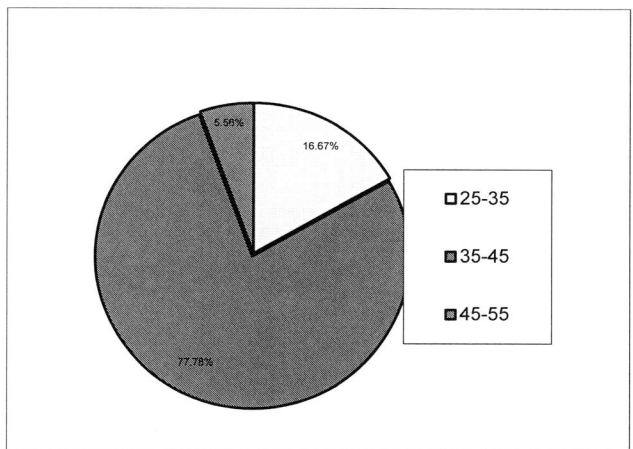

Fig. 23-1. Age of teachers in the sample

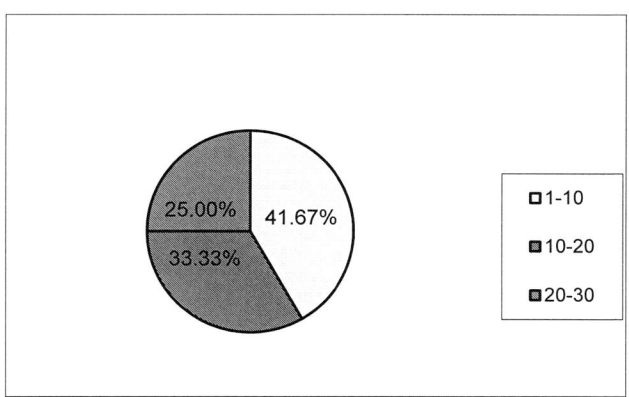

Fig. 23-2. Years of experience of teachers in the sample

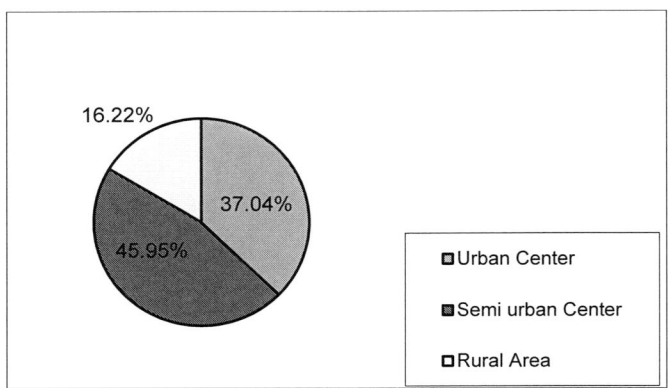

Fig. 23-3. Teachers' workplace

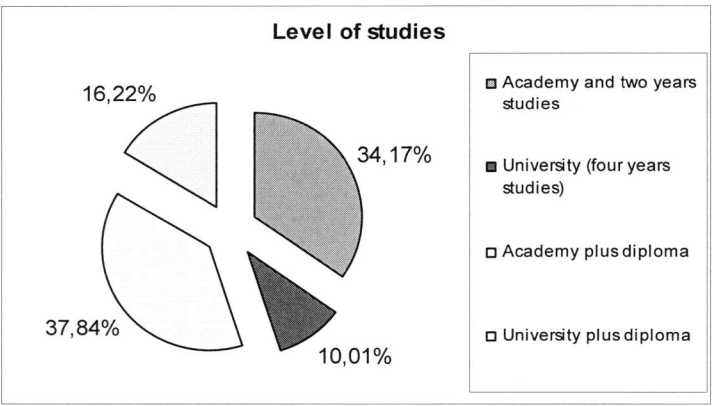

Fig. 23-4. Level of studies

| Studies | | |
|---|---|---|
| | **Diploma** | |
| **Basic Studies** | **YES** | **NO** |
| **Academy** | **51.9% (14)** | **48.1% (13)** |
| **University of Preschool Education** | **60.0% (6)** | **40.0% (4)** |

**Table 23-1. Diploma studies**

Table 23-1 shows kindergarten teachers can be classified with reference to the level of their studies as follows:

a. Teachers with basic studies (degree of the Faculty of Kindergarten, two-year duration (academy) and degree of the corresponding university faculty with a two-year study period or degree of the University Pedagogical Faculties with a four-year duration).

b. Teachers with further studies to diploma level.

This classification is useful for two reasons. The first category includes those who have graduated from the two-year faculties of kindergarten teachers and went on with their studies in the corresponding University faculties for another period of two years as well as those who have graduated from the University faculties with a four-year period of studies. The second category includes those who have conducted studies to diploma level. These categories show how teachers' cognitive level differs.

***Presentation and analyses of the results***

The data arising from the teachers' answers are presented in this chapter. The logismic SPSS 15 (Norusis, 2004) was used for the control of contiguity.

*Preschool teachers' suggestions for the type of in-service education they wish to have*

The most important type of in-service education which teachers want to receive refers to the models of teaching to a 100% percentage. The informative material and the seminars follow with the same percentage. Meetings with their colleagues and lectures by experts possess the last place in their preferences.

| Order of Preference | Type of Education | N | MEAN | S.D. |
|---|---|---|---|---|
| 1 | Models of teaching | 33 | 3.9 | 0.3 |
| 2 | Informative material | 29 | 3.4 | 0.8 |
| 3 | Seminars | 29 | 3.3 | 0.8 |
| 4 | Meetings with colleagues | 28 | 2.9 | 1.2 |
| 5 | Experts' lectures | 29 | 2.8 | 1.2 |

**Table 23-2. Teachers' preferences for in-service training**

*Teachers' perceptions of the content of their in-service education.*
The overwhelming majority of preschool teachers in our sample (94.5%) consider that in-service education orientated to daily practice is very important. Only one teacher considers it to be of average importance (2.8%) and another one a little. 86.1% believe that in-service education concerning new trends is very necessary, 11.1% of average importance and 2.8% a little. In-service education which focuses on theoretical training is considered to be very necessary by 34.4% and a little or not necessary by 21.99%. Some 31.1% agree that in-service education concerning administrative matters is very necessary, 28.1% of average importance and 40.79% a little or not at all necessary.

Finally, their opinion about in-service education connected with the sociological or political frame of education are of particular interest. Only 28.2% of the preschool teachers consider it to be very necessary, 21.9% average and 50% a little or not at all necessary.

| Order of Preference | Content of Seminars | N | Mean | S.D. |
|---|---|---|---|---|
| 1 | Orientated to daily practice | 36 | 3.6 | 0,7 |
| 2 | New trends in education | 36 | 3.6 | 0,8 |
| 3 | Theoretical training | 32 | 2.3 | 1,1 |
| 4 | Administrative issues | 32 | 1.9 | 1,1 |
| 5 | Issues of sociological and political interest | 32 | 1.5 | 1,4 |

**Table 23-3. Content of seminars**

*Preferred type of in-service education according to level of studies*
Table 23-4 shows that the teachers' perceptions of the type of in-service education they wish to have do not differ according to the level of their studies. It is worth noticing that in all cases there were lost indicators that might define the prior ascertainments.

| Level of study | | Seminars | Models of teaching | Meeting with colleagues | Experts' lectures | Informative material |
|---|---|---|---|---|---|---|
| Basic | Mean | 3.23 | 3.75 | 2.45 | 2.85 | 3.31 |
| | N | 13 | 16 | 11 | 13 | 13 |
| | S.D. | 0.832 | 0.447 | 1.293 | 1.214 | 0.855 |
| Additional | Mean | 3.44 | 4 | 3.24 | 2.75 | 3.5 |
| | N | 16 | 17 | 17 | 16 | 16 |
| | S.D. | 0.727 | 0 | 1.033 | 1.238 | 0.73 |
| Total | Mean | 3.34 | 3.88 | 2.93 | 2.79 | 3.41 |
| | N | 29 | 33 | 28 | 29 | 29 |
| | S.D. | 0.769 | 0.331 | 1.184 | 1.207 | 0.78 |
| Mann-Whitney | U | 89 | 102 | 57.5 | 98.5 | 90 |
| Level of significance | p | 0.53 | 0.231 | 0.091 | 0.81 | 0.56 |

**Table 23-4. Teachers' preferences for type of education they wish to have according to their level of study**

*The content of the in-service education the preschool teachers prefer according to the level of their study*

Table 23-5 indicates how the preschool teachers who have basic studies prefer the content of in-service education to be orientated to matters of daily practice while the preschool teachers with credentials to diploma level consider that matters concerning the sociological and political frame of education should be prioritized.

| Level of study | | Oriented to daily practice | Theoretical training | New trends in education | Administrative matters | Issues of sociological and political interest in education |
|---|---|---|---|---|---|---|
| Basic | Mean | 3.65 | 2.06 | 3.29 | 1.76 | 0.6 |
| | N | 17 | 16 | 17 | 17 | 15 |
| | S.D. | 0.606 | 1.181 | 0.92 | 1.147 | 1.121 |
| Additional | Mean | 3.47 | 2.5 | 3.79 | 2.07 | 2.35 |
| | N | 19 | 16 | 19 | 15 | 17 |
| | S.D. | 0.772 | 0.966 | 0.631 | 0.961 | 1.057 |
| Total | Mean | 3.56 | 2.28 | 3.56 | 1.191 | 1.53 |
| | N | 36 | 32 | 36 | 32 | 32 |
| | S.D. | 0.695 | 1.085 | 0.809 | 1.058 | 1.391 |
| Mann-Whitney | U | 142 | 99.5 | 106.5 | 107.5 | 33 |
| Level of significance | p | 0.55 | 0.29 | 0.08 | 0.46 | 0.0001 |

**Table 23-5. Teachers' preferences for content of in-service training according to their level of study.**

## Conclusion

Prior to the presentation of the conclusions of this study, it is necessary to state that the sample of this research was small and therefore the resulting data are indications of the preschool teachers' perceptions of the type and content of the in-service education they wish to have. These conclusions are as follows:

1. As far as the type of in-service education they wish to have is concerned, there are indications that the preschool teachers prefer the models of teaching while the informative material and the seminars follow. Their preferences concerning the content of in-service education seem to focus on issues of daily practice, new trends in education, theoretical training and administrative matters; the least important in their preferences is in-service education on

matters concerning the sociological and political frame of education.

2. The level of their studies does not affect their perceptions of the type of in-service education they wish to have. However, their perceptions of the content of in-service education do differ significantly according to the level of their studies. The preschool teachers who possess a greater number of credentials consider that in-service education should give priority to issues connected with the sociological and political frame of education.

Based on the data of the research and the Weberian approach (Blackledge and Hunt, 1995: 423), the indications which have arisen show that the preschool teachers' perceptions with a higher level of study respond to a broader model of professionalism through the expansion of their cognitive basis, in comparison with the preschool teachers with basic studies. It is obvious that there is need for preschool teachers' personal and professional evolution through a broader model of professionalism which would be reflected in the frame of their in-service education so as to enable them to meet the standards of the twenty-first century.

# References

Apple, M. W. 1983. *Education and Authority.* Thessaloniki: Paratiritis.

Asimaki, Koustourakis, G. and Kamarianos, I. 2002. "The Concepts of Modernity and Postmodernity and their Relation with Knowledge: A Sociological Approach", *The Step of Social Sciences* IE, 99–120.

Barton, L., Barrett, E., Whitty, G., Miles, S. and Furlong, J. 1994. "Teacher Education and Teacher Professionalism in England: Some Emerging Issues", *British Journal of Sociology of Education* 15(4), 529–543.

Ball, S. 1988. "Staff Relations during the Teachers' Industrial Action: Context, Conflict and Proletarianisation", *British Journal of Sociology of Education* 9(3), 289–309.

—. 1990. *Politics and Policy-making in Education: Exploration in Policy.* , London: Routledge.

Ball, S. J. 1994. *Education Reform: A Critical and Post Structural Approach.* Buckingham: Open University Press.

Bennet, W. S. F. and Hokenstand, M. C. 1973. "Full-time People Workers and Conceptions of the 'Professional'", in P. Halmos (ed.), *Professionalization and Social Change.* Keele: Keele University, 21–45.

Blackledge, D. and Hunt, B. 1995. *Sociology of Education.* Athens: Ekfrasi.

Cohen, L. and Manion, L. 1994. *Methodology of Educational Research.* Athens: Metaihmio.

Dale, R. 1997. "The State and the Governance of Education: An Analysis of the Restructuring of the State–Education Relationship", in A. H. Halsey, H.

Lauder, D. Brown and A. S. Wells (eds), *Education: Culture, Economy, and Society*, New York: Oxford University Press, pp. 273–282.

Darling-Hammond, L. 1997. "Restructuring Schools for Students Success", in A. H. Hasley, H. Lauder, D. Brown and A. S. Wells (eds), *Education: Culture, Economy, Society.* New York : Oxford University Press.

Diamantis, K. 2005. *The Sociology of Education as Content of Teachers' Iinitial Ttraining in the Pedagogical Faculties of Primary School Teachers (1984–2004).* Library of the University of Ioannina.

Furlong, J. 2001. "Reforming Teacher Education, Re-forming Teacher", in J. Furlong and R. Philips (eds) *Education, Reform and the State.* London: Routledge Falmer, 118–135.

Furlong, J., Barton, L., Miles, S., Whiting, C. and Whitty, G. 2000. *Teacher Education in Transition: Re-forming Professionalism.?* Buckingham: Open University Press.

Gialamas, B. 2005. *Statistical Techniques and Implementations in the Sciences of Education.* Athens: Patakis.

Giddens, A. 2001. *The Consequences of Postmodernity.* Athens: Kritiki.

Grolios, G. 1999. *Ideology, Pedagogy and Educational Policy: Speech and Practice of the European Programmes for Education.* Athens: Gutenberg.

Kossivaki, F. 2003. *The Role of Teacher in the Postmodern School: Expectations, Perspectives, Dreams.* Athens: Gutenberg.

Hargreaves, A. 1994. *Changing Teachers, Changing Times*, London: Cassell.

Hatcher, R. 1994. "Market, Relationships and the Management of Teachers", *British Journal of Sociology of Education* 15(1), 41–61.

Legatt, T. 1970. "Teaching as a profession", in J. A. Jackson (ed.) *Professions and Professionalization.* London: Cambridge University Press, 155–177.

Macdonald, K. M. 1995. *The Sociology of the Professions.* London: Sage.

Maurogiorgos, G. 1987. "Sciences of Education and Ppedagogical Research: Pedagogical Research, Educational Change and Social Change: Reading of the Dominant, Urban Ideology", *Contemporary Education* 35, 15–25.

Nixon, J., Martin, J., McKeown, P. and Ranson, S. 1997. "Towards a Learning Profession: Changing Codes of Educational Practice within the New Management of Education", *British Journal of Sociology of Education* 18(1), 5–27.

Norusis, M. 2004. *SPSS 13.0 Statistical Procedures Companion.* Upper Saddle-River, NJ: Prentice Hall.

Noutsos, H. 1993. "Teachers and the Ideology of Professionalism", Conference of OLME with the title *The Teacher in Front of the Changing Europe*, vol. 9. Thessaloniki-Athens: OLME, 38–49.

Ozga, J. (ed.). 1988. *Schoolwork: Approaches to the Labour Process of Teaching.* Milton Keynes: Open University Press.

Sacks, J. 1997. "Reclaiming the Agenda of Teachers Professionalism: An Australian Experience", *Journal of Education for Teaching* 23(3), 263–275.

Sakellariou M. 2002. *Introduction to the Teaching of Social and Pedagogical Labour in Kindergarten.* Athens: Atropos.

Sakellariou, M., Zempylas, A. and Petrou, A. 2010. *Ethics and Education: Dilemmas and Perspectives.* Athens: Kritiki.
Sianou, E. 1995. "The New Forms of Materialization of Curricula and the Dynamics of Social Control in Cchool", *Educational Society* 30, 35–39.

# Chapter Twenty-Four

# Supporting Change in Schools through Participatory and Reflective Teacher-Training Processes

## Vassilis Tsafos
### Assistant Professor, National Kapodistrian University of Athens
## and Eleni Katsarou
### Assistant Professor, University of Crete, Greece

**Abstract**

This paper presents an in-service training project developed in two different locations in Greece, a high school in Athens and an elementary school in Rethymno, from December 2011 to June 2012. The main goal of the project was to achieve school change though action that would assist participating teachers in each school to: a) become a professional team which gradually develops a sense of belonging and commits to joint action and change, b) explore their role and practices, c) seek common interests and, more importantly, areas for intervention and d) act in a continuum of planning – action – reflection – evaluation.

In this context, we discuss: a) common features of the organization of the project in each school, b) the perceptions and resistance of participating teachers regarding the project, and c) the difficulties and the potential of each context. Finally, we focus on the processes through which we, as their facilitators, managed to overcome the teachers' resistance to a certain extent. Through this discussion we highlight issues concerning action research processes that support professional development and school change at the local level.

**Keywords**
In-service teacher training, professional learning community, school change / innovation.

## Introduction: Theoretical Framework

In his trilogy on educational change (1993, 1999, 2003), Fullan introduced the perspective of a multidimensional development of change on three levels: school, community and state. It is a holistic approach to change, according to which the key for the success of any innovation is the participation of all stakeholders in a cooperative interactive framework, which allows them to enhance their relationships. Thus on a school level, Fullan focuses on changing the school culture, which mostly entails a change of relationships and values. He goes on to claim that no change can be achieved unless everyone shares the same vision and develops new understandings by jointly shaping the process of change.

One way to achieve this participatory and cooperative framework is to transform the school into a professional community of learning, id est to a group of teachers who recognize that they have to cooperate in order to lead all students to learning and who create structures that gradually weave a cooperative culture in the process. The development of such a community in the school involves "going from a situation of limited attention to assessment and pedagogy to a situation in which teachers and others routinely focus on these matters and make associated improvements" (Fullan, 2000). Developing a professional community of learning provides the basis for enhancement, in the context of true change.

According to relevant literature, the features of such a community can be summed up thus: the professional staff constitutes a community that:

1) has a common vision and common responsibility for meeting the learning objectives;
2) develops a collective and participatory climate;
3) inspires in its members a moral commitment to high quality learning for all and to continuous enhancement;
4) involves its members in a collective investigation of their practices and the underlying educational values;
5) develops interactive, investigatory and reflective practices.

(Nehring & Fitzsimons, 2011)

# In-service Training: Supporting Change

This paper aims to demonstrate how through an alternative in-service training intervention we endeavoured to transform a group of teachers into a professional community of learning in the context of school change in two locations, a high school in Athens and an elementary school in Rethymno, where we coordinated this programme. This specific in-service training was developed in the framework of the Education of Foreign and Repatriated Students programme. Similar training projects have been developed both in Greece (Androussou, 2008; Vekris & Hodolidou, 2004; Avgitidou, 2013) and abroad (McLaughlin & Talbert, 2006).

## Project Aims

- To support the involved teachers in their effort to form a professional group, gradually shaping a common perspective and collective educational values and taking joint decisions.
- To help teachers understand the processes of change and the conditions for its success, by: a) expressing their beliefs, values and practices, b) reflecting on the existing conditions in the school and their classroom, and c) seeking alternative action strategies.
- To enable teachers to work in an action research continuum of design–action–reflection–evaluation, in the logic of a circular, not a linear, development of change.
- To encourage teachers to approach training as a means of improving school life and the educational process in general, whether it involves the development of students or the professional development of teachers, which are interrelated in an action research framework.

## The Role of Facilitator/coordinator

In this training intervention, we undertook the role of facilitator/coordinator. Despite the obstacles posed by our academic status (with a latent element of power) and although we were external agents (relative to the school), from the beginning we tried to be critical partners to the teachers, adopting the reflective mentor model. We focused on how we could actively involve them in critical reflection on their teaching and training experience, promoting their learning in the framework of their community (Chapman, 2008). By discussions with the teachers, cooperatively designing their action, analysing their practices and asking critical questions about the practices, we tried to reveal teachers' tacit and implicit assumptions that guided their choices in the classroom (Athanases et al., 2008: 747–748).

## Project description

The project was developed around the following features:

- Plenary meetings, during which the teachers discussed educational issues and problems that had been diagnosed and required further investigation and action with the aim of improvement. Through such discussions and investigations, all teachers could both express and sometimes even realise the meanings and interpretations of the educational act.
- Design and action by teacher groups, who could pose questions and provide the stimulus for alternative perspectives. In this way, teachers could focus on issues that would later constitute the subjects of the training seminars they would attend.
- Experiential training seminars and workshops, which helped teachers gain deeper insight and expand their thinking, and supported them in their quest for new practices and general innovative interventions that would gradually reculture the school.
- Plenary meetings, during which the teachers reflected collectively on new perspectives and discussed new designs.
- Redesign and new action.

## Towards an Assessment of the Project

We will now focus on how the teachers perceived this in-service training, the expectations it created and the reservations they expressed, some of which were indicative of their resistance. Later in the paper we will attempt to outline the development in terms of their attitude towards both the training programme and change in general, focusing on the transformation stages of the professional community of learning and on the role they feel this intervention played in their professional development in general.

These points are based on data collected from: a) the journals we kept as coordinators, b) the assessment of the training programme by the teachers, both in the questionnaires we administered and in the final evaluation meeting, and c) the comparison of the teachers' attitudes at the beginning of the programme, as stated in an open-ended questionnaire, and after it was completed. These questions concerned the in-service training and the potential it offers for professional development and for improvement of teachers' everyday action in school and of the educational conditions in general.

## Difficulties

From the early stages of the project, both schools displayed considerable difficulties, which, according to the data we collected, related to:

a) *The teachers' expectations*, revealing the dominant views on in-service training: the trainers are qualified scientists who illuminate the trainees, who simply have to imitate these mainly teaching standards. Most teachers seem to embrace the training model of the treatment of deficiencies, which aims to reinforce theoretical knowledge, cultivate skills, and cover any gaps left by initial training or caused by time (Day, [1999] 2003: 291). So they ask for an instrumental kind of learning that will enable them to deal with their students in pedagogically acceptable ways and to efficiently manage any problems that emerge during the educational process.

   In such a context, almost everyone perceives change as the consequence of the transfer of ready knowledge, an external intervention that will change how they work and also influence the students' attitude. They simply seek to have external control of teaching effectiveness, adopting a technocratic approach to the educational process (Salteris, 2006: 48). The positive experiences they report having from previous training projects fall under this scheme. A colleague characteristically states:

> My best experience from the training was the model teachings. In my opinion, their advantages are: a) they truly refer to the teaching act, b) they allow you to observe which teaching designs are interesting to children and which will fail and c) they let you reflect on whether the new methodology is efficient.

b) *Their mistrust of theory and their tendency towards empiricism.* They demand that training be directly correlated to practice, often through their expectations of learning specific techniques, thus revealing an outdated perception of pedagogy as implementation.

c) *Their insecurity concerning possible destabilization*, and the consequent defensive attitude towards their investigative and reflective action in the project. Besides, the dominant individualistic school culture, summed up as "the educator and his/her classroom", appears well established in most of the participant teachers. The statement of a teacher after the first plenary discussion reveals how she perceives the exchange of views:

> We are a group of different people, just thinking and hanging around. I feel we are wasting our time.

This defensive stance is founded on various assumptions:

> About the co-teaching, I was informed, but I did not participate, as I had a heavy workload at the time. I haven't understood what purpose it serves. I am also suspicious that it will be used to reduce the teaching staff numbers.

Their fear of the new and of the destabilization it may cause is evident in their attitude when testing something new:

> Group cooperative teaching is very noisy and will disturb my colleagues.

> To do all that, I will have to disturb the teaching of my colleagues.

> The students develop expectations that we will fail to meet, as some things are only tried out once.

In order to cover this destabilization, they invoke the institutional discourse, using it as an alibi, although they often feel it opposes their own discourse:

> As a language teacher, I have a large syllabus to cover, my responsibility is great, I am responsible for how the children will learn the language, how they will speak if I do my job well. Some things need to have been tried out in practice many times, before I can feel confident to implement them.

## Reinforcing Factors

It is evident that, at the beginning of the in-service training, most teachers appear to resist the perspective of becoming an educational community of learning. However, despite this deterrent climate, certain reinforcing factors began to emerge, often developing parallel to the difficulties and shaping a contradictory action framework. Over time, these factors grew stronger, to a certain extent overcoming teachers' resistance.

These factors were:

a) *The gradual development of a reflective dialogue*, enabling the group of teachers to realise the value of: i) exchanging views and interacting, and ii) creating a professional learning community that gradually develops a sense of belonging and commits to joint action and change.

> We were given the chance to talk to each other, to discuss if we could implement some of these practices, even for a short time.

> The most useful part of the process was that I participated in meetings, in which all the opinions of my colleagues were discussed and debated. This enabled me to have a more comprehensive picture of the debates present in the school.

b) *The cooperative and participatory nature of the project.* The perspective of creating a community through the active involvement of teachers in the project inspired in many of them a sense of security, in terms of implementing innovation in practice, engaging in teaching experimentations, or even overcoming institutional limitations, which are usually considered overly binding. The climate of cooperation developed in the project opened the closed classroom doors and decreased the distances between teachers, enabling them to develop a common code, a common language in which to share their experiences. Perhaps the interactive framework of social and emotional support developed in the project helped the teachers decide to share their concerns over implementing change and even their failures (Zembylas & Barker, 2007: 246).

> I was able to cooperate with the teachers of other subjects, which is difficult because of my subject (I'm a gym teacher), and that was very good for the children. They started to view knowledge differently, they saw how it's all connected.

> We shared a common discourse. You know, say I have this problem, and this was an opportunity to start communicating and start understanding each other. And it is important that we did this in practice.

Through cooperation, one can get rid of individual stress about how to cover the syllabus, while also having time for tests and innovations.

I am very pleased to share a common discourse with others, and to feel that I am not alone in doing something different.

c) *The opportunity offered to teachers to co-shape the project* by cooperating with each other and with the facilitators / coordinators. This is a bottom-up approach to professional development, where teachers are actively involved (Day, [1999] 2003):

An originality of this training programme was that we chose the topics of the seminars we held. We would talk and try to link our classroom experience to the topic studied in the seminar. After each seminar, we would design, test, evaluate and then redesign, until our next seminar.

d) *The alternative forms of training implemented in the project*, which meet specific teachers' demands, are experiential in character, and relate directly to school activity:

The way we did that motivated me to act. The experiential character is what made the training different. And that was what triggered our interest. I hadn't experienced it like that before, and I felt it covered me.

This alternative form of training is not just about what we learn but also about how we learn it. And I don't mean just us, but also our students.

e) *Our role as coordinators.* Throughout the project, we made a point of constantly exploring our role, cooperating in our own action research, in order to gradually improve as facilitators/coordinators. At the same time, we acted as co-researchers along with the teachers, in all matters that concerned them, not as experts bringing ready solutions to the school. We only had tools that could help us understand the educational situation and find solutions to the complex problems faced by teachers. We didn't give any answers, but rather supported and encouraged them in their own effort to change. Moreover, we posed critical questions to encourage their reflection. Indicatively, these included:

- *Of all the things that happen in my classroom, what disturbs me most? Am I trying to stop it? How? Why does it keep happening?* (in order to reveal what each teacher viewed as problematic and why).
- *What did I achieve with my intervention? Which difficulties did I face in implementing it? What could I have done to overcome them? What knowledge and which skills would I need to do that? What other ways of action could I have chosen? Why didn't I choose them?* (in order to help them reflect on their intervention).

f) *The positive impact this process seemed to have on students*, mostly in terms of mobilising their interest:

The children responded positively; it was a positive experience for them. They too started to cooperate, to perceive the world around them and what's more important, it's not what I learn but how I learn it, how one can help with the other's weaknesses or shortcomings, entering an experiential process, assuming different roles...

My students were intrigued, they formed their own opinions, they expressed their views and even justified them. It was such a pleasure. I wasn't expecting something like that. It was a great change..."

## Conclusions

At the beginning of the in-service training project, the teachers expressed their reservations and resistance and seemed unwilling to get involved in a process that would link change and improvement with research and data collection and analysis. As they confessed, they often reacted defensively towards the innovative framework that was being shaped and the process of change. In this way, the teachers became part of the educational mechanism, which reinforces resistance to innovation (Sarason, 1982). Besides, in the first stages of the process of change, anxiety and fear of the unknown are intrinsic elements of the process (Fullan, 1993). In their attempt to limit the problems of this complex process, teachers tended to return to their usual practices and routines. They believed that in this way they could be liberated from the oppressive need to act, reflect and design, which was imposed by the process of change, and which they perceived as a threat.

However, through this training project, particularly through the gradual emergence of issues and needs, resulting from their action, the educators started to pose research questions and challenge problematic situations. An important fact that demonstrates how their attitude towards the research orientation of the training project, and the perspective of change and supporting processes started to alter, was that they realized the need to base their claims on specific data. More importantly, they started to utilize their data in a meaningful way, in order to improve their students.

As is evident in their requests to continue the project, a different culture started to evolve in the group. They gradually started to ask for steps that would allow them to reflect and research on their own. Although they did not explicitly express it, this shows that they started to trust their ability to learn from their research at the school.

Finally, they gradually realized our role not as an academic external factor, but as a coordinator, a critical partner who can support the collective construction of knowledge among educators and help them endow their community with a climate of mutual respect and trust.

# References

Androussou, A. 2008. "Teacher Training in Minority Education: The Dynamics of a Three-year Period", in T. Dragona and A. Fragoudaki (eds). *Addition, not Subtraction, Multiplication, not Division: The Reform Intervention in Minority Education in Thrace*. Athens: Metaihmio.

Athanases, S., Abrams, J., Jack, G., Johnson, V., Kwock, S., McCurdy, J., Riley, S. and Totaro, S. 2008. "Curriculum for Mentor Development: Problems and Promise in the Work of New Teacher Induction Leaders", *Journal of Curriculum Studies* 40(6), 743–770.

Avgitidou, S. 2013. "Supporting Professional Development through Action Research: Basic Principles and Ssuggested Pprocesses", in the proceedings of the Education Across Borders International Conference, Florina, 5–7 October 2012 (forthcoming on the website of the Florina Faculty of Education).

Chapman, R. 2008. "The Reflective Mentor Model: Growing Communities of Practice for Teacher Development in Informal Learning Environments", in C. Kimble, P. Hildreth and I. Bourdon (eds), *Communities of Practice: Creating Learning Environments for Educators,* Vol. 1. Charlotte, NC: Information Age, 39–64.

Day, C. (1999) 2003. *Developing Teachers: The Challenges of Lifelong Learning* [Greek translation by A. Vakaki]. Athens: Typothito – G. Dardanos.

Fullan, M. 1993. *Change Forces: Probing the Depths of Educational Reform*. London: The Falmer Press.

—. 1999. *Change Forces: The Sequel*. Philadelpheia: Falmer Press.

—. (2000). "The Three Stories of Education Reform", *Phi Delta Kappan* 81(8), 581–584.

—. 2003. *Leading in a Culture of Change: Personal Action Guide and Workbook*. San Francisco: Jossey-Bass.

McLaughlin, M. W. and Talbert, J. E. 2006. *Building School-Based Teacher Learning Communities*. New York: Teachers College Press.

Nehring, J. and Fitzsimons, G. 2011. "The Professional Learning Community as Subversive Activity: Countering the Culture of Conventional Schooling", *Professional Development in Education* 37, 513–535.

Salteris, N. 2006. *Continuing Teacher-Training: Seeking the Reflective Practitioner*. Athens: Taxideftis.

Sarason, S. B. 1982. *The Culture of the School and the Problem of Change*. Boston: Allyn and Bacon.

Vekris, E. and Hodolidou, E. (eds). 2004. *1ˢᵗ National Conference of Second Chance Schools, 28–29 June 2003*. Athens: General Secretariat for Adult Education, Institute of Adult and Continuing Education.

Zembylas, M. and Barker, H..B. 2007. "Teachers' Spaces for Coping with Change in the Context of a Reform Effort", *Journal of Educational Change* 8, 235–256.

# CHAPTER TWENTY-FIVE

# THE INNOVATIVE TRAINING MODEL OF THE "MELINA: EDUCATION AND CULTURE" NATIONAL CULTURAL PROJECT IN GREECE: CHANIA, CRETE (2001–2004)

## MARIA A. DRAKAKI
### SCHOOL COUNSELLOR, CRETE REGION, CRETE, GREECE

The cultural education for the growth and the cohesion of local society constituted the core of philosophy of national cultural project "MELINA: Education and Culture", as shaped through the new reality that resulted for the role and the prospect of local societies in the twenty-first century. Thus each school unit of experimentation elects itself in regional training centre for the cultural education and cultural cell of local society. The school as training centre is addressed in the teachers of first degree education of region and functions moreover at the same time as dynamic point of meeting of cultural institutions of region. (Paizis, 2002)

**Abstract**
The Chania region was the first prefecture in which the "Melina" project took place, during school years 2001–2004. A central co-ordinating committee took responsibility for its scientific, pedagogic and administrative operation and forecasted, activated and developed effectively all the operations and levels. The committee involved people from the locality, education executives, the educational community, school staff, local society, teachers' trade unions and parents.

**Keywords**
Education, culture, national programme, training of teachers, organizational model

## Introduction

The Melina project on education and culture was a joint action programme of the Ministries of Education and Culture with the General Secretariat for Adult Education as the implementing agency. It was a long-lasting national cultural strategy programme involving all three levels of education.

> "In 1994 informally before the death of the Minister of Culture Melina Merkouri, in the Ministry of Education a group of artists and teachers at all levels were trying to discern what may be the future of art in Greek education and its contents. A meeting of Melina with Jack Lanka has taken place at the end of 1993 where Lang conceived the idea of a systematic collaboration of five ministries in France (Education, Higher Education, Culture, Youth and Franks Speaking) in order to recast the heavy artillery of foreign policy of France: its art, civilization, culture," says project coordinator of "MELINA – Education and Culture" Nick Paizis. (Terezaki, 2008: 17)

At the same time, in the mid-90s, the tendency of socialist parties of Europe which functioned as governments for initiative-taking on the issue of interconnection between art education and local communities was strongly manifested.

> The countries characterized by this reasoning include the Netherlands, Denmark, Sweden, England, Austria, Belgium and Catalonia, each one for different reasons. Similar initiatives were undertaken by UNESCO and the Council of Europe, also for different reasons. Finally, the European Union announced plans for inter-school partnerships with an additional field, art and culture (Socrates, Comenius) and after several years proceeded to the consolidation of the General Administrations (the 22nd – Task Force – and 10th – of Culture) in one General Administration of "Education and Culture" with Mrs. Reding as the first Commissioner. In the first intervention message of the Commissioner, there was clear reference to the Greek initiatives on the subject. (ibid)

Thus, in several countries, programmes to strengthen cultural education in the educational system each had different practices but all had a common central axis: student encouragement in arts and culture within and outside the curriculum.

> In the six-year experimental implementation of the project "MELINA: Education and Culture" (1995–2001) in Greece, 92 primary schools (86 public and 6 private) from Greece and 2 from Cyprus (Nicosia and

Limassol) participated. At its training sessions about 2,500 teachers and educators of various specialisations participated, 350 book titles were published (teacher and student books) while the programme addressed a total of about 20,000 students in elementary school. (Paizis, 2002)

The ultimate teaching goal of the programme was the atmosphere of the arts with their polytechnic and polysemous expression, to enrich not only the curriculum, but also the educational visits, the classroom, the everyday life and the relationships converting the whole school community into a community of expression, communication and creativity. Teacher training in the arts revealed, through the MELINA project, new teaching standards that allowed teachers to intervene in everyday teaching practice utilizing a variety of methods and tools facilitating personal discovery, thrill and enjoyment. "The MELINA project is essentially a teacher motivation and training programme designed to increase their positive attitude towards Art and Culture and eventually the recognition of its pedagogical importance" (Paizis, ibid).

The work which the Central Coordination Committee of the programme undertook[1] was a common decision of Education Minister G. Papandreou and Culture Minister Th. Mikroutsikos :

- The training of cultural facilitators
- The production of teaching material on cultural issues in education
- The sensitization of public opinion and the production of relevant forms
- The formation of a cultural archive in schools for local opportunities and the development of school venues
- The creation of visit possibilities to school sites for art education
- The organization of educational visits to museums, archaeological sites, cultural organizations with cultural heritage sites.
(Vergidis & Vaikousi, 2003, citing protocol F 8/249, 309/28-2-1995/C1)

During the school year 2001–2002 the first phase of the programme was extended to all elementary schools in the city of Chania.

---

[1] The Central Coordination Committee was a Committee of experts consisting of representatives of the political leadership, management executives, the stakeholders (Ministry of Education, Ministry of Culture, General Secretariat for Adult Education), artists and teachers. The Central Coordination Committee made suggestions to the political leadership and generally oversaw the actions of the pilot implementation in collaboration with the Ministry of Education, Ministry of Culture and the General Secretariat for Adult Education (NGEE).

# Implementing the Melina Programme in the Prefecture of Chania

After the completion of the six-year pilot implementation of the Melina project in primary education, the Central Committee of the Programme decided during the school year 2001–2003 to focus its activities on the town of Chania. The proposed aims were:

- the thorough development of the training model for managers and primary school teachers of the city of Chania
- the activation of the educational institutions of the city and materialisation of parallel actions in the context of cultural education (emphasis on the cultural dimension of the regional educational policies of the institutions mentioned above)
- the activation of the cultural institutions of the city and the development of parallel actions in the context of cultural education (emphasis on the educational dimension of regional policy on cultural heritage and cultural development of the institutions mentioned above
- the coordination of these activities and visibility in the local community and the wider region.

(Melina – Education and Culture, 2001–2002)

By analogy with the operating model of the Central Coordination Committee, during the Chania programme a Regional Coordination Committee for the Prefecture of Chania was appointed with eight members: the School Counsellor of the School Accountability District (Education Centre for Cultural Education); the Director of Primary Education in the Prefecture of Chania; the Head of the Office of Environmental Education of the Prefecture of Chania to which the School Training Centre for Cultural Education belonged; the Director of the School Training Centre for Cultural Education; a representative of the Prefecture Administration of Chania; a representative of the Municipality Administration of Chania; a representative of the Association of Primary and Preschool Teachers of Chania; and a representative of the Association of Parents and Guardians of the School Education Centre for Cultural Education.

The School Counsellor of the Prefecture of Chania was appointed as coordinator of the Regional Coordination Committee in the Prefecture of Chania, also having the responsibility for convening the committee as well as for the communication with the Central Coordination Committee and the local media. The teacher employed permanently in the school training centre for cultural action who had the greatest educational experience in the programme during its pilot implementation was appointed as secretary administrator.

So the scientific responsibility for the implementation of the training sessions and educational programmes in accordance with the instructions of the Pedagogical Institute of the Ministry of Education and the proposals of the Central Coordination Committee of the MELINA programme was held by the School Counsellor of Primary School Education in the Prefecture of Chania who had in his education region the school training centre for culture education, namely the 8th Elementary School of Chania.

Administrative responsibility for the implementation of the action of the MELINA programme regionally in the Prefecture of Chania in accordance with the instructions of the Ministry of Education and the recommendations of the Central Coordination Committee of the programme, was held, as dictated by the law, by the administrative institutions and services of Primary Education in the Prefecture of Chania namely, the Primary Education Management Centre of Chania, the Administration Offices falling under this and especially the 1st Administration Office of Primary Education, to which the 8th Elementary School of Chania belonged, which served as the first Regional Centre of Cultural Education for the Regional Committee of Chania

The administrative responsibility for the operation of the 8th Primary School of Chania as a Regional Training Center for Cultural Education was held by its headmaster.

(Melina – Education and Culture, 2001–2002)

## Operation of Training Centres

During this stage of the project in Chania there were two training centres, one in the city of Chania, in the 8th and 20th Elementary Schools of Chania, which are housed in the same building, for the teachers of the schools in the city and one in the area of Kounoupidiana in the 1st and 2nd Elementary Schools of Kounoupidiana, which are housed in the same building, for the rest of the teachers of the city and surrounding municipalities.

The programme MELINA covered the costs for the purchase of additional material infrastructure at the training centers so that they could essentially satisfy their function role. It also covered the cost for food, soft drinks, coffees and lunch for the teachers participating in the training utilizing the canteens of the schools and local restaurants. It is worth noting that the MELINA programme took care of and covered all additional cleaning costs (cleaners payment, cleaning materials) on the days when the schools operated as training centers as well as the costs for the purchase of consumables materials, which the Executive Secretariat of the programme reported and described clearly in a document addressed to the secretariat of the Regional Coordination Committee before each training meeting. The headmaster ensured that the school unit purchased the necessary materials on behalf of the Institute of Continuous Adult Education (MELINA programme). Finally, for each workshop, the seating arrangements, the means and technological infrastructure and anything that would make the educational procedure in the particular workshop effective for the learners was clearly reported by the Executive Secretariat of the programme prior to the start of the training session.

(Melina – Education and Culture, 2003–2004)

## Organization and Content of Training

The training of primary school teachers in the city of Chania
- was designed by the Central Coordination Committee of the programme;
- was coordinated by the Central Coordination Committee of the Perfecture of Chania in cooperation with the competent administrative authorities of the Prefecture;
- was developed by the educators of the Central Coordination Committee of the Melina programme in collaboration with the School Counsellor and the Headmasters of the Schools Training Centres for Cultural Education as well as teachers from the 8th Elementary School who wished to act as helpers and associates of the educators;
- addressed the Headmasters, general education teachers and subject specialists (Physical Education, Music, Art and English) of the 22 elementary schools of the city of Chania (20 public and 2 private) and 10 schools of suburban municipalities (9 public and 1 private) with priority given to those having a permanent position at those schools;
- was primarily of a laboratory type for all subjects of the training;
- was continuous and repeated at regular intervals in order to be of an interactive nature and to function in an assistive way throughout the school year;
- relied on particular educational material which served as a model for action in the context of the curriculum of primary school subjects;
- was divided in the following five sections:
  - art workshops (music, art, dance, audiovisual expression, theatre and subject teaching material) (40 hours)
  - visits to cultural centres (5 hours)

- ○ group dynamics (7 hours)
- ○ teaching aids (7 hours)
- ○ local history and art (14 hours)
- developed in two annual cycles with a total duration of 130 hours that were implemented during two school years.

Participation in the training programme MELINA was optional and had no other motive but the quality of the content. However the "MELINA – Education and Culture" project completely covered all expenses for the proper functioning and organization of training sessions gradually equipping schools training centres with the necessary technological and educational means. Moreover, considering absolutely necessary to cover to the extent of its economic potential the beyond working hours work of the teachers who participated in the training (Friday, Saturday and Sunday), the programme paid to each teacher the amount of 150 Euros depending on the attendance rate. The training places for general upper A and 150 were teachers. Teachers who attended the training were bound by a declaration to attend the two-year training programme with a presence that exceeded 80% of the training hours.

(Melina – Education and Culture, 2002–2003)

## Distribution of Teaching Material

The school units that joined the training programme gradually purchased the entire educational programme material (more than 350 titles of books, records, slides and CDS) on the grounds that 40% of those serving in the school participated in the training.

## Cooperation with Cultural Institutions of the City. Production of Educational Programmes. Organization of Thematic Cultural Events

The Melina programme did not sponsor artistic events, but supported cultural institutions that wanted to implement training programmes. In particular, it worked with the Union International de la Marionnette (UNIMA) Crete, with the Visual Laboratory of the Municipality of Chania and the Municipal Regional Theatre of Crete. It also put together interdisciplinary writing teams of teachers, museum educators, historians and architects with the aim of writing and publishing educational files for the students of the final year of elementary school. At the same time, there was an effort to develop thematic cultural events in cooperation and with the support of local authorities focusing on the promotion of the educational dimension of art and culture.

## Local Teacher Conference: Informing the Media and the Local Community

At the end of each training cycle and with the support of local authorities and the Prefecture local conferences were organized in which model educational activities and educational material composed by teachers of schools educated in all areas of teaching intervention (model teaching of subjects of the curriculum) and parallel programmes (cultural education, environmental education, health education, consumer education, IT) were presented. At the same time, on the occasion of the attempt to highlight the continuous dialogue between Culture and Education the Central Coordination Committee investigated and implemented the potential of ongoing television and radio coverage and written promotion of the unit Education and Culture with special local broadcasts and tributes in order to further redefine the cultural and educational reportage.

(Melina – Education and Culture, 2003–2004)

## Conclusion

Cultural action for the development and cohesion of the local community was the capstone of the philosophy of the programme as that was formed through the new reality that emerged for the role and perspective of local communities in the twenty-first century.

The key to strengthening cultural policy is the local people of the area … So the interdisciplinary dialogue about cohesion and the development of the local community with the actions of various arts in the fields that are tight, for example that of Education, Culture, Youth, Health, Social Services with the aim of improving the quality of life in the family, at school, in the local community, in the wider community. (Williams et al., 2002: 39)

Nine years later, the teachers that were trained in the programme, building on the legacy of the programme, insist on resisting everyday school practice seeking "the aesthetic dimension of the curriculum being taught highlighting the cultural dynamics in education with the indestructible power of art and culture", aspiring to "restore an authentic communication between their students and the historical, social and cultural environment". In this context the curriculum is not treated as information only, but also as recorded human experience, as a final emotions stimulus (Paizis & Theodoridis, 1995: 12). It would clearly be of stronger research interest to investigate whether the target groups that received the impact of the programme and its innovative interventions (students, teachers, local community, cultural organizations) in Chania show any changes today in the way they manage the cultural stock of the place and how they communicate and express themselves through the arts and culture in their lives, in education and in their opportunities to meet with other cultures.

A modern cultural policy must promote its educational component in order to follow the evolution of society. The Melina project was the first major attempt at a national policy level in our country for a multi-level joint strategy of the Ministry of Education and the Ministry of Culture. In Greece, however, it is evident that there is no long-term planning of cultural policy and that is often attacked by reshuffles and changes of government.

In the large picture of the national educational policy of our country, human resources have never been treated as a resource worth investing the success of an innovation on it. However, the production of educational and cultural innovation, is the modern and safe way for the development of social innovation, cohesion and prosperity of local communities in a globalized economic environment eager to develop into a social and cultural one. The production of social innovation at the local level is there from the lower tier of the education system and develops lifelong, in an atmosphere of wonder and enjoyment, discovery and experimentation.

An important local innovation is the development of actions, not in one classroom , not in one school but in all classrooms, in all schools, in all educational and cultural institutions of the local community, the neighborhood , the district and the municipality. An important **local innovation** is grafting the national to the local, a major innovation is the existence of critical degrees of freedom in educational and cultural activity in the local community. Finally, an important, **educational, social and technological innovation**, is the emergence of composition and collegiality within the educational reality. (Paizis, 2010 )

The Melina programme constituted "an innovation that was created and developed through the procedures and processes of a Central Coordination Committee that functioned with self-commitment from its members and chemistry that was attributed to the high degree of collaboration in the leadership core and the high confidence. The Central Coordination Committee managed to face the challenges and changes of the programme which, as a system had a sensitive dependence on initial conditions and aimed at the internal reform of the school" (Vergidis & Vaikousi, 2003). The organizational dynamics of the programme, as is highlighted during its implementation in the Prefecture of Chania, does not simply mark an innovative proposal for additional teacher training. It is an example of a successful TQM strategy (Total Quality Management) that managed to "inspire and connect every member of different target groups with the vision" (Champouri-Ioannidou, 2003), of a substantial cultural development based on cultural pedagogy with educational perspective.

> Cultural action in this perspective suggests the value of the education of the individual, the facilitation of the creative as well as personal involvement of individuals (mental, emotional, communication) with the information, the creation of personal opinion through meeting and communicating with "other opinions" that are so different and so human. (Paizis, 2002)

The project rallied the educational community, the local community and the cultural organizations of the Prefecture of Chania in "total commitment to quality by involving everyone in the process of continuous improvement and services through the use of innovative scientific methods" (Logothetis, 1993: 20).

The vision of a genuine cultural development based on cultural education with pedagogical perspectives emerges in the new curricula for all levels of compulsory education "aimed mainly at the awareness of all students regarding the charm and possibilities provided by the alternative and emotionally rich communication ways based on artistic expression" (Pedagogical Institute, 2011) . The modern school incorporates, as its key components, the educative objectives/abilities incurring in all teaching and learning fields and subjects of the new curriculum with the words "knowing and understanding", "exploring", "communicating" and "connecting" which refer essentially to planning principles and the organization of teaching (Dukas, 2011) and which are derived from the principles of the 1996 UNESCO principles (Pedagogical Institute, 2011).

A question, though, that remains timeless and always timely is the way in which innovation in education will be able to finally bear fruit towards a substantial change in strategy and perspective.

# References

Champuri-Ioannidou, Aik. 2003. "Management Strategy of the Cultural Institutions" in Velopoulou, A. (ed.), *Cultural Policy and Management, Cultural Administration*. Patra: Hellenic Open University, 25–66.

Doukas, Chr. 2011. "Learning through Planning and New Curricula" in *New Learning and Transformative Mechanisms in Pedagogy and Assessment*, http://neamathisi.com/learning-by-design/pilot-greece/ (accessed 16 April 2013).

Drakaki, M. (2009). *"The supervisor of cultural activities in primary education: Management duties and relations with the headmasters of the school units. Contribution to the cultural development of the students"*, Thesis in the University of Crete, School of Education Sciences, Department of Pre-school Education, supervisor Pr. Argiropoulou El., Rethymno: 32

Logothetis, N. 1993. *Total Quality Management*. Athens: Interbooks Publications.

Melina – Education and Culture. 2003–2004. *Annual Activity Report 2003–2004*, Central Coordination Committee, Archive of 1st and 2nd Elementary Schools of Kounoupidiana, Chania.

—. 2002–2003. *Annual Activity Report 2003–2004*, Central Coordination Committee, Archive of 8th and 20th Elementary Schools of Chania.

—. 2002–2003. Activities Planning, September 2003–August 2004, Chania – Zakynthos – Drama – Kavala – Thessaloniki – Athens – Heraklion. Central Coordination Committee, Archive of 8th and 20th Elementary Schools of Chania.

Paizis, N. 2002a. "Course and Perspectives of the Programme MELINA-Education and Culture" in *Museum-School 6th Regional Seminar*. Kavala: Ministry of Life-Long Learning and Religions, Ministry of Culture, ICOM, Greek Department, Elementary School of Kavala, 49–51.

—. 2002b. "Travelling in Time with Programme MELINA: The Value of Cultural Education" in Kokkinos, G. and Alexaki, E., *Interdisciplinary Approaches to Museum Education*, METAICHMIO Publications, 239–243.

—. 2010. "Education Culture and Social Innovation: Social Innovation in the Epicenter of Local Societies", *Scientific Net of Adult Education of Crete* 1, http://cretaadulteduc.gr/blog/?cat=6 (accessed 16 April 2013).

Paizis, N. and Theodoridis, M. 1995. *Education and Culture Programme MELINA*. Athens: Ministry of Culture, Ministry of National Education and Religions, General Secretariat of Information and Communication.

Pedagogical Institute. 2011. *Major Training Programme: Basic Educational Material,* volume A, May 2011, www.epimorfosi.edu.gr (accessed 1 April 2013).

Pedagogical Institute, Ministry of Life-Long Learning and Religions, New Curricula, Scientific Field Culture, Art Activities, Recommendation B, http://digitalschool.minedu.gov.gr/info/newps.php (accessed 16 April 2013).

Terezaki, Chr. 2008. *Alternative Types of Communication and Learning: Cultural Education in Everyday Teaching Practice, From Theory to Practice*. Athens: Self-published.

Vergidis, D. and Vaikousi, D. 2003. *Programme MELINA- Education and Culture. Teacher Training.* Ministry of National Education and Religions, Ministry of Culture, General Secretariat of Adult Training, Athens.

Williams, J., Losito, C. and Cottingham, J. 2004. *Creative Community Building through Cross-Sector Collaboration : A European Mapping and Consultation Initiative.* Center for Creativity Communities in co-operation with the MELINA Project (IDEKE), GR Sponsored by Hellenic Ministry and Religious Affairs, Greece , The Melina Project, Greece, European Cultural Foundation, The Netherlands, Final Report.

# Chapter Twenty-six

## Teachers' In-service Training: Types of Training Institutions and Forms of Activities in Greece, Great Britain, Germany, Sweden and Finland

### Eleni Efthimiopoulou
#### Teacher, Graduate, Primary Teacher Education, University of Crete, Greece

**Abstract**

The important changes in the social and educational sector, due to the rapid development of scientific and technological knowledge, have created a pressing need for the teachers' enrichment with new knowledge in order to rise to these occasions. The teachers' in-service training – in most European countries – is the key element for the improvement of education, so it is an integral part of their educational policy. The training policies that are implemented by the member-states are of great importance, because they allow us to understand and interpret the educational data of other countries. The main concern is the modernization of knowledge, giving emphasis on the role of the educator, as well as on making sure that the specific needs of the school are met. In this document, we will refer to the European dimension of teachers' in-service training, focusing on the types of in-service institutions and on the forms of in-service training activities that Greece, Great Britain, Sweden, Germany and Finland adopt.

**Keywords**

in-service training, continuing professional development, in-service training institutions, in-service training forms

# Introduction

There have been a lot of challenges for teachers by the end of the twentieth century due to economic, social and cultural changes. These changes, together with the development of technological and learned knowledge, created something brand new for educational practice. Educators are asked to face these challenges and succeed in their difficult work at school.

Teachers' main education and training at university cannot meet the needs of today's school and it cannot be considered enough these days. In this profession lifelong learning, new research and enrichment of disposable knowledge are expected and are necessary.

In-service training is considered to be the main element for the improvement and modernization of teachers' knowledge; it is also necessary for teachers' professional development, so that the level of teaching can improve and pupils' knowledge can develop (Day, 2003: 23).

In recent years in-service training has come to be believed to be of more and more importance in Greece and in other European countries and it plays a very important role in teachers' careers. For most countries in the European Union the in-service training and lifelong education of teachers are considered to be a great challenge to their education system, but they are also very important parts of their educational policy.

In the education policies of the European countries, teachers' continuous professional development and their lifelong education are considered necessary to ensure effective and good-quality education (*Teachers Matter*, 2005: 10). There has developed a dialogue between the member-states lately that is mainly occupied in facing the problems of the educational system, searching for solutions, introducing lifelong education, meeting the needs of schools and improving the role of educators. Furthermore, a lot of documents have been adopted by the European Union concerning professional development and educators' training. However, the role of the European Union is more strategic and directing, because the issue of teachers' training is determined at national or sub-national level in each country, according to their educational system. Generally, a trend of decentralization of education has been noticed lately all over Europe and the same is happening with the in-service training.

The study of in-service policies in the EU is a very interesting exercise. There are many comparisons between the member-states as well as differences in issues of training with respect to the types of in-service training institutions and forms of in-service training, which will be analysed below. In this report I would like to draw your attention to the general trends that exist in Europe, by considering a few European countries.

## Types of In-service Training Institutions

Many types of institutions in Europe offer programmes for in-service training. They are mainly the universities or teacher-training institutions which organize specialized training or training in pedagogical disciplines. In some countries responsibility for the training is assumed by the state, in others we can see a trend of decentralization, where the role of the schools is maintained, improving its importance (Fig. 26-1).

In the 1990s the model of professional development put into practice was based on the school. This model was used by a lot of European countries. According to this model the training activities are organized and realized by the school, with experts' help and direction. This model recognizes the need for influence and effective cooperation of participants in group work with the aim of facing the problems of the school and meeting its needs.

The most important issue of the European states with regard to teacher training is that the needs of the school have to be directly met. In the literal sense of the word, the schools in Finland take responsibility for part of the organization and realization of training and they cooperate with the government or with in-service training institutions. The decentralization of teacher training in Finland started in 1968, when the education system of primary schools in Finland was reformed. The educators' training was considered of great importance for all teachers and according to the school leaders the development of the teachers' abilities was necessary for the enhancement of the educational quality of schools (Tuula Asunta, 2006, p. 142).

In Sweden, in 1991, responsibility for the organization and planning of training programmes was assumed by the municipalities. These reforms created a training policy in which the state accepted responsibility for access to quality training and the municipalities took on the organization and delivery of the training for the teachers, as well as for informing school directors about the training programme. The directors in Sweden and in Great Britain play an important role in the organization of continuous teacher training.

Furthermore, in Greece, in Finland and in Germany school leaders cooperate with teachers, teachers' counsellors and school supervisors and they organize the training and create activities together. In a great number of states teachers' counsellors assume responsibility for the biggest part of teachers' training, educating adults and doing research into the teachers' educational needs in cooperation with the universities and other training institutions (Longworth, 1999: 30). In Greece there have been teachers' counsellors since 1982 and according to Greek law N.1304/82 "he organizes and looks after the training and helps teachers in their research with the methods he considers right in his municipality" (Zografou-Tsantaki, 2005: 326).

| Types of training institution | Great Britain | Germany | Greece | Sweden | Finland |
|---|---|---|---|---|---|
| Universities | ● | ● | ● | ● | ● |
| State-owned training centres | ● | ● | ● |  | ● |
| Private training centres | ● | ● |  |  | ● |
| Schools | ● | ● | ● | ● | ● |
| Others (private companies, organizations, | ● | ● |  | ● |  |

Fig. 26-1. Main types of training institution

On the one hand, there are mature and experienced teachers especially in Great Britain. They are the so-called advanced skills teachers, who can take over the teacher training and can be responsible for teachers' improvement, either by giving advice regularly or by organizing specialized training. On the other hand, in Greece and in Finland the educators' associations are activated during the preparations for the training programme in each school, so that they maintain the teachers' improvement.

High level educational foundations, initial training foundations, universities and colleges are types of training foundations which we meet more often in European training practice, where they assume the initial role in teachers training. In Sweden, municipalities successfully cooperate with universities to organize and realize the training programmes. In Greece, the universities organize several types of teacher training in cooperation with the schools and other organizations which are maintained by their educators. Generally, the importance of high standards of teacher training is seen in a lot of countries, because it is considered to create a link between the university and the primary school, the reality of teaching practice, between the initial teacher training and pedagogical research and with production of knowledge, as well as between theory and school knowledge.

As in Great Britain, Greece has an Open University that offers teachers many opportunities for distance learning, with the improvement and evaluation of appropriate teaching material and offering various teaching methods. Moreover, in these two countries there are institutions which offer extra education for teachers. In England they are the Institutes of Education for postgraduate and continuing education; in Greece they are institutions at the universities, the so called Teaching Post graduations.

Furthermore in a lot of European countries, specialized training centres have been created to offer training for teachers and maintain their professional development. In Greece these are called Provincial Training Centres (PEK in Greek). The main aim of these centres is to conduct the training of candidates who want to start teaching, or teachers who have just started teaching (Kapsalis & Papastamatis, 2006: 259), teachers' periodic training and information for teachers about the introduction of new subjects, methods and school books with continuing training programmes (Chatzidimou & Stravakou, 2003).

Finland has professional training centres, adult training centres and national in-service training centres. In Great Britain there are local teachers' centres and independent centres for education, which began with a curriculum development programme. The main purpose of these centres is to inform teachers regularly about results of scientific research in their subjects, to give them a chance to discuss their problems in everyday school routine and to solve them, informing them about imminent changes in the educational system, in books or in detailed programmes (Nasainas, 2010: 143).

The situation in Germany is very similar to that in Great Britain. There are a lot of training centres depending on the ministries of education and they have different names in each state (Bundesland). Some of them are called State Academies (Staatliche Akademie) and Academic Institutes for Teacher Training (Wissenschaftliches Institut fuer Lehrerfortbildung) (Eurydice, 2009/10: 213).

Beyond the municipal and state-owned training centres, the private sector also undertakes teacher training in some countries. There are private companies in Finland and private centres in Germany that are certified to offer several programmes to improve the quality of education.

The types of training institutions mentioned above exist in almost all countries. But there are other training institutions, too, which are not so common as the types of training institutions shown in Fig. 26-1. Specifically, in Germany, there are institutions (not state owned) and churches which offer educational training for teachers concerning religious subjects and in Sweden it is planned to publish information and other digital material with the help of the Internet and in Great Britain there has been a digital channel since 2005 called "Teachers TV", which has educational and developing programmes, educational material, such as sources from the school class and educational news (Eurydice, 2007/08: 317–318).

All in all we can say that there are a lot of types of educational institutions and training organizations. Responsibility for teacher training cannot be taken over by only one training institution, so in most countries there is cooperation between different types of educational institutions to ensure a more sucessful, high quality future education.

## Forms of In-service Training

The forms of training activities chosen by EU member-states are either official or unofficial; they are different, depending on the training institution, the duration, their aims and the type of organization, but also on the teachers' professional needs.

Apart from this there are types of training activities, which we can meet more often in most EU countries. Some of them are:

- In-service training at school
- Distance learning
- In-service training tutorials
- Lectures
- Training journeys
- Introductory programmes for in-service training

As mentioned above, because of the decentralization of the education, schools play an important role in choosing the form and content of training activities. The in-service training at school and the training organized by the educational authorities are the most common forms of continuous professional development. This form is considered very important internationally and it is also indispensible and is created for the teachers of a certain school unit. This form is based on at least two facts:

a. The school is a seed, where the purpose of the education must be achieved.

b. The quality of the educational procedure in each school mainly depends on the quality of the teacher's work in class (Ksochellis, 2000: 11). The main purpose is to meet the teachers' individual and professional needs, as well as the needs of the school.

In most European countries in-service training at schools is of great importance. In Germany, in Finland, in Great Britain and in Greece the training organized by the education authorities mainly contains lectures, one-day class observation, group teaching and seminars. Seminars are the most common method of teachers training in Europe. These seminars are not offered only by the school unit; teachers have the opportunity of seminars abroad, in the form of training journeys.

Moreover with the organization of in-service training in Germany, in Finland and in Great Britain project groups are created and courses are offered. Specifically in Great Britain group teaching is organized, as well as other activities that give teachers the opportunity to discuss their opinions, focusing on teaching methods. In Finland a lot of in-service activities end with own-teaching. Similarly teaching in a real class is organized as a periodic, introductory and yearly form of training. Furthermore in these two countries teacher training is supported by visits to companies and other educational institutions (in Finland), and by teacher exchange with teachers from abroad (Great Britain).

Besides the data mentioned above, teachers in Great Britain have the opportunity to take paid holiday for one year to attend training lessons to improve their knowledge. Teachers in Great Britain can also attend training lessons on a higher (postgraduate) level, giving them the certificates they need. This form of training is an innovation in Great Britain and it is an important motivation for teachers who are willing to improve their individual and professional development.

Beyond the in-service training which is realized in the framework of the school, there is another form of in-service training, which is directly connected with the school unit and (whether happening in it or out of it) is called school-focused in-service training. This form is known in Greece, in Great Britain and in Finland and offers lectures, discussions and observations of teaching. The main purpose of this form of training is to face the direct and special needs of the school and is focused also on meeting the training needs of the school (Ross & Hutchings, 2003: 56). The main difference between in-service training at school and school-focused training is the place where it is organized. School-focused in-service training does not require the observation of activities at school, but it demands their teachers' education out of it. So this is a global form that takes some items from training at school and some from training out of school (Mayrogiorgos, 1983: 48).

Furthermore, in Greece, the form of the introductory training has been known very well in recent years. This form is necessary and compulsory for teachers who have just started teaching and its purpose is to cover the gap in these teachers' knowledge, which may exist because of the long period between obtaining the diploma at university and the moment they start teaching. This form of introductory training is claimed to add necessary facts to the teachers' former and deficient education (Ksochellis, 2001: 39).

According to research in Finland, there were positive results of an introductory training programme which offered workshops, teaching seminars, homework, analysis of articles in newspapers, experience at school after observing class and teaching in class working with projects and at the end some pieces of advice given by experienced teachers to the new ones (Villegas-Reimers, 2003: 61).

In the English educational system the introductory training or "probationary term" is an important step for the teachers at the start of their career. It is in new teachers' interest to be observed for a period of probation so that their ability in teaching can be diagnosed and they can be added legally to the teachers' profession. This period of probation has to agree with national practice in the education policy of the state, which can clarify the needs, the obligations, the knowledge and the ability teachers have to have at the end of this period (Villegas-Reimers, 2003: 53). Teachers who cannot reach the required level cannot teach but can be given other jobs in the educational system. Finally, an NUT (National Union of Teachers) essay is typical of the problems of the probationary period. In this essay a wide range of suggestions were presented concerning the organization of introductory training of 3–4 weeks in the summer, before school starts and teachers take up their work at schools. It suggested the teachers spend 2–3 days a week at school and the other days of the week they could use for their university work, where they could be supported by theoretical material.

| Forms of training institution | Great Britain | Germany | Greece | Sweden | Finland |
|---|---|---|---|---|---|
| In-service training at school | ● | ● | ● | ● | ● |
| Introductory training | ● | – | ● | – | ● |
| Distance learning | ● | ● | ● | ● | ● |
| Periodic | – | – | ● | – | – |
| Yearly | – | – | ● | – | – |
| School-based | ● | – | ● | – | – |
| Education journeys | ● | ● | ● | ● | ● |

Fig. 26-2. Main forms of training
(● = the form exists; – = there are no references)

Beyond these forms, there is the yearly or periodic training for teachers in Greece, which we cannot find in other countries in Europe. Periodic training lets the teachers know about educational innovations and changes, and takes place during the school year. We could consider this as similar to the training lessons for teachers in Sweden which are organized during the school year or in the holidays, their main purpose being to inform teachers and to improve their knowledge of certain issues.

Furthermore, there is distance learning. This is very different from the other training forms. This form is well known in all member-states in Europe and uses new technology, meeting the personal needs of each teacher and reducing problems of time and place.

Generally, the forms of training in EU member-states are abundant and inexhaustible due to the very complicated needs of each country's teachers and to the expectations of school in modern society. Apart from the similarities in choosing the forms of training in European countries, we need to state that each country applies each form of training according to its needs, expectations, economic situation and national policy in its education system.

# Conclusion

After collecting and studying the data mentioned above we can conclude that teachers' professional improvement and training is in line with the interest of educational reforms of each European country and they have accepted that it is useful and they need it. In spite of the fact that teachers' main education is deficient in some countries, teachers training is not compulsory according to the law. Furthermore, the lack of resources for training activities and the lack of supply teachers during training restrict the frequency of training. Often, these problems are combined with teachers' lack of motivation. Despite these weaknesses, training cannot be the responsibility solely of state education policy; teachers themselves have to accept responsibility for their personal improvement and professional development (ETUCE, 2008: 44). Finally, we must mention that all countries in Europe have to deal with problems and they present weaknesses, which they are called to get over, so that they can support their training policy.

# References

Chatzidimou, D. and Stravakou P. 2003. *PEK as Statutory Training Institute and their Contribution to Educational Practice: The Example of the First PEK in Thessaloniki*. Thessaloniki: Kiriakidis Publishing. (In Greek)
Day, C. 2003. *The Development of Teachers: The Challenges of Lifelong Learning,* translated by Anthi Vakaki. Athens: Tipothito publishing. (In Greek)
ETUCE. 2008. *Teacher Education in Europe*. An ETUCE Policy Paper.
Eurydice. 2009/10. "Teacher and other Staff in Education", in *Organization of the Education System in Germany*, 194–231.
—. 2007/08. "Teachers and Education Staff", in *Organization of the Education System in England*, 267–344.
Georgiadis, M. I. 2004. *Education and In-service Training of Secondary School Teachers in Greece and in England: Innovations in Education*. Athens: Kiriakidis Publishing. (In Greek)
Kakavakis D. 2005. "Open, Flexible and Distance Education and Adult Learning Principles: The Base for Effective Teachers' In-service Training and Further Education", in 3rd Congress of Syros, 11–13 May, TPE in education, http://www.epyna.eu/~agialama/synedrio_syros_3/ksenwn_glwsswn_epimorfo si/kakavakis423_429.pdf (posted 11 May 2011). (In Greek)
Kapsalis, A. and Papastamatis, A. 2006. *Professionalism in Continuing Education*. Athens: Tipothito Publishing. (In Greek)
Ksochellis, P. D. 2000. "In-service Teacher Training in Greece: An Innovation in the Continuing Education of Teachers", *Proceedings of the International Symposium on Continuing Education Teachers and School Development*, Thessaloniki, 15–16 December, 10–15. (In Greek)

—. 2001. "Teacher Education in Greece: Findings, Criticism, Suggestions", in Aristotle University of Thessaloniki, Proceedings of First National Conference on "Connecting Higher and Secondary Education", Thessaloniki, 35–46. (in Greek)

Longworth, N. 1999. *Making Lifelong Learning Work: Learning Cities for a Learning Century.* London: Kogan Page.

Mavrogiorgos, G. 1983. "Forms of In-service Training: Conceptual Clarification: The Political and Social Context-conditions", in *Contemporary Education* 9, 37–52. (In Greek)

—. 1989. "Teachers' In-service Training: The Ministry of Education and the Working Group", in *Contemporary Education* 46, 16–26. (In Greek)

Nasainas, G. 2010. *The In-service Training of Teachers in the Context of Lifelong Learning.* Athens: N. & S. Batsioulas. (In Greek)

OECD. 2005. *Teachers Matter: Attracting, Developing and Retaining Effective Teachers.* OECD Publishing.

Ross, A. and Hutchings, M. 2003. *Attracting, Developing and Retaining Effective Teachers In the United Kingdom of Great Britain and Northern Ireland: OECD Country Background Report.* London: London Metropolitan University Institute for Policy Studies in Education, http://www.oecd.org/education/school/2635748.pdf (accessed 2 January 2014).

Tuula Asunta. 2006. "Developments in Teacher Education in Finland: In-service Education and Training", in Pavel Zgaga (ed.), *Modernization of Study Programmes in Teacher's Education in an International Context.* Ljubljana: European Social Fund, University of Ljubljana, Faculty Of Education, 136–147.

Villegas-Reimers, E. 2003. *Teacher Professional Development: An International Review of the Literature.* Unesco.

Zografou-Tsantaki, M. and Boziki, A. 2005. "The Educational Role of School Directors: Early Childhood Education from the Perspective of Early Childhood", in Bagakis, G. *Teachers' In-service Training and Continuous Professional Development.* Athens: Metaixmio Publishing, 326–333. (In Greek)

# CHAPTER TWENTY-SEVEN

# THE ROLE OF SCHOOL PRINCIPALS IN TEACHER EVALUATION

## NAHED SHALABY

AMERICAN UNIVERSITY OF CAIRO, EGYPT

**Abstract**
The evaluation of teachers can be defined as a mechanism aiming to enhance teachers' instructional and management practices in the classroom by using methods to judge their performance based on specific standards that will be reflected in their promotion and job retention (Zepeda, 2007). In this respect, school principals and leaders can contribute positively to teaching practices through supervision and evaluation by enforcing goals, concepts of teaching standards and values to teachers through instructional supervision. This paper aims to analyse the nature and extent of the evaluation of teacher performance by school principals in international schools located in Northern and Central parts of Egypt, specifically Cairo and Alexandria. The study is qualitative, in-depth interviews being considered the most suitable approach. The study aims to reveal trends and motives behind teachers' behaviours and experiences.

**Keywords**
school principals, teacher evaluation, professional development

## Introduction

For decades, teacher evaluation in Egypt has been swirling between inspectors, head teachers and school principals, and more recently, exams. In the rebirth of the country, the evaluation process for teachers remains at the forefront of the education reform agenda. The influx of information on the importance of teacher evaluation performance has permeated the discussion on using the evaluation of teachers to improve the education of students (UNICEF, 2000).

The Ministry of Education regulates and norms the educational system. For many years, it has facilitated and encouraged the creation of private schools. The public schools follow the national curriculum of the government.

With regard to teacher evaluation in Egypt, it is based on standards set forth by the professional Academy for Teachers (PAT). There are five domains upon which teachers are evaluated (PAT, 2010). Each domain comprises a number of standards as listed below:

**First Domain: Planning**
Standard 1: Determining The Educational Needs of The Student.
Standard 2: Planning for Greater Targets Not for Detailed Information and Small Objectives.
Standard 3: Designing Suitable Educational Activities.
**Second Domain: Learning Strategies and Classroom Management**
Standard 1: Using Learning Strategies to Meet Students' Needs.
Standard 2: Facilitating Effective Learning Experience.
Standard 3: Involving Students in Solving Problems and in Critical and Creative Thinking.
Standard 4: Providing an Environment That Will Guarantee Equity.
Standard 5: Effective Utilization of Diverse Motivation Methods.
Standard 6: Managing Learning Time Effectively and Limiting Time Wasted (Time On Task).
**Third Domain: Knowledge of Subject Matter**
Standard 1: Being Fully Aware of the Basis and Nature of the Subject.
Standard 2: Fully Knowing Methods of Research in the Subject.
Standard 3: Being Able to Integrate his/her Subject with Other Subjects.
Standard 4: Being Able to Produce Knowledge.
**Fourth Domain: Evaluation**
Standard 1: Self-Evaluation
Standard 2: Student Evaluation
Standard 3: Feedback
**Fifth Domain: Teacher Professionalism**
Standard 1: Ethics of The Profession
Standard 2: Professional Development

The supervision, control and evaluation of teachers in Egypt have always been in the hands of inspectors. Their role is to visit schools and classrooms to observe teachers and collect data based on a set of criteria endorsed by the technical Academy for Education established in 1981 by the Ministry of Education. The inspectors' evaluation of teacher performance consists of judging teachers' classroom discipline and instructional practices in the classroom. They use standards and efficiency indicators which are later sent to the Ministry of Education. Generally, inspectors are subjective and biased in their reports (Torff & Sessions, 2009).

The topic related to the evaluation of teacher performance in Egyptian classrooms injects a new hope aligned with potential reforms in the educational system. The evaluation of teacher performance in Egypt is a serious need that must be met with best practice and dynamic modernization. If the classroom teacher's performance is good, students will achieve as well. In fact, it is imperative that Egypt's educational system moves forward and works diligently to increase success for all students and enhance a positive school environment that will favour the teacher and other participants (students, families and school leaders) working together at the local level, as school teams, for students' progress and for their own professional development. Ainsworth and Viegut (2006) suggest that educational systems must examine the cultural standards that are the basis for instructional standards. In Egypt, conducting the analysis of classroom teachers' performance evaluation would illuminate education policy makers.

The present research study shines light on the most needed practices in order to create the professional evaluation climate that will empower classroom teachers. Based on the previous argument, the purpose of this study takes two distinctive directions. First, to analyse the nature and extent of the evaluation of teacher performance in international schools located in northern and central parts of Egypt, specifically Cairo and Alexandria. Second, to identify and describe the use of clinical supervision components (pre-conference, observation and post-conference) in the evaluation process of classroom teachers of selected schools.

## Literature Review

Generally, recognition of the influential impact of teachers on enhancing student achievement is appreciated (Darling-Hammond and Ball, 1997; Wright, Horn and Sanders, 1997), while the role school principals play in framing the educational system for successful teaching results is on the whole unconsidered (Elmore, 2002). Through supporting new acquisition of knowledge, motivation of staff, selection of resources, involvement in progressive development, principals influence instruction indirectly (Berends, Bodilly & Kirby, 2002). School leaders can have their impact and effect on teaching practices through supervision and evaluation, by enforcing goals, concepts of teaching standards and values to teachers through instructional evaluation.

Teacher evaluation is considered compulsory in most schools. Common practices of teacher evaluation rely on the restrained competencies of teaching (Darling-Hammond, Wise &Klein, 1999). They are described as inaccurate and unsupportive (Peterson, 1995). Instead of serving the promotion of the organization goals, traditional evaluation programmes are usually regarded as superficial and stressful to both teachers and principals alike. In fact, there is evidence that weeding out low performing teachers is the objective of teacher assessment, rather than sustaining the accountability of all teachers or improving their performance (Darling-Hammond, Wise &Klein, 1999). Due to these limitations of scope and efficacy, teacher evaluation has limited influence on teacher performance and learning (Peterson, 1995).Teachers are often frustrated about their summative evaluation, as it is a product of cut and paste from a variety of scenarios. Both teachers and principals feel dismayed by the traditional method of checklist. Teachers believe that the process of their evaluation should undergo a fundamental transformation and that a new evaluation model must take place in lieu of the traditional method. For example, principals' walk-through and classroom observations for data collection purposes would be used to assess their performance. The use of teacher evaluation to judge knowledge, skills and practices in the classroom serves as a distracter of development. School leaders, especially those in charge of evaluating teachers' classroom performance, must reinforce the philosophy of supervision and evaluation for teaching development not for teaching penalization.

Instructional improvement can be obtained through instructional supervision when it is used as a mechanism to enhance and develop instruction (Glickman, Gordon & Ross, 2010). There are various instructional strategies that would be influential in relation to instructional goals and students' abilities. In this respect, it is the role of the supervisor to assist teachers to identify the instructional strategies that would allow classroom instructional objectives to be met through the design of constructivist teaching, co-operative learning, classroom dialogue and service learning, among others (ibid.). Using a variety of teaching methods aligned to different lesson goals and students' learning styles could help accomplish effective classroom instruction. Many attempts have been made to define the link between student achievement and effective teaching methodology. In seeking accountability, principals are starting to evaluate teachers with regard to student achievement and teaching. The role of the principal is to achieve a plan for the development of the teacher.

# Research Problem

Based on the literature review that confirms the importance of the evaluation of teacher performance, this study seeks to analyse the nature and extent of the evaluation of teacher performance in international schools located in northern and central parts of Egypt, specifically Cairo and Alexandria. It also identifies and describes the use of clinical supervision components (pre-conference, observation and post-conference) in the evaluation process of classroom teachers of selected schools.

# Methodology

This is a qualitative study, where in-depth interviews were considered the most suitable methods to conduct the study. The qualitative approach applied as the research design in this study helps reveal trends and motives behind teachers' behaviours and experiences.

## Subjects

The participants in this study were school principals of international schools located in Alexandria and Cairo. Schools were chosen for comparative purposes. Two international schools located in Alexandria and two international schools located in Cairo constituted the sites of this study. Because of the sensitivity of the topic and the risks the study might involve, I kept the names of the schools and participants confidential.

I aimed to determine if the geographical differences could have an impact on the principals' perception. Also, Alexandria and Cairo are the two major cities in Egypt where international schools are widely located. They could represent a good indicator for the vast majority of professional teachers.

## School Descriptions

Table 27-1 shows information concerning the four schools included in the study.

| Description | School A | School B | School C | School D |
|---|---|---|---|---|
| Year of establishment | 1992 | 1997 | 1988 | 1929 |
| International division start year | British 1996 | American 1997 | American 2000 | British 1996 |
| Number of students in international division | 613 | 560 | 650 | 300 |
| Number of teachers in international division | 21 | 22 | 23 | 20 |
| Number of classes | 25 | 20 | 21 | 15 |
| Average number of students per class | 20 | 20 | 20 | 20 |

**Table 27-1. School Information**

Data were collected through structured interviews in which school principals were formally interviewed with a specific set of questions that elicited information on similar topics from the respondents (Appendix 1). A standardized interview was used so that all participants were asked the same questions in the same order. I included both open-ended and closed ended questions to allow both lengthy and short responses. Interviews lasted approximately thirty minutes each for the four school principals representing the four schools. Appendix 2 illustrates the scheduled time for each school.

# Data Analysis

The following themes have been coded from the principals' responses:

### *Professional development*
The goal of teacher evaluation is to empower teachers to become good educators. Primarily, the four school principals agreed that head teachers are responsible for teacher evaluation. One principal added that principals observe teachers' speech time compared to students', the relationship between teachers and students, and the active participation of students.

Besides, observation should vary in number and aspects according to teachers' acceptance of observation.

They all tend to admit that teachers at the beginning of the year are reluctant and nervous because they are not familiar with the process and have negative notions about supervision and observation. When the process is applied and they improve and develop, they become more receptive, but not 100% receptive.

Observation is the step that helps evaluators follow up on the professional growth plan.

"When you adequately identify the strengths of a teacher, it's an opportunity to cherish them, and when you identify the weaknesses, it is an opportunity to help empower the teacher with proper guidance." Guidance is provided by workshops and training.

One principal seemed to be aware of restricted budgets and facilities that help teachers enhance their profession.

Only one principal referred to peer coaching as a fruitful tool for professional development. Teachers learn from each other by observing and discussing.

Further aspects that help principals determine the strengths and weaknesses of teachers are a pre-conference, holistic clinical, focused clinical, scripting analysis, post conference, and a professional growth plan for each teacher. Another principal suggested using audio visual aids in lesson planning and integrating extra curricula activities. Tangible and achievable plans should be taken into consideration.

### Teacher evaluation and student achievement

Three principals approved linking teacher evaluation to students' achievement and believe they are interrelated. One principal confined the link between teacher evaluation and students' achievements to primary stages. Children's fluency in languages and oral work are good indicators of what teachers are doing. At upper grades, private tuition is extensive, which eventually makes it difficult to link their achievements to the class teacher.

### Challenges of teacher evaluation

All principals are aware of the complexity of teacher evaluation – as one of them said, "They require a phenomenal amount of time, practice and work". It involves great responsibility in order to be fair, precise and accurate. This finding is aligned with the evaluation of teachers in Tennessee mentioned earlier in the literature review with regard to scripting and filling out papers that consume a lot of time.

Another principal recalled her experience when she was a teacher and how her head teacher had an authoritative attitude which made her discount all her remarks. Hence, she became very tactful and careful when she took her position. Therefore, trust and effective communication skills are necessary.

"Be objective, put personal feelings aside, make sure you end up with a win win situation." The success of the principal is the ultimate goal of teacher evaluation.

### *Principals' qualifications for evaluating*

Experience as a requirement for principals to evaluate teachers has been shared by all. Two principals received their training in their masters' programme as well as previous training from work. One of the principals was trained in England while working in an organization. They all agree that qualification is vital. One principal added that a sense of humour and patience are necessary requirements. Finally, they should not be fault finders.

## Discussion

Based on the above analysis of the four schools, I could tie in the research problem that directed the study to the findings. No doubt, school principals play a major role in the evaluation of teachers' performance. Principals can empower teachers by promoting motivation, guidance and facilitating work conditions. Professional development configured by principals ensures the enhancement of students' learning. Principals must possess certain knowledge, skills and experience to assess and promote teachers' performance.

The research findings reveal the importance and effectiveness of clinical observation that escalates professional growth plan, which in turn promotes students' learning and achievement.

## Conclusion

The research conducted in two international schools in Cairo and two in Alexandria on principals' perspective about the best strategies and techniques on teachers' evaluation did not reveal any significant differences among the participants. There seemed to be consensus about the importance of teacher evaluation if it is done for professional development and met the objective of learning for enhancing students' knowledge.

The study findings are directly related to the literature review. It sheds light and advocates the vitality of evaluating teachers' classroom performance as the main pivot for improving teaching quality. The process of evaluation requires investment in professional development that successfully enhances teachers' experience. Directing the philosophy of supervision to reinforce progress and practice is the core of evaluation. In an attempt to link teacher evaluation to students' achievement, some principals opposed the accountability of this measurement due to the nature of private tuition in the Egyptian culture.

Unlike public and private national schools, the study reveals that teacher evaluation though complex shows awareness of multiple strategies. However, the researcher advocates the importance of collaborative professional communities with peers through internet, seminars and meetings during school days. Helping teachers improve is highly recommended by continuously providing support that includes both moral and professional development.

# References

Ainsworth, L. and Viegut, D. 2006. *Common Formative Assessment: How to Connect Standards-Based Instruction and Assessment.* Thousand Oaks, CA: Corwin Press.

Berends, M., Bodilly, S. and Kirby, S. N. 2002. "Looking Back over a Decade of Wholeschool Reform: The Experience of New American Schools", *Phi Delta Kappan* 84(2), 168–175.

Darling-Hammond, L. and Ball, D. L. 1997. *Teaching for High Standards: What Policymakers Need to Know and Be Able to Do.* National Education Goals Panel.

Darling-Hammond, L., Wise, A. E. and Klein, S. P. 1999. *A License to Teach: Raising Standards for Teaching.* San Francisco, CA: Jossey-Bass.

Elmore, R. 2002. *Bridging the Gap between Standards and Achievement: The Imperative for Professional Development in Education.* Washington, DC: The Albert Shanker Institute.

Glickman C. D., Gordon, S. P. and & Ross, J. M. 2010. *Supervision and Instructional Leadership: A developmental Approach.* Upper Saddle River, NJ: Pearson Education.

Peterson, K. D. 1995. *Teacher Evaluation: A Comprehensive Guide to New Ddirections and Practices.* Thousand Oaks, CA: Corwin Press.

Professional Academy for Teachers. 2010. *Tools for Teacher Evaluation.*

Torff, B. and Sessions, D. 2009. "Teacher Training and Development", *Teacher Education Quarterly* 36(3), http://www.freepatentsonline.com/article/Teacher-Education-Quarterly/210591619.html

UNICEF. 2009. *Guiding Framework of Performance Standards for Arab Teachers.* Cairo.

Wright, P. S., Horn, S. P. and Sanders, W. L. 1997. "Teacher and Classroom Context Effects on Student Achievement: Implications for Teacher Evaluation", *Journal of Personnel Evaluation in Education* 11, 57–67.

Zepeda, J. Sally. 2007. *The Principal as Instructional Leader: A Handbook for Supervisors.* 2nd edition. Larchmont, NY: Eye on education.

# Appendix 1

*Interviewee: Principal*
1. Who will conduct the teacher observation?
   a) Principals
   b) Head teachers
   c) Peers
2. How often will observations be required?
3. Will observation vary according to teachers' levels of experience?
4. What do you think the teachers feel about the evaluation process?
5. What qualification should an evaluator acquire to evaluate?
6. What training, if any, have you had for evaluation?
7. Recall when you were a teacher. What is your memory and perception of the evaluation experience? How has that experience impacted how you do evaluations of teacher now?
8. What in your opinion are the challenges of evaluation?
9. What is your opinion about linking students' achievement to teacher evaluation?
10. How will evaluation results function to improve professional development?
11. Which tools do you use to determine strengths and weak nesses of teachers?
12. How many evaluation cycles will be used to ensure that opportunity for professional growth is provided?
13. What is it like to visit classrooms?
14. What is the most satisfying aspect of evaluation?
15. What is the least satisfying aspect of evaluation?
16. What would you change to the process if you could?
17. What is the goal of evaluation?
18. What opportunities and support do you provide to ineffective teachers?

# Appendix 2

*Interview schedule*

| School | Date          |
|--------|---------------|
| A      | January 2012  |
| B      | January 2012  |
| C      | February 2012 |
| D      | February 2012 |

# Chapter Twenty-Eight

# Readiness and Practices of Kindergarten Teachers in Crete with Respect to Evaluation in Preschool Education

## George Manolitsis
Associate Professor, University of Crete, Greece
## and Vasilios Oikonomidis
Assistant Professor, University of Crete, Greece

**Abstract**

The evaluation of the teaching process is one of the most interesting issues in education. The present study examined kindergarten teachers' attitudes towards the importance of three dimensions of educational evaluation: a) the evaluation of the kindergarten teacher, b) the evaluation of the teaching process in the kindergarten, and c) the assessment of the child in the kindergarten. The findings of the study showed that the kindergarten teachers considered the evaluation of the teaching process as the most important dimension of the educational evaluation. On the other hand, they do not feel confident and ready for implementing a self-evaluation of their own teaching ability. According to their views the evaluation of their teaching can be achieved by examining the accomplishment of the learning objectives rather than by using "objective" tools of assessment (e.g., tests, scales). The kindergarten teachers' attitudes did not vary according to their educational background or their teaching experience.

**Keywords**

educational evaluation, evaluation of the teaching process, preschool education, kindergarten teachers' attitudes

# Introduction

Evaluation in education is a particularly interesting area of the sciences of education and especially of pedagogy since there are many different approaches to evaluation in education (Mavrogiorgos, 2005). In addition, the necessity for evaluation is universally acknowledged (Kassotakis, 1999; Kapsalis & Haniotakis, 2011; Doliopoulou & Gourgiotou, 2008). Key questions about *what, where, how, when, who, why, by whom and with what purpose to evaluate* (Konstantinou, 2007) provide a space for making different responses to a variety of arguments, while the forms, methods, techniques, species, tools of assessment, analysis, interpretation and use of the evaluation results constitute an extensive literature of relevant articles and books (Doliopoulou & Gourgiotou, 2008).

The key issues involved in the debate on educational evaluation are the following: the evaluation of the student (Konstantinou, 2007; Kassotakis, 1999, 2010), the evaluation of the teacher (Mavrogiorgos, 2005) and the evaluation of teaching (Kapsalis & Haniotakis, 2011).

The position of evaluation in early childhood education is distinguished by a peculiarity which does not contradict the basic principles of design and implementation of educational evaluation, but rather enriches it and expands its horizons. The alternative forms of evaluation are consistent with the criteria and the evaluation types applied in the context of preschool education (Kakana, 2006; Epstein et al., 2004). The explicit reference to evaluation in the Greek curricula of 1989 and 2003 for kindergarten demonstrates that the implementation of evaluation is a clear choice of Greek educational policy on early childhood education. However, Greece is still in the early stages of finding out the views, attitudes, beliefs, knowledge, preferences and readiness of kindergarten teachers on the implementation of the evaluation (Kakana, 2006; Sivropoulou et al. 2006; Sakellariou, 2007; Botsoglou & Panagiotidou, 2006; Raptis, 2002). For this reason we planned a broader research project that examines the attitudes and the readiness of the kindergarten teachers about the evaluation, the practices, the difficulties faced and the sources from which relevant knowledge and support are derived. In this paper we present a part of this wider project.

# The Purpose of the Present Study

In this study we examined kindergarten teachers' attitudes towards the importance of evaluation in the educational process under three headings: a) the evaluation of the kindergarten teacher, b) the evaluation of the teaching process in kindergarten, and c) the evaluation of the child (student) in kindergarten. Specifically, we examined: (i) the attitudes of the kindergarten teachers towards the above mentioned three dimensions of the educational evaluation, (ii) their attitudes towards the procedure they follow when they evaluate the teaching process and students (evaluation elements and evaluation tools) and (iii) their readiness for the self-evaluation, the evaluation of the teaching process and of students. We also examined the association between the kindergarten teachers' attitudes towards the three dimensions of the educational evaluation, their educational background and their teaching experience.

# Method

## *Participants*

A sample of 107 kindergarten teachers (K-teachers) serving in public kindergarten schools in three cities of Crete (Chania, Heraklion and Rethymnon) participated in the study. It followed a snowball sampling procedure.

## *Measures*

A closed-type questionnaire was used to assess the K-teachers' attitudes towards educational evaluation. The questionnaire included:

(a) Three demographic questions requesting participants to provide information in a nominal scale about their (i) undergraduate studies background (whether they have obtained a college or a university degree), (ii) postgraduate educational background (whether they have continue their education after the Bachelor degree), (iii) years of teaching experience (0–10, 11–20, above 21).

(b) Two questions assessing the K-teachers' general attitudes towards the importance of evaluation in the educational process. First, K-teachers were asked to assess on an ordinal scale which one of the three educational evaluation dimensions (K-teacher, child, and teaching process) they valued as the most important. Second, the K-teachers were asked with a 5-point Likert scale to indicate their degree of agreement (0 = strongly disagree – 4 = strongly agree) with the necessity of evaluating the various aspects of early childhood education (children, teaching, K-teacher, educational infrastructures, educational administration).

(c) Two 5-point Likert scale questions assessing the K-teachers' attitudes towards the evaluation of teaching. Participants were asked (i) whether they considered as useful a variety of assessment strategies (such as standardized tests, worksheets, observation, psychomotor or sociodramatic activities, narration) and (ii) which elements were necessary for the evaluation of teaching (e.g., accomplishment of teaching objectives, children's participation, children's achievement in worksheets, task production, classroom discipline).

(d) Two 5-point Likert scale questions assessing the K-teachers' attitudes towards their readiness for the evaluation of themselves (self-evaluation), their teaching and their students. The first question asked the participants to indicate whether they feel prepared to evaluate their students, their teaching and themselves. The second question asked the participants to indicate whether they have benefited from the various courses that they attended in their undergraduate studies (e.g., Practicum, Pedagogy, Psychology, Sociology, Philosophy, Statistics).

## *Procedure*

The questionnaire was distributed by the authors to the K-teachers in their classrooms. One hundred and thirty questionnaires were distributed and 107 were returned (return rate 82.3%).

## *Results*

The distributions of the dependent variables assessed by Likert-type scales were examined. The Kolomogorov–Smirnov tests showed that none of the dependent variables of interest had a normal distribution. Therefore, non-parametric tests were used for further analyses. Particularly, the Friedman test was used for the initial comparison between the responses of each one of the Likert-type questions. A post-hoc multiple pairwise comparison of the responses' means with the Bonferroni adjustment was examined with the Wilcoxon test, when the initial Friedman test showed significant differences among the responses. In addition, the Mann-Whitney U test was used to examine the differences between the two categories of "educational background" (college or university degree vs postgraduate degree) on the mean of each dependent variable. The Kruskal-Wallis test was used to examine the differences among the three categories of the independent variable of "teaching experience" on the mean of each dependent variable.

| Dimension of educational evaluation | Hierarchical order of importance | | | | | | N |
|---|---|---|---|---|---|---|---|
| | 1st | | 2nd | | 3rd | | |
| | f | % | f | % | f | % | |
| K-Teacher's evaluation | 8 | 11.6 | 28 | 26.2 | 33 | 30.8 | 69 |
| Teaching process evaluation | 65 | 60.7 | 19 | 17.8 | 7 | 6.5 | 91 |
| Child's evaluation | 20 | 18.7 | 24 | 22.4 | 29 | 27.1 | 73 |

**Table 28-1. Absolute (f) and relative (%) frequencies of the participants' responses regarding the hierarchical importance of each of three dimensions of evaluation.**

The descriptive statistics for the K-teachers' attitudes towards the importance of the educational evaluation are presented in Table 28-1. Friedman's test on the K-teachers' responses regarding the importance among the dimensions of the educational evaluation showed that there was a significant differentiation ($x^2(2) = 25.59$ p < 0.001). In turn, post-hoc analyses with the Wilcoxon test showed that the teaching process evaluation was valued by the K-teachers as more important than the child's evaluation ($z = 4.16$ p < 0.001); however, the post-hoc comparison between the K-teachers attitudes towards the importance of the child's evaluation and the K-teachers' evaluation did not differentiate significantly ($z = 1.49$ p > 0.05). It seems that according to the most of the K-teachers the evaluation of the teaching process was valued as a more important dimension of the educational evaluation than the dimensions of the child's evaluation or the evaluation of themselves as teachers. It is noteworthy that a large part of the participants' pool did not answer the item regarding the importance of the K-teachers' evaluation or the child's evaluation. The response rates for these two specific items were 64.5% and 68.2% of the total sample pool respectively. On the contrary, the response rate for the item asked K-teachers to value the importance of the teaching process evaluation was higher (85%) than the previous two items.

Table 28-2 shows the participants' degree of agreement regarding their attitudes towards the evaluation of various components of the educational process. Friedman's test analysis on these items showed that the K-teachers degree of agreement for the necessity of evaluation of these educational process components was significantly different ($\chi^2(4) = 82.67$ p < 0.001). Post-hoc comparisons with the Wilcoxon test and the

| Educational process components | M | SD |
|---|---|---|
| Children | 2,69 | 0,80 |
| Teaching process | 3,06 | 0,75 |
| K-teacher | 2,84 | 0,82 |
| Infrastructures in Education | 3,44 | 0,60 |
| Administrative context | 3,36 | 0,66 |

*Note*: 0 = strongly disagree, 1 = disagree, 2 = uncertain, 3 = agree, 4 = strongly agree

**Table 28-2. Means (M) and standard deviations (SD) of the K-teachers' degrees of agreement for the necessity of evaluation of various educational process components**

Bonferroni adjustment (the modified alpha level for the four tests for K-teachers agree on the necessity of the evaluation of the infrastructures in education and the administrative context significantly more than they agree on the evaluation of the other components of the educational process ($z = 3.33$ p < 0.05). In turn, the K-teachers considered the evaluation of the teaching process as more necessary than the evaluation of themselves as teachers ($z = 3.32$ p < 0.05) or the child's evaluation. The participants' attitudes regarding the necessity of the K-teachers' evaluation did not differ from their attitudes to the necessity of the child's evaluation. It seemed that while most of the participants agree with the necessity of the K-teachers' or the child's evaluation, the degree of agreement for the necessity of these two components was significantly lower than their agreement for the necessity of evaluation of the other educational process components. It is notable that none of the participants disagreed on the necessity of evaluation of the infrastructure in the education and the administrative context. To sum up, the K-teachers' responses showed that they believe that the teaching process evaluation is more important in the context of preschool education than the K-teachers' or child's evaluation.

Next, further analysis of the teaching process evaluation showed that it was considered by the participants as a more important dimension of the educational evaluation than the child's or the K-teachers' evaluation. Table 28-3 shows the participants' attitudes towards the elements that were considered as necessary for the evaluation of the teaching process in kindergarten as well as the necessary tools for the effective implementation of the teaching process evaluation. Non-parametric analysis with the Friedman test showed that the mean scores of agreement between the various elements that the participants considered as necessary for the teaching process evaluation were significantly different ($\chi^2(4) =$

171.78 p < 0.001). Further analyses of the pairwise comparison of the participants' attitudes towards these evaluation elements implemented Wilcoxon's test and the Bonferroni adjustment. These analyses showed that "children's participation" and the "achievement of the teaching objectives" were rated by the participants significantly more important than the other evaluation elements reported in the questionnaire ($z = 4.45$ p < 0.001). The next important evaluation element was the "task production" by the children (students), which was rated as more important than the element of "discipline in the classroom" ($z = 3.78$ p < 0.001) or the student's "achievement on worksheets". Furthermore, the comparison among the participants' mean scores with the Friedman test regarding their attitudes towards the usefulness of the various tools for the educational evaluation showed significant differences ($\chi^2(6) = 107.21$ p < 0.001). Specifically, it has shown that the "combination of the evaluation tools", the "observation of the children's play", the "psychomotor", "drama" and "narration" activities were those evaluation tools that the K-teachers rated

| Teaching process evaluation | M | SD |
|---|---|---|
| **Evaluation elements** | | |
| Teaching objectives achievement | 3,32 | 0,59 |
| Discipline in the classroom | 2,22 | 0,96 |
| Children's participation | 3,31 | 0,65 |
| Tasks' production | 2,77 | 0,99 |
| Achievement on worksheets | 2,01 | 0,92 |
| **Evaluation tools** | | |
| Worksheets | 2,53 | 0,83 |
| Psychomotor activities | 3,02 | 0,73 |
| Drama activities | 3,15 | 0,61 |
| Narration activities | 3,20 | 0,49 |
| Observation of the children's play | 3,17 | 0,64 |
| Standardized tests | 2,42 | 1,01 |
| Combination of the evaluation tools | 3,17 | 0,74 |

*Note*: 0 = strongly disagree, 1 = disagree, 2 = uncertain, 3 = agree, 4 = strongly agree

**Table 28-3. Means (M) and standard deviations (SD) of the K-teachers' degrees of agreement for (a) the evaluation elements considered as necessary for the teaching process evaluation and (b) the tools of the teaching process evaluation.**

as more important for the evaluation of the teaching process. The participants' ratings on those evaluation tools did not differ significantly. However, the K-teachers reported that the worksheets and the standardized tests were less useful than the previous evaluation tools for the evaluation of the teaching process.

The descriptive statistics for the participants' responses regarding their readiness for educational evaluation are presented in Table 28-4. Friedman's test showed that the K-teachers did not feel equally ready for the evaluation of the three different dimensions of the educational evaluation ($\chi^2(2) = 24.79$ p < 0.001). Further analyses showed that K-teachers seemed to be more ready for the evaluation of their teaching process or their students than for the evaluation of themselves as teachers ($z = 3.53$ p < 0.001). It is notable that only 57% of the participants responded positively (agree or strongly agree) that they are ready for the evaluation of themselves as teachers (self-evaluation).

The K-teachers reported that the courses taken in their college or university education did not contribute equally to their readiness for educational evaluation ($\chi^2(5) = 87.41$ p < 0.001). Post hoc analyses with the Wilcoxon test and the Bonferroni adjustment showed that the "Practicum" and the "Psychology" courses were considered as the most important among the undergraduate courses for their contribution to the K-teachers preparation for the educational evaluation ($z = 2.72$ p < 0.01). The courses on "Pedagogy", "Sociology", and "Arts Education" were rated as more important by the K-teachers for their contribution to their preparation for the educational evaluation ($z = 2.87$ p < 0.01) than courses from other disciplines (e.g., philosophy, history, statistics).

It is noteworthy that the K-teachers' attitudes towards educational evaluation, as presented in the Tables 28-1 to 28-4, did not associate significantly with any of the study's independent variables (undergraduate studies background, postgraduate educational background, and years of teaching experience). In other words, the K-teachers who were graduates from a University did not differ significantly from those who were graduates from a College of Preschool Education. Similarly, the K-teachers' attitudes did not differentiate significantly between those who have attended or those who have not attended postgraduate studies (master's programme or school of further education for in-service preschool teachers). Also, the years of teaching experience did not have a significant effect on the K-teachers' attitudes towards educational evaluation.

| Readiness for the educational evaluation | *M* | *SD* |
|---|---|---|
| **a) Feel of readiness for the evaluation** | | |
| Self-evaluation | 2.63 | 0.83 |
| Children (Students) | 2.90 | 0.76 |
| Teaching process | 2.82 | 0.69 |
| **b) Undergraduate courses** | | |
| Practicum | 3.01 | 0.73 |
| Pedagogy | 2.76 | 0.77 |
| Psychology | 2.88 | 0.85 |
| Sociology | 2.53 | 0.95 |
| Other courses (e.g., philosophy, statistics) | 2.08 | 0.83 |
| Arts education | 2.41 | 1.05 |

Note: 0 = strongly disagree, 1 = disagree, 2 = uncertain, 3 = agree, 4 = strongly agree

**Table 28-4. Means (M) and standard deviations (SD) of the K-teachers' degrees of agreement for (a) their feel of readiness to implement the educational evaluation and (b) the undergraduate courses that contributed to their preparation to implement the educational evaluation**

## Discussion

The present findings showed that the kindergarten teachers consider the evaluation of the teaching process as more important than the evaluation of themselves and the evaluation of their students. Kindergarten teachers believe that it is more necessary to evaluate the "regional" structures of the educational process such as the infrastructures and the administrative context than to evaluate more "central" components such as the kindergarten teacher and the kindergarten students. Another interesting finding of the present study was that the accomplishment of the teaching objectives and the active participation of children were considered by the kindergarten teachers as more necessary elements for the evaluation of teaching than any other element. They also considered as more important evaluation tools the various types of authentic assessment than the use of objective tests, such as worksheets or tests. The kindergarten teachers' readiness for evaluation focuses more on the evaluation of teaching and on the evaluation of their students than their own self-evaluation as teachers.

The priority given by the kindergarten teachers to the evaluation of teaching towards student evaluation and their self-evaluation has been observed in previous research with participants from Greece (Sakellariou,

344 Chapter Twenty-eight

2007). This finding can be explained if one considers that the evaluation of teaching on one hand is guided by the kindergarten teachers without the direct involvement of other agents and administrators of education (school counsellors, parents, etc.); on the other hand the evaluation outcomes obtained are introversive, since the kindergarten teachers use the outcomes to redesign and reshape their own teaching practices (Doliopoulou & Gourgiotou, 2008). On the contrary, the evaluation of the student, although it is implemented by the teacher, provides extrovert outcomes, because they can be addressed to students, parents, teachers or even to the teachers of the next school grade. The moderate reluctance of the kindergarten teachers to agree with the need of students' evaluation may be attributed to a general doubt about the use of the outcomes of this type of evaluation (Sivropoulou et al. 2006) or a general question about the evaluation of young children (Raptis, 2002). It should be noted that previous findings have identified the difficulty kindergarten teachers have in evaluating children and the educational process, which was attributed to the teachers' limited knowledge about the evaluation (Doliopoulou, 2008; Goti & Dinas, 2008). The kindergarten teachers showed a similar degree of hesitancy about the evaluation of themselves. In this case, the outcomes of the evaluation are extrovert and it is unclear to the teachers who will be the recipient of the evaluation's outcomes and what the consequences will be for the appraisee (Kassotakis, 2003). Therefore, the unclearness of the evaluation's objectives seems to be reflected in the present findings that kindergarten teachers were suspicious for both the evaluation of themselves and their students. In line with the present findings, previous studies in Greece (Zouganeli et al., 2008; Mangopoulos, 2005) and elsewhere (Brown, 2006; Segeres & Tillema, 2011) have confirmed the cautious attitude of all teachers in their evaluation. However, it has to be noted that the three dimensions of evaluation (student, teaching, teacher) are interrelated. In other words the successful teaching corresponds to a successful student achievement and both could be indicators of the teacher's capability, or the reverse; a good teacher designs successful lessons and leads the children to higher educational goals (Kapsalis & Haniotakis, 2011; Ellet et al., 2002). In this perspective, it seems as a potentially oxymoron schema, the teachers' preference for one dimension of the educational evaluation and a dislike or rejection for another dimension (e.g., self-evaluation). Therefore, it is likely that the differences among the dimensions reflect the subjective interpretations of the kindergarten teachers regarding the introversive (results are controlled by the teacher) or the extroversive (the results are checked by others) direction of the evaluation's outcomes.

In line with the above interpretation were the findings which indicated that kindergarten teachers put priority on the evaluation of the infrastructure (e.g., school building) and the administrative context of education (governance structures, teaching staff, administrative procedures, school counsellors). Next, the kindergarten teachers reported that the teacher, the teaching process and the children (students) were components of lower importance for evaluation. These results are consistent with the findings of Sakellariou (2007) and showed that the kindergarten teachers were in agreement with the rating of "regional" components of the educational process, which affect directly the educational process both in terms of space in education (Germanos, 1998) and in terms of the organizational framework of the educational process. The evaluation of the building comforts of kindergartens plays an important role in the criteria for evaluating the quality of preschool education in several countries (Harms et al., 2004; Sanoff et al., 2004). However, the low quality building comforts of Greek kindergartens has been highlighted by several studies (Koulaidis, 2006; Oikonomidis & Linardakis, 2012; Koffas & Metochianakis, 1994). Also, administrative structures and interpersonal relationships between teachers and managers of education significantly affect the educational process directly and indirectly (Hitz & Wright, 1988). Therefore this element leads kindergarten teachers to agree on the evaluation of the administrative context as agreed by teachers from elementary and secondary education (Zouganeli et al., 2008; Mangopoulos, 2005).

In line with previous studies (Sakellariou, 2007), the kindergarten teachers' evaluation of teaching seems to be focused on the achievement of learning objectives, on children's active participation in the teaching process and on the production of children's work. Furthermore, the preference of kindergarten teachers for focusing on the achievement of learning objectives and on the children's participation in the evaluation of the teaching process indicates that the assessment implemented by the teachers is mainly grounded in the teaching objectives of the curriculum (Doliopoulou & Gourgiotou, 2008) and in a child-centred approach to teaching. A good knowledge of the curriculum and an appropriate use of the evaluation by the teacher contributes to the sufficient preparation of children for the next school grades and for successful later academic achievement (Campbell et al., 2002). The evaluation tools that kindergarten teachers prefer to use are diverse. The kindergarten teachers reported that they implemented them individually or in combination, but they did not rate all these tools with the same degree of preference. The kindergarten teachers considered that the evaluation tools that rated as the most contributive to the evaluation of the teaching process were those (psychomotor activities, drama activities, observation and recording children's play) which could be characterized as aspects of an authentic evaluation (MacBeath et al., 2000; YP.E.P.TH./Pedagogical Institute, 2003). These evaluation tools belong to the active forms (Sakellariou, 2006) or alternative forms of evaluation (YP.E.P.TH./Pedagogical Institute, 2003; Doliopoulou & Gourgiotou, 2008). The observation of children's play and the whole action of the child in school and the respective written records are the main tools of evaluation which are clearly evident in the last two Greek kindergarten curricula (Venizelou et al., 1991; Dafermou et al., 2006). These evaluation tools are considered as a comprehensive, effective and developmentally appropriate evaluation procedure (Avgitidou, 2001; Sivropoulou, 2006). Therefore, the priority of observation and other authentic forms of evaluation by the kindergarten teachers in the evaluation of the teaching process is probably influenced by the "pedagogical culture" cultivated in the last two decades in preschool education in Greece. Similar findings were reported by other studies in Greece (Sivropoulou et al., 2006; Sakellariou, 2007). These studies suggested that the evaluation of the teaching process is approached by kindergarten teachers through a holistic approach to the everyday reality of kindergarten and not through static and instantaneous assessment tools such as worksheets and tests. Furthermore, the international research has shown that the beliefs held by teachers for teaching and learning practices affect their options in educational evaluation (Remesal, 2006). Teachers of lower grades of education did not make frequent use of worksheets and tests (McNair et al., 2003; File & Gullo, 2002), but they prefer to use alternative forms of assessment. It is believed that the alternative forms of evaluation contribute to a deeper assessment of the child's potential, improving the educational process (Stiggins, 1997) and they are more appropriate for young children's education. However, other findings have shown that kindergarten teachers use worksheets more than direct observation of children (Botsoglou & Panagiotidou, 2006). These findings did not confirm that kindergarten teachers have a generic acceptance of alternative evaluation and a respective opposition to "objective" evaluation tools. Finally, the reluctance of kindergarten teachers to use standardized tests may be due to their lack of relevant psychometric knowledge, the lack of standardized evaluation tools in Greece and the lack of a culture and practice of a national evaluation system in young children (Eurydice, 2012; National Centre for Education Statistics, 2001).

In line with the present findings about the types of evaluation that are considered as important by the participants, the kindergarten teachers felt more ready to evaluate their students and their teaching than themselves (self-evaluation). These findings are not consistent with a previous Greek study (Sakellariou, 2007). Sakellariou showed that the kindergarten teachers felt more prepared to evaluate themselves than the children or their teaching ability. Readiness for kindergarten assessment is linked with the courses attended during their basic undergarduate studies, as demonstrated by the research of Sakellariou (2007). The findings of both the present study and Sakellariou's showed a similar hierarchy of the important courses for the teachers' preparation to implement adequately the educational evaluation process. The Practicum is regarded as the most important course that offers directly a lot of methodological elements (Oikonomidis, 2007) in preparing the kindergarten teachers for evaluation. During their Practicum in their undergraduate studies, the prospective teachers transmute their theoretical knowledge in practice in order to evaluate the students, the teaching process and themselves. Notable is the importance attached to psychology courses, since they can contribute to the children's evaluation, because the kindergarten teachers should know and understand their students' developmental characteristics (Kakana, 2006).

To sum up the findings of this study it appears that the kindergarten teachers were not very positive about the evaluation of themselves and their students. They considered as a priority the evaluation of "peripheral" components of the educational process (buildings' comforts, administrative context) and the evaluation of the teaching process. For the assessment of the teaching process most of the kindergarten teachers focused on data that contribute to the evaluation of children's learning. Although they reported a willingness to use a variety of evaluation tools, the kindergarten teachers seemed to trust the "alternative" more than the "objective" forms of evaluation. However, it is understood that the more "objective" evaluation tools are challenged for their appropriateness in the kindergarten. The confidence that the kindergarten teachers felt about their readiness to implement and participate in the evaluation of the educational process seemed to be moderate. Importantly, the kindergarten teachers acknowledged that they are based more on knowledge gained from courses (during their undergraduate studies) that brought them into a direct contact with teaching practice rather than from theoretical courses.

The present study has specific limitations on the generalization of its findings. The participants came from only one region of Greece in a particular time period, their answers derived from a questionnaire and the values may be inflated due to social-desirability bias; also the use of closed questions leaves much room for misinterpretation of the participants' answers by the researchers. In future, it will be good to consider the beliefs of kindergarten teachers through interviews and questionnaires which will include more aspects of evaluation or open-ended questions. Clarifying the aim and feasibility of the evaluation of teachers by the state should be in the direction of encouraging teachers to implement evaluation since they are going to have benefits for their teaching ability. Besides, the pressure for accountability of teachers and of the education system is powerful in society (Kersten & Israel, 2005; Kyriakides & Cambell, 2003).

Finally, the pedagogical implications arising from the present study indicate that the ability of kindergarten teachers to use a variety of evaluation tools must be cultivated and expanded in order to use multiple assessment tools including the "objective" tools. At the same time, the courses for kindergarten teachers' bachelor's degree must be enriched by educational evaluation courses (Sakellariou, 2007; Sivropoulou, et al., 2006; Kakana, 2006). The issue of the readiness of kindergarten teachers to evaluate the student, the teaching process and themselves as well as the evaluation practices they apply has to be studied further in order for the evaluation of the educational process in early childhood education to provide optimal outcomes.

# References

Avgitidou, S. (ed.). 2001. *Play: Modern Research and Teaching Approaches.* Athens: Typothito C . Dardanos. (In Greek)

Botsoglou, K. and Panagiotidou, El. 2006. "Forms and Technical Evaluation of Infants in the Kindergarten: Attitudes and Practices of Educators of Preschool Age", in S.-M. Kakana et al. (eds), *Evaluation in Education: Pedagogical and Didactic Dimension: 71 Texts for Evaluation.* Thessaloniki: Kyriakidis Bross, 149–155.

Brown, G. T. L. 2006. "Teachers' Conceptions of Assessment: Validation of an Abridged Version", *Psychological Reports* 99, 166–170.

Campbell, F. A., Ramey, C. T., Pungelo, E. P., Sparling, J. and Miller-Johnson, S. 2002. "Early Childhood Education: Young Adult Outcomes from the Abecedarian Project", *Applied Developmental Science* 6, 42–57.

Dafermou, Ch., Koulouri, P. and Basagianni, El. 2006. *Kindergarten Teacher's Guide: Educational Planning: Creating Learning Environments.* Athens: Organismos Ekdoseos Didaktikon Vivlion (OEDB). (In Greek)

Doliopoulou, E. 2008. "Kindergarten Teachers' Views of the Implementation of the Kindergarten Teacher's Guide", *Synchroni Ekpaideysi* 153, 165–180. (In Greek)

Doliopoulou, E., and Gourgiotou, E. 2008. *Evaluation in Education, with an Emphasis on Preschool Education.* Athens: Gutenberg. (In Greek)

Ellett, C., Annunziata, J. and Schiavone, S. 2002. "Web-based Support for Teacher Evaluation and Professional Growth: The Professional Assessment and Comprehensive Evaluation System (PACES)", *Journal of Personnel Evaluation in Education* 16, 63–74.

Epstein, A. S. et al. 2004. "Preschool Assessment: A Guide to Developing a Balanced Approach", *Preschool Policy Matters* 7, 1–11.

Eurydice. 2012. *Key Data on Education in Europe.* Brussels.

File, N. and Gullo, D. F. 2002. "A Comparison of Early Childhood and Elementary Education Students' Beliefs about Primary Classroom Teaching Practices", *Early Childhood Research Quarterly* 17, 126–137.

Germanos, D. 1998. *Buildings and Educational Procedures.* Athens: Gutenberg. (In Greek)

Goti, E. and Dean, K. 2008. "Kindergarten Teachers Judge the New Preschool Guidance and Proposals", *Synhroni Ekpaideysi* 153, 181–190. (In Greek)

Harms, T., Clifford, R. and Cryer, D. 2004. *Early Childhood Environment Rating Scale.* NY: Teachers' College.

Hitz, R. and Wright, D. 1988. "Kindergarten Issues: A Practitioners' Survey", *Principal* 67, 28–30.

Kakana, S.-M. 2006. "Trends and Practices of Assessment in Early Childhood Education", in D.-M. Kakana et al. (eds), *Evaluation in Education: Pedagogical and Didactic Ddimension: 71 Texts for Evaluation.* Thessaloniki: Kyriakidis Bross, 31–141. (In Greek).

Kapsalis, A. and Haniotakis, N. 2011. *Educational Evaluation.* Thessaloniki: Kyriakidis Bross. (In Greek)

Kassotakis, M. 1999. *Evaluation of the Performance of Students: Means, Methods, Problems, Prospects.* 7th ed. Athens: Grigoris. (In Greek)

—. 2003. "Evaluation of Educational Work and Teachers", *Leschi ton Ekpaideytikon* 30, 3–8. (In Greek)

—. 2010. "The Main Changes in how to Assess Students in the 1990s: Presentation of Relevant Efforts and Analysis of the Implementation Difficulties", in J. E. Pyrgiotakis & B. Economides (eds), *Dialogue On Education.* Rethymnon: University of Crete Department of Elementary Education, 139–165. (In Greek)

Kersten, T. and Israel, M. 2005. "Teacher Evaluation: Principals' Insights and Suggestions for Improvement", *Planning and Changing* 36(1/2), 47–67.

Koffas, Al. and Metochianakis, E. 1994. *Main Problems of Preschool Education: Empirical Pedagogical Approach of Kindergarten's Problems.* Rethymnon. (In Greek)

Konstantinou, Ch. 2007. *The Evaluation of Students' Performance as Pedagogical Logic and Classroom Practice.* Athens: Gutenberg. (In Greek)

Koulaidis, B. (ed.) 2006. *Depiction of the Educational System – School Grades.* Athens : Centre for Educational Research. (In Greek)

Kyriakides, L. and Campbell, R. J. 2003. "Teacher Evaluation in Cyprus: Some Conceptual and Methodological Issues arising from Teacher and School

Effectiveness Research", *Journal of Personnel Evaluation in Education* 17(1), 21–40.

MacBeath, J., Schratz, M., Meuret, D. and Jakobsen, L. 2000. *Self-evaluation in European schools*. London: Routledge Falmer.

McNair, S., Bhargava, A., Adams, L., Edgerton, S. and Kypros, B. 2003. "Teachers Speak Out on Aassessment Practices", *Early Childhood Education Journal* 31, 23–31.

Mangopoulos, G. 2005. *Teachers' Views of the Evaluation of Teachers' Work.* Masters' Thesis, University of Crete Department of Education. (In Greek)

Mavrogiorgos, G. 2005. *School: Teaching and Assessment.* Vol I. Ioannina: University of Ioannina. (In Greek)

National Centre for Education Statistics. 2001. *Early Childhood Longitudinal Study. Kindergarten class of 1998–99. ECLS-K base year public-use files and electronic codebook,* http://www.nces.ed.gov/pubs2001/2001029.pdf

Oikonomidis, V. 2007. "Students Judge the Practicum: Case Study", in D. Chatzidimou, K. Mpikos, P., Stravakou and K. Chatzidimou (eds), *Greek Pedagogical and Educational Research: Proceedings of the 5th Conference of Greek Educational Society, Thessaloniki, 24–26 November 2006.* Vol. I. Thessaloniki: Kyriakidis Bross, 205–214. (In Greek)

Oikonomidis, V., and Linardakis, M. 2012. "The Quality of the Classroom in Kindergarten: Activity Corners and Equipment", in Trilianos, Ath., Koutroumanou, G. and Alexopoulos, P. (eds), *Quality in Education: Trends and Prospects: Proceedings of the National Conference with International Participation.* Vol I. Athens: National and Kapodistrian University of Athens Department of Elementary Education, 770–781. (In Greek)

Rapti, M. 2002. "The Perceptions of Kindergarten Teachers of the Position and Role of Evaluation in Kindergarten", in E. Kourti (ed.), *Research in Early Childhood Education.* Vol III. Athens: Typothito G. Dardanos, 169–178. (In Greek)

Remesal, A. 2011. "Primary and Secondary Teachers' Conceptions of Assessment: A Qualitative Study", *Teaching and Teacher Education* 27, 472–482.

Sakellariou, M. 2007. Opinions of Preschool Educators and Future Educators about Authentic Assessment and Daily Practice in Kindergarten: Aa Comparative Approach", in D. Chatzidimou et al. (eds), *Greek Pedagogical and Educational Research: Proceedings of the 5th Conference of the Greek Educational Society, Thessaloniki, 24–26 November 2006.* Vol. I, 397–406. (In Greek)

Sanoff, H., Pasalar, C. and Hashas, M. 2004. *School Building Assessment Methods.* Raleigh: North Carolina State University.

Segers, M. and Tillema, H. 2011. "How do Dutch Secondary Teachers and Students Conceive the Purpose of Assessment?" *Studies in Educational Evaluation* 37, 49–54.

Sivropoulou, Ir., Tsakiridou, El. and Papadopoulou, Ag. 2006. "The Views of Kindergarten Teachers for the Evaluation Process in Kindergarten" in S.-M. Kakana et al. (eds), *Evaluation in Education: Pedagogical and Didactic*

*Dimension: 71 Texts for Evaluation.* Thessaloniki: Kyriakidis Bross, 217–225. (In Greek)

Stiggins, R. J. 1997. *Student-centered Classroom Assessment.* 2nd ed. Columbus, OH: Merrill.

YP.E.P.TH./Pedagogical Institute. 2003. *Cross Thematic Framework Curriculum for Kindergarten.* Athens: Pedagogical Institute.

Venizelou, G., Kalabaliki, Ef., Kalostipi, Aik., Kontaxakis, G., Lafrentaki, F., Mavroidis, G. and Patriki, Aik. 1991. *Activities Book for Kindergarten.* Athens: Ministry of Education/P.I. (In Greek)

Zouganeli, Aik., Kafetzopoulos, K., Wise, Efs. and Tsafos, B. 2008. "Evaluation of Educational Work and Teachers", in Pedagogical Institute, *Quality in Education.* Athens: Pedagogical Institute, 391–435. (In Greek)

# CHAPTER TWENTY-NINE

# TEACHERS' SELF-EVALUATION PROCESS IN FURTHER TRAINING PROGRAMMES IN GREECE

## MARIA I. KADIANAKI
SCHOOL COUNSELLOR, CRETE REGION, CRETE, GREECE

**Abstract**
Self-evaluation is the process by which individuals alone, often without external intervention, undertake to assess their own value or that of their works based on specific criteria. These criteria are shaped by subjective opinions and attitudes of the individual and of the objective data he/she receives from the environment.

In this study, the instructor collects objective data for teaching through students' evaluations of daily practice. These data constitute the criteria set up by the students, under which she has to place herself and her teaching, since the aim is the effective communication – teaching. The result of the self-evaluation process is that the instructor receives continuous feedback, notes the results of her teaching, controls the way towards her personal goals, makes decisions about herself and her behaviour and amends her practice. The aim is not finding success, but ensuring success.

**Keywords**
evaluation, teacher self- evaluation, self- evaluation process

## Introduction

Self-evaluation is a knowledge figure that includes knowledge statements, descriptions, judgments, beliefs of the individual himself/herself and may be right or wrong, may or may not be valid. The accuracy and validity of this knowledge depend on the image that the person has formed for himself, which has an objective and subjective side. Apart from the cognitive dimension, self-evaluation also involves the emotional evaluation the person makes, for these beliefs that he/she has for himself/herself and whether or not he/she has a favourable opinion of them. The third element of self-evaluation is what the person is or is not likely to do in response to this self-evaluation.

According to Towler and Broadfoot (1992: 137), self-evaluation is defined as the process by which the person "redefines his/her previous experiences, attempting to recall and to understand what has happened and trying to gain a clear idea of those that he/ she has learnt or achieved". They point out that this review itself is of little importance unless it is used by the person in order to formulate future decisions. Then the self-evaluation process acquires significance, since the review will define the planning, objective setting and action of the person.

Klenowski's definition (1995:146) mentions the purpose of self-evaluation: "Self-evaluation is the evaluation or review that the person performs in relation to his/ her actions, recognizing his/her strengths and weaknesses in order to improve the results of his/her actions."

It is also mentioned that "self-evaluation is the process by which the individual alone, often without external interference, undertakes evaluating the value of himself/herself or of his/her works based on specific criteria" (Andreadakis et al., 2007: 226). These criteria are shaped by the subjective views and attitudes of the individuals and the objective data they receive from the environment (Burns, 1982: 8). The opinions and attitudes are shaped by the same person, from the lifelong messages he/she receives from society. The objective evidences received are the criteria developed by the transmitter in which one must place himself/herself, since the purpose of the individual is to participate in the communication process (Kadianaki, 2006: 591).

According to Ziller (1973: 28), self-evaluation emerges from the opinions that the person believes the "significant others" have about him/her and this is why he/she integrates it in a social context. Coopersmith, however (quoted in Makri-Botsari, 2001: 23), places it in an emotional context that includes stances of acceptance or disapproval of the individual in relation to himself/herself, and is expressed through the satisfaction rate about his/her abilities, his/her personal success and worthiness. This satisfaction varies from one day to the other due to causes that are more idiosyncratic rather than rational (Leontari, 1998: 82). This does not mean that the self-evaluation is not stable with respect to its basic form, but its characteristics vary every single time.

Self-evaluation includes personal ambitions and subjective assessments and based on these: the individual decides what failure and success is. The subjective element is visible since what is considered a success or a significant achievement by one person can mean failure or an insignificant event for someone else (Leontari, 1998: 89).

## Teacher Self-evaluation

At all levels of education the person who teaches, often not in a systematic way or without external intervention, assesses the value of his/her work or in general of himself/herself and reviews, contests and repositions his/her actions aiming at self-improvement (Kadianaki, 2006:591). The teacher converses with him- or herself, forms judgments about the adequacy and effectiveness of his/her knowledge, of his/her performance, his/her beliefs and actions with the purpose of self-improvement (Airasian, Gullickson, 1997: 4). He or she focuses on personal practice and observes his/her thoughts, feelings and reactions. The focus of the observation is on his/her own professional development, his/her own experiences inside and outside the classroom, the declaration of what it means for him/her to teach in order to meet his/her own need to understand and improve everyday teaching.

The teacher is at the centre of the process of self-evaluation during which he/she is responsible for examining and developing his/her own professional practice. He/she collects, interprets and judges the information derived from personal practice, plans and establishes criteria and standards for comparison in order to determine the adequacy of his/her beliefs, knowledge, skills and effectiveness to decide on the nature of his/her professional development activity to be undertaken (Andreadakis et al., 2007: 227), he/she ascribes positive or negative consequences to himself/herself (Kalantzi-Azizi, 2002: 111). During his/her self-evaluation the teacher acts researching his/her own self.

The teacher, being a natural assessor of learning (MacBeath, 2000: 94), assesses an extensive list of behaviours of himself/herself and others and constantly takes diverse decisions. Most evaluation made in the classroom is not self-evaluation, because it does not focus on the teacher. These evaluations focus primarily on those who are entitled to learn (whether school or university students), on the classroom environment and the teaching methods, not on the teacher's behaviours, actions and beliefs (Andreadakis, Kadianaki, and others, 2007: 228). The teacher self-evaluation takes place when the focus of the evaluation is directed away from the students and the teaching materials towards himself/herself. During self-evaluation, the teacher poses questions and seeks answers. He/she discusses the teaching method and ponders about his/her triumphs and failures. When he/she asks: "are they interested in my lesson?" the teachers does not assess himself/herself. When he/she asks: "Is it because I do not mention examples from everyday practice that they are not interested in my class?" then he/she assesses himself/herself. The focus of the first question is on learners, whereas in the second one it is on the teacher.

Each behaviour aims towards a specific goal. The teacher chooses his behaviour – verbal or otherwise – among a number of behaviours, according to the criteria developed by himself/herself as a receiver or as those are formed by every single transmitter and under which he/she must place himself/herself if he/she wants to participate in the communication process (Andreadakis et al., 2007: 227). If he chooses to modify the behaviour deemed ineffective, he/she activates the self-regulatory procedures and, as a result, it is the teacher himself/herself that controls his/her behaviour. He/she can observe himself/herself, evaluate himself/herself – through defined criteria – and return positive or negative consequences to himself/herself (Koliadis, 1994: 58; Kalantzi-Azizi, 2002: 128). Self-evaluation leads him/her to compare, weigh, adjust and regulate his/her behaviour and leads him to get along with himself/herself. And the teacher gets along with himself/herself, when what he/she does is in harmony with what he/she is and feels, when he finds ways to express himself/herself (Kosmidou-Hardy, 1998: 40).

During the evaluation of a person, energy or project, judgments and decisions are formed regarding what is evaluated. This means, once they enter the procedure of assessing themselves, the teachers will not have to form judgments and decisions regarding themselves and their behaviour. It should be clarified that the questions possibly posed to themselves regarding their behaviour, the opinions that may be expressed or the interpretations of their behaviour, do not constitute self-evaluation, whether they are fragmentary or in combination. That is, while each of these processes can be used in the self-evaluation of the teacher, the self-evaluation emerges only when the questions, opinions and interpretations guide the teachers to make decisions about themselves, their behaviour, and their professional practice. Thus, the self-evaluation operates in a subsidiary way, for the teachers to recognize and make decisions on their strengths and weaknesses in order to improve them (Airasian & Gullickson, 1997: 8).

# The Self-evaluation Procedure

The teacher self-assessment process is a formative process (McColskey & Egelson, 1993: 42; Airasian & Gullickson, 1997: 3) which means that this is conducted throughout his/her educational course. It is the medium through which they not only realize the results of their teaching, but also check their progress towards the achievement of their personal goals. As a formative process, self-evaluation seeks the causes of the results, functioning in a regenerative way for the teacher, so that the teacher himself/herself makes decisions for himself/herself, his/her behaviour and modifies his/her practice (Kapsalis, 1994: 14; Kassotakis, 1998: 27). It is a continuous evaluation and an intrinsic part of every educational effort (Dimitropoulos, 1989: 13). Certainly, the context of self-evaluation is personal each time, and so is the personal information collected. During their self-evaluation, the teachers also monitor the aspects of the situation they evaluate and assessment method (Airasian & Gullickson, 1997: 3). The process of teacher self-evaluation, whether it happens spontaneously or deliberately, includes four stages (Kremer-Hayon, 1993: 130): focus on a specific situation, data collection, questioning and decision-making, development and implementation of action strategies.

# Focus on a Specific Situation

The particular teacher self-evaluation was conducted in the winter semester of 2010–11 in the Preschool Teachers Post Training Course in Rethymno, where a module on evaluation in education was being taught. The instructor, coming from primary education, was impressed when the preschool teachers in both years of the post training programme chose this particular module. In her diary, she says: "It is unbelievable. Do they care about evaluation? I did not expect them to take my module and eventually they take it in both years! This is a heavy burden, I have to meet their expectations, teaching them a subject that they have never been taught before. I want them to love it. How am I going to make it?"

Her strong wish to achieve her goals leads the professor to decide to focus on and to observe every three-hour teaching session. She chooses to assess herself, not to realize her success but to ensure it (Dimitropoulos, 1989: 14).

# Data Collection

A self-evaluation objective was set by the instructor to check if her teaching succeeded in making the post-trainees build knowledge, interest and a positive stance towards evaluation in education. To achieve this, she chose to use peer assessment among the trainees in every one of her teaching sessions. So, she asked the 22 post-trainee school teachers, optionally and without giving their name, at the end of every three-hour teaching session, to write on a simple piece of paper evaluation judgments regarding the subject, the professor and her teaching, their feelings and thoughts, concerns and comments.

This external information regarding the professor's tactic along with her diary constitute the data on which the questioning, interpretation and realization of her own practices is based. In her diary, notes are written down from unorganized observations, comments, discussions with the post-trainees, personal thoughts and feelings of hers and ideas related to matters arising throughout the semester.

Out of the 242 (11 three-hour teaching sessions × 22 post-trainees) expected evaluation reports, she received 176, a response rate of 73% over the semester.

# Questioning and Decision-making

The evaluation judgments were classified in four categories based on their content:

- Evaluative judgments about the object (K1)
- Evaluative judgments about the instructor and her teaching (K2)
- Feelings and thoughts of the post-trainees (K3)
- Concerns and various comments (K4)

Every report usually included more than one category, so the analysis is conducted in relation to the paragraph and what it refers to every time. There were some rather laconic reports, too, such as: "No comment", "Go on", "I am tired", which are not classified under any category since they are elliptical sentences and in some of them it is difficult to understand what they refer to.

In the first session, the category K1 gathered six judgments, K2 nine, K3 ten and K4 gathered five comments. The evaluative judgments regarding the instructor and her practice (K2) outnumber the others along with the thoughts (K3) of the post trainees and actually all 22 preschool teachers give their "little paper".

Post-trainee comment (K2) 1st lesson: "*I like the certainty, documentation of all you say. Good professional, person that will try, that feels like doing it, who does not say: 'I shall do it and whatever they learn'.*"

Post-trainee comment (K2) 1st lesson: "*You know how to be a listener but the discussion spreads too much sometimes.*"

Post-trainee comment (K2) 1st lesson: "*The introduction of the discussion left me speechless. It has not happened to me before that somebody would ask for my opinion on a topic like this.*"

The comments are mainly positive and the instructor sets as goal the point where most of the comments will be in the first category (K1), namely the judgments to refer to the teaching subject, only then will she consider that her goal is achieved. However, this is a long way off as she must first win them as a teacher.

## Development and Implementation of Aaction Strategies

In every lesson, there is initially feedback in relation to the anonymous correspondence kept by the instructor and the trainees. Answers and clarifications to questions and queries expressed anonymously are given. Everybody is involved in the process and this feedback excites both sides, the communication climate is positive and the interaction is continuous. The trainees are encouraged and are discreetly involved in the design of the teaching process.

Trainee comment (K1) 4th lesson: "*More contact with the preschool reality/everyday life is needed. What happens at the nursery school?*"

The instructor decodes the messages correctly and in the following sessions she makes sure to use examples from everyday reality, conducting research at a nursery school. In her diary she writes: "*They took me by the hand and led me into their world. That was beyond my expectations. I learn attempting to make them learn.*" The post-trainees write:

Post-trainee comment (K2) 3rd lesson: "*It is impressive how you utilize whatever is mentioned in the classroom. You do not forget what we request.*"

Post-trainee comment (K2) 6th lesson: "*No sooner do we write something on our 'little paper' and we send you to an interview at the nursery school. We have some power after all!*"

Post-trainee comment (K2) 6th lesson: "*I had a great time today in the lesson. The fact that you entered a . . . nursery school contributed to that!*"

In the eighth lesson, evaluative judgments will be made only regarding the subject; there are 17 of these and what is impressive is that there are no judgments related to the other categories. In this lesson, the instructor believes that her goal has been achieved. After an attempt at mutual respect, emotional understanding and sympathy between the two sides, she achieves the goal of her teaching. She achieves an effective communication, something that leads to effective teaching, where learning is planned by the teacher, the results are recognized and those entitled to learning modify their behaviour (Andreadakis et al., 2006: 81).

## Discussion – Results

Although the self-evaluation process began with the instructor's desire, over time it developed in a joint project between the instructor and the students. The two sides became partners, both learned from the process, but mainly both felt that they could exercise control over events that affect them (Koliadis, 1994: 166).

The instructor did not take either her practice or the expectations of the trainees for granted. She explored her knowledge and practice, examined the expectations of the persons entitled to learning, developing the ability of self-criticism and challenge of her teaching through self-evaluation. She considered it her professional responsibility to achieve the purpose of her teaching by changing her practice and herself. Noting that this goal had been achieved, she developed as a professional, while her morale and motivation were boosted.

As was revealed by the process, self-evaluation requires the teacher to be a lifelong student, to develop professionally, to experiment with new ideas. The ongoing review of activities within the teaching classroom and the pursuit of self-improvement through self-evaluation appears to be inherent in the professional responsibility of the teacher (Kremer-Hayon, 1993: 3). Several researchers (McColsey & Egelson, 1993: 47; Airasian & Gullickson, 1997: 7) indicate that self-evaluation is the core of professional responsibility and combines the satisfaction of all beneficiaries and especially of the teacher himself/herself.

The innate character of learning, the internal need for development and change, the importance of questioning for individual learning and development, and the devotion of the individual to what he/she creates are axioms of teacher self-evaluation (MacBeath, 2001: 140). A fifth axiom that can be added is that the most important evaluation of a professional is the one that is driven by himself/herself (Stufflebeam & Shinkfield, 1985: 17), since he/she creates and is responsible for his/her education or training (Kolettas, 1980:19 ).

# References

Airasian, W. P. and Gullickson, R. A. 1997. *Teacher Self-evaluation Tool Kit*. California: Corwin Press.

Andreadakis, N., Xanthakou, G. and Kadianaki, M. 2006. "Empirical Study of the Communication Context of the School Class", in H. Papailiou, G. Xanthakou and S. Chatichristou (eds), *Educational School Psychology, vol. C*. Athens: Atrapos, 78–94. (In Greek)

Andreadakis, N., Kadianaki, M. and Xanthakou, G. 2007. "Teacher Self-assessment: Consequences of his Work and Techniques that Contribute to its Systematization", *The Stand of the Social Sciences* 49, 225–250. (In Greek)

Burns, R. B. 1995. "Paradigms for Research on Teaching", in L. W. Anderson (ed.), *International Encyclopaedia of Teaching and Teacher Education*. 2nd ed. Oxford: Pergamon Press, 119–136.

Dimitropoulos, E. 1989. *Educational Assessment. Part Two: Student Assessment*. Athens. Grigori. (In Greek)

Kadianaki, M. 2006. "Communication Context of the School Class and Teacher Self-assessment", in D. M. Kakana, K. Mpotsoglou, N. Chaniotakis and E. Kavalari (eds), *Assessment in Education: Pedagogical and Teaching Dimension*. Thessaloniki: Kiriakidi, 589–598. (In Greek)

Kalantzi-Azizi, A. 2002. *Self-awareness and Self-management*. Athens: Ellinika Grammata (Greek Letters). (In Greek)

Kassotakis, M. 1998. *Assessment of Students' Performance*. 8th ed. Athens: Grigori. (In Greek)

Kapsalis, A. 1994. *Assessment and Marking in Primary School*. Thessaloniki: Art of Text. (In Greek)

Klenowski, V. 1995. "Student Self-evaluation Processes in Student-centred Teaching and Learning Contexts of Australia and England", *Assessment in Education: Principles, Policy & Practice* 2(2), 145–163, http://www.informaworld.com/smpp/content~content=a739133973~db=all (accessed 6 March 2006).

Kolettas, S. 1980. *People's Education and Illiteracy in Greece*. Athens: self-published. (In Greek)

Koliadis, E. 1994. *Learning Theories and Education Action, volume B*. Athens: Ellinika Grammata (Greek Letters). (In Greek)

Kosmidou-Hardy, H. 1998. "The Teacher as a Counselor in the Teaching-learning Appointment", *Counselling and Orientation Inspection* 46–47, 33–63. (In Greek)

Kremer-Hayon, L. 1993. *Teacher Self-evaluation: Teachers in their Own Mirrors*. USA: Kluwer Academic Publishers.

Leontari, A. 1998. *Self-awareness*. Athens: Ellinika Grammata. (In Greek)

MacBeath, J. 2001. *Self-assessment in School: Utopia and Practice* (Ch. Doukas & Z. Polimeropoulou, transl.) Athens: Ellinika Grammata. (In Greek)

McColskey, W. and Egelson, P. 1993. *Designing Teacher Evaluation Systems that Support Professional Growth.* Greensboro: South Eastern Regional Vision for Education.

Makri-Mpotsari, E. 2001. *Self-awareness and Self-respect: Models, Development, Operational Role and Evaluation.* Athens: Ellinika Grammata. (In Greek)

Stufflebeam, D. L. and Shinkfield, A. J. 1985. *Systematic Evaluation.* Boston: Kluwer-Nijhoff.

Towler, L. and Broadfoot, P. 1992. "Self-assessment in the Primary School", *Educational Review,* 44(2), 137–152.

Ziller, R. C. 1973. *The Social Self.* New York: Pergamon Press.

# CHAPTER THIRTY

# EVALUATION OF THE WORK CARRIED OUT BY THE TEACHER

## C. PAVLIDOU
### COMPUTER STUDIES TEACHER, GREECE

**Abstract**

The aim of the present assignment is to demonstrate the importance of evaluation of the educational work carried out by the teacher. Following this, we will refer to the continuous, non-continuous and influential evaluation and to educational objectives. Also, we will refer to the need for retraining and educating on matters of evaluation, specifically in educational work. Nowadays, there is a wide range of evaluation techniques which are recommended depending on the diversity and level of the educational objectives. Educators do not hold a positive attitude towards alternative methods of evaluation due to the absence of sufficient retraining and pedagogical guidance. The method and objective for its realization are issues that concern education. Of course, educational programmes should be responsible for the competence and readiness of the teacher on evaluation matters. After all, evaluation attempts to facilitate educational work and give feedback, locating any difficulties, enquiring for and implementing better methods of practice.

**Keywords**

evaluation, educational work, teaching, retraining, educator, feedback, types of evaluation

## Introduction

Modern economic, social, cultural and technological challenges in Europe and all over the world exert pressure for changes in educational institutions. School organization, the content of the educational work, the means used, the results it produces and the professional development and upgrading of teachers are main fields of study, criticism and review at a theoretical as well as at applied level. Especially matters such as the improvement of the quality of the educational work and the evaluation of educational practices are considered vital issues and priorities of European and international education policies.

Since the mid 90s in most European countries the quality and evaluation of educational work are considered interdependent concepts that are the main goals, axes and directions of educational reforms. Additionally, the evaluation of educational work is considered an essential factor in assessing the reliability of the educational system, as it is related not only to the organization, operation and effectiveness of the school but also to the effectiveness of the educational planning and implementation of education policies.

Today, the task of teacher evaluation is treated as the only priority of the policies of the Ministry of Education regarding "New School".

## General Framework of Evaluation

Technically, evaluation is a concept known to everyone: in our everyday life we evaluate ourselves or other people's actions, we assess the value of services or products and redefine our course viewing our actions with a critical eye. Evaluation is a new scientific field but also an ancient practice.

Especially, by "evaluation" we refer to the procedure aiming to define, as systematically, credibly and objectively as possible, the suitability, functionality and outcome of a teaching and educational activity regarding its objectives, as well as a certain methodology.

One of the obligations of the State towards its citizens, as cited in article 16 of the Constitution of Greece, is the provision of quality education. This service must be evaluated in order to ensure its quality. Educational evaluation was developed at the same time as the creation of the educational systems, while in many educational systems it is considered an integral part of education procedure. In our country the evaluation of educational work has remained basically inactive since 1982 with the abolition of the institution of superintendent (Law 1304/1982), to whom this task was assigned. Since then, despite the efforts made by the Ministry of Education through regulatory interventions (Laws 2525/1997 and 2986/2002) to restore educational evaluation, until this day the work of the educators is not officially evaluated. It should be noted that an unofficial evaluation of educational work as well as the work of teachers is being informally conducted by students, parents, colleagues and the teacher him/herself, though without being able to overcome any weaknesses.

Nowadays, the accession of Greece to the European Union, where educational systems have already developed evaluation systems, the public awareness of quality education, the change in teachers' attitude towards evaluation due to the institution of the superintendent and how it was exercised, have prepared the education body for the institutionalization of the evaluation of educational work.

Regarding evaluation, there are several differences between countries. Hungary has a more complicated institutional evaluation system than Greece has. More specifically, there are many parties involved, they share responsibilities and they operate in multiple levels of communication and implementation. Whereas in Greece the central administration defines uniform evaluation criteria, in Hungary each school establishes its own evaluation programme with the participation of independent experts and special consultants from private companies.

Sweden has for many years developed a stable evaluation system, where despite decentralization the state is responsible for the review, evaluation and subsequent assessment of the education system which are conducted by its public services. Sweden also takes into consideration national tests and statistics from all over the country, in order to have a complete view of the situation in education and thus to establish a proper education plan.

The situation in Greece is unique because even though an explicit framework for evaluation has been legislated for, it has never been implemented. The laws remain inactive. There are pressure groups opposing this state of affairs, and during recent years the need for evaluation in all sectors has become clear. Evaluation should take place in a larger sense, that presupposes that it will not only regard teacher and student but all the parameters that affect the educational process.

In general, it can be observed that the evaluation systems tend to adjust to the rapidly developing political socio-economical conditions, at a different pace in each country. However, during recent years voices calling for educational evaluation have increased both internationally and locally. This mainly results in the education system, schools units and teachers being accountable to society.

# Goal/objective of Evaluation

As can be seen, as far as the educational community is concerned evaluation is associated with the elaborate and multilateral education process. Therefore, it has regard to educational objectives, syllabus, learning means, teachers, students, teaching methods and the educational system as a whole. However, the term "evaluation", according to common belief in Greek society and schools, is associated with exams, grades, education qualification and, naturally, with school performance. Thus, evaluation has acquired a social meaning and prevails in the minds of students, teachers and parents. This development overlooks and marginalizes the real and clearly the ethical meaning of evaluation, as a procedure with certain objectives, certain techniques and certain means and measures.

It has been noted that in many cases the "objective" of the evaluation is confused with the "object" of the evaluation, and sometimes with the evaluation criteria. At this point, it seems necessary to refer to the concept of goal/objective, in order to point out another principle of the evaluation: That the evaluation is a means and is not in any case an end in itself. It does not exist only to exist. It is not being conducted only to be conducted.

According to the above, evaluation without a goal cannot exist. The goal or the objective of the evaluation reflects the reason why the evaluation is being conducted. At this point it is necessary to clarify the difference between the terms "goal" and "objective", because there is a lot of confusion regarding this matter. Thus, we talk about "general goal" and "specific objective" and "final goal" and about "intermediate objective" or "total goal" and "partial objective".

A position that states an inviolable principle in educational evaluation is that every evaluation should lead to an improvement of the evaluated object and of its role as a whole. If the evaluation and the measures implemented afterwards did not result in any improvement, this could mean that the evaluation, at least in most cases, was unnecessary if not harmful. This improvement may be of specific areas or the educational system as a whole. Therefore, improvement is the main goal of the evaluation.

In a well-designed educational enterprise, evaluation is an integral part, constituting the structural and operational part of the enterprise. Without evaluation, it would be impossible to ensure constant self-adjustment though feedback.

Some indicative objectives of the educational evaluation are stated below:

- To facilitate programming and planning of educational programs, activities, bodies, means etc.
- To facilitate the decision making process and to validate decisions regarding expenditures, means, materials etc. Such decisions may also consider employment, training, establishment, appointment etc. of the staff.
- To evaluate the students who participate in educational programmes or projects.
- To facilitate the adjustment of the education provided towards the requirements, needs or specifications of the socio-economic environment served by this particular educational system. These specifications can be viewed in their social, cultural, financial etc. dimension.
- To determine the need for improvement of the teaching staff and to define the framework of the actions that will lead to this improvement.
- To improve the school environment and the atmosphere prevailing in the school.
- When stating the objective one should refer to the conditions under which the desired behaviour should be expressed and the criteria for the evaluation of the outcome.

It should be noted that the educational objective:

- aspires to a behaviour based on the comprehension of the material selected by the educator and through it having the desired result.
- is functional. It is associated with the subject of learning, the student, and for that reason the level of development of the student should be taken into account as well as the learning conditions that can be offered to the student in within the frames of the possibilities of the environment. If the means and methods necessary for the realization of the objectives cannot be provided during teaching, the objectives cannot be functional in that environment.
- must aim at a result that can be measured or quantified, so that the information of the assessment can be used for feedback –necessary for the evaluation of the objective and the educational enterprise.
- should be complete. Completeness of the educational objective ensures the proper course of the educational work and the preconditions for its evaluation. According to that, evaluation

provides the educator and the student with information about the result.

It is a fact that in a set of objectives, cognitive objectives are easier to evaluate than affective or other objectives concerning aspects of the enterprise attempted. This should not lead us to setting only cognitive objectives.

Unfortunately, the school Act shows that the evaluation is focused on testing memorization of facts and acquiring mechanical skills and pays little attention to personal growth, creativity, insight, adapting values and regulation of personal and social life based on those.

## Types of Evaluation

One classification distinguishes between continuous and non-continuous evaluation.

By the term "continuous evaluation" we mean the evaluation realized by the teacher in his/her classroom at specific intervals with his/her students. The objective of this evaluation is to monitor the development of each student, recording their progress and regression and identifying their difficulties. Additionally, it is monitoring the course of teaching, identifying the obstacles presented to the educator, the imperfections of teaching and testing the suitability of programmes or teaching methods. Since it provides information to teachers and students during the educational process allowing for gaps to be filled or imperfections to be corrected, it realizes a truly pedagogic function.

On the other end lies "non-continuous" evaluation. By that term we mean evaluation during exams or competitions. The evaluators are not the same people that ensured the teaching of the group of students under evaluation. An example of this type of evaluation is the university entrance examination. Its objective is to account for a teaching period.

Another classification made by Bloom et al. is:

- Initial – Diagnostic: Determining the level of knowledge, interests, and possible problems of the student.
- Formative – Gradual: Monitoring the progress of the student regarding the educational objectives. Detection of potential modifications-interferences to the schedule or the teaching method.
- Final – Summative: Overall assessment of the achievement of the teaching and pedagogic objectives.

In the case of formative evaluation we try to achieve two kinds of feedback:

- Feedback to the student, in order to see the progress he/she has made in his/her learning and the difficulties he/she encountered.
- Feedback to the teacher, to see the course of his/her pedagogic plan and which obstacles he encounters. The learning difficulties can be caused by the content, the setting of the didactic objectives, the didactic methods and the means of teaching, or the teaching time dedicated. Many times learning difficulties can be caused by setting non-realistic pedagogic objectives.

Undoubtedly, formative evaluation completes the teaching process and makes possible a continuous and dynamic self-improvement. Moreover, it has been proven to be especially useful, because the student feels a real need to know the level of his/her progress and the ways to overcome his/her weaknesses, whereas the teacher feels the need to seek better ways to teach. The teacher's main concern is to create the best conditions possible for learning.

## Ways in which Educators Use the Results of Formative Evaluation for the Improvement of their Didactic Work

As far as primary education is concerned, many education counsellors point out that most teachers simply review the students' essays, without taking the results into account in order to planning the next teaching session or taking corrective measures. Particularly, students' performance is perceived as "evidence" when informing parents. Educators seem to have a negative attitude towards alternative approaches, perhaps due to lack of retraining and educational guidance concerning evaluation.

In secondary education, quantitative documentation of the students' performance seems to prevail. The objective of the evaluation should be the expansion and the facilitation of learning progress and the proper psychosomatic development of the teenager; however the evaluation has become a certification of qualifications for admittance to universities.

## Retraining in Evaluation

Retraining of an educator throughout his/her career and in matters of evaluation is considered necessary. The way in which the evaluation is being realized should be the object of retraining. Certainly, the objective of the retraining programmes should be the competency and preparedness of the educator.

Pivotal concepts in retraining programmes regarding evaluation are the following:

### Knowledge

Educators should comprehend the role of the learning evaluation and the evaluation criteria of their educational work.

### Skills

Educators should be able to participate in a self-evaluation of the school unit concerning student evaluation, and while planning the learning evaluation they should view with a critical eye the criteria of their own evaluation.

### Attitudes

Educators should have a positive attitude towards an evaluation aiming at the retraining and improvement of their work as learning evaluators.

## The Necessity for Evaluation of Educational Work

The necessity or otherwise of the evaluation of educational work has been the subject of great debate in our country. Many scientific studies regarding the evaluation of educational work have been published, members of the educational community have argued about this subject and many suggestions have been made by leaders of the education body. After years of discussions, disputes and endless debates, it has become clear that the evaluation of educational work is necessary for the promotion of the education provided.

Some of the reasons that make the evaluation of education necessary are the improvement of the quality of the educational system, the information necessary for making strategic and functional decisions, the feedback of educators regarding their work, the meritocratic selection of officials in education, the support of educators through retraining programmes, the moral satisfaction of the educators with their work and the reinforcement of their professional status. Educational evaluation as a means of assessing efficiency is a form of social control that is considered necessary for ensuring total quality in education.

In order for educational evaluation to perform its role, it should be characterized by transparent and meritocratic procedures.

In order for the evaluation to be valid, reliable and objective, we must:

- legislate clear evaluation criteria for effective teaching, which should be flexible in order to cover the whole range of the efficiency of the educational work;
- use credible and valid means, in relation to evaluation objectives, such as questionnaires, interviews or observation forms of the teaching process;
- get information from as many sources as possible – the most important information sources about teaching being the educator him/herself, the evaluator and the student;
- addressing the training of the people called to evaluate educational work, in order to minimize the subjectivity of the evaluation, which is an integral part of the evaluation;
- make constant attempts aiming at the consensus of all parties involved and mostly of the educators. No change can be effective if human resources are not involved or if the planning does not follow a hierarchy. Needless to say, the modern tendencies towards educational evaluation recommend participation models. The evaluation of educational work moves from supervision and the institution of the superintendent towards collaboration and reflection.

## Conclusion

In conclusion, the function of the evaluation must aim at testing the didactic measures with the prospect of maintaining, modifying or correcting them. The pedagogic function of the evaluation does not aim at an hierarchical judgment but at the assessment of the process of the educational work and the detection of learning difficulties, in order to take timely and preapproved pedagogic measures towards that direction.

In our country it seems that evaluation is a sensitive subject with social and political dimensions. It has caused intense reactions inside the educational community, pointing out that the form and type of the evaluation is not a matter of "techniquality" as far as education policy is concerned, but a matter with consequences in the political, social and educational body.

Despite the consequent regulations, the subject of evaluation is not closed, as it has not been dealt with in reality. In general, some could argue that the debate evolving around the evaluation of the educational work is focused, initially, on the issue regarding its necessity; there are many that consider evaluation necessary, while others argue that it will be used only to control and implement hierarchy in education. Additionally, it is focused on the issue regarding the objectives, the bodies and the methods.

The introduction of an evaluation system in any educational system is a social procedure that should be established gradually, systematically, by consensus and with great consideration.

# References

Björklund, A., Clark, M., Edin, P., Frederiksson, P. and Krueger, A. 2006. "The Market Comes to Evaluation", in *Sweden: An Evaluation of Sweden's Surprising School Reforms.* Russell Sage Foundation Publications.

Chaniotakis, N. and Kapsalis, A. 2002. "Evaluation and Professional Development", *Epistimes Agogis* 2, 27–37. [In Greek]

Charisis, A. 2007. *Evaluation of the Educators and Educational Work: Evaluation of School Learning and Retraining of Educators.* [In Greek]

Constantinous, C. 2004. *Evaluation of Learner Performance as a Pedagogical Logic and School Practice.* [In Greek]

Dimitropoulos, E. 1999. *Educational Evaluation: The Evaluation of Education and of the Educational World.* Athens: Grigoris. [In Greek]

Kapsalis, A. G. 2004. *Pedagogical Psychology.* Thessaloniki: Kyriakides. [In Greek]

Kassotakis, M. 1992. *The Request for Objective Evaluation of Educational Work and its Problems: Evaluation of Educational Work – Basic Training and Retraining of Educators.* [In Greek]

—. 2003. *Evaluation of Educational Work and of Educators.* [In Greek]

Kotthoff, H. G. 2006. *Discrepancies between Intended and Achieved Effects of School Evaluation in International Comparative Perspective: Empirical Comparison and Recommendations.*

Ksochellis, D. 2005. "Criteria of Validity, Reliability and Pedagogical Suitability of School Books", in Veikou (ed.) *Textbook and Educational Material in School: Concerns – Possibilities – Prospects.* [in Greek]

Lahdenperä, P. 2000. *From Monocultural to Intercultural Educational Research, Sweden.*

Lannert, J. 2004. *Strategies for Reform and Innovation in Hungarian Public Education.* National Institute for Public Education (NIPE).

Lannert, J., Martonfi, G. and Vago, I. 2006. "The Impact of Structural Upheavals on Educational Organisation, Attainment and Choice: The Experience of post-Communist Hungary", *European Journal of Education.*

Leontios, N. 1978. *Evaluation of Education.* Nea Paideia. [In Greek]

Makras, S. 1982. *Types of Evaluation in Education.* Sychroni Ekpaidefsi. [In Greek]

Mavrogiorgos, G. 2002. *Evaluation in Education – Who, Whom and Why.* Athens: Savvalas. [In Greek]

Mavromatis, I., Zouganeli, A., Kafka, D. and Stergiou, P. 2007. *Student Evaluation.* Epitheorisi Ekpaideutikon Thematon. [In Greek]

Mpouzakis, S. 2005. *Educational Reforms in Greece* Volume II. 4th ed. Athens: Gutenberg. [In Greek]

Pamouktsoglou, A. 2007. "Theory, Practice and Evaluation of Teaching", *Intercultural Education* 11(2), 201–207. [In Greek]

Papaioannou, A. 1978. *Educational Objectives and Evaluation.* Nea Paideia. [In Greek]

Papakonstantinoy, P. 1993. *Educational Work and Evaluation in School.* Athens: Ekfrasi. [In Greek]

Reppa, A. 2007. *The Evaluation of the Teaching Work of Educators in Greece: From Theory to Practice.* [In Greek]

Standaert, R. 2003. "Inspectorates of Education in Europe: A Critical Analysis", *Comparative Education.*

Zavlanos, M. 2003.*Teaching and Evaluation.* Athens: Stamouli. [In Greek]

Zouganellis, A., Kafetzopoulos, K., Sofou, E. and Tsafos, V. 2008. "Evaluation of Educational Work and Educators", in *The Quality Characteristics of the Pprimary and Secondary Educational System.* Athens: Pedagogical Institute. [In Greek]

# CHAPTER THIRTY-ONE

# TEACHING PRACTICE IN GREEK TEACHER TRAINING PROGRAMMES: THE CASE OF THE UNIVERSITY OF WESTERN MACEDONIA—INSTITUTIONAL DEVELOPMENT AND EMPIRICAL DATA

## DEMETRIOS THEODOROU,
LECTURER, PRIMARY EDUCATION DEPARTMENT,
DEMOCRITUS UNIVERSITY OF THRACE
## VASSILIKI PAPADOPOULOU,
ASSOCIATE PROFESSOR, PRIMARY EDUCATION DEPARTMENT,
UNIVERSITY OF WESTERN MACEDONIA
## IOANNIS THOIDIS
ASSISTANT PROFESSOR, PRIMARY EDUCATION DEPARTMENT,
UNIVERSITY OF WESTERN MACEDONIA
## AND SOFIA ARGYROPOULOU
PHD, SPECIAL TEACHING FELLOW OF TEACHING
METHODOLOGY AND TEACHING PRACTICE,
PRIMARY EDUCATION DEPARTMENT,
UNIVERSITY OF WESTERN MACEDONIA, GREECE

**Abstract**
In the present article we examine the institutional development of the Teaching Practice Programme of the Elementary Education Department at the University of Western Macedonia in the last two decades. Subsequently we present research data, product of our effort to investigate the way in which this development affects the programme's evaluation by

the students themselves. This research data was collected during the last
six academic years and proves that, despite the significant reduction of the
teaching practice programme, it seems to fulfil students' expectations to a
satisfying degree.

**Keywords**
teacher education, teaching practice programme, evaluation of teaching
practice programmes

# Introduction

The Teaching Practice Programme (TPP) is undoubtedly one of the
three main aspects of teachers' education, along with the pedagogical and
instructive training and training in the teaching of different subjects. The
value and contribution of teaching practice to the professional preparation
of student-teachers are internationally recognized in an ever-growing way
(Arends 2009, Britzman 2003). In various European countries these
teaching programmes have been expanded, which has meant that the
amount of time spent on them has increased as a proportion of overall
course time (Xochellis, 2006: 108).

The integration of a teaching practice programme into the initial
teacher education curriculum presupposes an awareness of the following
four points (Theodorou 1998: 65):

1) The programme's duration, as well as the proportion of course time
   this represents in relation to the other two main aspects of studies.
2) When it will be incorporated and how much study time will be
   apportioned to it.
3) The goals, content and structure of the teaching practice in relation
   to the most desirable profile of a future teacher.
4) How the teaching practice will be connected to the other aspects of
   studies for a more efficient correlation between theory and practice.

There is a wide array of teaching practice programmes, depending on
the approach taken to the aforementioned questions and also on the special
conditions in each teacher education university department, or other
academic institution. The variety of programmes available has been
commented on by many researchers (Caires, Almeida & Vieria, 2012).

> Research as well as relevant bibliography have not led to an in general
> acceptable structure of teaching practice. The various concepts of teaching
> practice thus are characterized by fluidity and lack of unambiguous
> theoretical character, while in many cases teaching practice is not an
> integral part of the studies. (Xochellis, 2006: 109)

In the Greek educational system, teaching practice in the preschool and primary education departments today constitutes an integral part of initial teacher education. Previous academic experiences (Pedagogical Academies and Faculties of Kindergarten), international ideas, perspectives and research results, and also experimentation during the first years of university education departments, were all utilized in the conceptualization of the teaching practice programmes (Theodorou, 1998: 12).

During the last few years teaching practice has become an increasingly attractive research field for Greek researchers (see Chaniotakis, Efthimiou, & Pirgiotakis, 2006; Kakana et al., 2007; Poulou, 2007; Bikos, 2011; Michalopoulou, 2011; Chaniotakis, 2011). In the Primary Education Department of the University of Western Macedonia in Florina, a longitudinal research project has, for the last six years, focused on systematic evaluation of the teaching practice programme by the students (Argyropoulou, 2005; Thoidis, Papadopoulou & Tsakiridou, 2005; Papadopoulou, Thoidis & Tsakiridou, 2007; Papadopoulou & Dimitriadou, 2007; Papadopoulou & Thoidis, 2008; Thoidis, Papadopoulou & Argyropoulou, 2011). Throughout the project students were asked to respond to a questionnaire about the degree of satisfaction they felt regarding the programme. Specifically they were asked for their feelings about the content, organization and implementation of the programme. They were further asked to identify any dysfunctional or problematic areas and to make suggestions for improvement in these areas.

In the present article, we initially delineate the institutional development of the TPP of the Primary Education Department in Florina over the last twenty years, while also exploring whether, and to what extent, the institutional changes regarding both the reduction of the programme's duration and the content of the teaching practice have influenced students' evaluation of the programme.

## Institutional Development of Teaching Practice in the Primary Education Department in Florina

The Primary Education Department in Florina was founded by the Presidential Decree 544/1989, but started its academic life during the academic year 1990–1991 as a part of the Aristotle University of Thessaloniki. The teaching practice programme was from the beginning combined with teaching methodology for a more efficient connection between theory and practice. It initially took up a large amount of course time, and was therefore allocated a correspondingly high number of course credits. Gradually, it was modified and to some extent narrowed down in length, duration and content, resulting eventually in its current form.

*First period: the stage of initial enthusiasm (1994–2000)*
    After a short period of academic effort and experimentation the teaching practice programme acquired a clear structure and content during the academic year 1994–1995 (see Table 32-1), both of which were retained until the end of the 1990s. The teaching practice programme, consisting of four phases, was divided into six semesters (starting with the 2nd semester and ending with the 8th semester), lasted for a total of 650 hours (or 30 weeks) and was awarded a correspondingly high number of credits (42 out of the 170 required for graduation, namely, 24.7% of the final degree). One of its essential aspects was its organic interweaving into the process of academic study, throughout almost the entire duration of the course, to the point that it was characterized as being experiential and workshop-like. It also brought the students into regular contact with the school from the beginning of their course, and gradually initiated them into a "methodological approach to the teaching process, from the instructional planning to the students' assessment" (Xochellis, 1997: 16). Taking these characteristics into account, teaching practice has a central and "keystone-like" role in the syllabus of the Department of Primary Education in Florina.[1]

    The 4th phase of these TPPs was characteristic for this atmosphere of initial enthusiasm: the Department aspired to prepare teachers who would be able to undertake the teaching of one of the aforementioned subjects in the future, despite the fact that from the 90s art, music and physical education were taught only by teachers specializing in these subjects, and not by the classroom teacher (see Program of Studies of the Department of Primary Education in Florina, 1995: 41).

----

[1] Given the advance in primary education teachers' studies in Greece, it was suggested that the teaching practice cover 25% of the course time and acquire a "keystone-like role" in the teachers' education programme: "Unless we assign a central, keystone-like role to the teaching practice ..., we cannot expect an improvement in the education of our teachers ... Only if we arrange the syllabuses around the central role of the teaching practice, we can be optimistic for the improvement of the teachers' education of all levels of our educational system" (Filippou, 1984: 45).

| Teaching Methodology and Teaching Practice | Semesters | Duration | Contents (activities and subjects) | Credits |
|---|---|---|---|---|
| 1st phase, Part I: Introduction to the theory and practice of school | 2nd | 2 days per week for 1 semester (at school: 2–3 hours, at university: 3 hours) | Each week, the following process takes place: At the university, a theoretical course for a school, or teaching related issue, with classroom observation focused on this issue, and teaching and classroom analysis based on the observation at the university. Topics: Methods of classroom observation. Pedagogical relationships and interaction in the classroom, School environment and School learning, Management of problems in school class, Climate of school class, discipline, verbal and nonverbal communication. | 4 |
| 1st Phase, Part II: Introduction to teaching theory and practice | 3rd | Same as Part I | Same process as in Part I. Topics: Aims, objectives and contents of teaching. Methods, strategies and teaching aids. Evaluation and learning environments. Alternative approaches to teaching. Main principles of lesson planning. At the end of the semester, a "model" lesson from the mentor, and optional teaching from students (planning - implementing – analyzing a lesson). | 4 |

| | | | | |
|---|---|---|---|---|
| 2nd Phase: Teaching of primary school subjects<br><br>1. Modern Greek<br>2. History<br>3. Religion<br><br>4. Mathematics<br>5. Physics<br>6. Elements of environmental education<br><br>7. Art<br>8. Music<br>9. Physical Education | 5th to 7th (3 credits per semester) | 2 days per week for 3 semesters | The second Phase for each subject includes two parts:<br>a. Theoretical, which takes place at the Faculty , lasts four weeks and focuses on the main issues for teaching each subject.<br><br>b. Practical, which is comprised of the mentors' "model" lesson(s), students' teaching and *teaching* analysis-evaluation at the university?<br>Each student teaches each of the subjects once, and at other times observes his/her colleagues (6-7 weeks: 1 hour at school, 2 hours at the university). | 27 (9x3) |
| 3rd Phase: Undertaking classroom teaching with theoretical preparation and provision of feedback | 8th | 3–4 weeks | a. Theoretical course about the school<br><br>b. Familiarization of students with school classes in an urban school (3 days) and teaching of all subjects for 1 week.<br><br>c. Meeting at the university to discuss experiences from the urban school.<br><br>d. Information about the organization of teaching at a rural school.<br><br>e. Familiarization of students with school classes in a rural school (3 days) and teaching of all subjects for 1 week.<br><br>f. Meeting at the university to discuss experiences from the rural school. | 4 |

| 4th Phase: Teaching Art, Music and Physical Education (informal specialization) | 8th | 1 semester | a. Theoretical course on these specific subject (the first 5 two-hour sessions)<br><br>b. 10 lessons from each student for each subject<br><br>c. 3 two-hour sessions on teaching analysis with emphasis on problematic teaching areas. | 3 |
|---|---|---|---|---|
| Total | 6 Semesters | | Overall: almost 655 hours of theory and practice (or approximately 30 weeks). More specifically: Theoretical hours: around 250 Classroom observation hours: of teachers around 100, of classmates around 50. Teaching analysis and evaluation hours: of teachers around 50, of classmates around 130 Hours of student teaching: around 75. | 42 |

(Source: Theodorou, 1998: 233)

**Table 32-1: Programme of teaching practice 1994–2000**

Effective management during this period made the organization of such an extensive teaching practice programme within the curriculum feasible. On the one hand, the number of students attending the lessons regularly remained low compared to the number of students entering the school, while on the other hand the supportive network of cooperating schools and of the mentors of the Department adequately covered the operational needs of the programme.

*Second Period: the "rationalization" stage (2000– present)*

The second phase began with the first decade of the new century and was characterized by rationalization, moderating the use of human resources as well as allocating hours more wisely for teaching practice within the curriculum of the Department and the cooperating schools. As a result, at the 115/28-6-2000 meeting, the General Assembly of the Department decided, first, to unify the two parts of the 1st phase in one semester and, secondly, to terminate the 4th phase and the informal specialization. However, these changes, although necessary considering the ever-growing number of students and the stable or reduced number of mentors, did not influence the main form or concept of the teaching practice programme.

The second major change took place when the General Assembly, at the meeting numbered 183/12-4-2006, decided the restructuring of the 2nd phase. The compulsory Teaching of the primary schools subjects were reduced from nine to four (Modern Greek, History, Mathematics and Physics), while from the remaining five (Religion, Elements of Environmental Education, Art, Music and Physical Education) the students would have to choose two from then on (see Table 32-2). This reorganization meant that, practically, during the 3rd phase, students would teach some subjects without any previous theoretical instruction on the subjects. This would result in their teaching without the experience of planning, implementing and evaluating a teaching situation of these specific subjects.

The structure and content of the new Teaching Practice programme are briefly described in Table 32-2.

| Teaching Methodology and Teaching Practice | Semester | Duration | Contents (activities and subjects) |
|---|---|---|---|
| 1st phase: Introduction to school and teaching theory and practice | 3rd | 2 days per week for 1 semester (at school: 2–3 hours, at university: 3 hours) | Each week, the following process takes place: At the university, a theoretical course on a school- or teaching related issue, classroom observation focused on this issue, teaching and classroom analysis based on the observation at the university. Topics: Formal prerequisites for teaching. School space and class observation methods. The theoretical basis of teaching. Curricula, the Cross-thematic framework. Aims, objectives and contents of teaching. Methods, strategies and teaching aids. Evaluation and learning environments. Alternative approaches to teaching. Main principles of lesson planning. Management of problems in school class. Climate of school class, discipline, verbal and non-verbal communication. Types of schools: Comprehensive, rural, full-day, Inter-cultural, Special schools. Evaluation of the Programme's 1st Phase. 5ECTS |

| | | | |
|---|---|---|---|
| 2nd phase:<br>a) 4 compulsory primary school subject<br>Teachings:<br>1. Modern Greek<br>2. History<br>3. Mathematics<br>4. Physics<br>b) Optional primary school subject teachings:<br>1. Religion<br>2. Elements of Environmental Education<br>3. Music<br>4. Art<br>5. Physical Education<br>(The students have to choose 2 of the 6 teaching options) | 4th through 7th | 1 day per week for each Teaching (morning: teaching at school, afternoon: theoretical instruction at the university and teaching analysis) | The second Phase for each subject includes two parts:<br>a. Theoretical,which takes place at the Faculty , lasts four weeks and focuses on the main issues for teaching each subject.<br>b. Practical, which is comprised of the mentors' "model" lesson, of sstudents' teaching and of teaching analysis-evaluation at the university.<br>Each student teaches each of the subjects once, while the other times observes his/her colleagues (6–7 weeks: 1 hour at school, 2 hours at the university).<br><br>30 ECTS |
| 3rd phase:<br>Undertaking classroom teaching with theoretical preparation and provision of feedback only at an urban school | 8th | 11 days | a.. Theoretical course on the school organization b. Familiarization of students with school classes in an urban school (3 days) and teaching of all subjects for 1 week.<br>c. Meeting at the university to discuss experiences from the urban school. |

**Table 32-2. Current teaching practice programme from the academic year 2006–2007 onwards**
**(Based on data from the study guide of the Department of Primary Education of Florina for the academic year 2006–2007)**

# Empirical Examination of the Effects of the Institutional Changes

*The research question and the data collection instrument*

The institutional changes in 2000 and 2006 raised interest in the examination of their consequences for the quality of the practice provided for the professional preparation of the students of the Department of Primary Education in Florina. Consequently, the emerging question was whether and to what extent these changes have affected the practical training of the students, as reflected mainly in the level of the students' satisfaction with the overall Teaching Practice Programme.

The purpose of the present research was to form a broader picture of the development of the Teaching Practice during the last six years through the students' perceptions. The sample consisted of 555 senior students from the academic years 2007–2008, 2008–2009, 2009–2010, 2010–2011, 2011–2012 and 2012–2013.

A structured written questionnaire was used for the assessment of the students' opinions. Its composition was based on the structure and content of the Teaching Practice programme. Similar research tools from other education departments were taken into consideration, as well as those of other research projects which had taken place previously in the Department of Primary Education in Florina. The questionnaire has been through various stages. It was used for the first time in 2005 and included 31 questions, 21 closed, 3 preconceived and 7 open questions (Thoidis et al. 2005). It was used again in a revised version in 2007 with this version consisting of 21 questions, 14 closed and 7 open (Papadopoulou & Thoidis 2008). In the 2009 questionnaire, the open questions were turned into closed questions, following a categorization of the corresponding answers of previous studies. Thus, the new questionnaire comprises 80 statements of the five-point Likert scale type (Thoidis et al., 2011). The scale is reliable since Cronbach's alpha coefficient of internal consistency is statistically significant ($\alpha = 0.92$).

Methods and indicators of descriptive statistics were used for data processing.

## Results

The majority of students seem to be quite satisfied with the organization and functioning of the current Teaching Practice programme (16.8% very much, 43.2% a lot, 33% somewhat, 6.5% little, not at all 0.5%). According to the students' responses, the main goal of the

Teaching Practice, which is to combine theory with "praxis", seems to be achieved (72.1% a lot and very much, 22.1% somewhat, 5.4% little).

For this reason its contribution is acknowledged when it comes to the issue of an adequate professional training (36.1% very much, 35.7% a lot, 23.2% somewhat). The Pearson consistency index $r$ was statistically significant in a positive way when it came to the satisfaction stemming from the Teaching Practice programme, with regard to the connection between theory and practice and the contribution of the Teaching Practice in terms of professional competence ($r = .479$, $p = .000$ και $r = .411$, $p = .000$).

According to the students' estimations of the first phase of the Teaching Practice programme, its topics and content to a large extent covered the basic aspects of classroom education and teaching, since 75.2% of the students responded with either "somewhat", "a lot" or "very much" (somewhat: 47%, a lot 23.9%, very much 4.3%). Still, the number of students responding with "little" satisfaction was also quite significant (23.4%).

Moreover, the students appeared to be quite satisfied with the classroom observation ($M = 3.06$, $SD = .836$) and its connection to theory ($M = 3.16$, $SD = .840$). The Pearson consistency index r was statistically significant in a positive way when it came to the question of the completeness of the contents of the first phase and the question of classroom observation ($r = .447$, $p = .000$). The same goes for the statements with regard to the connection with theory ($r = .415$, $p = .000$). According to students, the most serious problems they faced during the first phase had to do with the excessive emphasis on the theoretical part ($M = 3.04$, $SD = .902$) as well as with the organization of the classroom observation at schools.

In the second phase of the Teaching Practice programme and in relation to their preparation, the students appeared quite satisfied with the first contact with the classroom ($M = 2.49$, $SD = 1.023$), with the theoretical presentations $= 2.55$, $SD = .876$) and with their collaboration with the mentor ($M = 2.61$, $SD = 1.175$), while they considered the teaching preparation to be time consuming (somewhat 35.1%, a lot 29%, very much 20%, $M = 3.04$, $SD = .902$) and locating informative material rather difficult (somewhat 32.3%, a lot 31.3%, very much 18.8%, $M = 2.87$, $SD = .987$).

As far as lesson implementation during the second phase was concerned, the students' main problems centred on their feeling of anxiety ($M = 2.92$, $SD = 1.189$) and on the difficulties of classroom management ($M = 2.68$, $SD = .959$). During the teaching evaluation of the second phase, the students pointed out the excessive focus placed on lesson planning as a problematic issue, in contrast to their apparent expectation that the emphasis would be on lesson implementation ($M$ =3.29, $SD$ = 1.048), while the focus on the negative aspects of their teaching was pinpointed as the second most important problem that they faced ($M$ = 2.57, $SD$ = 1.143). In order to improve the second phase, they suggested a reduction in the teaching costs by creating a bank of informative/visual material ($M$ = 4.33, $SD$ = .964), better acquaintance with the classroom and more "model" lessons $M$ = 3.73, $SD$ = 1.098).

In the 3rd phase of TPP, the main problem remained the time-consuming preparation ($M$ = 4.34, $SD$ = .945), while the next two most serious issues were the search for informative material ($M$ = 3.58, $SD$ =1.150) and the lesson planning, that must be written daily ($M$ = 3.01, $SD$ = 1.207). In relation to lesson implementation during the third phase, the main problems were, once again, the students' anxiety stress ($M$ = 2.75, $SD$ = 1.291), time and classroom management, and also the density of the material ($M$ = 2.60 for all three problems, and $SD$ = 1004, 1128 and 1169 respectively). As far as the teaching evaluation of the third phase was concerned, the main problem was once more the excessive emphasis on lesson planning ($M$ =3.24 και $SD$ = 1.212), while the next most serious problem was the restriction of the evaluation results to broader judgments and the neglect of feedback ($M$ = 2.39, $SD$ = 1.096).

A considerable number of the students (33%, i.e. one in three students), estimated that the first phase of the programme did not prepare them adequately for their participation in the second phase ("not at all" 6.5% and "a little" 26.5%), while the theoretical and practical preparation of the students during the 2nd phase, in relation to their involvement in the third phase, pleased the majority (93.7%) of them (somewhat: 19.9%, a lot: 34.7% and very much: 39.1%). Only 5.7% of the students chose "little", while 0.7% chose "not at all" as an answer to this question.

With regard to the duration of teaching practice, half of the students (50.1%) believe that the amount of Teaching Practice was enough, while the rest believe that it was a lot (34.7%) or too much (9.7%) and only 5.5% consider it to be "little" or "too little". Although the satisfaction they derived from the Teaching Practice programme was positively associated with the satisfaction they gained from participating in the third phase ($r$ =.445, $N$ = 552, $p$ = .000), as well with the overall satisfaction associated with the organization and functioning of the programme ($r$ = .518, p = .000), the students stated that the practical exercises in the 3rd phase were many and too many (57%). In the second phase, the rate was markedly smaller ("many" and "too many" 29.2%) and in the first phase even smaller ("many" and "too many": 22%).

## Conclusion

A noteworthy result was that, despite its narrowing down, the duration of the Teaching Practice was considered to be quite lengthy by a considerable number of the students (44%). A further interesting finding was that, despite the reduction of its content and duration, the second phase prepares students adequately, both theoretically and practically, for their participation in the third phase. Conversely, greater difficulties emerge in the stage of transition from the first to the second phase, possibly due to the unification of the two parts of the first phase in one semester. This is something that needs to be reassessed.

A major problem for the students seemed to be the written planning of every lesson, which is something to be expected considering that planning is an element that draws from theory while, as other research also suggests, the students tend to underestimate theoretical matters, mainly focusing on lesson implementation and on more technical aspects of teaching (Thoidis et al., 2011; Kollias, 2007; Zanting et al., 2003).

It is characteristic that the anxiety which overwhelms students is considered to be the most crucial problem when the second and third phase takes place, a finding that is reaffirmed by international research as well (Caires et al., 2013; Head et al., 1996; Lamote & Engels, 2010).

The emerging overall conclusion is that, despite the shortening of its duration and the narrowing down of its content due to institutional changes, the new Teaching Practice Programme seems to fulfil students' expectations.

## References

Arends, R. 2009. *Learning to Teach.* New York: McGraw-Hill.

Argyropoulou, S. 2005. *Teacher Education: Evaluation of the Tteaching Practice Programme in the Department of Primary Education at the University of Western Macedonia.* Unpublished Doctoral Thesis, Florina.

Bikos, K. 2011. "Improvement Strategies of the Effectiveness of Teaching Practice", in V. Economides (ed.), *Initial and In-service Teacher Education: Theoretical and Research Approaches.* Athens: Pedio, 472–482.

Britzman, D. P. 2003. *Practice Makes Practice: A Critical Study of Learning to Teach.* Albany: State University of New York Press.

Caires, S., Almeida, L. and Vieira, D. 2012. "Becoming a Teacher: Student Teachers' Experiences and Perceptions about Teaching Practice", *European Journal of Teacher Education* 35(2), 163–178.

Chaniotakis, N. 2011. "Student-Teachers' Teaching Practice: Perceptions of the Teachers of the Collaborating Schools", in V. Economides (ed.), *Initial and In-service Teacher Education Theoretical and Research Approaches.* Athens: Pedio, 495–508.

Chaniotakis, N., Efthimiou, A. and Pirgiotakis, G. 2006. "Student-Teachers' Perceptions on Their Teaching Practice", *Social Sciences* 45, 185–212.

Filippou, D. K. 1984. "Teaching Practice in Teacher Education Programmes", *Pedagogical Review* 1, 39–61.

Head, J., Hill, F. and Maguire, M. 1996. "Stress and the Postgraduate Secondary School Trainee Teacher: A British Case Study", *Journal of Education for Teaching* 22(1), 71–84.

Kakana, D.-M., Mpotsoglou, K., Chatzopoulou, K. and Panagiotidou, E. 2007. "Connecting the University with the School Community through Teaching Practice", in E. Taratori et al. (eds), *Primary Education Departments: Past, Present, Future.* Thessaloniki: Kyriakidis Bros., 219–227.

Kollias, B. 2007. "Why Do Our Students Find Difficult to Objectively Evaluate the Challenge of Becoming a Good Teacher?" in E. Taratori et al. (eds), *Primary Education Departments: Past, Present, Future.* Thessaloniki: Kyriakidis Bros., 149–155.

Lamote, C. and Engels., N. 2010. "The Development of Student Teachers' Professional Identity", *European Journal of Teacher Education* 33(1), 3–18.

Michalopoulou, K. 2011. "Students' Formation of Opinions and Representations Regarding the Profession of the Kindergarten Teacher During Teaching Practice", in V. Economides (ed.), *Initial and In-service Teacher Education, Theoretical and Research Approaches.* Athens: Pedio, 534–542.

Papadopoulou, V., Thoidis, I. and Tsakiridou, E. 2007. "Teaching Practice in the Department of Primary Education at the University of Western Macedonia: Perceptions of Teachers as Collaborators", in E. Taratori et al. (eds), *Departments of Primary Education: Past, Present, Future.* Thessaloniki: Kyriakidis Bros., 241–250.

Papadopoulou, V. and Thoidis, I. 2008. "Teaching Practice Programmes in Greece: The Case of the University of Western Macedonia", in *Comparative Education Teacher Training, Education Policy and Social Inclusion* 6, 86–73. Sofia, Bulgaria: Bureau for Educational Services.

Papadopoulou, V. and Demetriadou, K. 2007. "Teaching Methodology and Teaching Practice in the Department of Primary Education of the University of Western Macedonia: Students' Evaluation of the First Phase", *Conference Proceedings: Primary Education towards Challenges of Our Times,* University of Ioannina: 17–20 May, 436–445 (in digital form).

Poulou, M. (2007). "Student-teachers' Concerns about Teaching Practice", *European Journal of Teacher Education* 30(1), 91–110.

Study Guides of the Department of Primary Education of the University of Western Macedonia for the Academic Years 1995–1996 (pp. 62–75) and 2006–2007 (pp. 130–147).

Theodorou, D. 1998. *Teaching Practice in Initial Teacher Training Programmes in Greece,* Unpublished Doctoral Thesis. Florina.

Thoidis, I., Papadopoulou, V. and Tsakiridou, E. 2005. "Teaching Practice in the Department of Primary Education in University of West Macedonia: Data and New Questionings", *Panhellenic Conference "Education and Society in the Modern World: Primary Education Departments 20 years later."* Rethymno, 15-17 April.

Thoidis, I., Papadopoulou, V. and Argyropoulou, S. 2011. "The Graduates of the Department of Primary Education in University of West Macedonia Evaluate the Teaching Practice Program", in V. Economides (ed.), *Initial and In-service Teacher Education, Theoretical and Research Approaches.* Athens: Pedio, 521–533.

Xochellis, P. 1997. "School and Teacher towards Current Needs", *Makednon* 4, 3–19.

—. 2006. *Teachers in the Modern World.* Athens: Typothito.

Zanting, A., Verloop, N. and Vermunt, J. D. 2003. "How do Student Teachers Elicit their Mentor Teachers' Practical Knowledge?" *Teachers and Teaching: Theory and Practice* 9(3), 197–211.

# CHAPTER THIRTY-TWO

# STUDENTS' EVALUATION OF THE TEACHING METHODOLOGY AND SCHOOL PRACTICE PROGRAMME (PHASE B) IN THE PRIMARY EDUCATION UNIVERSITY OF WESTERN MACEDONIA

## P. STAVRIDIS,
### PHD. CANDIDATE, UNIVERSITY OF WESTERN MACEDONIA
## Y. BOUNOVAS
### PHD., UNIVERSITY OF WESTERN MACEDONIA
## AND S. ARGYROPOULOU
### PHD., UNIVERSITY OF WESTERN MACEDONIA

**Abstract**
Contemporary reality sets high demands on education. Teachers' training should be based, among other things, upon a solid foundation of knowledge. Through the study of the guidelines for the training of teachers, we conclude that the Practical Internship of candidate teachers is necessary. In the Department of Primary Education of the University of Florina practical training (DiMePA), is provided to the student in three phases either in the form of observation or as personal instruction in the classroom. The second (B) phase aims at the provision of the basic theoretical training of the student in the actual teaching of each course, as well as the development of their capacity to design, conduct and critically evaluate their teaching efficiency.

In this paper we present the students' views on the usefulness of the theoretical training courses, the tools they are given to design and assess teaching and their utilization in the teaching process. To do so we used questionnaires and statistical analysis processing the findings through the use of a SPSS statistical program.

Data analysis proved that Primary Education Department students believe that the second phase of the Instruction Methodology and Practice provides them the opportunity to design efficiently and systematically a teaching session while they also stress that their detailed preparation helps them successfully overcome unexpected situations in the classroom. This Phase is a useful and necessary procedure which provided much needed experience and tools to the students in order to continue and complete their Practice Programme while giving them preparation techniques to implement in their future teaching careers.

**Keywords**
Teacher Training, Students' Practice, Teaching Evaluation

# Introduction

> To create a teacher means to enable him
> to take responsibility for his uncertainties.
> (G. Ferry)

The purpose of this research is to examine the views of the students of the Department of Education in Florina concerning the theoretical preparation, planning, analysis and evaluation of their teaching after their induction, as well as the relationship of the subject matter from the university courses with the corresponding school knowledge. The aim is to investigate these through the experiences of students at the end of the second phase of the programme of Teaching Methodology and Internships.

# Theoretical Framework

### *The concept of "School Practice"*
By "School Practice" we mean all the experiences that the prospective teacher acquires, either through observing experienced teachers or classmates at school, or by teaching themselves. We also mean any planned and orderly educational activity which, by bringing the student-teacher into direct contact with the school reality, aims to associate the act of education with pedagogical theory and to familiarize students with their future professional field. Furthermore, it enhances the students' understanding of the conditions and the requirements of the educational

work and the systematic introduction of the prospective teacher to the key areas of everyday pedagogical and didactic activity, i.e. the analysis, planning and implementation of teaching and pedagogical processes (Theodorou, 1998: 61). We also mean everything that the potential teacher observes or does inside or outside schools as opposed to the theoretical courses (Philippou, 1983). Finally, the practical exercise describes the aspect of training which refers to the transformation of a series of theoretical methodological choices into concrete actions and pedagogical practices of organization and implementation of the educational process, which allows schools to function (Papakonstantinou, 1991).

From all the above, it follows that "School Practice" has at least three meanings: a) practising teaching skills in order to pursue the role of educator, b) the whole range of experience gained by prospective teachers through their contact with the school and class and c) the practical side of their studies as opposed to the theoretical training. Usually the first concerns the evaluation of the internship, the second its implementation by the students and the third the need to combine theory and practice in the training of prospective teachers.

The DiMePA is consistent with the broader framework of European Education Policy, which is mainly designed to make European citizens able to cope with the needs of the new era through competitiveness, innovation, social cohesion, equal opportunities and active participation in the knowledge society (Organization for Economic Co-operation and Development, 2005).

Improving the quality and efficiency of education in all member states is vital for the success of Europe. The main call is to ensure the acquisition of key competences by all and especially by the teachers of tomorrow. At the same time, we have to ensure high quality teaching by providing adequate initial training of the teachers through diversification of teaching, collaborative learning and the application of good practices (Department of Education and Science, 2006). This requires continuous professional development for teachers and trainers, so as to make teaching an attractive career option, which is achieved through the practice of future teachers (Teaching Council of Ireland, 2009).

## The Teaching Methodology and Internships (DiMePA) programme of the Department of Primary Education, Florina

The Department of Primary Education of the University of Western Macedonia places particular emphasis on student internships and considers that this is more effective when combined with the theoretical course.

Through the continuous connection of theoretical knowledge with practical experience, the student, throughout the course of his studies, should gradually form a personal single theory of education and teaching, which will make him more and more capable of conscious, effective, refreshing and, ultimately, responsible personal implementation of teaching.

The programme is carried out in three separate phases as follows:
- Phase A: Introduction to the theory and practice of school
- Phase B: Teaching of primary school subjects (mandatory: Greek Language, Mathematics, History, Physics; elective with two of them mandatory: Environmental Studies, Religion, Arts, Music, Physical Education)
- Phase C: Appointment of pedagogic teaching assignments in the classroom for two weeks with theoretical preparation and feedback.

Phase B aims to provide students with basic theoretical training in the teaching of each course and, secondly, to develop the ability of students to design with imagination, to conduct with pedagogical consideration and evaluate critically their teaching, with the ultimate objective of linking educational theory and practice.

## Research Methodology

The questionnaire method of research was selected and applied to collect the views, preferences, expectations and attitudes of the students concerning Phase B of the programme.

The questionnaire was presented to students who completed Phase B of the programme until the end of the academic year 2009–10. Some 96 undergraduate male and female students from a total of 101 who completed Phase B of the Internship participated in the study. The questionnaire contains twelve closed-type questions the answers to which were then quantitatively analysed by statistical processing with the SPSS program.

The questions can be divided into four categories: The first examines student satisfaction with the theoretical training as well as the degree of readiness in the conduct of teaching. Thus it answers the question of how well prepared students feel from theoretical training to teach courses. The second category concerns the planning of teaching and investigates what were the elements that guided the students to realize their hourly teaching. The third category deals with the process of evaluation of the teaching after its completion, as well as the final evaluation of the semester course, through some additional work or written exams. It answers the question how students evaluate the process of analysis and evaluation of their teaching after its completion as well as at the end of the semester. Finally, the fourth category of questions concerns the students' evaluation of the theoretical courses of specific disciplines attended, compared to the elementary school subjects and their profession in general.

# Findings

## *Analysis of survey data*

Of the 96 students who answered the question whether the theoretical preparation courses in the teaching of primary school subjects were adequate, 88.5% responded they were, while 10.4% answered that they were few. Only 1% told us that the theoretical preparation courses were too much and none said they were too few. Thus, the number of theoretical courses is deemed as satisfactory in preparing students for implementing their first instruction in the elementary school subjects. Table 33-1 summarizes the results.

| *Subjects* | *very* | *enough* | *not enough* | *not at all* |
|---|---|---|---|---|
| Greek Language | 31.6 | 47.4 | 20.0 | 1.1 |
| History | 35.1 | 55.3 | 9.6 | 0 |
| Religion | 31.9 | 37.7 | 14.5 | 15.9 |
| Mathematics | 34.7 | 54.7 | 10.5 | 0 |
| Physics | 48.4 | 49.5 | 2.2 | 0 |
| Environmental Studies | 33.8 | 29.7 | 16.2 | 20.3 |
| Arts | 33.3 | 39.5 | 7.4 | 19.8 |
| Music | 11.7 | 31.7 | 15.0 | 41.7 |
| Physical Education | 33.8 | 36.4 | 15.6 | 14.3 |

**Table 33-1. Degree of satisfaction with the theoretical training**

In teaching physics the degree of satisfaction is overwhelming (97.9%) (very satisfied), while satisfaction is also very high in the teaching of history (90.4%), the teaching of Mathematics (89.4%) and the teaching of Modern Greek language (79%). We observe that the satisfaction of students with their theoretical training in the mandatory courses is great, while a small difference is observed in electives where rates are slightly lower (more specifically, in Religion 69.6% (very and enough),

Environmental Studies (63.5%), Arts (72.8%), Physical Education (70.2%)), while there is no significant variation in Music with 43.4%.

One limitation of the survey which is worth noting is that we are not able to know the interests of the students (as defined by their elective courses) or their preferences and their inclination towards "theoretical" (Language and History) or "positive" (Mathematics and Physics) courses. We could note, however, indicatively that the students chose the following subjects: Religion 69, Study 74, Arts 81, Music 60 and Physical Education 77.

In our question about whether the theoretical courses prepared the students appropriately and effectively for their teaching, the results were clear, since 88.3% responded positively, while only 11.7% responded negatively. Hence, it can be said with relative certainty that the majority of students consider the theoretical part of the second phase of the DiMePA programme to be quite effective and students feel that they are ready to implement their teaching.

In the planning stage of an instruction, we asked students on what coordinates they were based:

A. On the "model teaching plan" which is given for every teaching practice by the instructor: 63% of the respondents answered that they were assisted by it.

B. On the "book for the teacher" provided by the Ministry of Education: 47.8% of students used this book.

C. "Personal ideas" of the students: 73.9% said that they were based on their personal ideas and this indicates their autonomy and confidence about what they do, as well as the very good relationship with the posted (appointed) teachers who are willing to help students to experiment with their own ideas.

D. On the "lectures and notes" of the lecturer: Only 18.5% said that they used the notes from the lectures of their professors in preparing the plan of the module which they would teach.

However, since the answers to this question were combinatorial, some items arose that deserve mentioning: 14.6% of the respondents said that they used all of the materials above when planning their teaching, while 11.5% told us that they were based on the book of the teacher and their own ideas and 10.4% were based exclusively on their personal ideas. 18.75% of the students were based on the model plan as well as their own ideas, while just 3.1% were based only on the book of the teacher. Finally,

9.4% drew only upon the model plan, while a mere 3.1% used the model plan combined with the book.

When asked how much students were helped by the analysis and evaluation of teaching in relation to the way it was conducted, 31.6% thought that they were helped a lot, 51.6% said that it helped them enough, 14.7% of students replied that they were helped a little and only 2.1% felt that it did not help them at all. We therefore see that, collectively, attendees expressed a positive opinion about the process of analysis and evaluation followed by the appointed lecturer and by the responsible lecturer, by 83.2% (very and enough) of all students taught, while 16.8% (not enough and not at all) tells us that they were not satisfied and that something needs to change.

When asked who benefits by the process of analysis and evaluation of teaching, 75% felt that generally it helps all students involved in the teaching of the course, 19.6% believe that, apart from the instructor, fellow students who observe the teaching also benefited, while only 5.4% claimed that it helps only those who taught. It is clear therefore that the analysis and evaluation by the responsible lecturers greatly aids all those who attended the teaching of the course and not only the ones that taught.

Students were asked if they would like to try a second or even third instruction in each lesson, and 69.8% said that they would like this to happen while 30.2% responded negatively. We should note here that the students were teaching alone during the period of the completion of the questionnaire, something that changed in the following years and teaching is now performed in pairs, which means a decrease in the actual individual teaching time.

As far as the teaching of individual subjects is concerned, students hand in an assignment (on the planning and evaluation of their teaching) which accounts for one of the criteria for the total score of the students at the end of the semester. When asked if the writing of this work benefits them, 77.1% responded positively, while 22.9% felt that the work does not benefit them in particular.

Many teachers, at the end of the semester and after teaching in schools, require their students to be assessed with additional written or oral exams. This meets opposition from a large proportion of the students (82.1%), since they believe that this is not necessary while 17.9% think the opposite.

When asked what the most important criterion for their grading in teaching is, half the students (50.5%) believe it was the practical teaching, 39.8% the lesson preparation, while very small proportions give the other two responses (6.5% the evening evaluation at the Department and only

3.2% the written work at the end of the semester). Hence, we see that students consider the process of lesson preparation as the prime criterion for their assessment, as well as their effort and the successful implementation of their subsequent teaching. Generally, it appears that coursework and exams are not considered significant for the final scoring of students. Table 33-2 summarizes the findings.

| Subjects | great | some | little | none |
|---|---|---|---|---|
| Greek Language | 27.4 | 38.9 | 25.3 | 8.4 |
| Greek History | 32.6 | 33.7 | 24.2 | 9.5 |
| Religious Studies & Philosophy of Religion | 24.6 | 35.4 | 33.8 | 6.2 |
| Mathematics | 51.6 | 35.8 | 12.6 | 0 |
| Physics | 71.3 | 23.4 | 5.3 | 0 |
| Environmental Studies | 25.9 | 39.7 | 20.7 | 13.8 |
| Arts | 40.7 | 33.3 | 19.8 | 6.2 |
| Music | 19.4 | 47.2 | 13.9 | 19.4 |
| Physical Education | 45.0 | 38.3 | 8.3 | 8.3 |

**Table 33-22. Content of university courses related to the subjects of elementary school**

There is a strong correlation between the subject taught at university with those taught in primary school, with Science subjects and Physics in particular holding supremacy with 71.3%, followed by Mathematics with 51.6%. In contrast, theoretical subjects have notably smaller percentages: 32.6% in History and 27.4 % in Modern Language.

Looking at the elective subjects we observe that the relationship of the course with the elementary school subjects is large enough in Arts (40.7%) and Physical Education (45%). On the contrary, as far as music is concerned, just 19.4% said there is a relation between the theoretical courses and the school subject.

Finally, students were asked whether the knowledge they acquired in the disciplines of Greek Language, History, Mathematics and Physics, throughout the duration of their studies, was sufficient for their future profession. 56.8% responded positively and 43.2% negatively for the Greek Language, 74.7% said yes and 25.3% no for History, while for Mathematics positive responses reached 68.4% compared to 31.6% who responded negatively and finally, in Physics 79.8% of the participants was positive and 20.2% negative. There is a significant proportion therefore, which allows us to conclude that the knowledge acquired during studying, both through theoretical lessons and through teaching, are deemed as satisfactory by the students for their future profession and for the integrated handling of the teaching work which they will be required to undertake in the classroom .

## Conclusion

After the presentation and analysis of the results of this survey, we can proceed to drawing some general conclusions regarding the second stage of Teaching Methodology and Practical Training of Primary Education in Florina.

Originally the question of how well prepared students feel for teaching through their theoretical training on the courses was addressed. The results are clear and we can say that the theoretical preparation of the students for the mandatory subjects were sufficient, while the theoretical courses on the individual teaching subjects were judged as entirely satisfactory.

Since students were provided with the necessary theoretical training, we saw the elements that were employed in planning their teaching and implementing their hourly teaching sessions. It was found that the students used the model teaching plan which they were given during the course, they read the teacher's book to articulate the objectives of their subject, but they were also informed by the notes of the course and the instructor so as to be within the wider teaching framework. However, what they based their teaching on to a greater extent and what makes their teaching methods unique, are their own personal ideas, which they implemented in each module and in the philosophy of the subject, customizing their job and allowing them to gain experience and confidence for the future.

The completion of the teaching practice is followed by the analysis of both the hourly teaching practice lessons and the final evaluation of the semester, through some additional work or written exams. Interpreting the responses of students, we find that they have been largely satisfied with their evaluation processes and they do not want to change anything in it. Moreover, the students consider this process to be beneficial as it helps everyone who participates in the lesson and not just those who teach. We therefore conclude that the most important evaluation criterion for them is the preparation and implementation of teaching, whereas they believe that the written exam or the additional work at the end of the semester is not necessary and they would rather agree with the abolition of this particular exam. Also, participants appeared willing to teach more than once, and argued that this would help them, in conjunction with the work carried out after the teaching and relating to self-assessment (reflection).

Finally, we examined how students evaluate the theoretical courses of specific subjects attended in relation to their profession and the elementary school subjects. It has been found that there is a higher correlation between the theoretical courses at university and the subjects of Mathematics and Physics in primary school while this relationship is weaker for Greek Language and History. Also, the respondents have deemed the knowledge gained both through the theoretical courses on teaching and through the actual teachings as satisfactory for their future profession and their efficient handling of teaching in the classroom.

In conclusion, we conclude that the students of the Department of Education of Florina believe that Phase B of the Project of Teaching Methodology and Practice gives them the opportunity to prepare systematically and with ample time; the detailed preparation helps them to overcome the contingencies of class in the best possible way. It is a useful and necessary process which equips them with skills and experiences, not only for the continuity and completion of the teacher training programme but also for the more thorough preparation for the teaching profession.

# References

Argyropoulou, S. 2005. *Teacher Education: Evaluation of Teachers' Training Programme for the Students of the Department of Education in Florina.* Unpublished PhD thesis, University of Western Macedonia, Department of Primary Education, Florina, Greece.
—. 2007. "Evaluative Observations of Students on the Teacher Training Programme of the Department of Primary Education in Florina in the years 1995–1999", *Bulletin of the 5th Conference of the Hellenic Educational Society*, vol. B, 215–223.
—. 2008. "The Contribution of Teacher Training in Shaping a Self-theory from Candidate Teachers", *Kinitro* 8, 83–97.
Department of Education and Science. 2006. Learning to Teach: Students on Teaching Practice in Irish Primary Schools. Dublin,
http://www.education.ie/en/Publications/Inspection-Reports-Publications/Evaluation-Reports-Guidelines/insp_learning_to_teach_pdf.pdf (accessed 15 April 2013).
Organization for Economic Co-operation and Development. 2005. *Teachers Matter: Attracting, Developing and Retaining Effective Teachers.* Paris: OECD.
Papakonstantinou P. 1991. *Encyclopedia of Educational Psychology*, dictionary vol.7, ed. Ellinika Grammata. Athens.

Phillipou, K. 1983. "Internship programs in teacher education", in *Paidagogiki Epitheorisi 1/84, 1st International Conference of Hellenic Educational Society, 23–25/9/1983.*

Study guide (curriculum) of the Department of Primary Education, Florina 2009–2010.

Teaching Council of Ireland. 2009. *Learning to Teach and its Implications for the Continuum of Teacher Education: A Nine-country Cross-national Study,* http://www.teachingcouncil.ie/_fileupload/Teacher%20Education/LearningTo Teach-ConwayMurphyRathHall-2009_10344263.pdf (accessed 14 April 2013).

Theodorou, D. 1998. *The Teacher Training Programmes in the Curricula of the Departments of Primary Education.* Unpublished PhD thesis, Aristotle University of Thessaloniki, Department of Primary Education, Florina, Greece.

Thoidis, I., Papadopoulou, V. and Argyropoulou S. 2009. *The final-year students of the Department of Primary Education evaluate the teacher training program.* Speech in a scientific conference with subject "Education and training of teachers", Rethimno 23 May.